OLIVER WENDELL HOLMES AND
THE CULTURE OF CONVERSATION

Peter Gibian explores the key role played by Oliver Wendell Holmes in what was known as America's "Age of Conversation." He was both a model and an analyst of the dynamic conversational form that became central to many areas of mid-nineteenth-century life. Holmes' multivoiced writings can serve as a key to open up the closed interiors of Victorian America, whether in saloons or salons, parlors or clubs, hotels or boardinghouses, schoolrooms or doctors' offices. Combining social, intellectual, medical, legal and literary history with close textual analysis, and setting Holmes in dialogue with Emerson, Hawthorne, Melville, Fuller, Alcott, and finally with his son, Justice Oliver Wendell Holmes Junior, Gibian radically redefines the context for our understanding of the major literary works of the American Renaissance.

PETER GIBIAN is Associate Professor of English at McGill University. He is the editor of *Mass Culture and Everyday Life* (1997), and the author of articles in *The American Century: Art and Culture, 1900–1950* (1999), *American Modernism Across the Arts* (1999), and *The Legacy of Oliver Wendell Holmes, Jr.* (1992).

Recent books in this series

OLIVER WENDELL HOLMES AND THE CULTURE OF CONVERSATION

PETER GIBIAN

CAMBRIDGE
UNIVERSITY PRESS

PUBLISHED BY THE PRESS SYNDICATE OF THE UNIVERSITY OF CAMBRIDGE
The Pitt Building, Trumpington Street, Cambridge, United Kingdom

CAMBRIDGE UNIVERSITY PRESS
The Edinburgh Building, Cambridge CB2 2RU, UK
40 West 20th Street, New York, NY 10011–4211, USA
10 Stamford Road, Oakleigh, Melbourne 3166, Australia
Ruiz de Alarcón 13, 28014 Madrid, Spain
Dock House, The Waterfront, Cape Town 8001, South Africa

http://www.cambridge.org

First published 2001

Printed in the United Kingdom at the University Press, Cambridge

Typeset in Baskerville 11/12.5pt   System 3b2   [CE]

A catalogue record for this book is available from the British Library

Library of Congress Cataloguing in Publication data
Gibian, Peter, 1952–
Oliver Wendell Holmes and the culture of conversation / Peter Gibian.
p.   cm. – (Cambridge studies in American literature and culture; 125)
Includes bibliographical references and index.
ISBN 0 521 56026 8
1. Holmes, Oliver Wendell, 1809–1894 – Criticism and interpretation.
2. Literature and society – United States – History – 19th century.
3. Conversation – History – 19th century.
4. Table-talk – History – 19th century.
5. Conversation in literature.
6. Dialogue in literature.   I. Title.   II. Series.
PS1992.C67 G54 2001
818′.309–dc21   00-068945

ISBN 0 521 56026 8 hardback

For my parents

Socratic irony is the only involuntary and yet completely deliberate dissimulation . . . It originates in the union of savoir vivre *and the scientific spirit, in the conjunction of a perfectly instinctive and a perfectly conscious philosophy. It contains and arouses a feeling of the indissoluble antagonism between the absolute and the relative, between the impossibility and the necessity of complete communication . . . It is a very good sign when the harmonious bores are at a loss about how they should react to this continuous self-parody, when they fluctuate endlessly between belief and disbelief until they get dizzy and take what is meant as a joke seriously and what is meant seriously as a joke.*

(Friedrich Schlegel, *Lyceum* fragment 108)

Contents

Acknowledgments

"We must not begin by talking of pure ideas – vagabond thoughts that tramp on the public roads without any human habitation – but must begin with men and their conversation." These words from C. S. Peirce that introduce chapter three of this book also provide the most apt introduction to the true ground of the entire project. This analysis of the dynamics of talk was sparked by and is the product of a long series of collegial conversations and intellectual collaborations over a great many years. While I hope that my substantial debts to a wide range of foundational works in literary criticism and cultural history are made clear in the over-ample footnotes to this text, here I would especially like to remember debts that are personal as well as intellectual.

My initial fascination with the mercurial movements of conversation was stimulated by years of invigorating everyday converse with a truly exceptional cohort of graduate students in English, Comparative Literature, and Modern Thought and Literature at Stanford University. These primary intuitions then began to emerge as an argument grounding a revisionary reading of American cultural and literary history under the guidance of a very special group of teachers and thesis supervisors whose diversity of interests – literary, psychological, socio-historical, or philosophical – was ideally suited to the multi-faceted research involved in this project. Through his day-to-day counsel, through stimulating idea-exchanges in campus corridors, and through an incredible commitment of long-distance telephone time, Jay Fliegelman was a tremendous help at the thesis stage of this project. And he has remained a key source of enthusiastic encouragement over the long haul, always intervening at just the right moment to spur the next turn in thinking. With his generous, open, and creative critical mind, he has an extraordinary ability to sense the potential latent in even the most rough materials, and then to suggest ways of bringing those rich implications to the fore. David Halliburton influenced the dissertation greatly through the example of his own work and through his close readings of later drafts. And Albert Gelpi, who became a literary–critical model for me during the course of several classes I had with him, played a key role as a reader of this project, urging me to shape the sprawling thesis into a book for the Studies in American Literature and Culture series at Cambridge University Press.

Several other professors at Stanford contributed greatly to the definition of this new approach to Holmes and to conversation. During classes on the English Romantics and through several discussions of this project, Herbert Lindenberger influenced my sense of the relations between mid-century American literature and important lines of English and European writing; he remains for me a key model for his scholarly energy and his range of critical vision. Ian Watt, always a wonderful example of intellectual rigor, breadth, and generosity, helped me greatly as the Chair of my Program for many years; he also in effect commissioned the first version of the chapter on Holmes Junior for a Stanford Humanities Center conference on legal history, and then helped me to hone it for publication in The Legacy of Oliver Wendell Holmes, Jr., ed. Robert W. Gordon (Stanford, CA: Stanford University Press, 1992).

In the years since those first stages, the argument has broadened and shifted considerably, again with the aid of colleagues who were remarkably generous with their time. Mary Louise Pratt helped me look into parallels with some forms of conversational analysis in linguistics, and spurred new thinking with her provocative conception of "arts of the contact zone." Deborah Tannen provided keen responses to my initial notions about interruption and vocal diversity in Emerson, Alcott, and Fuller, influencing both this study of Holmes and a forthcoming companion volume surveying a wide range of mid-century authors. With characteristic kindness, Robert Ferguson brought forth challenging questions about early versions of the discussion about the legal vision of Justice Holmes. Faith Wallis' careful reading of sections on the history of medicine and psychology was clarifying. Thoughtfully commenting on the entire manuscript in great detail from the perspective of his broad vision of nineteenth-century literary history, Thomas Wortham provided invaluable insight and enthusiastic guidance. In another supportive reading, Thomas Gustafson sharpened my sense of the interactions between literary texts and cultural context here. And I am especially thankful to Bob Levine for his amazingly generous help at several stages of the revision process; his penetrating comments on many sections were crucial in giving shape to the final argument – both in this Holmes book and in the companion volume with its expanded treatment of Fuller, Douglass, and Truth. Finally, the overall conception of the "conversation of a culture" here was significantly developed in recent years through lively interaction with a number of colleagues in several departments at McGill University.

Even the institutional support for this project was often richly personal. At Cambridge University Press, the series editors (Eric Sundquist and Ross Posnock) and acquisitions editors (especially Susie Chang) were greatly encouraging as they expressed their real understanding of the goals of this project and their belief in it. In copyediting, Linda Woodward was efficient and scrupulous. Financial support from the Whiting Foundation provided much-needed help at the thesis stage, a research leave from Williams College made it possible early on to rough out the book project, and a Humanities Research Grant from the Faculty of Graduate Studies at McGill University helped me to complete the manuscript and prepare it for publication.

Throughout the extended gestation period for this project, the three women in my life played key roles in the stimulating and sustaining household conversation within which this book was developed. My daughters Rachel and Rebecca, twin figures of interruption, were always there to remind me to focus on the big picture. If, in everyday dialogues about this book, those two girls tended to ask "Why," my wife Wendy Owens was more likely to ask "When." She finally made this book happen, and makes it all worthwhile.

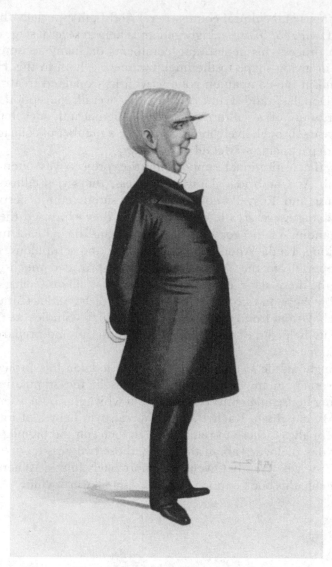

Figure 1 Oliver Wendell Holmes in a caricature by "Spy."
(*Vanity Fair*, June 19, 1886). Private collection.

Introduction

This business of conversation is a very serious matter.
Oliver Wendell Holmes, *The Autocrat of the Breakfast-Table*

This book brings to the fore – or, it brings *back* to the fore – both an author (Oliver Wendell Holmes, Senior) and a verbal mode (conversation) that have almost completely disappeared from our maps of American literary and cultural history. Losing Holmes, we have lost a brilliant writer and a provocative thinker. We have also lost a key representative figure in the American Renaissance, both the best model and the best analyst of the dynamic of conversation that came to pervade many areas of mid-nineteenth-century American life – in what was known, after all, as America's "Age of Conversation."

AN INTRODUCTION TO DOCTOR HOLMES

Holmes' life (1809–94) spanned most of the nineteenth century, and for much of that time he was a household name throughout America, recognized by his contemporaries as a national character, even a national institution. For foreign visitors like William Thackeray, Charles Dickens, or Oscar Wilde, a meeting with the tiny, hyperactive, loquacious Holmes became as much a part of the standard North American tour as a visit to Niagara Falls. Well into the twentieth century, the Holmes name still stood in most people's minds as a loaded, multivalent figure for a diversity of American possibilities. Playing a variety of parts on the national stage, he came to be celebrated as spokesman for and representative personification of American achievements in two very different fields – medicine and literature – and was acclaimed both as a voice of gravity and of levity, a Sage and a Jester, a man of reason and an irrepressible humorist, a neoclassical traditionalist and a free-thinking republican progressive,

I

a self-mocking provincial and an urbane cosmopolitan. But while Holmes played one role as the epitome of regional chauvinism – having given Boston its still-current title as "Hub" of the universe, and having named and defined the "Brahmin caste" of intellectuals so often associated with that New England center – he also made himself the embodiment of widely-shared national aspirations to intellectual advancement (unrestrained freedom of thought), sociability (the values of human association), and civility (the "etiquette of democracy" making possible broad participation in a common life) – all aspects of Holmes' ideal of a "conversation of the culture" that might help Americans to break down the barriers of atomistic individualism, social hierarchy, or local pride.

The mid-century's best-known doctor, Holmes was one of the fathers of modern American medicine, addressing and educating his countrymen as the leading spokesman for the medical field at a crucial transitional period in its development. At the same time, his poetry and prose works made him one of America's preeminent literary figures for more than a century – both in "high culture" and in "popular culture." Indeed, as the "Autocrat," Holmes became an American Humor type who would take a place next to (and in some ways opposed to) the Yankee and the Frontiersman in the nation's popular imagination. Much in demand as a traveling public speaker, the Doctor emerged as the most celebrated after-dinner talker in his day, defining a role (later taken up by Mark Twain) as unofficial poet laureate or toastmaster presiding over many of the huge banquets, mass ceremonies, and civic festivities so central to mid-century public life; he was also one of the trail-blazers in opening up the Lyceum lecture circuit at mid-century, becoming in that venue both widely popular as one of the first comic lecturers and widely controversial as a proselytizing Voice of Reason. When writing in this latter vein as a serious, free-thinking intellectual, the Doctor contributed a series of speculative essays about cutting-edge developments that placed him at the center of national debates in a surprising range of fields: in theology, psychology, and natural science, as well as in medicine and literature.

Doctor Holmes' medical career took him through a series of revolutionary changes in that profession. Studying medicine in Paris for two years (1833–35), the young Holmes was among the first Americans to be trained in the new "clinical" method being advanced by his French teachers, and became a leading advocate for this method on his return to the United States. Research along these lines led to several prize-winning medical studies in the 1830s and two controversial, ground-breaking medical essays in the 1840s: "Homeopathy and its Kindred Delusions" (1842) and "The Contagiousness of Puerperal Fever" (1843), the latter of which anticipated the germ theory of disease by fifteen years, and was ahead of its time both in its analysis of the problem of contagion and in its advocacy of antisepsis as a solution. After serving as Professor of Anatomy at Dartmouth in 1839–40, Holmes later taught at the Harvard Medical School where he served as Dean from 1847 to 1853 and was Parkman Professor of Anatomy and Physiology until his retirement in 1882. Promoting French clinical research and observation in his teaching, and following his personal fascinations with new technologies of vision (microscopes, telescopes, photographs, and the stereoscope that he invented), Holmes introduced microscopy and histology in American medical study. Always alert to the latest technological advances, he read in 1846 of early experiments using ether to reduce pain in surgery and instantly suggested the name – "anaesthesia" – that became permanently attached to this crucial medical breakthrough, while in later years he gave important and highly controversial speeches on the state of the medical profession – such as "Currents and Counter-Currents in Medical Science" (1860) – and on the philosophical implications of recent clinical and neurological research: such as "Mechanism in Thought and Morals" (1870). Because he was, throughout his medical career, a supporter of the revolutionary Parisian clinical method, which discredited earlier heroic medicine, undercut the principles behind current diagnosis and therapy as "myths" and superstitions, and questioned the usefulness of many drugs and therapies in the existing pharmacy, Doctor Holmes was left in a position of "therapeutic nihilism," promoting the need for close empirical observation of individual patients, broad statistical study of patient communities, anatomical investigation, and laboratory research (and thus breaking the ground for the bacteriological/laboratory revolution of the next generation in medicine) but offering little in the way of positive cures or treatments for patients. At the same time that he hailed the clinical movement to clear away old medical errors, however, Holmes was also associated with several of the important medical developments (germ theory, antisepsis, anesthesia) that would later lead out of the impasse of the clinical method, making possible key therapeutic advances of twentieth-century medicine. And, as Freud did, Holmes moved in his career from neuro-physiological approaches to verbal and psychological ones, with an increasing emphasis on the dialogic interactions of doctor and patient – writing on the placebo effect, the therapeutic uses of laughter, the importance of counseling and bedside manner, and stressing microscopically intense observation both of a patient's physiognomy and of the pulses and image patterns of his dynamic verbal exchanges with the physician, finally developing an experimental, conversational model for diagnosis and therapy that is still suggestive to medical explorers today.

In literature, too, Holmes passed through a series of diverse phases, producing very prolifically in a number of verbal modes and genres. Although he first came to national attention in 1830 with the poem "Old Ironsides," which gave voice and focus to early stirrings of nationalist fervor and was credited with having saved the U. S. S. Constitution from being dismantled, and in the 1850s he authored serious poems that instantly became standards to be memorized by generations of schoolchildren (especially "The Chambered Nautilus," a haunting meditation on intellectual progress, and "The Deacon's Masterpiece: or The Wonderful 'One-Hoss-Shay'," a humorous romp that reduces Calvinist dogma to absurdity), as a poet Holmes was finally most widely known as one of America's most reliable producers of light verse for ceremonial occasions. But poetry was only a minor part of Holmes' overall literary contribution. In the late 1850s, when he shifted his primary focus from medicine to literature, Holmes launched himself seriously into writing – and achieved sudden national and international celebrity as a man of letters – with a series of humorous essays presented as conversation around a boardinghouse breakfast-table: *The Autocrat of the Breakfast-Table* (1857), *The Professor at the Breakfast-Table* (1859), and *The Poet at the Breakfast-Table* (1872). These table-talk works are Holmes' most important and still-vital verbal productions. In 1857, James Russell Lowell had invited Holmes to become a regular contributor to a new journal he was founding. Holmes gave this journal its name – the *Atlantic Monthly* – and then assured its success as the nation's prime intellectual forum with these enormously popular columns that both recorded and shaped the talk of the town for a large American public. Inspired by these successes, Holmes also began to explore another hybrid genre, developing an early version of naturalistic fiction through a series of what he called "medicated novels" – *Elsie*

Venner (1861), *The Guardian Angel* (1867), and *A Mortal Antipathy* (1885) –
that combine his table-talk wit and personae with aspects of the
clinical case history to follow a series of anomalous life stories
(involving multiple personalities, repetition compulsions, trauma-
induced mental blocks, paralyzing erotic "antipathies," and so on)
that pose severe problems of diagnosis for the central doctor/
psychologist figures in the novels, raising questions about psychological and physiological determinism and generally challenging conventional thinking about the "normal."

HOLMESIAN TALK AND AMERICA'S CULTURE OF
CONVERSATION

The aim of this study is to show that the connecting thread, linking
all of the Doctor's multiple professional activities, his diverse forms of
literary and scientific work, and his active social life, was always his
interest in the base model of "conversation." First and foremost a
talker, Holmes was unusually well situated to sense the ways in which
talk or "conversation" had become perhaps *the* representative verbal
mode of his age – central to the era's spoken social discourse, to its
written literary discourse, and even to its changing medical discourse.
Even in his first professional triumphs – his Lyceum performances,
public verse readings, festival toasts, and the medical school lectures
that became phenomenally popular with a broad general public –
Holmes was already most celebrated for his gifts as a speaker. Then,
with his bustling social life centered around the verbal exchanges in
drawing rooms, boardinghouses, and elite clubs, he earned a national
reputation as America's most brilliant conversationalist. Contemporaries would rush home after social events to write down or to repeat
the Doctor's latest *mots*, with typical accounts describing him as "the
best talker ever heard," "the king of the dinner-table during a large
portion of the century," or "the greatest conversationalist in the
English language since Dr. Johnson left the scene." Holmes' witty
repartee would set the tone at literary salons and dinner parties, and
also make him a presiding figure at Boston's renowned Saturday
Club – where his sense of talk defined the verbal environment for
those important monthly conversations bringing together Ralph
Waldo Emerson, Nathaniel Hawthorne, Henry Wadsworth Longfellow, Louis Agassiz, Lowell, and many other prominent figures in
business, law, science, literature, and intellectual life. It was only

natural, then, that the Doctor would draw upon all of this salon and club experience when, in the 1850s, he committed himself to concentrated work on writing with his *Atlantic* "breakfast-table" essays. These imaginary, multivoiced dialogues now rank as classics in the "conversation" genre, and gave a new dynamic form to the English periodical essay. Rooted in the boardinghouse table-talk of nineteenth-century America, just as the early essays of Addison and Steele had been rooted in the coffeehouse discussions of eighteenth-century England, Holmes' essays were less a form for lyrical reflection or sequential argument than a social experiment, a verbal laboratory for studies of the volatile "associations" between diverse people and diverse ideas. Staging tea-table debates between a wide range of uncomprehending strangers speaking for divergent ideologies in divergent languages, Holmes presented his readers with a carnivalesque festival of verbal pyrotechnics and comic misunderstandings that also developed as a miniaturized, caricatural model of the "conversation of the culture" in these troubled years just before the Civil War, playing out the rational and irrational forces shaping public opinion in this period, and perhaps making possible some detached reflection on the explosive, interruptive, and multivoiced dynamics of the "public sphere" in mid-century America. Finally, all of this talking and conversational writing seems to have led Holmes to experiment with new kinds of medicine. In his medical career, the Doctor speaks for a major shift from mechanistic physiology and heroic interventionism to the verbal and conversational aspects of diagnosis, caring, and curing. Preparing his later, speculative medical essays, he increasingly took talk as the prime site for his research in "sentimental physics," and his medical treatments often took the form of a proto-Freudian "talking exam." In records of Doctor Holmes' medical sessions with his friends and "patients" Nathaniel Hawthorne and Herman Melville, or in his descriptions of the practices of the doctor characters in his "medicated novels," we will see how the physician's main activity comes to center on carefully managed and monitored verbal dialogue with the patient. Here the Doctor's work begins to verge on the new speculative psychology, and his most influential writings as a psychologist also reflect his grounding in the dynamics of talk: he became a prime theorist of the divided self (or of what his student William James would later term the "social self"), defining all mental process as an internal conversation.

OUTLINE: THE POLES OF CONVERSATION

Both as a scientist and as a writer, then, Holmes based his practice upon "talk" and the analysis of talk. Recent sociology in the line of Norbert Elias and Michel Foucault has reminded us how much is at stake in what goes on at the dinner-table, in table-talk and table manners; Doctor Holmes' model conversations can serve as a diagnostic tool in just this way, helping us to isolate the culture-specific pressure points in even the most mundane of mid-century verbal interactions. *The Autocrat of the Breakfast-Table* does for the mid-century American parlor, club, and Lyceum what Schlegel's *Fragments* did for the conversations of his Jena circle, or what Diderot's *D'Alembert's Dream* did for the salon discussions of eighteenth-century France: it recognizes in the era's dominant discursive form the symptoms of fundamental social and psychological concerns and then transforms the record of random talk into a structured enactment of these primary cultural themes. The characteristic Holmesian conversation, for example, can be seen to develop as a bipolar household dialogue building out of explosive oppositions between the forces of "gravity" and "levity" (to use the crucial terms which connect literary, theological, and scientific thought in the period), and between tendencies to "house-keeping" and "house-breaking" (to use the terms so common to the era of Victorian domesticity).

Part One of this book ("Opening the conversation") works to situate Holmes' talk form in its larger cultural contexts, drawing out the implications of this vision of talk as it relates to and participates in key developments in the social, medical, intellectual, and literary history of the era. Chapter One ("The conversation of a culture") begins with an overview of the oral culture of mid-century America, suggesting the many ways in which the speech forms of everyday social and intellectual life in this period – the "gestation period" for the literature of the American Renaissance – could serve as models for new forms of literary writing, and stressing through a broad survey of contemporary modes of oral expression that this could indeed be seen as the nation's "Age of Conversation" as well as its "Golden Age of Oratory." A wide range of mid-century American writers and artists were centrally inspired by the culture's obsession with dialogic talk – or centrally concerned with potential dangers or problems latent within this conversational ideal. Many (such as Emily Dickinson, Henry Thoreau, or most especially Hawthorne) focused on conversation as a prime site in which to observe and explore problems of the social in a culture devoted to the individual: hopes and fears about the invisible interpersonal powers at play during each exchange in a love relation or friendship; anxieties about the difficult negotiation of a balance between selfhood and sympathy in any effort to transcend personal limits either through intimate relations or association with a broader community. Others celebrated conversation as in itself a fundamentally progressive form: some (like Holmes or Emerson) seeing in the ongoing turns of talk the movement basic to intellectual progress and ideological experimentation, a fundamental challenge to static, monolithic, or monological notions of selfhood or of culture, while more activist figures (such as Margaret Fuller, Bronson Alcott, Frederick Douglass, or Sojourner Truth) looked to conversation as a privileged vehicle for their efforts at personal and political emancipation, community conscious-raising, or social change. But perhaps most widespread and most crucial was a shared sense of conversation as a model for the larger culture: in this period, as again in our own day, the problems of American diversity and American dividedness and the possibilities for American pluralism were often figured as problems and possibilities of American conversation.

Chapter Two ("To change the order of conversation") extends this contextualizing overview. Highlighting Doctor Holmes' distinctive vision of dialogue as a non-synthetic verbal form built out of explosive interruptions and continual alternations between the diverse voices of multiple speakers, this chapter then works to situate his dynamic vision of American talk in relation to models of dialogue inherited from eighteenth-century England as well as to talk forms developed by the most significant nineteenth-century theorists of conversation: Emerson, Alcott, Fuller, and William Hazlitt. Turning from Holmes' written table-talk to analysis of his everyday social conversation, Chapter Three ("The electrodynamics of conversation") defines in detail the Doctor's peculiarly physicalist sense of interruptive talk as an "electrodynamic" system, an "art of the contact zone" – the site of charged "collisions of discourse" across cultures and between truly polarized, heterogeneous voices – and explores his vision of the appropriateness and social uses of such a talk form in the fluid and fragmented culture of Victorian America. The following chapters then show how Holmes' emphasis on such a mode of talk could inform his theory and practice in a wide range of fields, serving as the fundamental model in social relations (Chapter Four: "The cultural work of Holmesian talk"), in philosophy (Chapter Five: "A conversational approach to truth"), in medicine (Chapter Six: "Conversation and 'therapeutic nihilism'"), and in psychology (Chapter Seven: "The self in conversation"), as well as in literary writing.

Part Three ("The two poles of conversation") traces more schematically what is involved in each of the two alternating poles in Holmes' conception of interruptive conversation as a bipolar system: analyzing the Doctor's vision of the dialogue between the voices of "gravity" and "levity" in Chapter Eight, and his sense of the dialogue between the related urges to "house-keeping" and "house-breaking" in Chapter Nine. Succeeding chapters then work to situate Holmes' conversational applications of and plays upon the culturally defined "levity–gravity" topos in the contexts of contemporary intellectual and literary history as Holmes is set in a series of "conversations" with other related writers: with Melville, Sterne, and Dickens in Chapter Ten; with Hawthorne in Chapter Eleven; and finally, in Chapter Twelve, with his son, Supreme Court Justice Oliver Wendell Holmes Junior, who speaks most strongly for the post-bellum urge to "close the conversation" opened by his father during New England's mid-century cultural flowering.

LEARNING TO READ AMERICAN TALK: HOLMES IN DIALOGUE WITH THE AMERICAN RENAISSANCE

Relearning how to read Holmes and how to read mid-nineteenth-century conversation required the definition of a broad new interpretive context – an interdisciplinary method combining legal, medical, social, intellectual, and literary history with close textual analysis. The approach developed here was stimulated by a wide variety of critical work on the dynamic of dialogue that has emerged in recent years, in a number of different fields: in philosophy (with the conversation-based models of Richard Rorty and Habermas, or with the concept of a dialogical ethics in Martha Nussbaum and others); in linguistics (with new trends in conversation analysis, and with Mary Louise Pratt's notion of "arts of the contact zone" providing a dialogic model for understanding and taking advantage of the sites of meetings between cultures); in medical history, psycho-analysis and psychoanalytic literary criticism (with work on therapeutic conversation, doctor–patient dialogue, transference, and verbal diagnosis); in social history (with an intensified focus on the activities and dynamic economies of domestic life); and in literary history (with studies of the influence of "dialogic" oral models – the salon, coffeehouse, or carnival – on early developments in British American *belles lettres* and in the English and Russian novel).

The resulting revaluation of Holmes as central to the "conversation of his culture" redefines the context for our reading of other major literary works of the American Renaissance. Counterbalancing our usual emphasis on the native heritage of American Puritanism, Holmes reminds us of important relations with the literature and culture of eighteenth-century England and Europe. (Most basically, the Doctor's literary and scientific writings highlight the ways in which the philosophy, psychology, and literature of eighteenth century Sensibility, which had evoked such a powerful response in early America, remained vitally alive through the early nineteenth century, serving as a crucial formative influence on the development of a national "sensibility" in this transitional period.) Expanding our traditional perspectives on mid-century conceptions of "Nature," he explores the implications of such beliefs as they might be applied in literary naturalism, in modern natural science, or in the "Nature cure" of contemporary medicine, and as they could be associated not only with defenses of the country virtues of Adamic simplicity but also with promotion of the metropolitan values of cosmopolitan cultivation. Complementing our notions of Romantic Organicism, he calls our attention to American versions of an alternative Romantic Irony. Broadening our sense of the scope of American Humor, he defines the place of the over-civilized, self-conscious, and self-important figure of pedantry and urbanity who always stood as necessary foil to the Yankee and Frontiersman in the folk imagination, while also speaking for the vitality of a tradition of scientific and philosophic comedy coming out of Rabelais, Swift, Sterne and Lichtenberg, and continuing in America from Irving and Twain on into the present day. Finally, Holmes' talk-based works complicate our stereotyped vision of Victorian America as dominated by a genteel culture of complacent optimism, leaving us with a very different sense of the spirit of the age and of its genteel culture. Developing out of a continual alternation between opposing voices, which means that every question opens into a multiplicity of possible responses in a process that unsettles fixed standards and involves an almost pathological avoidance of direct statements or conclusions, the multivoiced table-talk writings which made Holmes a major cultural spokesman can be seen as representative expressions of the profound anxieties and indecisions of an "age of uncertainty."

PART ONE

Opening the conversation

CHAPTER I

THE CONVERSATION OF A CULTURE
Strange Powers of Speech

It must always happen that the true work of genius should proceed out of the wants and deeds of the age as well as the writer, and so be the first form with which his genius combines, as sculpture was perfect in Phidias' age . . . Do that which lies next you, O Man!

Emerson, *Journals*

If a man wishes to acquaint himself with the real history of the world, with the spirit of the age, he must not go first to the state-house or the court-room. The subtle spirit of life must be sought in facts nearer. It is what is done and suffered in the house, in the constitution, in the temperament, in the personal history, that has the profoundest interest for us . . . Is it not plain that not in senates, or courts, or chambers of commerce, but in the dwelling-house must the true character and hope of the time be consulted?

Let us then come out of the public square and enter the domestic precinct. Let us go to the sitting-room, the table-talk and the expenditure of our contemporaries.

Emerson, "Domestic Life," *Society and Solitude*[1]

THE "CULTURE OF SHEER VERBOSITY": ORATORY AND CONVERSATION

If each age sees the flowering of its own representative art form, it was clear that in Emerson's America the first forms for new art could only proceed out of one powerful, popular, and pervasive medium: the spoken word. The period between the 1830s and the 1850s in America – a crucial period for the emergence of distinctively American modes of expression in a wide range of popular writing and public performance, and also the "gestation period" for the literature of the American Renaissance – was an overwhelmingly oral age; its wants and deeds in almost every domain were formed by the fundamental dynamics of speech. In fact this mid-century explosion of American speech seemed to burst out simultaneously in two modes that extended its influence into two normally separate spheres. Since this was both an age of oratory and an age of conversation, the spoken word could decisively inform activity both in state-houses and private-houses, in court-rooms and sitting-rooms, in chambers of commerce and in the chambers of a "domestic economy."

Of course the rolling, exhortative rhetorical periods – what Harold Bloom calls the "interior oratory" – of the first Emerson journal passage cited above reflect his early enthrallment with Daniel Webster's example of Man Speaking in the public square. Inspired by his personal experience of "moments of Eloquence" while listening to sermons and lectures by Edward Everett or orations by "the godlike Daniel," Emerson had made the crucial counter-Augustinian conversion from theology to rhetoric, from a calling as minister to a new vocation as lecturer. And the young Emerson could recognize this personal progress as a type of the progress of the age: "I look upon the Lecture room as the true church of today."[2] When the Golden Age of the Revolutionary Heroes was succeeded by the Golden Age of American Oratory, the channeling of civic energy into new forms of heroic action in the verbal arena would serve as a powerful stimulation for all citizens – including, as Emerson was well aware, many aspiring writers.[3]

To foreign visitors like Alexis de Tocqueville, Harriet Martineau, or Dickens, the American democracy seemed indeed to be developing as a huge lecture room or debating hall, loud with the cries of competing orators; this widespread fascination with the powers of public speech stood out as one of the new culture's defining traits. And certainly public speaking *was* central to the vital ferment of mid-century American social life. This could be seen in the celebrations of voice and vocal self-culture inspired by the mobbed tours of Italian opera stars or of singers like Jenny Lind; in a widespread enthrallment with the exaggerated gestures and virtuoso vocal stylings of traveling thespians in the mold of Edwin Forrest; in the remarkable proliferation of elocutionary rhetoric manuals and rote prep-books preaching self-advancement through the magnetic powers of speech; in the increasing centrality of speech training in mid-century American schoolrooms, where new textbooks stressed memorization and practice in oral delivery as the best training for the oral performances of public affairs; in the mania for public lectures that launched the Lyceum movement in cities, towns, and even villages across the land, bringing out large, diverse crowds of people who had obviously been hungering for the broadening of horizons offered by this new form of declamatory adult education; and in the consequent growth of the new profession of lecturer, a sort of secular ministry that opened stimulating and lucrative new opportunites for Americans aspiring to make their way as authors, or as verbal performers. At the same time, other testing grounds for new forms of oral self-expression emerged with the trend toward dramatically personal testimonials now given top billing at increasingly large and spectacular meetings of reform groups, as the movements for abolition or womens' rights came to depend upon and to be dominated by the powerful voices and magnified personalities of charismatic platform performers whose speeches made them not simply spokespeople for their political vision but embodiments of it. And crowds of listeners were apparently as thrilled as the speakers were with the possibilities of these new modes of vocal performance. In all regions of the country, a distinctly American enthrallment with the collective drama of public speech was expressed in a mass passion for verbal fireworks on every Fourth of July, for sonorous display rhetoric at almost every civic or educational ceremony in even the smallest localities, for booster talks and toasts at increasingly popular public dinners and conventions, for spell-binding histrionics in the court-room, and for a new mode of gushing grandiloquence from the pulpit.[4]

Whether outdoors in revivalist camp-meetings or indoors in big-city churches, religion in the mid-century came to center upon public, communal experiences of emotion spontaneously overflowing through the spoken word: during the Second Great Awakening, a revived faith revolved around neither good works nor doctrinal study but rather around sensationalistic vocal enactments of the experience of direct personal revelation – since the signs that a speaker was possessed by the Truth and thus in possession of the Truth were here primarily oral – and the new wave of itinerant evangelical preachers (such as Charles Grandison Finney) would arouse and possess their giant audiences through frenzied and theatrical performances of ecstatic inspiration; at the same time, for established, urban congregations the prime example of the new ministerial eloquence was the fiery, compelling Henry Ward Beecher, whose large Brooklyn church was said never to have had an empty seat during his thirty years as its pastor, as his rhapsodic interchanges with his listeners offered them immediate experience of his "new religion of sentiment," carrying them away upon waves of unrestrained emotion and thrilling them with sudden, searing transitions from hope to despair, laughter to tears. And these irrational powers of public speech also came to dominate the process of legal argument in the mid-century American court-room. Court days in smaller communities became highlights on the entertainment calendar, as rowdy packed houses would gather to hear local talents square off and display their forensic powers; many people would also travel long distances to larger court-rooms just to hear a well-known advocate argue a case. Among lawyers, Rufus Choate was the most celebrated speaker, an exotically cloaked "wizard of the court-room" who held listeners spellbound through the vehement intensity of his performances, and whose almost eery mastery of rhetoric and psychology, it was said, helped him to charm juries the way a snake charmed birds.[5]

A mesmeric or mellifluous voice was also the key to a political career in this period. Without question, the preeminent political orators in this Golden Age of Oratory were Daniel Webster, Henry Clay, John C. Calhoun, and Edward Everett. Though a speech by one of these full-voiced politicians could often last for many hours or even days, huge throngs would stand on tiptoe to try to pick up even the echo of their rolling periods in an actual performance. Then, at a second stage, these addresses were also attended to throughout the nation as the centerpieces of American public ritual; texts of commemorative speeches and Congressional orations by the major national orators were often reprinted and widely distributed, to be reviewed, studied, recited from memory, and applauded as the cultural equipment most basic to every citizen in the new democracy. Because of this wide dissemination of speeches through pamphlets, newspapers, and school readers, as Daniel Boorstin observes, "American history began to seem a series of events connecting famous orations . . . Oration seemed almost to displace legislation as the main form of political action."[6] Webster, the "Great Stone Face" whose granitic presence spoke for his immense political force as he sought to hold the Union together and enforce his construction of the Constitution through the exercise of his sublime, magniloquent voice, came to epitomize the era's sense that national self-definition must be achieved and defended through the verbal performances of powerful speakers. And experiencing such an eloquent orator's words seemed to offer isolated, divided Americans rare glimpses of the possibilities of commonality; a Golden Age address was not only often about collective vision but offered – through the dynamic process of its own performance and reception, the emotional collaboration between speaker and listeners, the public expression of shared sentiment – a defining experience of participation in the nation's collective life. During a successful speech, for what Emerson termed a "moment of Eloquence," speaker and audience might feel themselves to be transformed, responding together as a loving community, a united "body politic." But if public speech was a site for the sharing of sentiment, it was also seen as a battleground, a test of power. And epic oratorical duels between political campaigners or between verbal gladiators like Webster, Calhoun and Clay – struggles over the most solemn and crucial questions of national vision – also became the spectacular mass entertainments of the day. This nineteenth-century stress on the primacy of rhetorical action and agonism could then also be projected back into the past: even the Founding Fathers were now refashioned as verbal gladiators, with their new-found (or newly fabricated) Revolutionary speeches revered as "classics" defining an American heritage – a verbal "tradition" largely invented by the later generation, reflecting its own desires and its own special needs.[7]

In America's beginning was the spoken word. It was in the nineteenth century that a great new emphasis was placed on the widely shared sense that this nation had been, as one 1842 journalist put it, "spoken into existence."[8] And if it was given its founding impulses by the voices of Revolutionary orators, born out of a rhetorical "Declaration" of independence and a written Constitution, the nation was a linguistic construct that would depend for its definition and its continued vitality on public speakers – arguing about constructions of those founding words, interpreting the law for the people, and interpreting the people's will before law-makers. "To the extent that America had been spoken into existence, it had to be maintained and consolidated by constant eloquence," observes Tony Tanner: "America and public speaking were, then, coeval." In this spirit, John Quincy Adams urged Americans, in his 1810 *Lectures on Rhetoric and Oratory*, to "yield the guidance of a nation to the dominion of the voice." And, as Robert Ferguson notes, lawyers and orators then took very much to heart the "solemn obligation to speak and to speak often."[9]

"Oratory," writes F. O. Matthiessen, "was, as Emerson recognized while still a boy, the one branch of literature in which America then had a formed tradition."[10] But it was not until this later Golden Age that public speaking came to be appreciated as literature – not only as legislative action but also as a creative art – and celebrated as a distinctively American form. It seemed to Henry T. Tuckerman that mid-century Americans were only belatedly discovering the first forms of a representative tradition of national expression:

Orations constitute our literary staple by the same law that causes letters and comedies to attain such perfection in France, domestic novels in England, and the lyrical drama in Italy. They spring from the wants and developments of our national life.

Soon, though, a noisy pack of anthologists sprang forth to fill this gap in our knowledge, codifying this tradition as they celebrated it: "In no other country have orators and oratory played so conspicuous a part as in America," boasted one anthology editor; "Athens did not produce more than fifty-four distinguished orators and rhetoricians. We have produced more than that number within half a century," exclaimed another mid-century editor/booster.[11] Surveying this past, Bronson Alcott like many others would find here further evidence of a glorious national ingenuity and originality: in an effusive journal entry, he hails "the lecture" as "the American invention." And young Emerson was quick to pick up the infectious spirit of such hyperbole: "If ever there was a country where eloquence has a power," he asserted in one of his two enthusiastic lectures on the subject, "it is the United States." "Eloquence," one of Emerson's favorite words, recurs as a pervasive key word and enthusiastic refrain in many speeches and writings of the antebellum era – speaking for the age's fundamentally vocal model of the mystery of interpersonal power and of the hope for national Union.[12]

    In this era, then, Americans on every level of society seemed to become infatuated with the sound of their own voices – or with the collective ecstasy seen to be available to listeners standing for hours amidst huge crowds to be swept away by the voice of a celebrated speaker. And finally this astonishing national obsession with eloquence left many observers deeply ambivalent. By the 1850s, Emerson himself would feel the need to temper his attitudes both toward Webster and toward this American obsession with oratory.

Post-war comic lecturers (including Bill Nye, Petroleum Nasby, Artemus Ward, Orpheus Kerr, Mr. Dooley, Mark Twain, and Doctor Holmes) would find this pre-war mode of inflated, over-heated, and often bellicose rhetoric – what Twain termed "yell-ocution" – to be a rich mine for their own tall tales and deflating verbal tricks. As Finley P. Dunne's Mr. Dooley put it, ". . . whin [a man] has nawthin' to say, an' has a lot iv wur-ruds that come with a black coat, he's an orator." Even the crusading reform lecturer Wendell Phillips could admit that perhaps this nascent culture had given birth to more than its share of such orators: to an outsider, joked Phillips, it might sometimes seem that the first act of any lisping Yankee baby, as soon as it could sit up in its cradle, would be to call the nursery to order and then launch into an extended address to the house.[13] In a nation that seemed to have been spoken into existence, each child might now seem to be born into grandiloquent public speech. But many foreign visitors to mid-century America – such as Dickens, Trollope, Martineau and Tocqueville – would simply be annoyed when confronted with this pervasive local habit of speechifying. The standoffish Tocqueville seemed to find himself buttonholed by bombastic monologists at every turn; after his 1831–32 tour he concluded that this preoccupation with oratory seemed to bring with it a sad impoverishment in the ability of Americans to engage in casual, nuanced, or intimate conversation:

An American cannot converse, but he certainly can orate; even his intimate talk falls into a formal lecture. He speaks to you as if he were addressing a meeting; and if he should chance to become warm in the discussion, he will begin to say "Gentlemen" to the lone person with whom he is conversing.[14]

Looking back upon this oral culture from the perspective of the twentieth century, many culture critics have found themselves, very much like Tocqueville, baffled and unsettled. While Constance Rourke seems to find an intoxicating pleasure in entering into this mid-century scene, catching the era's contagious fever in her own words –

In this era of shattering change, many shrill or stentorian voices were lifted; orators appeared on every platform; with their babel arose an equal babel of print; perhaps there never was such a noisy chorus or so fervid a response. Words – the popular mind was intoxicated by words; speech might have provided liberation; sheer articulation apparently became a boon.

As if in response to a powerful wish, a broad sonority was rolling all around; the country was filled with an oratory which seemed to catch and hold a multitudinous feeling. Here and there an irritable critic might be heard declaring that eloquence was the curse of the country; but the demand for a broad and moving overflow of speech only crested higher.

– others like W. J. Cash can only observe America's oral age with an ambivalent awe:

A gorgeous, primitive art, addressed to the autonomic system and not to the encephalon, rhetoric is of course dear to the heart of the simple man everywhere. In its purest and most natural form, oratory, it flourishes wherever he forgathers – and particularly in every new land where bonds are loosed and imagination is vaulting. It flourished over the whole American country in these days of continental expansion, as it has rarely flourished elsewhere at any time.

More recently, in her polemic against the loss of intellectual and theological rigor in a mid-century culture of consumption pandering to the narcissistic desires of a sentimental public, Ann Douglas has responded with unconcealed horror at the specter of what she describes, most fundamentally, as a "culture of sheer verbosity."[15]

THE "ANIMATING SPIRIT OF THE AGE": AMERICAN FORMS OF TALK

But, Tocqueville and Dickens and other foreign visitors to the contrary, mid-century Americans knew that not every discussion in the land turned inevitably into a one-way harangue; not every American came on as an Ancient Mariner monologist. Though it may have been quieter and more complex than many Senate or soap-box expressions, and though it may not have been so obvious to the tourist's eye and ear, dialogue was vitally alive during the nation's socially mobile oral age. Indeed just as oratory was peaking as a mass phenomenon, the more private art of conversation – a speech form related to oratory but also in some ways its complement – was enjoying a rebirth of its own, subtly expanding the range of the voluble native tongue as it too became a popular craze and national obsession.

Recognizing the parallels between these two emerging modes of speech, Bronson Alcott wanted to put in a patent claim on the domestic form of talk:

> Emerson made the *Lecture*,
> and
> Alcott is making the *Conversation*.[16]

Having considered the path of oratory, Alcott was sure that spontaneous, interactive talk offered a more powerful and more democratic
means for establishing a true, heart-to-heart collaboration between
speaker and audience: "The lecture is too formal. It is, beside,
presuming. Man doth not meet his fellow on equal terms . . . Only
the living, spoken, answered word is final." At peak moments, such
conversation could open out of the prosaic world of monological
truths uttered by monadic selves into an experience of communal
inspiration – developing as a multivocal sharing of spirit, an ecstatic
"pentecost of tongues, touching the chords of melody in all
minds."[17]

But the second Emerson epigraph cited at the beginning of this
chapter shows that he too noted that the "genius" which had begun
to speak on the public stage through the age's representative art of
oratory could also be found lying nearer to him, in a more local
habitation; the "spirit of the age" could also move through the
subtle cross-currents of sitting-room table-talk: "Let us then come
out of the public square and enter the domestic precinct. Let us go
to the sitting-room, the table-talk and the expenditure of our
contemporaries."[18] After his youthful ventures into the new arts of
lecturing, the Concord bard would also recognize that "Wise,
cultivated, genial conversation is the last flower of civilization, and
the best result which life has to offer us, – a cup for gods, which has
no repentance."[19] Intoxicating, free-flowing dinner-table dialogue
might bring out, within our daily lives in the civilized city of man,
resonances of an original *sacra conversazione*: it incorporates within its
call-and-response movement the structure of the Christian conversation with divine spirit. While Emerson recognized that on most
days the talk at the sitting-room tea parties of Victorian America was
stiff and stilted – "In common hours, society sits cold and statuesque.
We all stand waiting, empty" – he nonetheless dreamed, like Alcott,
that this conversation could potentially become a sort of Pentecostal
talking-in-tongues, an eruption of the divine within everyday parlor
life: "Then cometh the god and converts the statues into fiery men
. . . and the meaning of the very furniture, of cup and saucer, of
chair and clock and tester, is manifest."[20] Helping us to rise above
ourselves, to interact with others, to recognize our places as parts in
a larger whole, the back-and-forth "wave" movements of such
dialogue open access for Emerson into an oceanic spiritual
experience:

The Beatitude of Conversation . . . I have no book & no pleasure in life comparable to this. Here I come down to the shore of the Sea & dip my hands in its miraculous waves. Here I am assured of the eternity, & can spare all omens, all prophecies, all religions, for I see & know that which they obscurely announce.[21]

We miss fundamental aspects of Emerson's thought and writing if we define him too simply as the promoter of an atomistic self-reliance and fail to note that, throughout his career, he celebrates the rhetorical movement of multivocal talk – with its enforced alternations between successive speakers – as a necessary counter to the spiritual and political oppression inherent in oratorical monologism. "Conversation is a game of circles," he writes in the key passage in "Circles": "When each new speaker strikes a new light, emancipates us from the oppression of the last speaker, to oppress us with the greatness and exclusiveness of his own thought, then yields us to another redeemer, we seem to recover our rights, to become men."[22] Emerson's two essays on "Eloquence" are then balanced by those on "Clubs" and "Domestic Life" which promote "society" as a necessary complement to self-reliant (and self-enclosed) "solitude."[23] Working to fathom the dynamics of conversation, these later essays – following up important suggestions in earlier essays like "Circles" – read the dialogic turns of domestic talk as the most basic type of intellectual and spiritual progress. "For . . . Alcott, Fuller, and Emerson, conversation was not just a pastime but also a fine art and fit subject for philosophy," observes Lawrence Buell: "And as an art form, the conversation came as close to a truly transcendental utterance as the movement ever attained." Mason Wade explains that

to the intellectual New Englanders of the forties conversation was indispensable and a weighty matter. Conversation was the method of Transcendentalism, the animating spirit of the age, and the great conversationalist was as manifestly a genius as a great writer, preacher, or orator.[24]

But the Transcendentalists were certainly not alone in their fascination with this "animating spirit of the age." In their excitement about the spiritual and philosophical applications of dialogue, Emerson, Alcott, and Fuller were not dreamers on the fringes of society but enthusiastic participants in a broad-based tendency of the larger culture, making important contributions to a general, and crucial, cultural debate about the place of various speech modes in

American life. A wide range of mid-century Americans – from diverse backgrounds, social classes, and regions – were as intrigued by the mercurial movements of conversation as they were by the magnetism and charisma of oratory. Indeed, they could not help but be affected by the workings of conversation. In this period, meeting and talking with others became not only a fundamental aspect of everyday private life but also a dynamic central to the workings of a number of public activities at the heart of civil society. Whether in elite salons or in working-class saloons, an explosion of talk forms pervaded and shaped many diverse areas of mid-century social experience. In their homes, their schools, their doctor's offices, their hotels and boardinghouses, their restaurants and public houses, their steamboats and trains and other forms of public transportation, their conversation clubs, literary societies, reform meetings and other voluntary associations, Americans everywhere seemed to be finding a new release in dialogic talk.

First of all, of course, this was an era that epitomized many of its cultural ideals in the image of the Victorian parlor. In the "parlor culture" of the nineteenth century, the "salon" ideal of the seventeenth and eighteenth centuries – a model that had actually been enacted only in rare and rarefied talk sessions of small circles of aristocrats and *philosophes* – was democratized and domesticated as it filtered down to become the pattern for everyday home life of a very broad spectrum of the middle class, in every region of the country.[25] Now almost everyone aspired to have their home filled with "salon style" conversation – or at least with stilted and clumsy attempts at such talk. For the social intercourse within these half-private, half-public parlors (named from the French *parler*) always centered on verbal dialogue. Many Americans came to see training in the "salon style" of talk as a key cultural attainment – a prime tool for social success.[26] Thus, parlor conversation was seen not as a retreat from public life but as a preparation for it; the dynamic of talk was seen as fundamental to social intercourse both inside and outside of the home – and as an important medium of connection between private and public worlds.

And this talk-based "parlor culture" was certainly not restricted to the domestic sphere. Mid-century America was, as historian Katherine Grier observes, "a world full of parlors."[27] Indeed, in this era many public and commercial meeting places – waiting rooms at the fanciest photographers' studios, public rooms at the newest city hotels, meeting rooms of leading social clubs and associations, and group seating areas on the most advanced steamboats and trains – were made over as breathtakingly extravagant versions of the domestic parlor, thus making the model parlor experience accessible even to those who could not afford a full-scale parlor at home. And these hybrid "public parlors" were very popular attractions. European travelers to the United States were astonished to see how many Americans chose to come in off the streets and pass their free time in the splendid public rooms of urban hotels, and how many families actually chose to live in these hotels – and thus had to use these strangely open public arenas as the sites for their more private talks and visits. (And these foreign visitors were similarly shocked by a key innovation at the huge new American "palace hotels" being built at many vacation spots: the common dining system of the "American Plan," which forced conventioneers, tourists, and traveling tradesmen to share their meal-tables [and their sometimes nervous, strained table-talk] with strangers. Speaking for the mid-century fascination with new venues for conversational exchange that might test the boundaries of public and private life, the American Plan made a hotel stay not a get-away to privacy but an experience of experimental interaction with the temporary and diverse community of hotel guests.)[28] Like hotels, boats and trains were also sites in which people were often forced into fascinating or uncomfortable conversations with disparate groups of strangers. The magnificent reception rooms on "palace steamboats" of the 1840s and then the much-advertised "parlor cars" introduced on mid-century trains (their woodworked interiors, draperies, carpets, and salon seating associated with the name of George Pullman) offered travelers the comforting sense that, despite the potentially fearful geographical and social mobility of mid-century American life, the boat and the train were still Victorian homes. Many middle-class citizens wanted to believe that the parlor ideal of refined and civilized talk could be imposed upon and control the increasingly unavoidable and increasingly baffling social confrontations of everyday public intercourse.

While unplanned meetings with strangers in impersonal public spaces would of course not always be governed by parlor etiquette, versions of parlor talk did crucially define most people's involvements with the smaller "publics" of their own cohort. For mid-century Americans of all classes, genders, regions, and ethnicities, social life outside the home and the workplace was a series of meetings, centering around a highly developed network of talk communities: political clubs, reform associations, coffeehouse discussion groups, salons, Lyceums, debating societies, literary and philosophical societies, militias, trade associations, fire companies, and so on. The astonishing proliferation of such voluntary associations from 1830–60 was, as Stuart Blumin observes, "one of the [era's] outstanding characteristics . . . without parallel in American history."[29] In eighteenth-century America, a vital tradition of metropolitan conversation had been kept alive through the oral performances of an aristocratic elite at select clubs, salons, tea-tables, and coffeehouses across the country, but the tradition was crucially transformed as it went public over the course of the nineteenth century. No longer set apart from the larger society, "private societies" became central to its functioning – engaging a broad spectrum of the population in their varied activities, and developing a variety of modes of discourse in their discussions that became instrumental in shaping public opinion in public sphere. (These emerging societies included, in Nancy Fraser's apt formulation, a vital network of "competing counterpublics" – from "elite women's publics" to "working-class publics" – formed at the same time as the groupings of an "official" or "liberal" public sphere, operating separately from it but always understanding themselves "as part of a potentially wider . . . 'public at large'.") Whether they were reformist "projecting" societies or clubs that were primarily social, mid-century associations developed as small-scale social experiments each designed to encourage a certain mode of conversational interaction and to explore the form of community brought about by such a talk mode.[30] But the talk that was both means and end at these meetings was now not always that of the classic "salon style"; with the great expansion in venues for dialogue came a great expansion in the diversity of talk modes explored. Clubs, for example, became immensely popular in this period, but their meetings were organized around a very broad range of interactive practices. Freewheeling festival wit and brilliant repartee were the central attractions at select, all-male conversation clubs like the Sketch Club or the Century Club in New York, or the Saturday Club in Boston, that emerged as the pride of every mid-century metropole, and were designed to test the dialogical possibilities in bringing together disparate groupings of a city's social and intellectual elite. At the same time, a more precious and decorous *badinage* became the dominant style at the genteel literary salons that were becoming the height of fashion in urban centers. In new-formed talk circles like the Transcendental Club in Concord, though, talk was seen less as a stylish and pleasurable form of social exchange than as a provocative form of intellectual inquiry, and club meetings featured dauntingly abstruse philosophical dialogues on moral questions. Consciously opposed to the pretension and prudishness of this sort of New England intellectual discourse, the metropolitan sophisticates in New York's informal Knickerbocker Circle, or later in the "Bohemian" Circle at Pfaff's Restaurant, saw themselves less as philosophers than as worldly, epicurean *boulevardiers*, developing a verbal style based on bawdy, Rabelaisian humor and loud, free, sometimes violent argument. Departing from "polite" speech in a talk form vitalized by their contact with a mix of middle-class and working-class people, these sorts of circles brought the literary discussion session closer to the more rowdy working-class culture of the political club, the saloon, and the fire company.[31]

Among the many men's clubs that arose at mid-century, for various classes and trades, the firemen's societies were perhaps the most notable social centers for working men. Though some such Firemen's Halls were built on the model of elite clubs as splendid "public parlors," these associations were best known not for "polite" talk so much as for their competitive brawling and for the sort of boisterous discussion so loved by visitors like Walt Whitman.[32] Less organized than the trade association, the saloon (another newly important institution of the mid-century) could also serve as a private club for its regular customers, functioning as a working-class version of the salon as it offered conversation and an important sense of community to often isolated young men, bringing together a "public" of workers from a trade, an ethnic group, or a neighborhood through interactions organized around storytelling, joking, rough debating, and singing as well as drinking – what one commentator describes as "rough masculine conviviality" rather than feminized parlor-room delicacy.[33]

But mid-century American women were themselves not confined to the traditionally feminine domestic realms of the parlor or the salon. Over the course of the century they became very active in establishing a whole network of women's talk groups: tea societies, reform societies, aid societies, literary societies, reading circles, and clubs. Indeed some estimates suggest that, despite the exponential growth of men's clubs in the period, women's clubs actually came to outnumber men's by the end of the century.[34] In the eighteenth century, elite women had already begun to carve out a distinctive domain for themselves within an emerging public sphere through tea-table dialogues that arose as counters and rivals to the discussions of the all-male coffeehouses – establishing a tradition of women's sociability revolving around a different talk form, a different venue, and a different stimulating beverage.[35] But the possibilities for women's talk circles developed dramatically from these beginnings with the explosive growth of a "counter civil society" of women's associations over the course of the nineteenth century across diverse classes, in diverse venues, and exploring diverse conversational styles.[36] Mid-century tea parties might tend to light, personal gossip; aid society meetings might tend to the self-righteous tones of a moral crusade; reading circle discussions might be either sentimental or pedantic. But mid-century women's talk groups were generally distinguished by their concern with the development of their own distinctive forms of discourse and by their stress on the centrality of communal talk to their enterprise. Indeed a main goal in all of these experiments was helping women to develop their own powers of articulation, first in "private societies" and then in the larger public sphere. Margaret Fuller's landmark Boston Conversations for Women of 1839–44, though they were set up in some ways as a serious philosophical alternative to the social chatter dominant in many genteel ladies' groups, nonetheless epitomized the fundamental aspiration shared by many mid-century women's societies: they were meant to help women come to see their own conversation not as decorative but as critical and consequential. The searching, effusive, and self-serious "consciousness-raising" Conversations led by Fuller broke the ground for modern feminism, exploring both the issues and the dialogic meeting mode that would define a new women's movement to come. But whether at Fuller's lofty Women's Conversations or at stuffy Ladies' Club teas, mid-century women aspired to give birth to new voices, new thoughts, and new selves through the maieutic process of dialogic talk.[37]

The widely shared mid-century mania for self-culture through conversation led to many experiments in the educational uses of dialogue. Vaguely Platonic teacher–pupil dialogues were the shocking, influential innovation at Bronson Alcott's experimental nursery school, and his book *Conversations with Children on the Gospels* of 1836–37 trumpeted the results of his letting young children work to

discover the truths of the Bible stories for themselves, in their own
words, through group discussion, rather than simply learning to
repeat the already revealed Truths forced upon them through the
lectures of a teacher or the sermons of a minister. And Alcott then
also applied this same revolutionary method in the many adult
education groups he sponsored. In the late 1830s and 1840s both
Alcott and Fuller began to travel widely as "professional conversationalists" offering to lead public conversations – in which talk begins
to become a form of show – and found large audiences ready to buy
pricey tickets to attend these solemn, organized "panel discussions"
now being tested as a new forum for intellectual development.
Thrilled with the financial and philosophical success of these early
talk sessions, Alcott came to believe that his "parlour teaching"
would emerge alongside the Lyceum lecture as a powerful new force
for cultural reform, a vehicle for awakening the masses, and so
extended his "ministry of talking" in demanding, months-long tours
that had him conversing in cities and towns across the Northeast and
the Midwest during the 1840s, 1850s, and 1870s.[38] Soon, high-
minded public exchanges were set up in Academies or music halls
across the country so that eager citizens could strain to utter
profundities in imitation of these Transcendentalist experiments. At
the same time, learned societies began to offer interactive assemblies
called "conversazione," at which they would offer an interested
general audience varied demonstrations of their work. And earnest
but plodding discussion sessions were beginning to offer a way out of
lecturing, memorization and rote learning at Mechanics' Institutes,
liberal churches, and some Lyceums, paving the way for revolutionary changes in American pedagogy. Indeed, with the expansion
of literacy through the nineteenth century, both speaking and
reading began to be learned through and associated with talk. A
newly "conversational" speech education in public schools was based
upon earlier Lyceum experiments with discussion.[39] And, to an
extent we may now find hard to imagine, reading in the mid-century
was a profoundly social, collaborative activity. Not only in the
children's conversational readings of the Bible at Alcott's school and
in the family reading circles in many Victorian parlors, but also in
the more public reading–discussion groups that multiplied rapidly in
this period – library associations, literary and author societies,
women's book clubs, Chautauqua Circles, and so on – Americans
read together and then discussed their reading together, hoping

through such talk sessions to gain middle-class culture and cultivation, but also in the process developing skills in rational–critical
debate that made them more effective "public-oriented" subjects
and then significantly shaped the modes of public discussion in the
larger society.[40] The mid-century Chautauqua movement was built
upon a public hunger for just this sort of self-culture – an earnest
desire to work continually on cultivating or improving the self, even
during holidays. Begun as a vacation school for Sunday school
teachers but opening its doors to the demand for general adult
education in the 1870s, the Chautauqua Institution in New York state
pioneered the "learning vacation" concept, with its American Plan
resort hotel, the Athenaeum, and surrounding community of ginger-
bread cottages, amphitheaters, and Halls of Philosophy offering
guests a full weekly curriculum of artistic performances, Lyceum-style
popular lectures, question-and-answer sessions, and "conversations."
Indeed a broad notion of conversation was (and still is) central to the
Chautauqua's mission: bringing together (generally middle-class)
people from diverse fields to discuss serious ideas in a civilized or
genteel environment, in response to diverse (though generally middle-
brow) programming, as members of a temporary model community
devoted to serious debate about the state of contemporary culture.
The Chautauqua ideal became a nationwide movement as its
founding book club, the Literary and Scientific Circle, spawned a
network that by the end of the century included 10,000 local reading
circles – about 2,500 of them in villages with populations of less than
500, and some even formed in prisons – and some 300 independent
Chautauqua centers in addition to the original Institution.

If the Chautauqua movement grew out of the discussion sessions of
liberal church groups, talk models also shaped other crucial shifts in
the modes of mid-century ministry and teaching. Many liberal
clergymen, for example, developed a newly "feminized," cosmopolitan form of polite Christianity as they adopted their parishioners'
self-conscious, refined "salon style" of conversation, turning away
from monological sermons to center their ministry on the "Christian
conversation" of sentimental drawing-room tea-talk with the
ladies.[41] Oliver Wendell Holmes' novel *Elsie Venner* shows how both
mid-century churchmen and doctors had begun to take drawing-
room conversation as the prime site for their various forms of
ministration. And indeed some leading physicians, like Doctor
Holmes himself, drew upon their experiences with the drawing-room

talk of the mid-century to reorient notions of medical conversation as
they experimented with forms of proto-psychoanalytic verbal dialogue in the "talking exams" now just beginning to emerge as key
elements in both diagnosis and therapy.

The mid-century was, then, crucially marked by an incredible
expansion in the discursive public sphere; Americans found themselves faced with ever-increasing opportunities to join others in social
talk. And those who couldn't talk could always read about it.
Upwardly mobile but tongue-tied newcomers, unaccustomed to
these new speaking roles in the social theater, could arm themselves
with toasts, aperçus, and retorts from a host of best-selling prompt-
books or parlor primers, formulaic guides to easy speech and correct
pronunciation. Others too timid even to test the waters of the new
spoken arts could content themselves with the casual company of
great minds in written form – Coleridge, Goethe, Hazlitt, and
Madame de Staël were but a few of the authors celebrated for their
published table-talk. Indeed, the published conversations of these
authors, as those of Dr. Johnson recorded by Boswell, were now often
ranked as their most valuable works. On the more local level, too,
the best conversational moments of each new day would be highly
prized and always quickly recorded in letters, diaries, and in multi-
plying minor collections of printed talk. At the height of this
fashionable interest in drawing-room conversation, cultural commentators and anthologists – like Rufus Griswold in his *The Republican
Court* (1855) – also sought to fill in the history of a native tradition of
such talk, looking back especially to the "republican court," a
continental network of affiliated salons for the new nation's governing classes established in the 1790s by Martha Washington, in an
effort to recreate a sense of the distinctive character of this new sort
of para-political talk arena developed to suit the needs of the young
democracy – combining polite sociability with a republican simplicity of manners, and giving elite women as well as men some voice in
the public sphere. While some might worry that the mid-century
proliferation of salons was based on dangerous imitation of a
European tradition of aristocratic luxury, Griswold and others were
keen to reclaim salon talk (along the lines of Martha Washington's
model) as an American form with American antecedents that could
stand alongside political oratory as a mode of speech with an
important place in the development of republican society.[42]

Fuller translated Johann Eckermann's *Conversations with Goethe* in

1839, but perhaps the clearest sign of the times was the American popularity of Hazlitt's 1846 translation of *The Table-Talk of Martin Luther*. As Emerson observed, "It is not [Luther's] theologic works . . . but his Table-Talk, which is still read by men." The mid-century wanted to know the doctrine in the life, the religion in social relations, the "spirit" in what Emerson called the domestic "facts nearer." "Conversation is the vent of character as well as of thought," he explained; and many people in this period certainly seemed less interested in reading the end results of thought – presented as universal truths or doctrines – than in following an individual's process of thought, and feeling, in a particular context, finding there the most telling lived examples of wisdom, ethics, or good sense. Moving away from the formal monological sermon, the age of conversation responded most strongly to the voice – in Wordsworth's or Emerson's gendered terms – of a man speaking to men, revealing in the homely dress of his extemporary reactions his character, his affections, his readiness, his mind in its intercourse with the immediate world.[43]

Certainly, as these references to Goethe, Dr. Johnson, Coleridge, and de Staël suggest, interest in conversation was by no means unique to America in this period. But in a young nation just developing its own literature and a sense of its own culture, the arts of talk could be especially exhilarating and important – what begins here as an imitation of old-world values can then form the basis for experiment and expansion in unexpected directions. In the early nineteenth century, Russia was probably America's closest relative in this regard. Through recent studies that emphasize how literary history here merges with social history, William Todd has shown that the era's "privileged mode of language use, 'talk'," came to serve as the "cornerstone" of the ideology of polite society in nineteenth-century Russia, "with a decisive impact upon the aesthetic activities, psychological self-awareness, social rituals, and political aspirations of the period." Offering its Sentimentalist vision of the author–speaker surrounded by family and friends, the conversational "salon style" modeled on the French salons and the English coffeehouses of the eighteenth century had a catalytic effect on Russia's Westernizing gentry. "Talk" gave a voice and a stance to the nation's nascent profession of letters, helping writers to begin to define a literary discourse distinct from the rigid, tradition-bound languages of the Orthodox church or of the specialized professions, and thus giving form to the strong impulses soon to bring forth the "Golden Age" of Russian literature – in the talk-based works of Pushkin, Lermontov, and Gogol.[44]

In America during these same years conversation could never be contained in the salons of one class – as we have seen, it proliferated through many levels of society in a democratic diversity of forms. But the example of Russia makes it possible for us to appreciate the possible catalytic effects of the talk phenomenon. Even the emergence of the "salon style" itself cannot be judged too quickly as merely the symptom of foppish, "feminized," Europhile, or stultifyingly genteel pretensions, for in America as in Russia the outpouring of this talk had a liberating effect on aspiring writers struggling with the "Problem of Vocation" in relation to a dominant, orthodox national church. Offering an alternative to the urgent "callings" of a long verbal tradition of American Calvinism, "talk" could serve here, then, as a crucial formative influence on early efforts by men and women of letters to forge a native voice and literary identity separate from that of the clergy – efforts that would suddenly ripen at mid-century into the first broad-based movement of American literature: our own Golden Age.

TALK-BASED WRITING IN AMERICA'S "AGE OF CONVERSATION"

Indeed, a wide range of mid-century American writers and artists found themselves caught up in the culture's obsession with dialogic talk – though what was for some a prime source of inspiration became for others a prime source of anxiety. While some of these artists, wholeheartedly sharing the general exhilaration with the possibilities of talk, made conversational dynamics central to both the form and theme of new works, others (or often the same artists in other moments, expressing second thoughts) came to focus on talk as a way in to some of the most vexed issues of contemporary American life, centering their aesthetic works on scenes of dialogic interaction in an effort to gain critical distance from broader societal tendencies, and then raising disturbing questions about potential dangers or problems latent within the conversational ideal. Although mid-century oratorical theory – highlighting the power dynamics involved in the interaction of a speaker and his audience, and raising the possibility of an ecstatic merger of this solo speaker with his rapt listeners in peak moments of eloquence – could stand for contemporary artists as one exhilarating oral model for interpersonal or social dynamics, a great many mid-century American authors – from humorists, journalists and popular novelists to belletrists, philosophers, and the major now-canonized writers of serious fiction – finally found that the form of the era's conversation, bringing to the fore the power dynamics involved in interactions between successive speakers, seemed to offer an even more sensitive and telling register of the dynamics of contemporary social and psychological life, and of the culture's most basic hopes and fears about interpersonal interaction.

One telling and characteristic innovation came in journalistic writing. The modern "interview" format was first introduced and developed by American newspapers in this period, as journalists (following the lead of Horace Greeley, who published verbatim his dialogue with Brigham Young in 1859) responded to the same reader desires that had made *The Table-Talk of Martin Luther* a success: the public seemed especially keen to see the character of important personalities expressed "live" in the give-and-take of supposedly spontaneous conversation.[45] (As the traditionally private mode of conversation begins in the mid-century to be developed for public uses, becoming a form of mass entertainment, we can often feel we are observing the first steps in the genesis of what will emerge a century later in hybrid forms like the "talk show" or "talk radio" or "newstalk" – those peculiarly American hybrid phenomena which merge "talk" and "show" elements to make a simulation of impromptu and revealing personal talk the basis for mass-media spectacle.) This widespread fascination with talk as the site for the most crucial revelations of individual character as well as of interpersonal dynamics was also reflected in mid-century trends in popular literature. Drawing-room intercourse takes the place of heroic action at the center of the period's best-selling prose fictions; the plots of the new style of domestic novels reaching a huge audience of women at mid-century develop mainly through intense, intimate "interviews" between leading characters or through the complex verbal interplay of larger, mixed social gatherings. (If journalism was beginning to explore one form of "interview" – as a new form for self-expression before a mass public – these popular fictions often find their crux in "interviews" of another sort: the especially solemn question-and-answer sessions now seen as the privileged scenes of

some of the most intense moments in private life.) Though many
domestic novels also speak for the dream, apparently widely shared
by mid-century women, of finding a conversational "safe haven"
where one could share secure, supportive, heart-to-heart talk with an
especially close female friend (or a network of such "bosom" friends),
their overall plots reflect the reality that for most of their lives women
felt the need to be ever-vigilant as they faced difficult, testing verbal
interactions with hosts of threatening or alluring interlocutors – and
with a great deal at stake in each exchange. Here each conversation
emerges as a highly charged negotiation; each personal encounter in
the private sphere plays out and makes manifest the power dynamics
that structure and limit life in the surrounding public world; the give-
and-take of even a seemingly minor verbal interaction is seen to
enact the drama of dependence and independence so central to the
concerns of female readers.

When Henry James set out, in *The Bostonians* (1885), to recreate and
analyze retrospectively the culture of mid-century America, he took
that era's newly emerging talk forms – the salon style developing in
aristocratic New York drawing rooms; the genteel mode of refined,
sentimental interchange now shaping the intimate talk of fashionable
youth; the rougher, less-restrained forms of verbal interplay erupting
in the free-ranging debates and mock-trials of young men's college
clubs; and especially the new modes of high seriousness and self-
revelation explored in Transcendentalist discussion sessions, in
reform groups, and in the early public Women's Conversations of
feminists like Margaret Fuller – to be the phenomena most crucial to
an understanding of the period. In *The Bostonians*, the divided nation's
struggle over shifting notions of public and private life is defined,
most fundamentally, as a struggle between two modes of speech: in
each exchange, here, public oratory meets private conversation, or is
seen to infect it and disrupt it from within. Drawing out the
implications of such shifts in speech modes, James' novel works as a
heightened, self-conscious return to the form and concerns of
popular mid-century domestic fiction: following the verbal power
struggles between Verena and Basil, we see how every conversation
about the redistribution of power in American social life also itself
enacts a small-scale redistribution of power; here tea-table chats,
lovers' dialogues, drawing room discussions, and the communal talk
of womens' societies are revealed as force-fields in which the grand
battles of national politics are being waged.

Even an anti-sentimental and anti-domestic novel of the mid-century, like Fanny Fern's *Ruth Hall* (1855), with its caricature of Fern's brother Nathaniel Willis as a dandy who "recognizes only the drawing-room side of human nature," progresses through a series of "interviews," discussion sessions retrospectively interpreting previous "interviews," a "revolution" that breaks out during the conversation at a boardinghouse breakfast-table, passages from the strained tea-table talk that expresses one couple's difficult marital relation, probing dialogues with doctors that reflect the form of the talking exams emerging in contemporary medicine, and social scenes that both imitate and mock the high-toned chatter of the conversation clubs now fashionable among the urban American literary set – with these verbal interactions often building out of just the sort of levity–gravity opposition explored by Doctor Oliver Wendell Holmes in his series of table-talk books – launched with *The Autocrat of the Breakfast-Table* – which gained a similarly broad popular readership in these years.[46]

More self-serious and stilted efforts at philosophy or *belles lettres* in the mid-century often developed out of very high aspirations for the critical or creative powers seen to be inherent in the dialogue form. Several more highbrow authors took up the writing of "imaginary conversations" on the model of Landor: Channing published *Conversations in Rome* and "Fashionable Dialogues," Lowell wrote *Conversations with a Critic*, working in the same mode as Taylor's *Diversions of the Echo Club*, while Margaret Fuller printed in the *Dial* a number of her exploratory literary dialogues with muse figures.[47] And many of Fuller's best-known written works – such as *Woman in the Nineteenth-Century* (1845) – can be seen to have been modeled upon the theory of dialogic form she developed during a period of intense conversational interactions with Emerson and then tested during her leadership of the experimental feminist Conversations in Boston. Emerson himself, though profoundly influenced by this period of interaction with Fuller – an interpersonal debate about dialogue – finally took the possibilities of conversation in a very different direction. In "Circles" and other essays, he articulates a radical vision of "conversation as a game of circles" – a model of multi-vocal, interruptive, and non-synthetic dialogue which becomes the core dynamic element in his thought and in the rhetorical form of his writing.

So not all mid-century talk took the form of parlor pretension, and not all mid-century talk groups were simply insulated bastions for a

threatened social elite or conservative fortresses defending against
the rise of new discourses or new ideas. As Carolyn Porter notes,
"Women, Afro-Americans, and working people all participated in
the national conversation that emerged" between 1830 and 1860.[48]
And in fact mid-century talk groups often served as privileged venues
for radical or unorthodox thinkers wanting to test new spiritual
visions – liberal theologians, Swedenborgians, mesmerists, spiritual-
ists, phrenologists – or new plans for social reform: Fourierist
associationists, socialists, feminists, abolitionists.[49] Activists such as
Frederick Douglass and Sojourner Truth, for example, influenced by
their experiences of the discussions and lectures at abolitionist meetings, developed radical aspirations for the emancipatory power of
dialogue form. Like Fuller, they then made such dialogic talk central
both to their lifelong campaigns for personal or collective liberation
and to their conceptions of life-writing – highlighting dialogue, along
with oratory, as cruxes in the development of their landmark
autobiographies.

But while some literary figures were excitedly rushing to carve out
a place for themselves within the era's talk, and to make use of it in
their writing, for others this proved almost impossible. If Whitman
perhaps defined one end of the spectrum with his enthusiastic
immersion in popular talk forms, Emily Dickinson, Thoreau, and
Hawthorne stood at the other end – each becoming in their own
idiosyncratic way obsessively fearful of conversation, finding it to be
fraught with problems both in everyday life and as a model for
writing.

Ever the ambivalent fence-straddler, Nathaniel Hawthorne shared
some of the enthusiasm of Emerson, Fuller, and Whitman for the
subtle, interpersonal forces seen to be available through the dynamics
of conversation, but, temperamentally closer to Dickinson, the
famously retiring Hawthorne was also deeply troubled by what he
saw as grave potential dangers in such powerfully charged verbal
interactions. His writings, then, return obsessively to scenes of
conversation. In "The Minister's Black Veil," the bachelor Reverend
Hooper gains his power as public spokesman for the community only
as he dons the dark veil that prevents full, unmediated, face-to-face,
private conversation with the woman who was to have been his wife.
In "Rappaccini's Daughter," young Giovanni is both obsessed by
and hysterically fearful of the possibility of opening himself to an
uncontrolled and unprotected "free intercourse" with Beatrice –

where the intimate sharing of words would also involve the sharing of breath, of bodily touch, of unexpressed desires. Intimate conversation always implies for Hawthorne not simply a rational exchange of viewpoints but the dream of a marriage of minds, a total interpenetration of souls – while also calling up deep fears of such intimacy: "He felt conscious of putting himself . . . within the influence of an unintelligible power by the communication which he had opened with Beatrice."[50] Scarcely daring to draw her fragrant breath into his lungs, Giovanni fears these interviews might "communicate" a deadly disease, drain his vital energies and fluids, or infect him with a poison. Verbal interaction builds upon a potent white magic of erotic attraction (romance) that is not easily distinguished from the black magic of witchcraft (necromancy); such a psychological and sexual merging of two selves can develop as a struggle for dominance between Romance powers and threaten the sense of independent or rational self-identity. The climactic moment of *The House of Seven Gables* is an intimate verbal encounter in which Holgrave – both necromancer and Romancer, and experienced as a lecturer on Mesmerism – threatens to use his magnetic powers of speech to violate the virgin Phoebe, and thus to reenact through the irrational dynamic of his oral tale-telling the plot of the legend of Alice Pyncheon: an abuse of the influence and interdependence in verbal intimacy which can make it the scene of erotic enslavement. "Our souls, after all, are not our own," observes Coverdale near the end of *The Blithedale Romance*, summarizing his experience of the mesmeric powers latent in both oratorical and conversational speech. Though finally he is able to withstand the spell of Hollingsworth's words, earlier, when he lay in bed delirious with fever, he had felt the quasi-erotic attraction in the bedside voices of both Zenobia and Hollingsworth, in his weakened and dependent state almost giving himself over to this form of doctor–patient conversation which offers the solace of a new sort of secular confessional at the price of possible enslavement to the mesmeric minister. But Hawthorne develops his obsession with these dynamics latent in talk most fully in *The Scarlet Letter*. As part of its study of the efficacy of various modes of verbal expression or confession, this novel traces the complex workings of a number of different forms of conversation: a play on the catechistical interview as Pearl meets the magistrates; a play on the Alcott-like "conversation with children on the Gospels" as Hester struggles to contact and to rear her lawless daughter; a play on the mode of the

Fuller–Emerson interaction as Hester and Dimmesdale exchange impassioned exhortations during their walk in the woods. But probably the most extended and detailed attention is given here to one complex series of conversational interactions which seems to many readers to become the central focus in the novel: the proto-psychoanalytic doctor–patient dialogues between Chillingworth and Dimmesdale. Throughout the novel, Chillingworth uses his marked powers of conversation to pry information out of everyone he meets – Indians, sailors, magistrates, children – and it is this verbal power which he then turns on his rival Dimmesdale. Chillingworth's interminable "talking exams" with the minister mime the total intimacy of marital intercourse only to pervert it – to destructive ends; his verbal powers allow him to touch psychic wounds, to experiment with them, to keep them open, but not to heal them. While the doctor's freethinking conversation seems initially vivifying to the over-orthodox minister, finally this liberating effect is deceptive; though his talk form seems to offer the release of full confession, a means of breaking out of crippling introspection, finally these dialogues seem only to reinforce a self-destructive interiority.

American Humorists in the mid-century were similarly concerned with the implications of breakdowns and failures in the conversational ideal. But while such problems became the matter of a grave obsession for Hawthorne, for many humor writers they also offered rich possibilities for comedy. And if for Hawthorne conversation figured forth sad psychological truths about interpersonal intimacy and interdependence, most humorists saw conversational form as a model of social relations in the larger culture. The collisions of discourse in multi-vocal talk become a core element in various forms of American Humor as they seem to play out in miniaturized form many of the major problems and disruptions confronting the fluid and increasingly diverse culture of the expanding nation. Charles Mathews and "Yankee" Hill, dialect comedians and impersonators who brought the first versions of several classic American Humor characters to the popular stage, made their fame with one-man shows in which they first explored the image of America as a collection of wildly divergent types and voices and then thrilled audiences with their ability to speak for several of these native characters at once – bringing those diverse voices together in a sort of virtuoso miming of the ideal "conversation of the culture" while also pointing up the ways in which the new nation's regional and racial and educational diversity could threaten that ideal. In his "Trip to America," Mathews (as a sort of proto-Whitman) celebrated the possibility that a self could contain the voices of multitudes, opening out of its privacy to become a site for a form of public interaction. In his "At Home," Mathews (here like a proto-Holmes) brought all of the nation's voices indoors, setting them in the table-talk of a boarding-house drawing room (presided over by a Coleridgean monologist) and then testing the comic possibilities as the insular privacy of a Victorian drawing room is invaded by the unruly and perhaps incompatible multiple voices of the American public sphere.[51]

A few decades later, this now-standard comic image of the nation continued to be developed in frequent stage representations of America as a caricatural "Debating Society," full of loud, self-serious, and divided amateur orators whose attempts at dialogic interchange lead only to wild confusion because they are unable to understand or even to hear one another. And genre painters in the mid-century – most notably George Caleb Bingham and Richard Caton Woodville – shared the stage humorists' fascination with American talk as a revealing social theater, developing a native form of the painterly "conversation piece" in which the verbal interactions between diverse speakers as they debate current events, trade goods, or trade stories at the village store, the election-hall, the barroom, or the country dance are taken, as art historian Elizabeth Johns has noted, as prime sites for study of "the politics of everyday life."[52] In Woodville's "Politics in an Oyster House" (figure 2) of 1848, for example, the slice-of-life glimpse of a moment in one everyday conversation between two men in a chowder house is heightened as it is set on a sort of stage (within the curtained, proscenium frame of a restaurant booth) to be read as a symbolic portrait of the American public sphere, a representative image speaking for many of the intellectual, aesthetic, social and political divisions currently threatening the life of the nation. Most basically, the diametrically opposed physical appearances of these interlocutors function as visual icons representing dynamic aspects of the verbal stances associated with each speaker: one over-heated, the other reflective and detached; one an irrepressible lecturer turning the dialogue into a one-way harangue, the other relishing his silence; one immersed in the messy controversies of the daily newspaper, the other attempting to guard some space for meditation on more lofty concerns; one

Figure 2 Richard Caton Woodville, *Politics in an Oyster House*, 1848.
The Walters Art Gallery, Baltimore.

dressed in all-black, neo-Puritanical garb reflecting his single-minded
fervor for his cause, the other presenting a more aristocratic appearance with an elegant ensemble balancing light and dark; one
apparently a Democratic advocate of the common man, the other a
Whig defender of genteel traditions; one perhaps a fervently nationa-
listic member of Young America, the other an Irvingesque cosmopolitan of the Knickerbocker Circle. While one character appears
ready for impulsive action as his unbalanced body spills out imper-
ialistically into the world (a foot on the table-leg, face and finger
beginning to intrude upon the private space of his partner), the other
adopts a pose of classical balance, repose, restraint, and self-contain-
ment; while one throws his paper and his still-lit cigar messily and
dangerously onto the floor, the other is rule-governed, orderly, and
careful enough to keep his ashes in the can provided; while one is a
bearded "natural man" who, like Whitman, dares to wear his hat
indoors, the other is cleanly shaven with his hat placed on its proper
hook and his umbrella neatly folded in its place (reflecting his
caution, his sense of the need to protect himself from natural
elements, and perhaps his commitment to political forms of protec-
tionism like banks and tariffs). In every detail of this dual character
study, Woodville is portraying the collusion between two archetypally
opposed cultures of mid-century conversation. Painters like Woodville, then, shared the contemporary tendency to figure the problems
of American diversity and American dividedness and the possibilities
for American pluralism as problems and possibilities of American
conversation. But the lack of light in the gas lamp between the two
speakers in Woodville's "Oyster House" suggests the painter's conclusion that, finally, while the collisions of discourse figured in this
scene may produce sparks, they will never produce much illumination; we are not given the sense that the antithetical poles of this
dialogue will soon reach any harmonious synthesis or common
ground. Indeed Woodville's vision seems to match that of Tocqueville
in his descriptions of the impoverishment of America's interpersonal
life – here again, the exaggeration of an oratorical impulse makes
genuine conversational interchange difficult or impossible. Certainly
this Oyster House is far removed from the coffeehouses of
eighteenth-century England celebrated by Jürgen Habermas as the
birthplaces of the smoothly functioning rational discussions which
constituted the modern "public sphere"; this is an image of a
conversation – and a culture – that cannot cohere.[53]

Most written forms of American Humor in this period are also fundamentally dialogic; very often, the point of departure for their verbal flights is the breakdown in conversational communication or coherence which apparently can be expected whenever diverse Americans meet and try to talk to one another. Almost every yarn or tall tale begins with the framing plot of an attempted conversation between speakers from different regions. In Twain's classic "Jumping Frog" or "Old Ram" tales, an Eastern, educated ministerial voice tries to open discussion with an uneducated, drunken Western gambler, and the story then gains its charge as it exploits the collisions of discourse between these opposed figures. The hunt plot at the center of most tall tales works as the most apt analogy for the conversational dynamics which are the true subject here – as the teller hunts and traps his unsuspecting listener, preying upon his "confidence," and the listener is then lured into the hunt for some meaning in the web of the teller's words. In T. B. Thorpe's "The Big Bear of Arkansas" (1841), for example, the effete narrator from the urban East is initially afraid of contaminating interaction with the wide range of Americans aboard his riverboat, and tries to protect himself from the wild swapping of oral tales by hiding behind his newspaper (and his association with written language). Finally, though, the tales being swapped all around him have a seductive power, and he becomes a lone listener enthralled by Doggett's vernacular story of a bear-hunt on the frontier – in the end, his strangely intimate conversational interaction with Doggett mirrors the relation between Doggett and the bear.

In "The Big Bear" as in other works of American Humor, the riverboat becomes the classic locus for these sorts of dialogic con-games or bragging matches – all tests of verbal power. The river represents the geographical and social fluidity which is always bringing diverse groups of mid-century Americans together, forcing them to learn how to confront or to interact with a wide range of strangers; the riverboat then emerges as a microcosm of this mobile democratic society, a lowly version of the ship-of-state, an image of the melting pot and of its potential dangers, an apt site in which to test the possibility of a "conversation of the culture." Herman Melville's *The Confidence-Man* develops as an extended, deeply troubled meditation on just this possibility. Taking up the topos of riverboat dialogue to follow with cynical, debunking insight the turns of talk between a classically diverse collection of voyaging

Americans, Melville tests mid-century America's social constitution through close analysis of what he takes to be the era's representative verbal form: the conversation between strangers. In 1857, the same year in which Holmes launched his highly popular series of *Autocrat* papers based upon boardinghouse table-talk, Melville apparently felt it crucially important to develop in *The Confidence-Man* an analysis of the fundamental dynamics of the nation's talk. This novel's exhaustive survey of commercial, pedagogical, medical, proto-psychoanalytical and philosophical forms of dialogue is, as Aaron Fogel observes, part of Melville's depressed, obsessive attempt to present a detailed "ethnography of American dialogue," indeed to "define the typical American dialogue scene."[54] Finally Melville wants us to see that, despite the surface differences in all of these talk styles, the base dynamic remains the same: here all mid-century American talk emerges as a cruel power-play, a deceptive manipulation of human sympathies, a con-game.

Melville's short works from this period – presided over by the figure of the uncommunicative Bartleby in his "Dead Letter Office" – develop the same preoccupation with conversation as a key register of the dynamics of American social relations, and also explore a similar anti-conversational stance. The fundamental problem in Melville's "diptychs" or paired tales of the mid-1850s – like "The Paradise of Bachelors" and "The Tartarus of Maids" – is always the impossibility of dialogue or communication between the two unnaturally separated story parts; in this bleak vision, the culture is seen to be divided into all-male bachelors' clubs (repeating the standard republican critique of clubs as secret brotherhoods of aristocratic, Europhile homosexuals pursuing corrupt pleasures in their moneyed leisure) and all-female factories, which makes for literary and sexual impotence.[55] And major stories such as "The Lightning-Rod Man," "Bartleby, the Scrivener," "I and My Chimney," and "Benito Cereno" all develop most basically as failed conversations. "Bartleby," for example, is at root the tale of Bartleby's refusal to enter into conversation with the story's talkative narrator. Here each character's worldview is epitomized in his attitude towards conversation, and the breakdown of conversation between these two characters enacts in miniaturized form the larger breakdown in the coherence of the culture. The narrator's sense of talk reveals him to be a company man, a team player, a social self informed in every way by commerce with the surrounding culture; in refusing to talk,

Bartleby is refusing his implication in that social contract, seceding from it like a caricature of Thoreau in "Civil Disobedience." The opposed visions of talk here then enact irreconcilable oppositions within mid-century American culture between Union and Liberty, interdependence and dependence, a philosophy of sympathy and fellow-feeling and a philosophy of self-interest and self-reliance. "I and My Chimney" also centers on the breakdown of an attempted conversation, though here the breakdown serves not as a register of deep problems in the American public sphere but as a register of deep problems in one family's domestic sphere. When the narrator and his wife try to resolve their ongoing debates about his psycho-somatic illness and about the remodeling of their house's chimney, the wife calls in a proto-psychoanalytic Doctor Scribe (clearly modeled on Melville's Pittsfield neighbor Doctor Holmes) to engage her husband in a series of talking exams. The main opposition here then pits the narrator, whose pathological attachment to the chimney (and refusal to talk about the secrets it hides) becomes an impediment both to circulation and to communication in the family house, against Doctor Scribe, whose purpose in his dialogic exams is to revive the dynamic process of household conversation. In this case, when the narrator rejects the Doctor's talk form as a prying invasion, it is clear that this will mean a final failure to expand out of his thick-walled, hyper-privatized atomism into any form of social intercourse. A peak moment for this thematics comes in "Benito Cereno," a story structured (along the lines of "Bartleby") around the failures of conversation between a social, sentimental, naive, and garrulous Captain Delano and his double, the mysteriously uncommunicative Cereno. At the story's end, we learn that, initially, Cereno could not speak directly because full communication of the explosive truth here would have meant instant death for both speaker and listener; but even in the final scene, when Cereno is free to attempt an intimate, retrospective dialogue with the American about the tragic lessons of his experience of the system of slavery, the talk is suddenly interrupted as it becomes clear that Delano is still absolutely incapable of comprehending such a dark message about this tragic history – and so will be condemned to repeat it.

But not all of Melville's analyses of conversational interactions end so simply and bleakly in failures or breakdowns. Indeed, part of what saves Ishmael in *Moby-Dick*, giving him the flexibility and the buoyancy to avoid sinking with the ship, and thus making possible his narration of the Pequod's story, might be broadly described as his ability in conversation. The humorously detailed analysis of his initial interactions with Queequeg shows that Ishmael, in contrast to a monological truthsayer like Father Mapple or to an autocratic orator like Ahab or to his regionally and ideologically provincial shipmates, can at least begin to be social with the cultural Other. In his timid gestures of verbal and non-verbal intercourse with Quee-queg, we see him first trying to apply the limited model of polite drawing-room talk and then finally expanding the possibilities of that model dramatically as he opens up an inter-cultural conversation with this "savage" across the boundaries of race, religion, ideology, language, and so on. In the novel as a whole, Ishmael emerges through his structuring of this encyclopedic narration as a writer–librarian–anatomist who is able to comprehend a multiplicity of perspectives on the doubloon, a variety of approaches to the whale and to the world. The character who rises out of the shipwreck to compose *Moby-Dick* can tell his tale only by setting the voices of a wide range of opposed dogmas and ideologies in conversation – without committing himself to any one of these anthologized positions. Melville's greatest work, then, can in some ways be read as an ambitious test of the possibilities for cross-cultural or cosmopolitan conversation in an increasingly diverse and interdependent world.

Doctor Oliver Wendell Holmes was perhaps the era's key spokesman for such a conversational ideal, and his life and work can tell us a great deal about the ways in which models of talk developed in eighteenth-century England and France would be transformed to suit the needs of the mobile, diverse, democratic culture of mid-nineteenth-century America.

AMERICA'S BOSWELL: DOCTOR OLIVER WENDELL HOLMES

When we think of eras defined by their conversation, we most commonly call up visions of the salons and coffeehouses of eighteenth-century France or England. As we have seen, though, a significant number of mid-century American authors, artists, and culture critics recognized the mid-nineteenth-century as America's "Age of Conversation," and took the dynamic American talk forms emerging in the era as crucial barometers of the dynamics of mid-century American life. But if Alcott saw "Conversation" as one of the American inventions, and if Emerson sensed in Boston table-talk the characteristics of a special native spirit, what *were* the crucial local inflections of this international impulse to speech? If we would take up Emerson's invitation (cited as this chapter's epigraph) to "enter the domestic precinct . . . go to the sitting-room, the table-talk" of the American mid-century, how can we establish any contact with such an ephemeral oral phenomenon? If we hope now to become attentive to the "subtle spirit of life" in such "real history," how can we attune ourselves to the tones and textures of domestic converse from the distant past?

Today it may in fact be impossible for us to recreate the atmosphere of the many Conversations in Emerson's Transcendentalist circles; they are almost entirely lost to us because, as Lawrence Buell observes, "The fact is that Transcendentalism lacked a Boswell."[56] But for a broad spectrum of its emerging talk, America did indeed have a Boswell: Doctor Oliver Wendell Holmes, whose enthusiasm for the democratic possibilities of the many modes of conversation he heard all around him was expressed in his famous motto, "Every man his own Boswell."[57] Holmes can serve as a key to help open up the closed parlors of Victorian America, bringing out the major cultural forces involved in this very volatile interior life, and leading us in for close dynamic analysis of the pulses and pressures of its characteristic speech. For if one of the best "ways in" to the spirit of a culture is through its conversation, certainly one of the best "ways in" to the conversation of the mid-century American household, club, boardinghouse, schoolroom, Lyceum, or doctor's office is through the life and works of Doctor Holmes.

Like the Protean Emerson, the Doctor wanted to play all the roles, to speak all the languages, to try to see all the sides. Preeminent in both American medicine and American literature, he was somehow able to combine the stances of grave scientist and light humorist, Sage and Jester, traditionalist and progressive, Voice of Reason and confirmed ironist. A strange new sort of cultural spokesman, he could express himself as an autocratic voice dictating the standards of Victorian gentility or as the author of multivoiced table-talk works that respond to every issue from a spectrum of opposing positions, avoiding singular conclusions, unsettling fixed standards, and challenging the old verities. As the dazzling allusiveness of his written table-talk suggests, Holmes' free-thinking curiosity led him to hone in on moments of revolutionary rupture in a wide range of fields – theology, psychology, visual technology, natural science, as well as medicine and literature – with his colorful or catalytic remarks (often speaking, in successive moments, for multiple perspectives on a vexing issue) making him a key participant in vigorous contemporary conversations in all of these areas. (This seems to be what Alcott, a rival in the talk field, is objecting to when he says that the rationalist Holmes "knows too much," or what Van Wyck Brooks means when he compares the Doctor to the virtuoso Erasmus, finding him "the most intelligent man in New England." In the same vein, noting how the Doctor's talk gave him wide contact with shifting developments in many diverse areas of life, Henry James, Sr., said to him, "Holmes, you are intellectually the most alive man I ever knew.")[58] Crusading all his life against an encroaching specialization among lawyers, clergymen, scientists, and doctors, Holmes was one of the last of the true generalists. If we can come to see how he could bring together the diverse strands of his wide-ranging interests, it may help us to bring together many diverse strands in the literary and intellectual history of his era.

For Holmes' contemporaries it was clear that the connecting thread was the dynamic of talk. Over the course of his long life (1809–94), the Doctor had become the nation's representative figure for sociability, civility, cosmopolitanism – and, above all, a figure wholly identified with talk: the living embodiment of the era's aspirations for American conversation. "They have a new term nowadays . . . for people that do a good deal of talking; they call them 'conversationists', or rather 'conversationalists'; talkists, I suppose, would do just as well," noted Holmes' persona the Poet, half complaining about the current fascination with talk and people's heightened expectations of him as a leading performer in that arena:

It is rather dangerous to get the name of being one of these phenomenal manifestations, as one is expected to say something remarkable every time one opens one's mouth in company. It seems hard not to be able to ask for a piece of bread or a tumbler of water, without a sensation running round the table . . . (*CW*, III, 44)

But the Doctor certainly could not escape such recognition as *the* model "conversationalist" is his day – he was "the king of the dinner-table during a large part of the century," according to Annie Fields; "the best talker ever heard in Boston," in accounts of Barrett Wendell; "the greatest conversationalist in the English language since Dr. Johnson left the scene," to a more recent biographer – and he apparently did reward his many eager interlocutors met during an extremely active social life at clubs and dinner-tables with an astonishing, sometimes "overwhelming," flow of spontaneous repartee and witty *bon mots*: as Van Wyck Brooks observes, "His talk was the eighth wonder of the Boston world."[59] As a literary figure, too, Holmes' best writing developed out of his explorations of talk form. The works that earned him instant celebrity with a large international audience, and broad recognition as one of America's leading authors, were his series of classic written conversations, framed as multivoiced, interruptive, imaginary dialogues arising out of the scene of boardinghouse table-talk – *The Autocrat of the Breakfast-Table* (1857), *The Professor at the Breakfast-Table* (1859), and *The Poet at the Breakfast-Table* (1872) – that transformed the English essay by giving it a new, dynamic rhetorical form.

To adapt a line from Emily Dickinson, Holmes' business was conversation. And Holmes would want to stress, in the first number of his "Autocrat" papers, that, for him, "This business of conversation is a very serious matter" (*CW*, 1, 5). While celebrated not only in Boston but across the United States as the most brilliant talker in America's "Age of Conversation," and recognized internationally for his experiments in conversational writing, he also emerged as one of the era's leading theorists of the implications of dialogue form, and one of the most probing analysts of conversational dynamics. We will see in succeeding chapters how Holmes' particular vision of talk would inform his theory and practice in many of the diverse fields in which he was active, serving as the fundamental model in social relations, in philosophy, in medicine, and in psychology, as well as in literary writing. Indeed, with conversation so central to his contributions in so many areas of social or intellectual life, the Doctor stands as a perfect example of the ways in which talk can serve as, in Todd's words, the "cornerstone" of a culture.

DOCTOR HOLMES' BOSTON: THE TALK CONTEXT OF THE "AMERICAN RENAISSANCE"

During America's "Age of Conversation," Boston was the center of the nation's outpouring of talk, and Doctor Holmes' place was always at the center of that city's ongoing conversation. (In fact, he gave the city its nickname – the "Hub" – to foreground and mock its sense of its own centrality; he also named and defined the Boston

"Brahmin caste" to spark a dialogue about the role of the intellectual in New England.) An overflowing fountain-of-words, the Doctor dominated Boston's everyday verbal intercourse, defining its terms and its tone; notebook in hand, he made himself the Boswell of this brilliant oral culture; and finally, in the eyes of many, he came to be seen as the epitome of this New England flowering in fine and explosive talk.

At the turn of the twentieth century, when many Americans began to look back and realize how far they had traveled from the world of their fathers, Doctor Holmes often emerged as the symbol of all that had been lost. For Barrett Wendell, in retrospect, Holmes stands as the figure most truly "representative" of antebellum Boston –

Among Boston lives the only other of eminence which was so uninterruptedly local is that of Cotton Mather. The intolerant Calvinist minister typifies seventeenth-century Boston; the Unitarian physician typifies the Boston of the century just passed.

– while for the same reasons *The Nation* would observe: "He belongs to old Boston now – an historical period of the city that cannot be recalled without his name." Then, in the late 1920s, Vernon Louis Parrington would put a lightly mocking accent on the same point, noting an outmoded provincialism in that old Boston Renaissance:

For upwards of half a century, throughout the prime and on past the Indian Summer of the New England renaissance, Holmes was Boston's own wit, inexhaustible in clever sayings, bubbling over with satire and sentiment, the autocrat of her social gatherings, the acknowledged head of her mutual admiration society.

On the other hand, Mark DeWolfe Howe could later locate the true significance of the Doctor's "embodiment of the Boston spirit" in his "comprehensive capacity": his virtuoso's ability to see himself and his local culture on a universal scale, with reference to a broad world culture:

Dr. Holmes was not only the embodiment of the community's energetic spirit but contributed distinctive elements to its vitality. He was the one man of letters whose education in the sciences had been rigorous and professional; he was the one scientist whose cultivation in the humanities was lively and alert.

Howe seems here to be building upon the initial insights of Van Wyck Brooks, who, only a few years after Parrington's critique, had made the crucial critical breakthrough by refocussing attention on Holmes as "conversationalist," recognizing that it was the Doctor's role as a talker that gave him so central a place in the "conversation of his culture," and thus emphasizing the cosmopolitan breadth of his interests and relations over any localism in giving us this picture of "Doctor Holmes' Boston":

The focus of culture in Boston was the Saturday Club, the club that Dr. Holmes would have invented if spontaneous generation had not produced it. There, once a month, the illuminati . . . met for the talk in which the town excelled. For Boston abounded in good conversation. Experienced outsiders . . . were struck by the quality of this conversation. Sometimes, at two successive dinners, the same men talked for eight hours without a sign of fatigue, and the conversation never fell off in interest.

. . . the Autocrat was not only Bostonian but more than anything else a talker, . . . in his airy way, he had scattered freely . . . the ideals that had made his town a center of culture. The Autocrat stood for Boston in its hour of triumph. For Boston was indeed triumphant. Its conversation bore witness to this.[60]

Late in his life, when Henry James, Jr. wanted to make a pious imaginative return to this "triumphant" Boston of his youth, he too would find Doctor Holmes' talk to be the memorial center of the city at its peak moment: "the admirable liberality and vivacity of Dr. Holmes' *Atlantic* career quite warranting . . . no matter what easy talk about a golden age." James remembers that Lowell's gamble – bringing the bustling, hyperactive anatomist and former dean of the Harvard Medical School in as the first regular contributor to his new literary journal – had paid rapid dividends: the Doctor quickly came up with a name for the journal, *The Atlantic Monthly*, and then launched the "Autocrat" papers that assured the success of this venture so important as catalyst to an emerging American literature. Almost literally overnight, in his first try at regular authorship, Holmes had transformed himself into what would be his lifelong persona; suddenly this whimsical, idiosyncratic talker – whom everyone now called "the Autocrat" – had become a figure on the national stage and a voice in the national debate.

Dr. Oliver Wendell Holmes had been from the first the great 'card' of the new *recueil*, and this with due deference to the fact that Emerson and Longfellow and Whittier, that Lowell himself and Hawthorne and Francis Parkman, were prone to figure in no other periodical . . .

Though his topic is the house of the publisher Fields, James here surprises himself with "unspeakable vibrations" and "ghostly breath" as, again and again, his reverie on the house of his fathers (full of images of fathers and sons reuniting after long separations) finds itself diverted into meditation on the house of Holmes, with its lively spirit embodied in the Doctor's multi-leveled table-talk:

The Autocrat's insuperable sense for the double sense of words . . . to say nothing of all the eagerest and easiest and funniest, all the most winged and kept-up, most illustrational and suggestional, table talk that ever was . . .

Finally, rising with the winged, champagne glow of these scenes, James can even surprise us by describing *The Autocrat of the Breakfast-Table* as "the American contribution to literature . . . most nearly meeting the conditions and enjoying the fortune of a classic."[61]

Of course not long after James wrote this, when critics in the stridently "modernistic" 1920s became determined to declare their independence from the sway of "old Boston," Holmes' high-flying fortunes were brought down with a jolt   his once-large national readership abruptly dissolving into a small, scattered club of devotees and this mysteriously imposed, near-total neglect then making almost impossible any further attempts at critical revaluation. But whether or not we now feel, with James, that Holmes' work in itself "meets the conditions" of a "classic," if we want, for our own literary–historical purposes, to make our own return to the Golden Age of mid-century New England and to get a fuller sense of the "conversation of its culture," we would do well to begin with the epitomes of Boston talk in Holmes' breakfast-table papers. To develop an ear for the dynamics of the Doctor's conversation is to develop an ear for the everyday verbal environment of many of the age's central authors. For Holmes' talk always put him into intimate and revealing relations with many of the major figures of the American Renaissance – both in the public gatherings where the irrepressible Doctor would set the tone at club meetings, steal the show at dinners, and manage the collisions of discourse at formal or informal group festivities, and in more private moments, when Holmes would arrive alone for a conversation which was medical and diagnostic (as we will see later, in analyzing the Doctor's proto-psychoanalytical "talking exams" with his patient-friends Hawthorne and Melville).

This is not to say that Holmes was "just like" these other New Englanders – quite the contrary. For though he often seemed to position himself at the center of each function, the Doctor was also always resolutely eccentric, a strange bird in his surroundings: in some ways an eighteenth-century Man of the Enlightenment looking in on America's first stirrings of Romanticism; or an Old World Gentleman taking up the pose of a marginalized aristocrat to gain a new perspective on the "era of the common man"; while also in many ways like a twentieth-century modern, somehow caught in a time warp, wandering around with eyes and ears wide open in a strange, foreign nineteenth-century culture. Holmes' talk form is resolutely dialogical because he always set himself in dialogue with the voices around him; he is always a devil's advocate, always oppositional, so that his comments (or those of his personae) very often emerge as true interventions – working to break up the trains of any currently established discourse or thought. When among lab scientists or doctors, Holmes could interrupt in the voice of a literary man or humorist; among writers and humanistic intellectuals, he could speak for the "other" voice of modern physical science. It is highly characteristic of Holmes, then, that his first table-talk work, *The Autocrat of the Breakfast-Table*, is structured to mine the collisions of discourse of a conversational confrontation between the classic image of Old World absolutism – the Autocrat – and the epitome of the New World's democratic diversity: the mid-century American boardinghouse or hotel.

But Holmes' willfully marginalized personae, his antithetical stances, only make the Doctor's close observations of mid-century America's most intimate life more telling and interesting. And recognizing Holmes' central place in the cultural conversation can help us to redefine the context in which many American Renaissance writers developed, reminding us of important relations with the literature and thought of eighteenth-century England and Europe, of significant American traditions of scientific and learned humor coming out of Rabelais and Sterne and continuing from Irving on into the mid-century, and of vital voices within American Romanticism developing less out of the conventions of Romantic Organicism than along the lines of an alternative Romantic Irony.

The central discovery of Holmes' life and the moment of his conversion to writing – something akin to Emerson's experience and recreation of that moment when he felt himself converted into a "transparent eyeball" – seems to have come with the first recognition that the written, multivocal "conversation," built out of found fragments of overheard talk, could develop as a microcosmic enactment both of his own multivalent, ambivalent inner life and of the dynamics of the culture at large. In the *Autocrat* he found that what Friedrich Schlegel termed the "ironic" form, seemingly so quirky and idiosyncratic, constructed out of a chaotic "dialogue" between note-fragments, can become a most illuminating form of material history: "It alone can become, like the epic, a mirror of the whole circumambient world, an image of the age."[62]

Just a few years after Whitman had introduced his giant Self as a public site in which to gather up the nation's many languages, Holmes introduced his giant Breakfast-Table as the site for a potential, utopian "conversation of the culture." In several scenes, as in the following passage written in 1858, Holmes makes clear both his hopes for such a national conversation and his strong awareness of the radical differences in regional languages and ideological "tastes" that would soon destroy these last antebellum attempts to achieve conversational harmony. The breakfast-table is a very fragile common ground; it can only offer so much tea and sugar water when confronted with the potentially warring voices of its diverse guests:

This table is a very long one. Legs in every Atlantic and inland city, – legs in California and Oregon, – legs on the shores of 'Quoddy and of Lake Pontchartain, – legs everywhere, like a millipede or a banian-tree . . .

Sit down and make yourselves comfortable. – A teaspoon, my dear, for Minnesota. – Sacramento's cup is out.

. . . Pepper for Kansas, Bridget. – A sandwich for Cincinnati. – Rolls and sardines for Washington. – A bit of the Cape Ann turkey for Boston. – South Carolina prefers dark meat. – Fifty thousand glasses of *eau sucrée* at once, and the rest simultaneously. – Now give us the nude mahogany, that we may talk over it.[63]

Within this gay scene of conversational pleasure, Holmes includes self-mocking recognitions that the older ideal of tea-table civility – originally conceived as a means of building personal bonds through converse between strangers, across social divides – may not be able to stand up to the sectional strife, class divisions, partisanship, and competing provincialisms of mid-century America. Indeed, we may already sense here an impending turn (to come during and after the Civil War) from the model of a free play of ideas (talk as an intellectual and emotional interchange) to the model (defined by Judge Oliver Wendell Holmes, Jr. in a significant move away from his father's world) of a free market of ideas (talk as a test of the power of competing forces) – a turn from the drawing room to the battlefield. But Holmes' image of this ideal for antebellum conversation is nonetheless a compelling one – even if its operation must be recognized as more poetic than political, defining a purely literary site for a form of visionary social connection.

Of course Whitman and Holmes in many ways define the most distant poles of the literary spectrum in their period: one assuming the barbaric stance of "one of the roughs," the other a highly civilized, neoclassical pose; one inventing an inflated self, "Walt," who claims to include almost all other American voices, the other inventing an inflated persona, the "Autocrat," who pretends to exclude all other voices. While Walt tells us that he sees all the voices in his song as equal, and wants to explore the possibility of establishing a harmonious coherence between these constituent elements, the Autocrat stresses the inequality of the voices at his table, so that his conversations emerge as struggles for power between people speaking different languages, full of dominations, interruptions, misunderstandings, and marked exclusions. But finally we must recognize that both of these writers, in translating talk into written, printed form, were responding to a felt need in the 1850s to attempt a textual miming of an ideal public sphere, making it possible for their readers to imagine themselves in the act of reading to be entering a national arena for dialogue – an imaginary dialogue between textual voices, and between various readers, that perhaps could only be realized through the mediation of a written, printed, fictional construct. More than any other American authors of their day, Whitman and Holmes developed new literary forms which could "contain multitudes."[64]

Holmes' dialogic anthologies of his age's voices, his carnival collections of contemporary ideologies, are never simply direct mimetic mirrorings of mid-century talk. The *Autocrat* is much more than a mere transcription of the genteel talk of Boston salons or the intellectual wit of Saturday Club meetings. Indeed it can be seen as one of the most self-reflexive, truly "ironic," literary works in nineteenth-century America.

Like most jokes in Holmes, the humorous motto, "Every man his own Boswell," has its serious side. It implies the basic self-doubling which would make the Doctor such an insightful participant in and observer of the talk of his day: for Holmes, the self-in-conversation contains both speaker and listener, writer and critic, poet and scientist, enthusiast and analyst. (This seems to be what Holmes' English admirer Oscar Wilde recognized and valued in the

"Boswell" motto, which he repeats near the opening of his "The Critic as Artist," thus placing his own self-reflexive dialogue on the duality of the artist, a defense of self-consciousness or "criticism," directly in the line of the Doctor's conversations.)[65] Holmes can both enact the dynamics of mid-century conversation and then step back for self-conscious analysis of those dynamics. For Holmes-the-virtuoso-talker, the parlor was a favorite stage for impromptu performances; for Holmes-the-scientist, it could serve as his laboratory for verbal experiments in a sort of "sentimental physics." (A writer-scientist like the Doctor could come quite naturally to sense deep relations between the charged interactions in the electrical experiments he observed in laboratories and clinics, and the human attractions and repulsions he observed everyday in the conversations of clubs, boardinghouses, and drawing rooms.) Holmes-the-poet loved to play out the intoxicating dance of metaphor, but Holmes-the-psychologist would then want to study the patterns of such mental movements, to try to explain the "associations" between ideas or between people, the mechanical workings of our "trains" of thought or "currents" of feeling.

If Holmes' giant Breakfast-Table conversation could then develop, along the lines of Schlegel's "ironic" ideal, as "a mirror of the whole circumambient world," it would allow him not only to reflect the voices and ideas of his period but also to reflect *on* them. In this way, *The Autocrat of the Breakfast-Table* does for the talk of the mid-century American parlor, club, and Lyceum just what Schlegel's *Fragments* did for the conversations of his Jena circle, or what Diderot's *D'Alembert's Dream* did for the salon discussions of eighteenth-century France: it both records the dominant mode of contemporary discourse and develops as a structured re-enactment of that discourse – giving the talk a telling shape, making fundamental social and psychological themes available for analysis. Holmes' dynamic vision of talk builds out of explosive oppositions between the forces of "gravity" and "levity," "house-keeping" and "house-breaking." And, as we will see in the next chapter, his distinctive mode of interruptive, multivocal, and non-synthetic conversation makes it an especially apt form for verbal expression in mid-nineteenth-century America.

PART TWO

Holmes in the conversation of his culture

CHAPTER 2

"TO CHANGE THE ORDER OF CONVERSATION"
Interruption and vocal diversity in Holmes' American talk

I was just going to say, when I was interrupted . . .
Holmes, *The Autocrat of the Breakfast-Table*

The man finishes his story, – how good! how final! how it puts a
new face on all things! He fills the sky. Lo! on the other side rises
also a man, and draws a circle around the circle we had just
pronounced the outline of the sphere. Then already is our first
speaker not man, but only a first speaker.   Emerson, "Circles"

"I was just going to say, when I was interrupted . . ." – the first
phrase in the first installment of the *Autocrat of the Breakfast-Table*,
launching Holmes' series of table-talk works in the *Atlantic* – focuses
our attention on the talk element perhaps most fundamental to his
vision of conversational form: the dynamic moment of "interruption" that allows one speaker to take the floor from another and so
makes possible the changes of voice, of tone, and of topic that define
the most basic difference between dialogue and monologue.[1] Traditionally, the arbiters of "polite speech" have sought to smooth over
and control the potential unpleasantness of these necessary moments
of alternation between voices through carefully defined rules for
proper turn-taking in talk. But in mid-nineteenth-century America
the issue of interruption asserted itself with a special force. With the
dramatic expansion in the discursive public sphere (or spheres), and
great numbers of diverse new speakers – not all sharing the same
rules for conversational coherence – clamoring to break into the
conversation, dialogue would only rarely approach those traditional
standards of continuity and uniformity. Indeed, a focus on interruption – on turn-taking that is not polite or proper, not based on
agreements between familiars, but arises out of unruly, aggressive
confrontations between interlocutors from very different backgrounds – distinguishes many of the talk forms that emerged in the

socially fluid, diverse, and divided democratic culture of mid-nineteenth-century America from the classic models of conversation
developed in eighteenth-century England and France.

But Holmes' special stress on the interruptive turns in talk – his
foregrounding of a sense of conversation as an ongoing struggle
between urges to "autocratic" monologism and periodic bursts of
revolutionary interruption, highlighting the explosive potential in
collisions of discourse between diverse speakers and always focusing
our attention on each changing of the voice – also defines the most
crucial difference between his talk form and those of many of his
American contemporaries. For if the "Age of Conversation" brought
a widespread fascination with the dynamics of conversation and a
proliferation of experiments in the practice of talk, this certainly did
not mean that all mid-century Americans talked alike, or that all
Americans in the period shared the same approach to talk. Indeed,
what the mid-century outpouring of American dialogic speech
suggests, most basically, is that in this period the cultural vision on
any issue could not be summed up in a single voice. And this was
certainly true of contemporary visions of conversation. Throughout
the mid-century, the leading conversationalists and theorists of
conversation in America were engaged in a significant debate about
the forms and goals of dialogue – a debate about dialogue that
centered upon opposed attitudes toward or uses of interruption.

THE MID-CENTURY DEBATE ABOUT DIALOGUE

To some degree, of course, all conversation is founded upon interruption: by definition, dialogue is a collective verbal expression that
develops through breaks in its continuity, alternations between its
successive voices. But, as linguist Deborah Tannen points out in her
recent studies contrasting the conversational practices and expectations of men and women, or of Jewish New Yorkers and Catholic
Californians, different "conversational communities" or "conversational cultures" often are distinguished from one another by their
very different attitudes toward interruption. While the basic act of
"beginning to make verbal sounds while someone else is talking"
might be interpreted in one talk circle as a rude violation of someone
else's speaking rights, an aggressive attempt to assert dominance and
control, in a second talk group it might be celebrated as a sign of
vitalizing engagement in the loud, energized agonism of dialogic

debate, and in a third group it might be appreciated as "cooperative overlapping": a means of expressing not disagreement but sympathy and connection amongst talk participants who thus display an almost telepathic ability to finish one another's sentences or at least to murmur in anticipation and approval.[2] Some talk communities, then, develop conversation forms that stress vocal continuity, sympathetic agreement, and homogeneity, keeping interruptive elements to a minimum in the hope that such talk will serve as a unifying common ground, a verbal "melting pot" – bringing many people together to speak as if with one voice, one shared vision. On the other hand, other talk communities cultivate forms of verbal interchange centering around vocal discontinuity and sometimes aggressive disagreement, viewing talk as a heterogeneous site for experimental meetings between a multiplicity of voices and visions, a noisy carnival of contradiction and interruption. (And the most explosive interruptive moments can often come during attempts at dialogue between members of such different "conversational cultures.") At stake in such differences of opinion about the uses of interruption – or about the degree to which interruption may be allowed to define a mode of talk – are fundamental questions about the goals of conversation: do we value talk more for its harmonies and coherences, or for its vitalizing discontinuities? Do we see conversation as a cooperative venture in which all participants merge as one in sympathy and love, or do we see dialogue more as the site of telling struggles for power and opportunities to "talk for victory"? Do we want conversation to bring all contributing voices together in a new homogeneous whole, or do we want dialogue to develop as a polyphony of heterogeneous voices, bringing out and expressing the differences between its participant speakers? Do we want to highlight and protect the role of one central speaker as guide and master in the dialogic process, or do we find more interest in alternations between successive speakers? Do we value consistency and continuity in the seamless flow of one central argument leading to a clearly summarized conclusion, or do we stress an ongoing process of alternations between antitheses over any final synthesis? Are we most interested in closing the conversation, or in opening it and in keeping the turns of talk going?

Such large questions about the implications of various approaches to interruption divided mid-century thinking about conversation. If we were to recreate these debates about dialogue very schematically, we would find that the Doctor's dynamic conception of talk – defining an interruptive, multivocal, non-synthetic talk context as the site for attempts at dialogue between speakers from divergent "conversational communities" – places him, along with Emerson, as the clearest representative of one pole in this debate, while the conversational theories and practices of William Hazlitt and Alcott argue powerfully (though in different ways) for the opposed position. Fuller would then emerge as one of the most important and interesting figures on both sides of this debate, as her explorations of talk form were divided between an anti-interruptive oral practice (usually in pedagogical contexts, or in her Conversations with Women) oriented to the development of a singular new voice, and ground-breaking work in written dialogue (especially in *Woman in the Nineteenth Century*) that was crucially founded upon multivocality and interruption – indeed developing in the largest sense as an attempt to open up a new speaking space within the closed, patriarchal conversation of the larger culture, to interrupt the monolithic expression of some of the dominant discourses in the era.[3]

DISTINGUISHING ENGLISH AND AMERICAN TALK FORMS: HOLMES' TRANSFORMATION OF EIGHTEENTH-CENTURY MODELS OF CONVERSATION

Holmes' conversational writings – the *Autocrat*, the *Professor*, and *The Poet* – may initially seem to speak for many talk ideals that had remained unchanged since the days of the *Spectator*. Like most eighteenth-century English literary works influenced by conversation, the Doctor's table-talk books are characterized by colloquial phrasings, by an obsessive fascination both with the careful recording of common dialects and with the promotion of the norms of correct speech, by the preoccupation with manners and socialized gestures that is so often linked to descriptions of or prescriptions for talk, by a fondness for aphorism, and by a rambling structural looseness which conveys some of the spontaneity of rapid living speech – the fragmentariness of many of Holmes' table-talk passages have clearly been shaped by the fragmentariness of his varied and distraction-filled social life in a talk-crazed culture. This is a literary form that still seems closely connected to its sources in everyday spoken conversation. And the Doctor's breakfast-table speakers also often seem to want to put a special stress on values usually associated with

Augustan or neoclassical conventions of conversational discourse. Making the standard distinctions between talk and oratory, Holmes' Autocrat can speak the praises of familiarity over sublimity, geniality over genius, and ease over eloquence. Conversation has always sought to replace rigid rhetorical rules with the vaguer (and perhaps thus more exclusive) dictates of a fashionable "taste," and Holmes' elitist Professor adds some nicely-turned words to the eighteenth-century traditions which favor the *noblesse* of pleasing over disputing, rational coolness and modesty over passion or dogmatic heat – which, most basically, put forth conversation as the ideal model of a harmonious and static society: the image of society as "polite society."[4]

But finally this neoclassical posturing seems quite removed from Holmes' most characteristic literary qualities; these surface gestures go against the grain of his deepest conversational impulses. In fact, the Doctor's table-talk works are set up as dramatic conflicts in which the static world of the aristocratic salon is invaded by all the forces from below which it had been designed to keep out – by new voices speaking for the positions and experiences of diverse classes, genders, ages, regions, specialized professions, political factions, educational backgrounds, and so on. Here we see what happens when the eighteenth-century model of a "converse among equals" of like and like-minded men (all of the same class, gender, and background) must open to include a host of singular speakers very aware of inequalities.

In the dynamic world of mid-nineteenth-century America, "talk" cannot avoid differences, competition, power relations, contradictions, frictions, or interruptions.[5] So, in Holmes' breakfast-table works, we find that an upwardly mobile young "Ben Franklin" moves his way through what might have been intended as a calm coffee-house circle in the line of Addison and Steele; like his namesake, this scheming, self-fashioning, modernizing American will only recognize the old conversational habits of deference to hierarchy so far as he can manipulate them to his advantage. But in this newly fluid verbal setting, all speakers find it very difficult to maintain the prescribed "easy" poise and detachment; far from effacing their own personalities before the shared norms of Reason, order, and propriety, talkers here seem to take the floor mainly to ride the hobbyhorses of their private eccentricities and enthusiasms. As another major sign of the changed circumstances of this talk, we note that women are now active participants in what would have been an all-male group of philosophers at the Lockean club – bringing a whole new set of possible expectations and values into the conversational mix. (When their talk group includes both men and women, speakers here seem to be even more inclined to allow their remarks to be shaped by passional influences – love, jealousy, courtesy, desires to impress, desires to dominate – rather than solely by austere philosophical rigor. And the subjects of discussion expand also: dutiful discussions of political or public issues now can merge with talk about matters that might earlier have seemed purely personal or private.) In Holmes' diverse boardinghouse assemblies, a "genteel" tone can never be kept up for long. For example, between one long disquisition on breeding and manners by the moralizing female Model, and a windy series of archaic guidelines to "polite" conversation dictated by the Professor, Holmes lets young John break in, interrupting the Professor's vision of an ideal conversational harmony with vulgar jokes about his unredeemable passion for cigars. When the censorious Model urges that all cigars be damned and committed "to the flames," John achieves his usual inflammatory effect by literalizing her stale metaphor and agreeing to "burn" his cigars – but one at a time, and probably while blowing the smoke in her face. Once again, in Holmes' American talk setting the victory clearly goes to the vital forces of ill-mannered interruption (*CW*, II, 137).

Though he might like to be seen as a neoclassical, eighteenth-century figure, then, the Doctor nonetheless always feels that the best conversation is combustive, full of dynamic collisions, and based on ongoing alternations between speakers; his works also recognize the shaping influences of eloquence and affection in what might, in other eras, have been defended as the Enlightenment realm of Reason. In a rising passage describing his highest ambitions for his own written conversations, Holmes clearly marks his break from the talk of the Augustan salon – with its static conception of an extra-dialogical "Truth" and its chaste "academic" tone and atmosphere – as he returns his table-talk dialogues to their classical roots in the "glorious license" of a Dionysian *symposium* in which the interactions are sometimes rude, sometimes explosive, sometimes wildly enthusiastic – and always truly multivocal:

[This truly intellectual banquet] . . . calls upon Truth, majestic virgin! to get off from her pedestal and drop her academic poses, and take a festive garland and the vacant place on the *medius lectus*, – that carnival-shower of questions and replies and comments, large axioms bowled over the mahogany like bomb-shells from professional mortars, and explosive wit dropping its trains of many-coloured fire, and the mischief-making rain of *bons-bons* pelting everybody that shows himself, – . . . (*CW*, 1, 64)

Behind all of this cheerful celebration of dialogic collisions of discourse, though, lie some sad recognitions about the possibilities for public discussion in mid-century America. In challenging and transforming eighteenth-century ideals of conversational coherence, Holmes also articulates a sense of the actual dynamics of verbal interaction in an emerging American "public sphere" that contrasts markedly with Jürgen Habermas' idealized vision of the smoothly-functioning, rational, pluralistic discussions seen to constitute the "public sphere" in early modern democracies – a vision grounded in Habermas' social–historical study of the eighteenth-century English model of "converse among equals." Habermas' *The Structural Trans-formation of the Public Sphere* holds up the experiments in talk at eighteenth-century coffeehouses as egalitarian innovations which brought together a diverse cross-section of the larger society for interactions in which the normal rules of social intercourse (laws of the market or laws of the state; political or economic status) were temporarily suspended: lord and commoner could begin to converse on equal terms in this newly defined public sphere dedicated to free inquiry – where in theory the only authority was that of the better argument. At least in the ideal, these new institutions for reasoned discussion were to be inclusive – the participants would represent all elements of the "larger public" and their talk would include all subjects of "common concern." In Habermas' view, the emergence of such talk groupings in a "public sphere" separate from both the market and the state expressed most clearly the shift in political life from absolutism to democratic participation, from a governmental structure in which a ruler's power is simply represented before the people to a state authority monitored through informed discussion in "centers of criticism" which represent a new conception of the "public."[6]

Of course on some levels Holmes' table-talk works can serve in many ways as classic, caricatural dramatizations of just the transfor-mations highlighted by Habermas. Here a series of Autocrat figures speaking for vestigial impulses toward absolutism confront the demo-cratic diversity of voices at a boardinghouse breakfast-table – and so discover the new situation of cultural authority as it must enter into and respond to public conversation. But while the broad outlines of Habermas' theory of the social–political functioning of eighteenth-century English talk are very useful and relevant here – speaking directly to some of the Doctor's own hopes for a pluralistic "conversation of the culture" in mid-century America – Holmes' works, in their struggle with and against eighteenth-century models of talk, also suggest the outlines of an important critique of the historical grounding of Habermas' conception. First, Habermas' analyses seem to miss some crucial aspects of actual conversational practice in eighteenth-century England: the apparent freedom and equality of interaction in the coffeehouse ideal of a "converse among equals" was made possible only by some crucial originary acts of linguistic and social exclusion (voices of women and working-people were not included, for example); its order was based upon unwritten rules about deference to existing social hierarchy; and, generally, it was promoted by contemporaries as a means of safeguarding the social status quo – intended to serve for all participants as the exemplary image of harmonious social relations in a static society. In contrast, the Doctor's dynamic and explosive American talk form shows how a more genuine diversity of speaking voices can threaten to turn any attempts at "reasoned" or coherent eighteenth-century argument into a "carnival-shower of questions and replies and comments"; and his foregrounding of social conflicts, power plays, attempts at exclusion, and collisions of discourse in conversation brings to the fore key questions about the practicability of Habermas' eighteenth-century-based ideal of truly unrestricted, inclusive, and egalitarian public discussion free from the intrusions of social or state power.

THE AMERICAN STERNE

At least one contemporary reviewer hailed Holmes as the "American Sterne," and clearly Sterne is the author closest to Holmes in "conversational style" – as in many other aspects of literary form and philosophical concern.[7] These two authors work out of and against Augustan conceptions of talk in similar ways, and to very similar effect.

Like *Tristram Shandy*, the *Autocrat* provoked in a huge, diverse audience an immediate sense of loyal fellowship and intimacy – and an unending flood of letters to the author – which from the first issue of the *Atlantic* guaranteed a long run for both the Breakfast-Table papers and the magazine. It is easy to imagine the reasons for the instant success of Holmes' transplantation of Sterne's form to the United States. In an increasingly privatized, lonely American mid-century, isolated citizens and alienated writers would be especially receptive to the Doctor's "invention" of a way of talking that seems to create its own community, to his revitalization of the Sentimentalist scene of author and readers in a close social relation – conversing easily as members of the same family or of the same convivial club.[8] In one passage (cited earlier in another context) characteristically addressed to his new company of fellow readers, Holmes invites them to imagine their own breakfast-tables, at which they are seated in their own homes across the nation, as linked to his in a utopian "association" of breakfast-tables spanning the country:

This table is a very long one. Legs in every Atlantic and inland city, – legs in California and Oregon, – legs on the shores of 'Quoddy and of Lake Pontchartrain, – legs everywhere, like a millipede or a banian-tree . . .
   Sit down and make yourselves comfortable. – A teaspoon, my dear, for Minnesota. – Sacramento's cup is out.

At the same time that he seems to be thus opening up his literary conversation democratically to all Americans, though, Holmes like Sterne can offer each individual member of this vast readership a curious sense of belonging to a small charmed circle – what he defends in the first *Autocrat* paper as a "Mutual Admiration Society" – able to laugh together at the many dullards and dogmatic outsiders seen unable to follow the trains of such whimsical and metaphorical talk.

But when Holmes takes the Shandian household as his model of mid-century America, he does so finally not so much to promote the eighteenth-century coherences of familiar conversation as to stress its functional disturbances – thus leaving us with quite a different picture of the American Union. Though his domestic table-talkers share a basic grasp of the English language, they nonetheless always speak, like the Shandys, in private dialects and at cross purposes. Their carnivalesque dialogues are constantly being derailed by misunderstandings, hobbyhorsical idiosyncracies, and effusive enthusiasms. Locke may have hoped with his studies of and prescriptions about language to purify the flow of communication, but scientific humorists like Sterne and Holmes take as the territory for their linguistic play all that the philosopher would wish away: the creative or even explosive disruptions of our verbal and our social "associations." Indeed the Holmes passage quoted above, which begins with the benign, quaintly utopian vision of a multi-legged breakfast-table conversation as a national common ground, quickly turns to a more ominous recognition of the sectional differences in "taste" and in language which in late 1858 obviously threaten severe disharmonies to come:

... Pepper for Kansas, Bridget. – A sandwich for Cincinnati. – Rolls and sardines for Washington. – A bit of the Cape Ann turkey for Boston. – South Carolina prefers dark meat. – Fifty thousand glasses of *eau sucrée* at once, and the rest simultaneously. – Now give us the nude mahogany, that we may talk over it.[9]

We are here left to wonder if any amount of refined parlor etiquette or Sentiment – or even these massively applied emergency doses of *eau sucrée* – will be able to hold together this fragile verbal association during the ensuing talk.

In the nineteenth and twentieth centuries many literary critics would refer to Tristram Shandy's definition of writing – "Writing . . . is but a different name for conversation" – as the basis for their new and quite restricted ideal of "conversational style."[10] But while we do at times seem simply to be eavesdropping on Tristram's singular voice as he speaks aloud to himself, actually Sterne is more truly described, in Ian Watt's phrase, as a "dramatic monologist specializing in multiple impersonation." For the author who could praise a preacher for "the variety of his tones [which] would make you imagine there were no less than five or six actors . . . together," conversation serves most often as a literary model of multivoiced dialogue rather than of monologue.[11] Indeed, in Sterne the parentheses, dashes, and syntax breaks often taken as stylistic marks of direct "talk" – signs of the spontaneity of one voice speaking off-the-cuff – are pushed to the limit, to the point that any interior monologue can suddenly break out in crazy multiple voices. And these are just the elements of "talk" most stimulating to Holmes. He too makes the sudden tonal shifts of Sensibility – interruptive turns between gravity and levity, tears and laughter – something of a trademark; he too mines the colloquial style for its inherent ruptures and discontinuities, exploiting the metaphorical leaps and grammatical ellipses of scattershot improvisation, the gaps which open up between plain impromptu talk and grandiloquence, the dualities involved in speech and its transcription, as the best ways to mime the perpetual multi-voiced conversation that is human thought.

While today we use the term "conversational style" to describe aspects of literary style and diction – the realistic recreation of a casual, colloquial voice, often in a regional dialect – for Holmes "conversation" refers to an overall rhetorical structure: not to successful miming of one speaking voice or regional dialect but to the alternation between many voices. In fact, his conversational writing is intended precisely as an alternative to and a "cure" for the limits of singlevoiced "conversational style." The idealistic goal here is to help people to see beyond linguistic (and thus ideological) provincialism, to define through dialogic literary structure a forum or perspective which might allow all the diverse national languages to come together – with at least some tolerant civility. In many works, Holmes presents people's spoken idiom as the clearest symptom of their limitations (blocking their self-development as well as their social advancement), and he constantly raises the hope that some larger general structure will allow some sort of liberating "conversation" between America's separate, specialized, regional voices. In the *Autocrat* and other table-talk works, the reader may attain such a perspective, though perhaps none of the individual speakers can; in Holmes' psychological novels – *Elsie Venner, The Guardian Angel,* and *A Mortal Antipathy* – the doctor–confessor–psychoanalyst hero is, as we will see, usually marked by this conversational ability: he can understand a wide variety of idioms; he can moderate between provincial speakers.

CONVERSATION AND CULTURAL AUTHORITY

Some mid-century cultural leaders may have wanted to hold up Doctor Holmes as a model of parlor refinement, and some mid-century readers may have wanted to use his table-talk writings as "parlor primers" giving them instruction in the new dominant style of genteel, middle-class verbal behavior. But while he may have been a leading talker, Holmes finally was far from serving as a sort of parlor policeman – an authoritative custodian of the salon style. In fact his written works tend toward deliberate subversion of that official model – mocking both coffeehouse sobriety and genteel politeness; sending up the parlor-room values of prudence, self-control, stability, and order; always showing that free talk is a very slippery ground on which to try to establish cultural dominion. Rather than serving as the epitome of a monolithic vision of the mid-century cultural ideal – the port of entry into a newly prescribed "parlor culture" – conversation for Holmes is built upon dialogical breaks, changes in voice and perspective, that take one out of the limits of one's provincial language and home, forcing recognition of the multiplicity of cultures – and also serving as a site for possible meetings between these cultures.

For Holmes, then, the literary conversation does not operate simply as a *tour de force* of cultural centralization – with a Boston Brahmin from the metropolis through his definition of "civility" subtly controlling and judging all peripheral languages – but can open up as an arena of carnivalesque vocal diversity. The very title of his first table-talk work, *The Autocrat of the Breakfast-Table*, brings out the fertile joke, full of ramifications for the culture of mid-century America, which will underlie all of Holmes' later conversations. For here the classic image of totalizing Old World authority – the Autocrat – meets the era's prime symbol of democratic decentralization: the American boardinghouse or hotel. And the cap is that even in this reduced realm – of just one small table – no Autocrat can hold much sway. At every turn in the Doctor's table-talks, the efforts of any figure of moral authority – whether the Autocrat, the Professor, the Master, or in the 1880s the Dictator – to monopolize the conversation, to define its terms or its tastes, to impose Robert's Rules of Order on its debates, or in any way to assert an ominously integrative centralizing power, will always soon be unsettled by explosive outbursts from the Babel of surrounding boardinghouse voices. Miming a sort of perpetual revolution, these conversations give the floor to a succession of "carnival kings" – not only to the title characters but also to the many more minor players like the Scarabee, or the Model, or Little Boston, or the Member of the Haouse – who each develop their hobbyhorses in an over-elaborate personal prose only to be quickly mocked and dethroned by the rabble constantly waiting on the fringes to interrupt.

While the *Autocrat* may then reflect a strongly felt desire for some unifying authority, its also speaks forcefully for antebellum America's central ambivalence to such authority. In a decade marked by Disunion Conventions and Congressional debates, the conversation of a Shandian household can indeed serve as a "representative" literary form. For the Autocrat's failure to control his boardinghouse can be seen to mirror the failure of Daniel Webster to control the "House Divided" of the Congress: neither one of these assertive talkers can hold such diversity together simply by the power of his voice. And Holmes' breakfast-table is then divided by a series of clashes which develop as matchbox versions of the Webster–Hayne or Webster–Calhoun clashes in the Senate. In scenes full of resonant allusions to the increasingly hostile and uncomprehending "conversation" then breaking down throughout the culture at large, the Autocrat is always confronting "secessions" and "revolts" from other restless and independent boarders. Like most Americans of the day, the Doctor had closely followed Webster's obsessive attempts to restore an interpretive common ground to the proliferation of factional and regional languages, but the sectional and class-based misunderstandings in his table-talk always imply on this small scale the failure to find any common linguistic authority. Indeed both *The Professor* and *The Poet* face this issue directly when they introduce the dynamic of Holmesian table-talk in early chapters by showing the speakers at the breakfast-table reenacting the mid-century "war of the dictionaries": when an argument erupts, each speaker runs for his dictionary to prove his point, only to find that all of his interlocutors have done the same thing and each has turned to a different linguistic authority, which only triggers a further unresolvable debate about the validity of each dictionary. Holmes' talkers speak such different languages that they cannot even agree about which lexicon to use to resolve their problems:

"Mr. Webster couldn't spell, Sir, or wouldn't spell, Sir, – at any rate, he didn't spell . . ."

The little gentleman with the malformation . . . shocked the propriety of the breakfast-table by a loud utterance of three words, of which the two last were 'Webster's Unabridged,' and the first was an emphatic monosyllable.

"Do you know Richardson's Dictionary? . . ."

"Boston has enough of England about it to make a good English dictionary."

"Don't let us deceive ourselves, – the war of the dictionaries is only a disguised rivalry of cities, colleges, and especially of publishers" (*CW*, II, 40–45).

Here the Doctor takes the contemporary "war" between supporters of Noah Webster's *New American Dictionary* and promoters of Joseph

Worcester's *Universal Dictionary*, or the clash of linguistic philosophies brought to the fore when Webster's *American Dictionary* first challenged the hegemony of Samuel Johnson's *English Dictionary*, or the charged series of debates about language in general that preoccupied America throughout the nineteenth century, as the most fundamental cultural models for the clashes and misunderstandings in the conversation at his breakfast-table.[12]

Holmes seems to have found a rich mine of humor in this predicament, as his writings join those of other American Humorists who had already begun exploring the multivocal potential in the now commonplace picture of America as a "Debating Society." And he also seems to hold up the movement of conversation itself as a site for some compensatory form of cultural interaction. What emerges here is an attempt to define through the talk form an alternative, utopian model of a social whole that would not necessarily impose homogeneity, a sort of "association" that would not necessarily trample upon individual rights and expression – in short, a way out of the impasse faced by Daniel Webster, the debaters in Congress, and the nation as a whole. Such a potential "conversation of a culture" would not seek a final resolution in monologue, but would hope to operate – very much along the lines of Mikhail Bakhtin's vision of a "dialogic" literary form that suggests the utopian possibility of a non-homogeneous social whole – as a creative dialogue between nationalities, between subcultures, between diverse factions, between insiders and outsiders; its language would not conform to one standard, but would develop its richness as a struggle between and overlapping of regional dialects, professional jargons, the intonations of different age groups, and so on.[13]

Such a vision of talk form differs in fundamental ways not only from the theories of conversation dominant in eighteenth-century England or in mid-nineteenth-century America, but also from the model of conversation put forward in much twentieth-century conversation analysis. Indeed, Holmes' conception of the workings of such dialogue forms can stand as a rough experimental ancestor of what Mary Louise Pratt has called for as an urgent need in our own divided era: an "art of the contact zone." According to Pratt, most theories of conversation now current in linguistics see it as the art of a seamless "speech community," an "orderly, coherent exchange . . . held together by a homogeneous competence or grammar shared identically and equally among all the members," by "a single set of rules or norms," and by "principles of cooperation and shared understanding," thus imaging forth the utopian ideal of a "unified and homogeneous social world." Alternative "arts of the contact zone," on the other hand, would arise to meet the needs of a very different social world and a very different (though increasingly common) sort of social interaction, hoping to make possible "communication across lines of difference and hierarchy" and to help us to negotiate those heterogeneous "social spaces where cultures meet, clash, and grapple with each other, often in contexts of highly asymmetrical relations of power."[14] Holmes' table-talk works – distinguished from many other written "conversations" by their special stress on interruption and vocal diversity and by their rhetorical structure valuing the continual alternation of antitheses over any final synthesis – can be seen in this way as quirky attempts to define a verbal arena for exchanges *between* communities, between speakers of different languages – and thus to approach the pressing mid-nineteenth-century problem of cultural mediation.

AN "ART OF THE CONTACT ZONE": TALK IN THE AMERICAN BOARDINGHOUSE OR HOTEL

French conversationalists in the seventeenth and eighteenth centuries had perhaps seen their salons as offering a special preserve for the free-play of ideas between ideally equalized speakers, and some eighteenth-century English talkers may have celebrated their coffee-houses as privileged spheres bringing together a cross section of society on special terms that suspended the normal rules of a status-based social intercourse, but Holmes, in a master stroke, distinguishes his utopian ideal of a "conversation of the culture" by setting it in a radically different milieu. His talkers meet not in an aristocratic salon or in a private, insular literary club but in a newly emerging and peculiarly American institution: the public boardinghouse. His conversations thus achieve their special effects by a surprising juxtaposition of talk-tones and talk-context: the Doctor transplants the best gems gathered from his salon life among the elite into the very different atmosphere of the boardinghouse (which he knows well from his college days) and of the small hotel (which he knows only too well from his travels on the Lyceum circuit).

When the boardinghouse was just peaking as a mid-century phenomenon, and the hotel was in the midst of a cross-country boom

– what has been called a "hotel mania" – many Americans celebrated these specifically American inventions as the clearest epitomes
of democracy in action. Like Holmes, the salon wit Nathaniel Willis
could recognize the American style of hotel as a microcosm of the
nation's life: for Willis, the new-style hotel stands as an image of "the
tangible republic – the only thing palpable and agreeable that we
have to show in common life, as republican."[15] For even the word
"hotel" was an American creation, borrowed from the French "hôtel
de ville" to name a new sort of community center, a new kind of
public "palace" for a migratory people. Historian Daniel Boorstin
notes that "hotels were among the earliest transient facilities that
bound the nation together. They were both the creatures and the
creators of communities, as well as symptoms of the frenetic quest for
community." In Holmes' Boston, the central hotel grew out of the
"Exchange Coffee-House," where the converse and commerce were
presided over by a famously autocratic hotel-keeper known as "the
Metternich of all hosts" and "the emperor of American landlords."[16]
But the new-style hotel-keeper could no longer be expected to be the
genial "host" of the eighteenth-century inn or coffeehouse; he ruled
over a newly diverse and dynamic realm, with splendid public parlors
attracting crowds of visitors and common dining rooms of the
"American Plan" bringing together a new temporary "community"
of strangers from across the land. Many foreign travelers, expecting to
be able to retire to protected interactions with their chosen familiars,
were shocked by a hotel system that seemed to force them into such
diverse and unnaturally close public associations, and commented on
the dangers of this plan: in the mid-1850s, one Englishman was
shocked at the way this "peculiar institution" dissolved the boundaries between "public and "private" life; Mr. Trollope was amazed at
the consequent loss of privacy for the intimate life of the family.
Boorstin summarizes their understandable reaction:

A western traveller who found himself sharing his dinner table, and called
upon to chat familiarly, with a miscellaneous company of common soldiers,
farmers, laborers, teamsters, lawyers, doctors, ministers, bankers, judges, or
generals, soon discovered that Americans considered the desire for privacy
akin to pride.[17]

The boardinghouse, another sort of "home away from home" for
mid-century Americans, though involving smaller and less transient
groups of people than the hotel, could be seen to represent an even

more insidious threat to the privacy of the family. The clearest symptom of a rapidly expanding urban life, an unfortunate side-effect of American mobility, the boardinghouse brought the hotel's heterogeneous quasi-public life into the heart of the home. Certainly the trend to these new forms of "surrogate family" structure was undeniable: in the 1850s one American family in five was found to be taking in lodgers, and in Boston between 10 and 30 per cent of all homes had opened themselves to these "strangers in the family" (with the most common arrangement just the one Holmes describes – a female Irish host taking in migrants of a higher social status who were willing to pay rent in order to find some independence from their families).[18] Foreign travelers were often horrified to see how many Americans now lived as lodgers, rubbing elbows with groups of strangers at each day's family-style boardinghouse meal. Even many native observers, like the playwright William Northall, surveying New York boardinghouses in 1851, could begin to worry that the spread of this living arrangement might allow the cold, amoral, anonymous life of the large cities to destroy the "bonds of union" of a true "family circle."[19]

When Holmes takes the boardinghouse or small hotel as the setting for his table-talk, then, his conversational form speaks for a social theory which would stress public life, public cooperation, and a sense of the self as formed by its relations to the social whole. It thus works as an implicit attack on Jacksonian atomism, and especially on the increasing insulation of the Victorian family home. His boardinghouse also celebrates the diversity of the public sphere, the vital addition of "strangers" within the haven of family privacy, the unsettling but provocative forces of dialogue. When he places his Autocrat, a man preoccupied with social distinctions, in the boardinghouse, which Boorstin describes as "the classic locale for . . . the dissolving of old distinctions," and when he then seats this would-be monologist amidst a table-full of people of such various ages, genders, and ranks, Holmes gives us what could be a perfect parody picture of the visiting Old World Englishman – the imagined scene of "Mr. Trollope in the American Hotel" – in much the same way that earlier American humorists were inspired to make the prudish Mrs. Trollope a foil character to energize their emerging Yankee theater.[20]

Building out of this fundamental tension between Autocrat and boardinghouse breakfast-table, though, Holmes' depiction of the free interactions between multiple discourses here is not so utopian as to imply that all of its participant voices have an equal sway, or to pretend that in the carnival of talk all power relations are suspended. Each person at the breakfast-table has to develop the conversational equivalent of a "boardinghouse reach," learning to fight to have a vocal share in the talk just as they have to fight for a fair share of the food. Holmes' imaginary boardinghouse is like a "sook," loud with the sounds of competing cries. Its talk builds as a model of the power struggles in the surrounding social world, with the distinctions of rank, gender, wealth, education, and so on, foregrounded by the Autocrat's attempts to rule. This verbal struggle gains its charge and its humor as it bares the mechanisms behind each assertion of power and, at the same time, it opens a wide variety of points for resistance and interruption. In the ebb and flow of this talk, we are made sharply aware of who has the floor, who asks the questions, who sets the vocabulary, the tone, the issues; who interrupts, and who is silenced or excluded. We also become keenly attuned to subtle differences in spoken styles that reflect widely differing approaches to conversation.

AN ANTHOLOGY OF MID-CENTURY TALK STYLES

Studying as well as enacting the dynamics of his age's talk, the Doctor structures his table-talk sessions to give us an historical anthology of conversational forms. And these voices are, indeed, surprisingly diverse. We meet: the Autocrat who, often as bluntly opinionated as his hero, Doctor Johnson, warms at every prospect of contradictory opinion as an opportunity to "talk for victory," or who, having silenced any opposition, tries to monopolize the free flow of dialogue, reflecting the popular image of Coleridge as, in De Quincey's words, "the autocrat who presided" over his worshipful admirers in endless soliloquy;[21] the Professor, who usually represents an older Addisonian tradition of casual, plain-style, instructive discussion, but who, after a glass of wine, can become quite the Shandian sentimental humorist, and who also verges at times on the scientific humor of another Holmes model, the scientist–humorist– conversationalist and founding Scriblerian, Doctor Arbuthnot; a shrewd "Ben Franklin" who, like his namesake, will use conversational skills to present himself in multiple masks as he moves along the road to social advancement, and who thus reflects the Mechanics'

Institute auto-didact's approach to self-culture in talk; the Divinity Student, who speaks for the newly "feminized" ministry now engaging itself in the self-conscious, aesthetic talk of refined urban parlors (and who clearly hopes that such sensitive reflections might lead to later more intimate talks with the Schoolmistress); the Poet, who takes this one step further, and so enters in at times with the sort of self-serious, purple-prosey effusion which was characteristic of some Transcendentalist experiments in Conversation; Little Boston, who epitomizes the sort of boosterish American stump orator that so bothered Dickens and Tocqueville; the Lady in Black, who invokes the age's urges to censorship of much free-thinking and free-talking; John, whose brief words link him with the prankish children at the table as an anti-conversationalist, filling any intervals with the down-to-earth jokes and bad puns that tend to deflate and derail the trains of too-serious talk; and of course the several less educated speakers who can't seem to make "respectable" sentences at all, but whose frequent interruptions in dialect become the matter for many Autocratic lessons in "elocution."

The Professor ends with a tonal shift as it moves into one-on-one conversations at Little Boston's deathbed, and so it adds to this collection of talk forms an explicit comparison between the bedside manner of nurses, doctors, and clergymen. But even when the comparisons are not elaborated, all of Holmes' table-talk works invite us to observe the divergences between the great number of juxtaposed speaking styles. The masters-of-ceremonies here frequently lead us through these long anthology-lists of guests – the Doctor's versions of the Whitmanian catalogue – noting the multiplicity of voices that are "contributing" to the life of this large table. *The Poet* even gives us diagrams to point up the variety of possible mixes: at the third breakfast-table we hear from The Capitalist and The Salesman (a lower Capitalist); The Master (old-style generalist's science) and the Scarabee (specialized science) and the Astronomer (abstract science); That Boy and Dr. Benjamin Franklin (having pulled himself up from a Boy's roots); the Register of Deeds (a scribe in a Dickensian bureaucracy) and the Man of Letters (an aesthetic "bachelor") and a female Novelist (author of works of popular sentiment) and the Poet; the conservative Western Member of the Haouse and the radical Easterner, Little Boston; the Lady (a fallen aristocrat) and the Irish Landlady; and so on. After one of these surveys of his full table, the Poet remarks, in a typical understatement, that while this may never be a frictionless assembly, neither is it specialized or one-dimensional:

I think we have a somewhat exceptional company . . . There is more individuality of character than in a good many similar boarding-houses, where all are business-men, engrossed in the same pursuit of money-making, or all are engaged in politics, and so deeply occupied with the welfare of the community that they think and talk of little else. (*CW*, III, 48)

Normally each of the speakers gathered at Holmes' breakfast-tables would converse only with others speaking very much the same language and preoccupied with the same matters, but this unusual boardinghouse brings them out of their comfortable everyday contexts into hilarious and revealing new combinations. Holmes' continued stress on this vitalizing diversity of voices as the fundamental prerequisite to any true conversational interaction allies the Doctor with Emerson, who at least in theory celebrates the invigoration of the sort of cross-fertilizing conversation which makes possible out-of-the-ordinary exchanges between workers and scholars, men and women, children and adults, thus drawing each participant out of himself and out of his everyday social and professional sphere to provoke fresh thought. And the basic structure of Holmes' table-talk clearly differentiates his vision in important ways from that of William Hazlitt, the era's best-known spokesman for "conversation." Influencing a major transformation of the talk tradition, Hazlitt's early nineteenth-century essays (including "On the Conversation of Authors" and "On Familiar Style") marked a crucial turn away from the earlier eighteenth-century conversational ideal of the public life. In Hazlitt's formulations, the model setting for talk shifts from a quasi-public place (a coffeehouse, a boardinghouse, or a hotel) to a more private sphere (like that of a select club); the goal in talk shifts from interaction between diverse strangers to interaction between familiars (those who are like one another, as intimately close as a sort of second family); and the privileged talk mode shifts from "civility" (an older set of norms designed to facilitate exchanges between those of different ranks, professions, sexes, ethnicities, religious affiliations, and localities) to "familiarity" – Hazlitt's famous "familiar style."[22] But Hazlitt's notion of the "familiar style" is in fact a prescription for writing more than for speech; his definitions of "conversational style," which have been taken as promoting an identification of speech and writing, are in fact pointedly concerned with stressing the differences between these realms. Finally, he is most concerned to show how writers might transfer the energies of spoken discourse into written form – what might be described as an aestheticization of talk. Founding the tradition still dominant today, then, Hazlitt turns away from the multi-vocal and interruptive model of public talk to redefine "conversational style" as the easy colloquialism of a single, private voice.[23]

MONOLOGICAL AUTOCRACY AND REVOLUTIONARY INTERRUPTION: HOLMES' "LIVELY DEMOCRACY OF A DINNER-TABLE"

But at the same time that Hazlitt was influencing this crucial turn towards the aestheticization of talk, many others in Holmes' era found themselves preoccupied with a completely opposed vision of talk – as they began to take very seriously the political dynamics inherent in the conversation form, and to analyze the talk forum as a microcosm of the operations of public life. On the one hand, for American Unionists the philosophical model of thought as a warring dialogue of voices was coming to have distressing implications in the political sphere. In a mid-century climate of increasing disunity, such thinkers worried obsessively about the linguistic breakdown at the root of this breakdown in the bonds of society. On the other hand, though, many wondered how order and civility could be restored to talk in the barroom and the drawing room, or more generally to the "conversation of the culture," without risking the imposition of a monolithic central authority. The subtle Arts of Conversation, then, became increasingly valued as a privileged site for study of the social Arts of Government. How should listener and speaker interact in a democracy? We find these political dynamics latent in Emerson's thought about dialogue when, in the peak passage of "Circles" defining conversation as a "game of circles," he celebrates the movement of continual interruption in which "each new speaker emancipates us from the oppression of the last speaker" – and in the ongoing process of these small-scale revolutions "we seem to recover our rights, to become men."[24] But Emerson's vision of a dialogical release from monological oppression leads to just the sort of radical vision likely to induce panic in those concerned with social, institutional, and governmental order.

Thomas De Quincey became interested in the close connections between the "Art of Conversation" and the "*uses* of social life" for similar reasons. Recognizing in talk the movements of a mysteriously potent force in social relations – a "secret magic" or "contagious ardor" in the "electric kindling" of affinities among people – he began to meditate anxiously about possible autocratic abuses of that power. The problem was epitomized for De Quincey in the spectre of an "autocrat" like Coleridge, who could soliloquize through a whole evening for four or five hours; more than a mere problem of salon etiquette, such uninterruptable talk reflects "a systematic trespass upon the conversational rights of the whole party": this was "not *colloquium*, or talking *with* the company, but *alloquium*, or talking *to* the company." But De Quincey then can envision few effective remedies (this side of "violent interruption") for such threats to our liberties: perhaps the turning of an egg-timer at the center of the table would serve as a reminder that talkers should turn over the floor at regular intervals; or perhaps a ruling *symposiarch* could be randomly chosen at each session to assure the "active commerce of question and answer, of objection and demur" so essential to free conversation. A governing *symposiarch*, though, might himself pose anew the problem of autocracy. Even in the Greek symposium, De Quincey notes, the "rules" of dialogue still allowed a *symposiarch* to govern as a tyrant: "Elected democratically, he became, once installed, an autocrat no less despotic than the King Of Prussia."[25]

In the very naming of his first and best-known character, the Autocrat, Holmes shows that he recognizes, and is in fact preoccupied with, just these issues of conversational despotism. Certainly the Autocrat bears a strong family resemblance to the "autocrat" Coleridge as described by De Quincey; or he might be taken as a caricatural parody of another early nineteenth-century conversational despot: Napoleon, who could dominate the salon the way he dominated the battlefield, whose "urge to talk was stronger than his urge to conquest," and whose demagogic monologues – the "Gespräch mit Napoleon" – flow on with almost no interruption to fill ten huge volumes.[26] And in his role as an after-dinner speaker Holmes could often take up this "autocratic" stance, introducing himself with fanfare at banquets as "master" of the *symposia*, highlighting his position as ruler of the unruly realm of banquet-table discussion, and playing upon analogies between the government of table-talk and of the larger society: his topic will be, he says in one typical toast-introduction, "the art of ruling, whether it be the council of a Nation, the legislature of a State, or the lively democracy of a Dinner-table."[27]

The political dynamics in talk would always be the Doctor's special terrain. But even in the years just before the Civil War, Holmes does not put these elements into play in a spirit of great anxiety. For him, the oppositions between monological autocracy and periodic revolutionary interruption can generate a vital compensatory humor. For, unlike a Coleridge or a Napoleon, Holmes' autocratic speakers always have a great deal of trouble with resistances to their magnetic authority; the "lively democracy of the Dinner-table" always provides a strong resistance to their attempts to rule the discussion. From those famous opening words, "I was just going to say, when I was interrupted," the Autocrat, proclaiming himself king of his conversational court, makes explicit the political resonances of his attempts to rule. But when he then announces that he will allow the Divinity Student "to take a certain share of the conversation, so far as assent and pertinent questions are concerned," he is immediately served notice that more rude interruption will also always play a major role – perhaps *the* major role – in this verbal battleground: "[The Divinity Student] abused his liberty on this occasion by presuming to say that Leibniz had the same observation." Like Webster in the Senate, the Autocrat soon finds that he is under siege. And he cannot protect himself behind Rules of Order or the by-laws of a Constitution; in fact the more he talks the more he meets such assertions of the liberties of conversation – resistances, "rebellions," and even movements of "secession" at the table.[28]

Just as he is gearing himself up for an elaborate defense of plagiarism, for example, the Autocrat is again rudely interrupted – by an audience that is apparently far from captive:

This is the philosophy of it. (Here the number of the company was diminished by a small secession.) (*CW,* I, 31)

Then, when he later continues to develop his philosophical defense of plagiarism after this breakfast-table "secession," the Autocrat finds he must also defend himself against other forms of vocal insurrection:

You need not get up a rebellion against what I say, if you find everything in my sayings is not exactly new. (*CW,* I, 51)

Now he must continue in the face of a deflating, almost defiant inattention,

[. . . After this little episode, I continued, to some few who remained balancing teaspoons on the edges of cups, twirling knives, or tilting upon the hind legs of their chairs until their heads reached the wall, where they left gratuitous advertisements of various popular cosmetics.] (*CW*, 1, 31–32)

A guerilla para-language of non-verbal signs and gestures often asserts itself here, as it does in Sterne, to disrupt the already fragmentary and fragile flow of any monologist's words, and to lead digressive minds further and further into metonymic lists of details. Ready to launch into the distinction between poetry and pun, the Autocrat makes the mistake of offering a slight opening to his listeners – and again confronts a non-verbal form of interruptive intervention:

Will you allow me to pursue this subject a little further?
    [They didn't allow me at that time, for somebody happened to scrape the floor with his chair just then; which accidental sound . . . broke the charm, and that breakfast was over.] (*CW*, 1, 50)

Another time he is droning on about the true irrationalism in human nature when he finds that his interlocutors have "understood" this message all too well, as they have discovered a private passion for one another and so are not even listening to him:

[Nobody understood this but the theological student and the schoolmistress. They looked intelligently at each other; but whether they were thinking about my paradox or not, I am not clear. . .] (*CW*, 1, 42–43)

    Much of the most charged life of this table-talk goes on between those brackets. For even when the Autocrat's voice does monopolize the floor, the bracketed scenes show how deeply he has internalized his interlocutors' reactions. Everything he does works in dialogue with that ever-present larger audience of creative, suspicious listeners, even if these hearers are usually recalcitrant –

I want to make a literary confession now, which I believe nobody has made before me. You know very well that I write verses sometimes, because I have read some of them at this table. [The company assented, – two or three of them in a resigned sort of way, as I thought, as if they supposed I had an epic in my pocket, and was going to read half a dozen books or so for their benefit.] (*CW*, 1, 30)

– or at times directly censorious:

[I think these remarks were received rather cooly. A temporary boarder from the country . . . left the table prematurely, and was reported to have been very virulent about what I said.] (*CW*, 1, 30)

Despite all the bluster in his own dull discourses, then, the Autocrat does not want to stop all debate. And indeed in the long run the main role of any monological voice in these table-talks is to invite explosive rebellion.

Holmes' second table-talk work, *The Professor at the Breakfast-Table*, also opens along just these lines – with a pointed parody of conversation in the mode of Alcott's or Fuller's Transcendentalist version of Socratic method. In the first paragraph, The Professor *begins* the table-talk by admitting that his goal is to lead us to his prepared speech on "The Great *End* of Being," which he believes provides a "universal formula of life." Realizing that an instructor must signal his intentions through an initial "large statement," he first solemnly intones: "I will thank you for the sugar. Man is a dependent creature." But even the Divinity Student ignores the weighty maxim, and simply passes the sugar. Then, when he turns to leading aphorism number two – "Life is a great bundle of little things" – the Professor is met only with laughter, and suddenly John jumps in with a loud, earthy interruption that opens the way for a rambling childhood reminiscence by the grotesque Sculpin. At this table, those who are always rhetorically or metaphysically oriented towards the end (and so simply pay lip service to the turn-taking of dialogue) lose control of the living, multivoiced, interactive talk that continues to flow on all around them (*CW*, II, 1–2).

All through the breakfast-table papers, John is the character who spearheads the movement which assures that in this talk there will always be at least some interruptive openings for vocal diversity. He is the one who breaks up the Professor's attempts to sum up "The Great End of Being," and whose crude jokes interrupt the Professor's long disquisition on the art of pleasing in harmonious Augustan conversation. He is the one who intervenes to break off the Autocrat's monological set-speech about the "carnival-shower of questions and replies and comments" in table talk; he is the one who makes "a very unphilosophical application" of the Autocrat's philosophical argument about "the three Johns" by taking the last three peaches in the basket for himself – "just one apiece for him" (*CW*, II, 1–2, 137; I, 65, 54). Apparently modeled on Holmes' real-life brother John Holmes, who accompanied Oliver everywhere and became better than anyone at getting irreverent words in edgewise to stop the flow of autocratic talk, the "John" of the written works interacts with the Autocrat the way many dummies interact with their ventriloquist companions. He is the Autocrat's double, a sort of alter ego. For while the Autocrat always remains wrapped up in the rather limited realm of words, John pops up with rude retorts, bawdy double-entendres, and terrible puns that violate all conversational decorum at the urgings of unrestrainable, non-verbal, libidinal impulses. He dares to gesture, to act; he dares to eat a peach. A key element in the bipolar battery of these electrodynamic conversations, he insures the continual flow of alternating currents. In the rhetoric of this table-talk, he is the main defender of dialogue, making sure that the tables will continue to turn.

John becomes the ringleader of a small gang of naughty children, armed with squirt-guns, whips, popguns and firecrackers, that is always ready to enforce the festival rule of explosive interruption at this breakfast-table. Though his main interventions involve only noise and gesture, the arsenal of his fireworks also includes the loud, irreverent remarks that he uses to disrupt all self-serious conversation and to send up its too ponderous, pedantic, or police-like partici-pants. But John's special verbal domain is the pun; he loves to pop one of them in any silent interval, and delights in the way puns literalize the metaphors of the most effusive speakers. When, in a *tour de force* of ironic wordplay, the Autocrat puts on the mask of gravity, pretending to banish all puns as enemies of the coherences and continuities of fine conversation, his pun-filled polemic – itself a carnivalization of all forms of judgment and of univocal authority – dismisses John's form of verbal levity as mere childishness:

People that make puns are like wanton boys that put coppers on the railroad tracks. They amuse themselves and other little children, but their little trick may upset a freight train of conversation for the sake of a battered witticism.

At the same time, though, he recognizes that such wantonness carries a powerful revolutionary potential: "Political double-dealings natur-ally grew out of verbal double meanings . . . What was levity in the time of the Tudors grew to regicide and revolution in the age of the Stuarts." But John can never be silenced. Even here he has the last word, whispering something about "the Macaulay-flowers of literature" just after the Autocrat's resounding rhetorical conclusion (*CW*, I, 12–13).

And John's spirit lives on in the retorts and misunderstandings that derail the freight trains of heavy, linear conversation more and more frequently throughout the later works of Holmes' breakfast-table series. By the time of *The Poet*, Holmes clearly recognizes the fundamental role of this interruptive power at his table. Now, in fact, the characteristic outbursts and interjections are perhaps even too consciously worked out. Becoming a caricatural running gag, the irrational jack-in-the-box uprisings of these rude, abusive voices of the "other" may be a bit too easily figured forth. For here Holmes gives us one character who stands as Interruption incarnate. Known as "That Boy" to the boarders, this *enfant terrible* is introduced by the Poet as "a sort of expletive at the table," meaning that his mono-syllables only "stop the gaps" in the larger sentences of adult conversation, but also implying that his loud, profane interjections can in fact open up gaps as well – and so often stop the functioning of those sentences altogether. First appearing just after the Master's warning that, "Boys should not touch off their squibs and crackers too near the powder magazine," That Boy carries a Popgun that he uses to shoot down any highflown speech: "This audacious child . . . is like to become a power among us, for that popgun is fatal to any talker who is hit by its pellet" (*CW*, III, 63). Just as he is about to tell us more about this child, the Poet is, aptly enough, interrupted. And when he resumes, something about that irreverent spirit leads him to imagine a seemingly unrelated scene showing how another poet found himself deflected from one question to another as he tried to compose at table:

> *"To be or not to be: that is the question: –*
> *Whether 't is nobl – "*
> "William, shall we have pudding to-day, or flapjacks?" (*CW*, III, 8)

Later in the conversation, That Boy touches off squibs to detonate the Poet's own fine, self-serious, overly "written" phrases – to make him stop talking like a book:

Why, a day or two ago I was myself discoursing, with considerable effect, I thought, on some new aspects of humanity, when I was struck full on the cheek by one of these little pellets, and there was such a confounded laugh that I had to wind up and leave off with a preposition instead of a mouthful of polysyllables. (*CW*, III, 63)

But the mischievous child has the same effect on the Master during a disquisition on Music:

Pop! went a small piece of artillery . . . it took the Master full in the forehead, and had the effect of checking the flow of his eloquence. How the little monkey had learned to time his interruptions I do not know, but I have observed more than once before this, that the popgun would go off just at the moment when some one of the company was getting too energetic or prolix. The Boy isn't old enough to judge for himself when to intervene *to change the order of conversation* . . . . (*CW*, III, 63, emphasis added)

And the youth also attacks the Member of the Haouse during a meal-time repetition of one of his most fiery congressional orations. Here again the popgun functions like a verbal retort, interrupting the speech flow by literalizing its metaphors – and thus exposing some of its dangerous latent tendencies:

The Member of the Haouse was just saying that his bill hit the constitooents in their most vital – when a pellet hit him in the feature of his countenance most exposed to aggressions and least tolerant of liberties. The Member resented this unparliamentary treatment by jumping up from his chair . . . seizing the implement . . . and breaking it into splinters. (*CW*, III, 236)

With all of these interruptions paradoxically providing one of the few continuous threads in the narrative of *The Poet*, then, we are not surprised when, at the book's end, as the Master tries, like Fuller at the end of one of her Transcendentalist conversations, to sum up all of his preceding points into one pithy concluding statement, the Poet can repeat for us only the first fragment of "the substance of this final intuition":

"The one central fact in the Order of Things which solves all questions is – "
    At this moment we were interrupted by a knock at the Master's door . . .
(*CW*, III, 339)

The mechanism may now be only too obvious, but That Boy's repeated non-verbal, prankish interruptions, derailing all monological attempts at pre-planned, over-literary eloquence, at high-serious treatment of the great themes, or at any coherent movement toward summation or closure, and forcing continual violations of the "proper" decorum supposedly prescribed by the "genteel style," may stand here as the clearest examples of the crucial dynamic qualities which distinguish the "collisions of discourse" throughout Holmes' conversations from the talk of Boston's polite society. Even the Master finally admits that, after the experience of this breakfast-table, he often finds himself mentally exclaiming "Popgun!" in the midst of monotonous drawing-room chatter:

In short, so useful has that trivial implement become as a jaw-stopper and a *boricide*, that I never go to a club or a dinner-party, without wishing the company included . . . That Boy with his popgun. (*CW*, III, 237)

And the Poet comes to feel the same way. In another scene late in *The Poet*, when two earnest lovers are gazing at their own images in a reflecting pool, trading fine sentiments in an epitome of the sort of high-minded, self-conscious, and fundamentally narcissistic "Christian conversation" that Ann Douglas takes as definitive of the genteel culture of mid-century Boston – "'There is no place too humble for the glories of heaven to shine in,' she said" – the Poet is happy to note that another naughty boy soon invades this lakeside scene to break up the "reflections" in such tepid talk: " – just then a lubberly boy threw a great stone, which convulsed the firmament, – the one at their feet, I mean" (*CW*, III, 315–16).[29] If the lovers' phrases always reach for Higher meanings, reading the pool's reflections as figures of the firmament above, the boy's gestural retort quickly brings them back down to solid ground. And the tiny explosion that arises as he literalizes their metaphors has the power of a miniature apocalypse: it "convulses the firmament," making the earth seem to move under the restrained talkers' feet. Holmes hopes that as it "convulses" us in laughter it may also, on its small scale, like That Boy's Popgun in almost every table-talk scene, serve to "change the order of conversation."

Finally, all the firecrackers and popguns that explode throughout Holmes' multivoiced, interruptive table-talk works must lead us to revise our received notions of him as a model of the "genteel style" – or perhaps indeed to revise our notions about the dynamics of this "genteel style." When we recall once again the Doctor's description of the most exhilarating moments around his breakfast-table as a festival of fireworks – in the well-known set-piece cited at the beginning of the chapter – we have to admit that this bears little resemblance to the stereotyped image of a staid, pale-faced, indoor literary form:

– that carnival-shower of questions and replies and comments, large axioms bowled over the mahogany like bombshells from professional mortars, and explosive wit dropping its trains of many-coloured fire, and the mischief-making rain of *bons-bons* pelting everybody that shows himself, –

When the Autocrat calls here for "Truth" to "get off her pedestal and drop her academic poses, and take a festive garland," he certainly does not speak as your standard *symposiarch* or your standard Victorian Sage. Delighting in the way "axioms" are unsettled by the turns of talk, he is hardly the usual maxim-moralist, or the normal "Fireside Poet" preaching about cultural coherences. Most basically, we have to recall that Holmes never speaks with a single voice. For at the end of this rising celebration of conversation as a Dionysiac revel, the Autocrat is again interrupted by an example of dialectic in action:

> . . . – the picture of a truly intellectual banquet is one which the old Divinities might well have attempted to reproduce in their –
> "Oh, oh, oh!" cried the young fellow whom they call John, – "that is from one of your lectures!" (*CW*, I, 64–65)

Because he is presenting this monological celebration of dialogue not at the Saturday Club but at the boardinghouse, diverse voices are always waiting for any opportunity to push their way in and take the floor. Characteristically, it is John who here creates the opening, insuring that this conversation will continue as a game of circles, so that new voices can contribute to the dialogic movements of permanent *parabasis*. Exploiting the problem points of the talk genre – this time the moment when distinctions between dialogue and monologue, and between spontaneous talk and pre-planned oratory, begin to break down – John always enters to make certain that this table-talk will build out of gaps, interruptions, and alternations as much as out of univocal coherence. At the end of this passage, the Autocrat himself recognizes the rightness of John's intervention. The "fountain-columns" of his words, he says, must after each rise sink back down to water level; the table-talk must flow on.

CHAPTER 3

"COLLISIONS OF DISCOURSE" I: THE ELECTRODYNAMICS OF CONVERSATION
A Carnival of Verbal Fireworks

> We must not begin by talking of pure ideas – vagabond thoughts
> that tramp on the public roads without any human habitation –
> but must begin with men and their conversation.   C. S. Peirce

In Victorian America the "separate sphere" of the Castle-Home was
never as insular, fortified, static, or coherent as its occupants might
have wished. Holmes' written conversations help us to regain a sense
of the dynamism of mid-century domestic life as they bring out all
that is at stake in table-talk and table manners, showing how even the
most mundane moments of verbal intercourse in the parlor, the
dining room, or the club can become charged encounters, sparked by
ongoing alternations between polarized voices struggling for power:
assertion continually meets counter-assertion, dominance meets
resistance. Through his structured reenactments of parlor talk,
Holmes points out that the champagne-pops of repartee within
genteel salon walls can have far-reaching repercussions; the
matchbox explosions that divide debaters at his boardinghouse can
be seen as warning shots predicting the much larger explosions soon
to erupt across the entire "House Divided" of America.

"THIS CARNIVAL-SHOWER OF QUESTIONS AND REPLIES AND COMMENTS"

Almost every reader of Holmes' works, in every era, thinks of some
form of fireworks when trying to describe the "explosive" literary
effects of his witty extended metaphors and juxtapositions and his
unusually interruptive table-talk form. In the mid-century vision, the
effects of wit can be very literally "bright" or "brilliant": the Doctor's
talk form could make Lowell think of a fountain of "Catherine-
wheeling" phosphorescent rockets; Annie Fields remembers that "his

wit left the world sparkling with the shafts it . . . let fly on every side";
Vernon Parrington notes that in his written table-talks each aphorism
or pun "explodes with a shower of sparks"; even the cautious S. I.
Hayakawa here erupts in an apt scientific analogy, comparing the
Doctor's wide-ranging and surprising figures of speech to the electrical figures which emerge in a charged experiment, "like a myriad
of flying atoms in an electrical tube, ready to light up at the slightest
current of thought"; and biographer Tilton sees in the dizzying,
centrifugal tendencies of this "whirling firecracker style" the most
characteristic reflections of Holmes' "pinwheel mind."[1] Holmes
himself seems to invite such readings of his table-talk as a form of
verbal fireworks. Hadn't the Autocrat introduced as the totem for his
talk the fountain-like water-sprinklers on street-cleaning carriages,
then picturing himself as a "thought-sprinkler" forever working to
open up the public highways of the culture's intellectual life as he
drives through with his words spraying out endlessly in all directions
(*CW*, 1, 27)? And hadn't he also described the most exhilarating
eruptions from this conversational fountain as a deafening and
dizzying festival of fireworks – a "carnival-shower of questions and
replies and comments" punctuated by the "bombshells" of major
contradictions and interruptions, with wit emerging at every opening
to scatter its "trains of many-coloured fire" (*CW*, 1, 64)?

Certainly the fountain-of-fireworks image captures something of the
carnival spirit so central to Holmes' sense of conversation. Indeed,
for the Doctor "carnival" becomes a mode of life and of thought, as
well as of writing. He often reminds us that he was born amidst the
exploding noise and color of a Cambridge academic carnival, and
the impression of that formative first scene seems to have influenced
much of his later development. In fact, even in his adult life as a
celebrated man of letters, Holmes never really left that carnival
scene: from his college days on through most of the century, he
presided as Master of the Revels at almost every Harvard festival –
and was also in constant demand as an after-dinner speaker or
toastmaster at the large, celebratory banquets that became increasingly popular throughout post-war America. (The festive ebullience
of the occasional opulent set-pieces introduced at the breakfast-table
by the Autocrat or the Professor shows how one mode of Holmes'
"talk" could be inspired by this "banquet" setting – with the
effervescent "star-foam" of his elaborate, multi-leveled wordplay

here clearly modeled on the pops and frothy foam of the champagne poured freely at these black-tie *symposia*.) And the most characteristic qualities of Holmes' written conversations seem to have been crucially formed by what he experienced, in his college days, as the "festive indulgences and gay license" of the "revelries" among other "young bacchanalians" in the life of student groups like the Hasty Pudding Club at Harvard – which turned his own world upside down, bursting apart the "sober habits" of his Calvinist upbringing. Seen by the young Holmes as directly descended from the saturnalian *symposia* of classical Rome, these club "revelries" centered on riotous wordplay at mock trials, mock debates, and mock spectacles featuring burlesque parodies of the pompous speech mannerisms of professors and politicians, crude imitations of the varied dialects of workers and country folk, and wildly costumed travesties merging the solemnities of mock academic processions with forms taken from music hall stage shows.[2] (These sorts of saturnalian influence erupt in Holmes' writings with detonations that are much less elegant and elaborate than the "carnival-showers" of his banquet set-pieces; as we saw in the last chapter, the arsenal of his fireworks also includes frequent sophomoric pranks: loud irreverent outbursts that interrupt self-serious speeches, and bad schoolboy puns that can derail whole trains of high-flown conversation.)

In fact, Holmes' connections to traditions of literary "carnival" follow quite closely the pattern defined by Mikhail Bakhtin in his speculative histories of this mode of "dialogic" writing. According to Bakhtin, the roots of the "polyphonic" or "dialogic" modern novel – exemplified in works by Dostoevsky and others that are seen to develop out of a dynamic interplay between multiple discourses tending to unsettle the attempts of any one authoritative voice to impose seriousness, coherence, or closure – can be found in the ritual forms of thousand-year-old folk traditions of "carnival": periods of holiday feasting and merry-making during which a saturnalian logic turning the conventional world "upside down" brings a general suspension of social and intellectual hierarchies. First of all, then, Bakhtin's carnival, like Holmes' table-talk, is always defined as a scene making possible unusual contacts between diverse figures: "people who are in life separated by impenetrable barriers enter into free, familiar contact on the carnival square."[3] But, for Bakhtin as for Holmes, the resulting mixture of diverse voices is certainly not "free" from conflict; Bakhtin finds forms of "oral carnival folk genres" and "conversational folk language" emerging here which reflect a "primordial struggle between tribes, peoples, cultures, and languages" and define two crucial aspects of the verbal life associated with saturnalia, both highlighting the explosive results of this mixture of languages and both also central to Holmes' vision of talk: *laughter* (rooted in a "primordial" folk tendency to imitate the linguistic habits of others in order to ridicule them) and *polyglossia* (the more highly evolved artistic and ideological uses of an "interanimation of languages").[4] The power struggles latent in these festival meetings between different cultures can often be expressed through the staging of "bloodless carnival wars" – in much the same way that Holmes describes the "carnival-showers" of verbal fireworks in his interruptive table-talk as like but not like the "bombshells" that explode in actual battle – or in another very common carnival plot: the mock crowning and discrowning of a carnival king. Like the reign of the Autocrat or of any other self-important "master" of the turns of talk at the Holmes breakfast-table, the reign of the carnival king is always by definition ambivalent and ephemeral – in such a "dialogic" context, it will not last long without interruption: "the idea of immanent discrowning is contained already in the crowning: it is ambivalent from the very beginning."[5]

When Bakhtin turns to the history of literary uses of these carnival dynamics, the touchstones of his vision of the tradition are also often Holmes' prime models for writing. Among the ancients, Bakhtin finds that a rich grounding in the life of folk carnival gave vitality to the elaborate, learned humor in a long line of Menippean satires – works usually structured as banquet *symposia*, often involving parodic uses of the philosophic mode of dialogue, and frequently bringing medical and scientific speculation into the mix with diverse literary genres and philosophic themes: the parodic dialogues of Plutarch; the saturnalian travesty of a symposium in Macrobius; the satiric miscellanies setting up dialogic juxtapositions between scientific aphorisms in Atheneus' *Doctors at Dinner*. In the Middle Ages, though the carnival spirit may have waned somewhat, it nonetheless continued to express itself in saturnalian forms of public life in the line of the "Feast of Fools." According to Bakhtin, important and influential medieval "school festivals" – forerunners of the carnivalesque commencement festivals and "bacchanalian" club spectacles at Harvard that so shaped Holmes' literary style – allowed students to ridicule "everything that had been the subject of reverent studies during the course of the year." And Bakhtin sees the ancient interest in parodic *symposium* dialogues continuing in a series of works of learned humor through the Middle Ages and on into the Renaissance, when the tradition of carnivalesque Menippean satires culminated in a great flowering: the appearance of the "complexly dialogized," hybrid "novels" of Rabelais and Cervantes.[6]

Holmes was an avid collector of just the carnivalesque works of learned humor studied by Bakhtin: Renaissance anthologies of table-talk *facetiae;* unorthodox, antique anatomy texts or literary compendia like Robert Burton's *Anatomy of Melancholy*; encyclopedic seventeenth-century collections of scientific para-doxa and aphorisms (dialogic juxtapositions of various unpopular, abnormal, or disproven scientific views); and a first edition (1532), in Greek, of the "Aphorisms of Hippocrates" (with the *Hippocratic Novel*) edited by the French doctor–writer–humorist François Rabelais. Rabelais' *Hippocratic Novel* and "Aphorisms" – a highly evolved Menippean parody of Socratic dialogue attributed to the ancient doctor, Hippocrates, and reworked by the French doctor-writer centuries later – is highlighted as one of the key, foundational works in Bakhtin's history of "carnivalization" in literature; and it was also apparently the most cherished book in Holmes' personal library. (Holmes bought this book – his "most exciting find" – during his student days in France, although he then had very little money to spare; and at the end of his life he felt he could not part with it, even when he had donated the rest of his library to various schools.)[7] Bakhtin's work can then help us to understand Holmes' senses of scientific–medical humor and of learned forms of the carnivalesque as "Rabelaisian" in very specific and crucial ways. Clearly the anthology of Hippocratic aphorisms and the *Hippocratic Novel* came to stand for Holmes as a sort of emblem of his goals, both in medicine and in literature; in his hybrid career as a doctor–writer–humorist, Holmes could see himself to be working very much in the line of Rabelais – much more profoundly than other contemporary authors of burlesque or sentimental humor who have been called "Rabelaisian" – though he was writing in another culture, in a very different era, and in a different literary genre.

And Bakhtin is also useful here as he explains how the base dynamic of carnival can transform itself to reemerge in different historical periods in a variety of literary genres. In his view, for several centuries after the Renaissance the dynamic of carnivalesque polyphony was kept alive only in the highly mediated forms of some traditions of aristocratic "chamber masquerade" and in certain forms of oral or written salon conversation or table-talk. But he does stress that certain modes of salon conversation – especially those modes which retain some contact with the free mixtures of carnival life on the public square, and so develop as dialogic struggles between diverse voices and opposed stances which tend to explode official ideologies and turn any assertions of single-voiced authority upside down – can be seen to operate as small-scale, upper-class, indoor translations or reenactments of the dynamics of saturnalia in an earlier folk life.[8] When Holmes foregrounds the "carnival-showers" of fireworks touched off by the talk at his breakfast-table, then, he seems to be suggesting a similar conception of the "blood-less" clashes between voices, genres, and discourses in his own verbal form, attempting to return our sense of the dialogic intercourse at his *symposium* – "this truly intellectual banquet" – to its roots in popular carnival.

THE BIPOLAR DYNAMICS OF ELECTRIC TALK

But we must not overlook the setting out of which those carnival-esque explosions arise: the Holmes scene is always that of conversa-tion, and it is always the movement of breakfast-table conversation itself that is combustive. In the alternations between speakers enforced by the perpetual revolutions of this breakfast-table, the rising rhetoric of each conversational enthusiast (those with "minds like firecrackers") is countered by the deflating retort of a harshly sceptical critic (brandishing some sort of popgun to shoot down each over-inflated idea). No wonder, then, that this table-talk will always be full of fireworks.

Everything in Holmes' world emerges in a tension of polarities. For him, as for the Scottish rhetoricians of the eighteenth century, the dynamic fields of rhetoric and electricity are intimately related. (Though probably only Holmes would yoke together so playfully the metaphors from science and speech, as when, for example, he elaborates his "hydrostatic paradox of controversy" [*CW*, 1, 114].) In rhetorical terms, every statement works dialogically against its antithesis; in electrical terms, all things operate and interrelate through a system of attractions and repulsions, and the energy of the lightning spark increases with the distance between the two poles.

Holmes may have been influenced in his application of this last electrical theory to "sparks" in the field of conversation by some sayings of Franklin, a talker–writer–scientist much on his mind. But his friend Emerson also speaks for the contemporary American interest in such an electrodynamics of talk. The Doctor would want to test far more literally and materially the scientific metaphors invoked by the Concord bard as he muses about "the metaphysics of the antagonisms, or, shall I say, Elective affinities observed in conversation," or asserts that "Society exists by chemical affinity," and again that "All conversation is a magnetic experiment."[9]

When in his element, in an endless round of parties, conventions, and club meetings, the Doctor was often seen as a "battery" or a "little dynamo" because of his boundless vitality, because of his whimsically physicalist sense of talk as a way of "experimenting" with new ideas, and because of his interest in all conversation as a laboratory for these chemical or electrical mixes. At salons or boardinghouses, on the train or at the circus, Holmes would always be verbally testing for flashes of laughter, for sparks of strong friction, or for all-out explosions. Thomas Appleton, wittily associating the Saturday Club's small scientific sprite with the Promethean image of the kite-flying Benjamin Franklin, said that his friend Holmes had "put the electricity of the climate into words." Along the same lines, James Russell Lowell, the Doctor's Saturday Club sounding board, presents in "A Fable for Critics" the perfect caricature of the Autocrat, and of his ability to electrify any group by drawing it out in diverse talk:

> There's Holmes, who is matchless among you for wit;
> A Leyden-jar always full charged, from which flit
> The electrical tingles of hit after hit;[10]

Holmes himself could later complain about being burdened with this reputation of being a "conversationalist" in an age so enamored of every nuance of daily conversation; the universal expectation that he would be able to produce unending streams of electric talk "every time [he opened his] mouth in company" could become quite a drain on his energies:

It seems hard not to be able to ask for a piece of bread or a tumbler of water, without a sensation running round the table, as if one were an electric eel or a torpedo, and couldn't be touched without giving a shock. A fellow isn't all battery, is he? (*The Poet at the Breakfast-Table, CW*, III, 44–45)

But both in his serious scientific writings, such as *Mechanism in Thought and Morals*, and in the *Autocrat*, the Doctor observes – repeating the insight in almost exactly the same words each time – that the base dynamic of all conversational interactions is bipolar and electrical:

I have often noticed . . . that a hopelessly dull discourse acts *inductively*, as electricians would say, in developing strong mental currents. (*Autocrat, CW,* i, 29)

The *induced current* of thought is often rapid and brilliant in the inverse ratio of the force of the inducing current. (*Mechanism, CW,* viii, 292)

Of course the coupling of speaker and listener need not always involve these two poles of dullness and brilliance; strong currents of talk seem to be sparked by almost any large gap between two cross-fertilizing discourses. Recognizing that he has been in religious controversies all of his life, Holmes finally admits that he really would not want this debate to end; if a truly "un-polarized" religious language were invented, things would be very boring. So, in his view, even a church will always need the electrical resistances of an "other" voice against which to define its own charge:

Why, the very life of an ecclesiastical organization is a life of *induction*, a state of perpetually disturbed equilibrium kept up by another charged body in the neighborhood. If the two bodies touch and share their respective charges, down goes the index of the electrometer! (*CW,* ii, 297)

In the same way, in *The Professor at the Breakfast-Table*, Holmes' "Professor" imagines a first conversation between an American and a Britisher as a volatile scientific experiment:

We begin skirmishing with a few light ideas, – testing for thoughts, – as our electro-chemical friend, De Sauty, if there were such a person, would test for his current; trying a little litmus-paper for acids, and then a slip of turmeric-paper for alkalies, as chemists do with unknown compounds; flinging the lead, and looking at the shells and sands it brings up to find out whether we are like to keep in shallow water, or shall have to drop the deep-sea line; in short, seeing what we have to deal with.

Finally, though, it is clear here that for Holmes true talkers would quickly avoid the timidity of such testing and head out of these shallow waters for uncharted seas – whatever the risk of unexpected clashes or explosions. Even if the Yankee is a chauvinist, hick booster and the Englishman a pompous prude, such polarizations or contrasts in culture and in language can only add to the interest of a verbal exchange – an exchange which is seen once again on the naturalistic model of the Doctor's "hydrostatic paradox":

After all, here is a great fact between us. We belong to two different civilizations, and, until we recognize what separates us, we are talking like Pyramus and Thisbe, without any hole in the wall to talk through . . .

This confronting of two civilizations is always a grand sensation to me: it is like cutting through the isthmus and letting the two oceans swim into each other's laps . . .

How much better this thorough interpenetration of ideas than a barren interchange of courtesies, or a bush-fighting argument in which each man tries to cover as much of himself and expose as much of his opponent as the tangled thicket of the disputed ground will let him! (*CW*, II, 35–37)

Here we have the ur-image of any Holmesian dialogue: for him, talk is always (in Pratt's apt phrase) an "art of the contact zone," a "confronting of two [different] civilizations"; its verbal dynamic will always develop, most fundamentally, as a version of Bakhtin's "polyglossia" – its vitality arising out of the "interanimation" of two or more "national" languages.[11] But if the conversational goal is the achievement of a fertile interaction, a truly "oceanic" interpenetration of ideas charged by the separations between the voices of two polar civilizations, it will not always be easy to maintain such a delicate balance, to avoid slipping into blank civility on the one hand or intransigent hostility on the other.

Holmes certainly had more than his share of experience with this particular sort of Anglo-American cross-cultural conversation – as by the mid-century a visit with the Doctor had become a standard stop on any literary Britisher's American tour. Boston had called upon Holmes to welcome Dickens with festive wit and occasional poetry on the novelist's first visit to America in 1842. And the two hit it off so well that, on a later visit, Dickens insisted on calling upon the Doctor – as they shared their mutual interests in melodrama and medicine while then taking a tour of the scene of the infamous Parkman murder at Harvard. Thackeray, on his own visit, understandably found Holmes – a "man of sensibility" with a sly, erudite wit – very congenial company. Back in London, he started an enthusiastic Holmes cult as he declared the Doctor the best thing he had seen in America, adding that "no man in England" could now do better than the *Autocrat*. But one meeting with Trollope exposed some of the limits of Holmes' rather idealistic conception of conversation as the site for an "interpenetration of ideas" between civilizations which

recognize their fundamental differences. In this encounter, whenever
the hummingbird-like Doctor tried to start an alcohol-inspired
"interpenetrative" romp, the beefy, red-faced Englishman would
abruptly bring things back to the ground, cracking coarse, heavy-
handed jokes in a roaring voice, thus pulling in his defenses in a fine
example of verbal "bush-fighting." Lowell describes this famous,
funny moment of failed cultural exchange: Dr. Holmes, he writes,
"charged, paradox in rest – but it was pelting a rhinoceros with seed
pearl." The Autocrat opened with a typically pointed challenge,

> You don't know what Madeira is in England.
> I am not sure it's worth knowing.
> Connoisseurship in it with us is a fine art. There are men who will tell you
> a dozen kinds as Dr. Waagen would know a Carlo Dolci from a Guido.
> They might be better employed!
> Whatever is worth doing is worth doing well.
> Ay, but that's begging the whole question. I don't admit it's *worse* doing at
> all. If they earn their bread by it, it may be *worse* doing (roaring).
> But you may be assured –
> No, but I may n't be asshored. I *won't* be asshored. I don't intend to be
> asshored (roaring louder)."[12]

No matter what the Doctor said, Trollope would mimic him with a
verbal retort, and then laugh so loud that no one could hear Holmes'
ripostes. Lowell remembers that, "Meanwhile Emerson and I, who
sat between them, crouched down out of range and had some very
good talk, the shot hurtling overhead." Surprisingly, in the end,
when Trollope began a hearty praise of English peaches, it was
apparently the quiet Hawthorne who got in the best word – which
seemed in fact to sum up the entire situation: "I asked an Englishman
once who was praising their peaches to describe to me what he
meant by a peach, and he described something very much like a
cucumber." With this, we get a sense of the difficulties in achieving
Holmes' ideal of vitally "polarized" conversation between widely
separate languages and civilizations: talking with such a utopian goal
can often seem as futile as comparing apples and oranges.[13]

Actually, much mid-century American discussion of the problems
and potentials in talk between Englishmen and Americans seems to
have served as a cover for reflection on a subject much closer to
home: the problems and potentials in talk (or in any interaction)
between increasingly divergent groups of Americans. In fact, as
Holmes was writing his *Professor* passage above, in 1859, this sort of

volatile, polarized talk situation would be increasingly common in any American's everyday life, with chance meetings between the different languages and "civilizations" of city and country, poor and rich, male and female, Whig or Democrat, narrow church or broad church, East and West, or, most obviously, between North and South, probably more likely to erupt in "bush-fighting argument" than in any ideal freeplay of conversation.[14] And the Autocrat's physicalist model of verbal interaction offers no real restraint to this tendency; indeed it often leads him to accent the elements of dispute that make a war of words sound very much like an actual fight. At times he wants to imagine talk resolving itself into a boxing match, with the controversialists stripping off their clothes for a full bodily engagement in the issues. But a similar sort of brute force can be involved even in normal parlor-room intercourse:

Every real thought on every real subject knocks the wind out of somebody or other. As soon as his breath comes back, he very probably begins to expend it in hard words. These are the best evidence a man can have that he has said something it was time to say.

This is the Autocrat in one of his Doctor Johnson moods – making blunt assertions, seeking and relishing strong contradictions. In fact he goes on here to recall Johnson's words of disappointment at the mild response to one of his pamphlets: " 'I think I have not been attacked enough for it,' he said; – 'attack is the reaction; I never think I have hit hard unless it rebounds' " (*CW*, I, 113–14). What Holmes values in this commonplace about fighting words is not simply the antagonism between speaker and listener but the implied sense of their strong interconnection: true controversialists become two poles of a single symbiotic system. Below the level of verbal content, talk here operates as a sort of two-stroke engine, its pistons moving back and forth with the pulses of physical action and reaction – wind out, breath in, hot air expended, and so on. And the Doctor was always much more interested in the process of such dialogue – the movements of this mental exercise often compared to the in-and-out movements of healthy breathing – than in its results in written form or in any static, quantifiable "thought": which he describes elsewhere as "the excretion of mental respiration" (*CW*, II, 24). No thought, and no speaker, can stand alone – each only takes its shape against the energizing resistance of a strong antithesis and a strong interlocutor.

We must always be careful, then, not to take single-sentence Holmes statements out of their conversational contexts as evidence of his permanent thoughts, firm ideological positions, or static beliefs. Most often, in reports of the Doctor's own everyday conversation or in our reading of "bombshell" interventions from the Autocrat or the Master in the table-talk books, it is clear that Holmesian speakers are always talking in opposition, seeking out a position of devil's advocacy, just to prime the conversational pump.

Explaining how the actual multivoiced dialogues of banquets or carnivals could be translated into the "polyphonic" discourse of the novel, Bakhtin is especially concerned to show how even seemingly single-voiced utterances can be "internally dialogized" – so that every phrase must be read as part of a discussion with one or more absent interlocutors (as in a "diatribe," for example), and every word can be seen to have arisen out of a complex "dialogical" interplay with other words in other discourses and languages – even if those other words remain unspoken.[15] The Autocrat's utterances epitomize such a process. Much of his talk and his verse is "dialogical," in Bakhtin's sense, not only in its larger rhetorical structure of rapid alternations between antithetical stances, but also in the texture of almost every word. The first chapter of the *Autocrat*, for example, contains that well-known set-piece in which the Autocrat's diatribe against punning itself develops as a tissue of puns – so that the grave condemnation of light wordplay also operates as a celebration of such subversive language games, and as a carnivalization of all efforts at univocal judgment. In a similar way, one of the Autocrat's poems, a paean to wine "accidentally" composed for performance at a temperance society meeting, is presented to us as a palimpsest combining the original work and its radical revision – so that we can see how most of the words have been crossed out and replaced by the poem's institutional sponsor. Here every "doubled" word emerges as part of a dialogue between a speaker and an internalized or externalized censor – and the Autocrat finally jokes that for such a doubled work he should have gotten double pay (*CW*, 1, 48). Another poem, "Aestivation," develops as a springtime carnival of jibberish – a surprisingly close anticipation of Lewis Carroll's "Jabberwocky" – and a bawdy defiance of tutor-censors as it exploits a similar doubleness (or Bakhtinian "polyglossia") that emerges in the problems of translation between the two very different national languages – low English and high Latin – of which it is constituted (*CW*, 1, 263):

No concave vast repeats the tender hue
That laves my milk-jug with celestial blue!

Me wretched! Let me curr to quercine shades!
Effund your albid hausts, lactiferous maids!
Oh, might I vole to some umbrageous clump, –
Depart, – be off, – excede, – evade, – erump!

The same sort of dissonances or collisions of discourse also erupt in "De Sauty: An Electro-chemical Eclogue," as the dialogic mix between two other very distinct languages – this time Virgilian *topoi* and the chemical table of the elements – is seen to be literally electrical and explosive, leading by the poem's end to a general disintegration of language and of the central character:

Nothing but a cloud of elements organic,
C. O. H. N. Ferrum, Chor. Flu. Sil. Potassa,
Calc. Sod. Phosph. Mag. Sulphur, Mang. (?)
   Alumin. (?) Cuprum, (?)
Such as man is made of.   (*CW*, II, 28)

And everything that is said as part of these combative breakfast-table dialogues is doubled in this way. The Autocrat becomes so preoccupied with the many voices that he criticizes or banishes – often giving extended play to repetitions of their "outrageous" statements – that finally their presence (or their structuring absence) is felt everywhere in his talk. His rebuttals of dogmatists and literalists and censors, and his close critical analyses of the non-standard dialects of the less educated and less practiced speakers that surround him, lead us to begin to feel all of these figures as resistant virtual voices latent within his every phrase – always ready to pounce whenever the polemical or hyperbolical talk goes too far. Far from being the imperial self of his dreams, then, the Autocrat is clearly very much a creature of the conversational setting; certainly he is never able to stand outside of that setting to make monological pronouncements *ex cathedra*. Indeed his talk reveals him to be radically "other-directed," often sending up his playful trial balloons simply to draw out a specific interlocutor, obsessed with predicting and recording the responses to his remarks – from his auditors around the table and from his readers around the country. The Autocrat suspects how each of his turns of phrase, each metaphor, will affect the Schoolmistress, the Lady in Black, the Divinity Student, Benjamin Franklin, or Little Boston. Hoping to get a rise, he points his talk toward their particular soft-spots or mental ruts: "They all stared. There is a divinity-student lately come among us to whom I commonly address remarks like the above . . ." or again, "Here is another remark made for his especial benefit," and then later, "I try his head occasionally as housewives try eggs, – give it an intellectual shake and hold it up to the light, so to speak, to see if it has life in it, actual or potential, or only lifeless albumen" (*CW*, i, i, 83, 85). And his conversational experiments in this particular case, with this egghead Divinity Student, finally prove successful: the young man becomes an active, suspicious, disruptive listener. After he has been fishing so long for some vitalizing response, the Autocrat can at last report,

[The divinity-student honoured himself by the way in which he received this. He did not swallow it at once, neither did he reject it; but he took it as a pickerel takes the bait, and carried it off with him to his hole (in the fourth story) to deal with at his leisure.] (*CW*, i, 84)

The Autocrat obviously has a great need for such conversational company; by all reports this was also the great need of Doctor Holmes' life. Famous for his witty repartee – to the point that the best retorts at every gathering would often later be attributed to him, even if he had not been present – he became the nation's symbol of Sociability. And his close friends kept up running jokes about his almost pathological need for interlocutors to help him keep up the flow of his incessant talk. (His schoolteachers remembered that, even as a child, Oliver had found it impossible to stop whispering to classmates all around him; and Silas Weir Mitchell recalls how difficult it was to leave the house after visiting the voluble Doctor Holmes: like many others, he would often get trapped standing in the doorway with his coat on and his carriage ready as the Doctor launched into just a few more last-minute jokes and observations.)[16] Holmes himself could lightly mock his own insatiable "fondness for society," and then speculate about the effects on his inner life of such a lifelong emphasis on the dynamic of conversation at an endless round of parties, salons, and conventions. Beginning with tongue in cheek, this passage from his late-life "Autobiographical Notes" goes on to describe the internalization of parlor-room dialogue in a fragmented, polymorphous personality – where again the talk can be charged and explosive.

Thus, though fond of society at times, I have always been good company to myself, either by day or by night. The "I" and the "me" of my double personality keep up endless dialogues, as is, I suppose, the case with most people, – sometimes using very harsh language to each other. One of them, I am sorry to say, is very apt to be abusive and to treat the other like an idiot, with expressions which, if uttered, would make a very bad figure in these pages. (*AN*, 43)

CONVERSING WITH ONESELF

We can easily understand that a man of Holmes' disposition, finding himself alone with no one to talk to, missing the "rebound" of Dr. Johnson's "attack," might well begin talking to himself – taking up the voices of all sides of a debate. And we can best understand the overall structure of his written table-talk works if we imagine them arising in just this way: as an internal dialogue, an interior debate modeled on the debates of the culture at large. We cannot fix Holmes to any one position taken by the Autocrat, or the Professor, or the Poet, or Little Boston, or the Schoolmistress, for he "himself" is always a Shandian household full of all of the figures, loud with noisy breakfast-table debates between warring voices which both forever oppose and forever need one another.

Many mid-century Americans came to feel that they did their best thinking in company – while also observing that the process of thinking itself seems to create an internal sort of conversational "company." "Conversation is my natural element," wrote Margaret Fuller, "I need to be called out, and never think alone, without imagining some companion."[17] But this was always especially true for Holmes. He found that, in internal conversation, the self can indeed be its own society. The Master opens *The Poet at the Breakfast-Table* with a meditation on these implications in the Doctor's lifelong motto, "Every man his own Boswell":

The idea of a man's "interviewing" himself *is* rather odd, to be sure. But then that is what we are all of us doing every day. I talk half the time to find out my own thoughts, as a school-boy turns his pockets inside out to see what is in them. One brings to light all sorts of personal property he had forgotten in his inventory.

The characteristically boyish playfulness of this idea of talk seems innocuous enough, but as usual it is spoken dialogically as a pointed statement – directed at a perceived soft spot in the "honest legislative soul" of a conservative Western Congressman at the breakfast-table.

And the remark succeeds in sparking an immediate interruptive response:

– You don't know what your thoughts are going to be beforehand? said the "Member of the Haouse," as he calls himself. (*CW,* III, I)

The ensuing scene enacts Holmes' theme, as the Master's initial musing monologue develops into a wild, polarized exchange between very different voices. If we pause here to trace more closely the turns in this particular talk passage, we find that this scene can serve as a clear epitome of many Holmes discussions, suggesting where his electrodynamic model of bipolar, cross-cultural conversation might lead. As the Master draws the Member out here, he introduces this new breakfast-table volume with a talk about talk which helps us to draw out the literary, political, and psychological ramifications of Holmes' characteristic form.

As one aspect of his celebration of the literary forms associated with carnival, Bakhtin observes that even the soliloquy should be read as a form of "discussion with oneself" that speaks for a radically "dialogized" conception of human subjectivity – evoking a sense of the self "which is accessible not to passive self-observation, but only to an active *dialogical approach to oneself,* an approach which destroys the naive integrity of one's conception of oneself . . . [and] breaks down the outer shell of the self's image that exists for other people."[18] And in this passage from *The Poet* the Master's elaboration on the implications of "interviewing oneself" develops as just such a "carnivalization" of the Member's "naive" self-image, demonstrating how conversation can indeed serve as the most basic model for mental process as his defense of the talk form here becomes a more general defense of a vision of life and thought as continual, dynamic, organic movement. First, responding to the Member's entrance into the table-talk, the Master stuns the visiting politician with this provocative answer to his questions about an internalization of the process of dialogue and about not knowing "your thoughts . . . beforehand":

– It's a very queer place, that receptacle a man fetches his talk out of . . . Some kinds of thoughts breed in the dark of one's mind like the blind fishes in the Mammoth Cave. We can't see them and they can't see us; but sooner or later the daylight gets in and we find that some cold, fishy little negative has been spawning all over our beliefs, and the brood of blind questions it has given birth to are burrowing round and under and butting their blunt noses against the pillars of faith we thought the whole world might lean on. And then, again, some of our old beliefs are dying out every year, and others feed on them and grow fat, or get poisoned as the case may be. And so, you see, you can't tell what the thoughts are that you have got salted down, as one may say, till you run a streak of talk through them, as the market people run a butter-scoop through a firkin. (*CW,* III, 2)

The Master seems to sense that the small-minded Member's rigidity makes him fragile, a tinderbox ready to explode. Every aspect of his shifting, imagistic talk then works as a challenge to the Member's reactionary attempt to remain fixed in set legalistic, rationalistic opinions – indeed as it develops it threatens the very foundations of the legislator's world. The Master's sort of conversation unsettles any conception of ideas as a form of unchanging "personal property" that can be "inventoried" or "salted down," or that can somehow preexist its expression in words. In the same way it puts into question the notion of a "proper" Self which can stand outside the dialogic flux: I do not make my talk, rather my talk makes me. For the flowing, changing metaphoric texture basic to such ever-developing talk introduces the Member to the unpredictable trains of association in unconscious or "sub-conscious" thought, miming the workings of what Holmes as psychologist would term the "underground workshop of the mind."[19]

As we immerse ourselves in the Doctor's "oceans of similitudes" here, we find that one metaphor seems always to breed another, in the same way that one dark, repulsive fish here can "breed" or "spawn" or grow organically into the nightmare vision of an entire school.[20] And somehow the movements of such metaphor and of talk in general seem to be evidence of a corrosive skepticism latent in unceasing thought: like those mental fishes, we are constantly erupting in new questions and new "negatives," forever burying old ideas and conceiving new ones. No static Truth or belief is exempt from this process of continual death and rebirth, of naming and renaming; as every word in the Master's talk takes on multiple meanings, even the solid, "proper" image of those old "pillars of faith" becomes caught up in the play of metaphor. Moving through dizzying leaps of analogy – from a "library comparison" (omitted in our excerpt) through raisins and then fishes to a firkin of salted meat – we eventually realize that no single one of these images can ever stand for the movement of thought in interruptive dialogue: it is in the leaps of metaphor, the ceaseless changing of names, that talk most effectively approximates the dynamic of "that receptacle" – the mind.

Any dialogue with the Doctor then has Enlightenment as a goal; he always hopes that discussion will, like a psychoanalytic "talking cure," "bring to light" the "dark" unspoken or unanalyzed elements neglected or hidden in the "cave" of our "underground work-shop."[21] But this exchange with the Member, like most of Holmes' verbal exchanges, reminds us that mental probing rarely results in such a straightforward triumph of sweet Reason. If talk should open us to the motions of the active mind, it can at the same time seem to open a sort of Pandora's box. If rigid thoughts have been too long repressed, their release in physicalist ex-pression can be funny, confusing, terrifying, irrational or explosive.

Though it began harmlessly in clear daylight with a schoolboy cooly emptying his pockets, the dialogue between Master and Member develops into a soaring, searing twilight Carnival. For the turning inside out of pockets leads through an escalating series of related "house-breaking" images to a final, fearful vision of the Member's world turned both inside out and upside down. And, as he slowly slips into slumber in the face of all this flowing talk, the Member serves as another classic example of Holmes' theory about the electrical potential in any contact between a dull discourse and a very charged mind. The Master's unpredictable images trigger a private train of nightmare associations in this Congressional inter-locutor. When the Master describes the way that talk can break down the old order in the shelves of the "mental library," his listener conjures a fearful disorder in the library of his State-House. When the Master's next metaphoric set-piece then adds house-breaking pictures of unconscious life opening out of its dark cave, cutting open its sealed market barrels (a traditionally carnivalesque folk-image), and under-mining the very "pillars of faith," the politician's deepest unconscious fears seem suddenly to be tapped as, falling into a strange reverie which internalizes the carnival dynamics of the external conversation, he dreams that he is engaged in a psychologically-charged debate with a multivocal "committee" which threatens to turn his entire world upside down, to destroy his material "property" and his "proper" self (the "ego" typically invested in his hat), and indeed to shake the very foundations of society as he knows it:

He thought a certain imaginary Committee of Safety of a certain imaginary Legislature was proceeding to burn down his haystack, in accordance with an Act, entitled an Act to make the Poor Richer by making the Rich Poorer. And the chairman of the committee was instituting a forcible exchange of hats with him, to his manifest disadvantage, for he had just bought a new beaver. (*CW*, III, 2–3)

In our dreams as in our talk, we discover unknown new ideas as we open ourselves to the multiple voices of interior dialogue – to what Holmes the scientist describes elsewhere as the "committee of the self."[22] And even when it is internalized, the structure of explosive conversation can seem to carry the charge of the larger social and political debates dividing the culture of mid-century America. But now, though, the Congressman shakes himself awake; his adrenalin is flowing; he is primed for the engaged intercourse of Holmes' talk ideal. Leaving behind quiet courtesy or brute complacency, he enters the fray to speak in defense of his very different form of "civilization," adding a new language to the breakfast-table mix with a question that interrupts the master's stream of thought:

Do you think they mean business? . . . those chaps that are setting folks on to burn us all up in our beds. Political firebugs we call 'em up our way. Want to substitoot the match-box for the ballot-box. Scare all our old women half to death. (*CW*, III, 3)

Through long passages of metaphoric talk, the Master has been probing and testing for a charged response from the Member, and here he gets it. This frenzied diatribe about "political firebugs" who "want to . . . burn us all up in our beds" was clearly incited by the Master's earlier comments about argumentative "nitro-glycerine," political "barbequing," and "inflammatory" political oratory. So when the Master continues to inflame this hothead with multileveled plays on all the "combustible" words in his vocabulary, his final statement in the passage can only be ironic: "Boys," he warns us, "must not touch off their squibs and crackers too near the powder-magazine" (*CW*, III, 5). For the Master's metaphoric language here has brought to the fore the explosive potential in a conversational form that mines the "collisions of discourse" between different "civilizations" speaking in polarized voices. Throughout the *Poet*, as throughout all of the Doctor's breakfast-table works, the carnival conversation often does just that – touching off "squibs," "crackers," and even "bombshells" in highly charged situations; and we will see that the unsettling detonations of this sort of Holmesian verbal fireworks can knock the hat off the Master's head as well as off the Member's.[23]

CHAPTER 4

"COLLISIONS OF DISCOURSE" II: ELECTRIC AND OCEANIC "CURRENTS" IN CONVERSATION
The Cultural Work of Holmesian Talk

> There lies the gold, and there it has slept, and will sleep, unless you can manage the collisions of discourse . . . to overcome the strong cohesion and detach the sparkling atom to the day.
> Ralph Waldo Emerson, "Clubs"

Vernon Parrington seems far off the mark when he takes the Master's final word from the *Poet* passage examined at the end of the last chapter – "Boys must not touch off their squibs and crackers too near the powder-magazine" – out of its conversational context, citing it as the main piece of evidence for his influential 1927 revaluation of Holmes:

If the mind is free other things will take care of themselves – this pretty much sums up Holmes's social philosophy . . .
    Unfortunately his Brahminism sealed pretty tightly certain windows of his mind that might better have been kept open. A radical in the field of theology where personal concern brought him to serious grappling with the problem, a tolerant rationalist in the realm of the intellect, he remained a cheerfully contented conservative in other fields. He was unconsciously insulated against the currents of social and political thought flowing all about him.[1]

But it is difficult to sum up the social philosophy of a very complex written *oeuvre* and of a very self-divided man. To do so Parrington must ignore the irony of the Master's final phrase, its implication in the dynamics of wild, free-ranging talk, and its relation to trains of imagery developed through the passage and throughout Holmes' works. After so much pyrotechnical play on "fireworks" imagery, it would be unlikely that the Master could univocally damn such combustibles; in the terms of electrodynamics, Holmesian talk always works not to "insulate" but rather to "charge" and "electrify" its participants by allusion to the most inflammatory issues of the day.[2] And Parrington's unconscious adoption of Holmes' infectious "house" metaphors – implying that the Doctor's salon-inspired writings are hot-house flowers "sealed" off behind domestic windows and "insulated" by those salon walls – in fact moves in the opposite direction from the "house-breaking" imagery which we have traced in the Master–Member passage, and which (as we will see in Chapter Nine) pervades the Doctor's written conversations, perhaps speaking for the most characteristic tendencies of his expansive, explosive talk form.

One of Holmes' most basic lifelong efforts, and a goal central to the very form of his conversations, was a "house-breaking" crusade to break down the walls and barriers of all narrowness or special-ization, of any "fenced-in" intellectual, social, and even geographical provincialism. Though it goes against the grain of his argument, Parrington himself has to recognize the breadth of Holmes' interests, extraordinary for any writer in the era:

This major intellectual interest appears most adequately in his picture of the Master . . . A dabbler in the law, theology, and medicine, a philosophic contemplator of the Order of Things, who refused to permit "the territory of a man's mind" to be "fenced in," who agreed with the Poet in thinking somewhat ill of the specialist who dedicated his life to the study of beetles, preferring to range widely through time and eternity, who followed Darwin and was deep in bacteriology, trying "curious experiments in spontaneous generation" – this was Holmes on the intellectual side, a genial disseminator of the latest scientific speculations, a tolerant amateur of the things of the mind, a friendly dabbler in absolute moralities, who hoped "to do some sound thinking in heaven" if he ever got there, but who was too pleasantly engaged with Beacon Street to settle things now.[3]

And, whatever the ambivalences of the Master–Member dialogue, it does indeed, contrary to Parrington, show Holmes in touch with (and perhaps soothing his deep-felt anxieties by playing upon) the psycho-logical resonances of the most revolutionary social and political "currents of thought" in his era. Parrington's imagery of universal mental progress as a supra-personal oceanic "current" is also frequently played upon by the Doctor, but Holmes always clearly wants to see the "currents" of free conversation as active agents of these larger "currents" of social and intellectual change.

A representative passage from *The Professor at the Breakfast-Table* sets the unsettling skepticism inherent in such conversation as a direct challenge to any rigid, insular judgment:

. . . all persons who proclaim a belief which passes judgment on their neighbours must be ready to have it "unsettled," that is, questioned, at all times and by anybody, – just as those who set up bars across a thoroughfare must expect to have them taken down by every one who wants to pass, if he is strong enough.

When this all-corrosive power of conversation – under Holmes' banner of "the freedom of ideas" – is then pushed to its extreme limits, its movement, as the Member realized, clearly tends to undermine the authorities most basic to governmental order:

If to question everything be unlawful and dangerous, we had better undeclare our independence at once; for what the Declaration means is the right to question everything, even the Truth of its fundamental proposition.

And, just as it is beginning to sound truly dangerous, this continual conversational disruption of human law is typically justified by reference to a higher "law," the natural law of gravitation "governing" the planetary "revolutions" and oceanic "currents" of an ongoing evolutionary progress. Holmes' Professor continues,

The old-world order of things is an arrangement of locks and canals, where everything depends on keeping the gates shut, and so holding the upper waters at their level; but the system under which the young republican American is born trusts the whole unimpeded tide of life to the great elemental influences, as the vast rivers of the continent settle their own level in obedience to the laws that govern the planet and the spheres that surround it. (*CW*, II, 295)

What is "unsettled" by the levity of free talk should then "settle" back down at its "own level" in obedience to the elemental and historical "tides." Holmes' "currents," like Parrington's, are assumed to have a democratic thrust, as their house-breaking force dissolves each successive enclosure: opening bars on the public highways of thought, flowing over locks, gates and other impediments to the "tide of life." Gravity is a great "leveler," dissolving class barriers just as it mixes waters from upper and lower canals – in the same way that, as we saw in an earlier scene, a truly "interpenetrative" conversation between contrasting English and American civilizations is analogized to the merging of two oceans: "it is like cutting through an isthmus and letting the two oceans swim into each other's laps" (*CW*, II, 36).

The young Lowell, after having listened to and participated in many of the Doctor's multivoiced conversations, continued to wonder where his friend really stood on many matters. Finally, wanting like

Parrington to sum up Holmes' relations to the "main currents" of the era's progressive social thought, he wrote him a challenging letter. Holmes' response to Lowell can stand as the best answer to Parrington's judgment; in unusually blunt, direct terms, it makes explicit the Jeffersonian republicanism latent in the conversation passages we have just surveyed:

It is a mistake of yours to suppose me a thorough-going conservatist; . . . I am an out-and-out republican in politics, a firm believer in the omnipotence of truth, in the constant onward struggle of the race, . . . In a little club of ten physicians I rather think I occupy the extreme left of the liberal side of the house. The idea of my belonging to the party that resists all change is an entire misconception. I may be lazy, or indifferent, or timid, but I am by no means one of those (such as a few of my friends) who are wedded for better for worse to the *status quo* . . .[4]

Holmes shouldn't have had to spell it out. Building out of an electrodynamic force, moving with what are seen to be the "currents" of large natural forces, his conversation could never be contained within an insular drawing room. The champagne-pops of "squibs and crackers" around the Doctor's small, domestic breakfast-tables can bubble up to become more than a tempest in a teapot – with an unsettling force which begins by rattling china, opening "secret" closets, snooping through drawers, and then can throw open windows and doors to burst out of that neat Victorian confinement as it expands with a ripple effect reducing all walls to rubble. In Holmes' writings, we meet such sudden transformations even in the rhetorical turns – the conversational alternations between voices – of one speech by a single speaker. The Professor can, quite characteristically, enter a discussion in quiet tones, stating that he is "*ex officio*, as a Professor, a conservative," but then wind himself up, through a few paragraphs expressing a mounting pressure against the confines of the salon's domestic walls, to the point that he finally bursts out in a revolutionary "house-breaking" fervor:

We the people, Sir, some of us with nut-crackers, and some of us with trip-hammers, and some of us with pile-drivers, and some of us coming with a whish! like the air-stones out of a lunar volcano, will crash down on the lumps of nonsense in all of them till we have made powder of them like Aaron's calf!
     If to be a conservative is to let all the drains of thought choke up and keep all the soul's windows down, – to shut out the sun from the east and the wind from the west, – to let the rats run free in the cellar, and the moths

feed their fill in the chambers, . . . [then] I, Sir, am a *bonnet-rouge*, a red-cap
of the barricades, my friends, rather than a conservative. (*CW*, II, 14–15)

Such turns appear everywhere as the most basic element in
Holmes' talk and in his thought – and these alternations between
what we will call "house-keeping" and "house-breaking" will be the
focus of the analysis in Chapter Nine. But here, as this passage
continues, we get a nice sense of the possible ripple effects of such
wild conversational movements, when diverse voices from around
the breakfast-table now enter the fray for a newly energized debate.
Aroused by these perpetual dialogic alternations between the downward, confining, gravitational tendencies of "house-keeping" and the
upward thrust of an impulse to "house-breaking," a first boardinghouse guest interrupts the Professor's speech above to rephrase the
sentiment along the lines of his own hobbyhorse: "But this [Boston]
is the great Macadamizing place, – always cracking up something"
(*CW*, II, 15).

This little voice – to use Emerson's phrase from "Circles" – draws
another circle; the Professor is now only a first speaker; the conversation turns again and moves on. After a soaring effusion like this one
from the Professor, Holmes will always be sure to let another word
interject – quickly bringing us back down to earth. And here, as
usual, the derailing is verbal, the interruption is based on a Shandian
misunderstanding. For the breakfast-table contains a multitude of
private languages and interpretations. While the Professor's words
were tending toward a metaphysical "crack up" of the entire solid-
seeming world, his first interlocutor can only think grossly and
mechanically about his own city's local progress in making new
Macadam roads. (Though this in turn would be sure to mesh with his
earlier uses of the "highway" metaphor in celebrating the revolutionary impetus of Boston talk: "I tell you Boston has opened, and
kept open, more turnpikes that lead straight to free thought and free
speech and free deeds than any other city of live men or dead men"
[*CW*, II, 3–4].) But then another foreign-accented voice enters to
provide a vivid example of the powers of conversation to crack things
up. He deflates that small-minded Boston boosterism with his own
retort – "Cracking up Boston folks" – implying that *all* of this
highfalutin' talk is just "cracked" anyway. And now, when these
metaphors become violent and pointed with the ugly provincialism
of the little man's reply – "Cracking up all sorts of things – native and

foreign vermin included" – we are back in the full swing of everyday agonistic table-talk. If the Professor's initial message is lost in all the electric "crackling" of this background noise, perhaps the most lasting effect of all of this "cracking up" is on the reader – who is meant to be cracking up in laughter (*CW,* II, 16).

THE MISSION OF CONVERSATION

Certainly in Holmes this "cracking up" is never destructive or nihilistic. In place of the solidity of the old dogmas and certitudes, he speaks most positively and enthusiastically for the value of what Lowell (in his review of the *Autocrat*) describes as the "universal Catherine-wheeling of fun and fancy" in a free-play of ideas, and of the need in antebellum America for what Richard Rorty has been promoting in much the same terms as an open, pluralistic "conversation of the culture."[5] In his intuitive enthusiast's essays of the late 1930s, Van Wyck Brooks began to suggest important relations between the dynamics of the Doctor's talk and the dynamics of antebellum society. Stressing the psychological rather than the political implications of the "house-breaking" movements of this conversation, Brooks situates Holmes in an era of mounting tensions, of pressures building toward explosive release. Paraphrasing the Doctor's own words, he pictures him against the background of a society in need of someone to "break up the ice of mental habits," to unblock the flow of currents in its mental batteries – to clean its terminal poles, try new connections, and perhaps then shock it into expression. Travelling from Lyceum to dinner to club, the Doctor in Brooks' view was a peripatetic "moral physician," ministering, with his therapeutics of laughter and of conversation, to a grotesquely repressed community:

What was his mission? It was very simple: the mission of conversation. Was it not very bad to have thoughts and feelings, which ought to come out in talk, *strike in,* as people said of certain diseases? There was the great American evil, morbid introspection, class-distinctions that were unconfessed, scruples of conscience, secrets that ought to be exposed to common sense, forms of speech and phrases, ugly and distorted, the outward and visible signs of the twisted life within. Fruits of the old religion of Calvinism, fruits of isolation and provincial conditions, fruits of unconscious living. Out with them, and talk them over! The boarders knew they could trust . . . a doctor who was used to dealing with secrets and who, without hurting their feelings, could give them the right prescription to set them on the road to mental health.

. . . Expression was the greatest need of this unexpressed New England, which almost seemed to enjoy its cold and taciturn ways, ways that concealed what tragic depths! Emotions that can shape themselves in language open the gate for themselves into the great community of human affections.[6]

In his medical work as in his everyday speech and writing, then, the Doctor's desire seems to have been to draw introverted Americans out: not so that they might begin to preach like the early American ministers, or to orate like the Golden Age politicians, but so that they might, in a quieter way, simply begin to talk.

In the essay "Clubs," his most extended meditation on the meanings of his era's new interest in conversation, Emerson is especially concerned to explore this process of "drawing out" which seems inherent to the talk form. His contemporary account of life at the Saturday Club then can serve as a helpful complement to Brooks' retrospective vision of Holmes' role within the emerging conversation of "unexpressed New England." For Holmes was of course the "*genius loci*" of the Saturday Club, and his spirit hovers over Emerson's entire essay – influencing both the dynamism of its scientific, physicalist imagery and the general tendencies of its treatment of talk. The essayist must surely have his Club companion the Doctor in mind when he begins his appreciation of the social values of company and sympathetic association – addressed to the spirit "too long shut in" – in such quirkily mechanical, medical language:

We are delicate machines, and require nice treatment to get from us the maximum of power and pleasure. We need tonics . . . But . . . of all the cordials known to us, the best, safest and most exhilarating, with the least harm, is society.

What makes interactive conversation the best "medicine and cordial," the best compensation for too much oracular "solitude," is its ability to help us draw out our thoughts, to externalize them. We have seen that Fuller too recognized the mind's need for self-doubling and ex-pression in dialogue, but Emerson's elaboration of this idea has a peculiarly Holmesian ring to it:

Conversation is the laboratory and workshop of the student . . . Every time we say a thing in conversation, we get a mechanical advantage in detaching it well and deliverly. I prize the mechanics of conversation. 'T is pulley and lever and screw. To fairly disengage the mass, and send it jingling down, a good boulder, – a block of quartz and gold, to be worked up at leisure in the useful arts of life, – is a wonderful relief.

Using the strange invented word "deliverly" in this passage, Emerson may intend to associate verbal "delivery" with a doctor's "delivery" of a new-born child – an association common to discussions of the action of dialogue ever since Plato's insistence on the *maieutic* (obstetric) goals of his dialectical method: Socrates would act as "midwife" to his students, drawing them out and thus helping to bring their latent "conceptions" to birth. But "deliverly" could also carry other apt and related connotations as well: suggesting that to "deliver" a message, to convey it into another's possession, is also to "deliver" it from bondage – explaining Emerson's final stress on the "wonderful relief" in articulation.

Of course Plato would never so literalize the medical image of the obstetrician's forceps, or the mechanics of the dialogist's levers and pulleys, and he might also then be shocked at the final definition of ideas not as static and eternal, but as fundamentally relational and active. But for Emerson as for Holmes, the symposium banquet (or, in the mid-nineteenth century, the party) works as a volatile electro-dynamic field:

Wisdom is like electricity. There is no permanently wise man, but men capable of wisdom, who, being put into certain company, or other favorable conditions, become wise for a short time, as glasses rubbed acquire electric power for awhile.

Wine glasses become Leyden jars in the ritual of the toast, but only rare conversation in fact rubs people together to achieve such moments of charged cordiality. In the lectures on "Clubs" and "Table-Talk" in which Emerson worked out his ideas for the "Clubs" essay, he admits that even at the Saturday Club the desired free flow of talk often found itself impeded by "insuperable obstacles" – an example in small-scale of what Brooks had described as the general problem throughout this "unexpressed New England":

We have found insuperable obstacles in the attempt to obtain the knowledge which others possess, and were willing enough to impart. Barriers of society, barriers of language, inadequacy of the channels of communication, all choked up and disused.

Each man has facts I am looking for, and, though I talk with him, I cannot get at them, for want of the clew. I do not know enough to ask the right question . . . Here is all Boston, all railroads, all manufactures and commerce, in the head of this merchant . . . Here is a philologist who knows all languages. Here is the king of chemists. Here is all anatomy, fossil and contemporary, in the mind of this zoölogist. All electro-magnetism in the next man; all geology in the third; all mechanism in the fourth; all American history in a fifth; and I cannot, with all my avarice of these facts, come at any fragment of all their experience.

The Saturday Club is the distillation of a brilliant university – but it thus throws into relief the need for a common ground to make possible some communication between the separate, specialized "departments" of American thought. Lamenting the increasing "atomization" of mid-century American life, Emerson then calls for the development of an art of conversation which might help to release the resources of all of this pent-up, now-inaccessible natural energy – leaving us with an image of talk as a sort of electromagnetic atom-splitter:

There lies the gold, and there it has slept, and will sleep, unless you can *manage the collisions of discourse* . . . to overcome the strong cohesion and detach the sparkling atom to the day.

Finally, Emerson suggests that perhaps, in his best moments, the Doctor is the speaker most likely to be able to manage the mining operations of such successful talk. Certainly Holmes often seemed to know how to ask the right question; he often served as the philosopher-dilettante who could begin to bring all of the Saturday Club's specialized languages together, helping both to spark interactive conversation and then to keep it going. And Emerson takes special note of the Doctor's mysterious ability to generate explosive "collisions of discourse" through whimsical wordplay, without arousing the belligerence of an all-out verbal "bush fight." In his view, Holmes achieves his liberating effects mainly because he is by nature just the opposite of those disputatious, Johnsonian conversational "gladiators" who always "fight for victory":

How delightful after these disturbers is the radiant, playful wit of – one whom I need not name, – for in every society there is his representative. Good nature is stronger than tomahawks. His conversation is all pictures: he can reproduce whatever he has seen; he tells the best story in the county, and is of such genial temper that he disposes all others irresistibly to good humor and discourse.

While his editor, Edward Waldo Emerson, provides quite definitive evidence in footnotes that the essayist here has Holmes in mind, it says a lot about the Doctor's national reputation that Emerson can assume that any contemporary reader would be able instantly to identify the subject of his portrait of America's most "representative" conversationalist.[7]

The pictures presented by Brooks, Emerson, and Lowell lead us to imagine the Doctor as a tiny, hyperactive scientist buzzing around at every Boston gathering, rubbing the glasses of all celebrants, managing and mining the collisions of discourse at all ends of the table, and hoping each time that clean contacts between the most distant poles would set off the fireworks that were the best sign of a successful household festivity. By all accounts he had a knack for "polarizing" the talk in any group, serving with his antithetical remarks as a sort of ice-breaker-*cum*-devil's-advocate. At one dinner, for example, while Lowell occupied the rather stereotypically Victorian, teetotaling Harriet Beecher Stowe with lengthy praises of champagne and of *Tom Jones*, Holmes would shock her husband, the pious Calvin Stowe, by testing on him the theory that all profanity originates in the pulpit. Then, before he could fully recover from that novel idea, Stowe would be amazed to find Holmes cheerfully insisting he knew of whole families in Boston who had remained unaffected by Adam's fall. Even in 1893, at a dinner for the three surviving alumni of Harvard's Class of 1829, the Doctor was still at it: he spent the time trying to convert one classmate, a Baptist preacher, to Unitarianism, and reported that he might have succeeded if only his interlocutor had not been so deaf.[8]

But the Doctor's performance on August 5, 1850 at the famous writers' picnic in the Berkshires organized by Duyckinck and Fields might stand as the summary example of this general tendency: here he set a range of intellects in motion by playing upon latent tensions between New York and Boston writers, city-wits and nature-mystics, jingoistic American nationalists and cosmopolitan internationalists, and even between authors and publishers. Cornelius Mathews later reported that, as Holmes, Hawthorne, Melville, Duyckinck, Henry Sedgwick, the Fieldses, and host Dudley Field began their climb up Monument Mountain – "rambling, scrambling, climbing, rhyming – puns flying off in every direction, like sparks among the bushes" – the talkative Doctor made quiet, romantic contemplation very difficult. "Mr. Town Wit" made the ascent carrying his black India-Rubber medical bag, which becomes in the accounts a perfect emblem of the two sides of his nature (a dark scientific gravity which frames and is balanced by a potent levity bubbling up from within) when, at the summit, he opened the bag to surprise everyone with its contents: bottles of Heidsieck champagne. Soon these would help give the Byronic setting the more familiar atmosphere of a parlor. For though the Doctor only feigned horror as Melville perched heroically on a jutting rock, pulling mock ropes as an example of life at the mast-head, he later admitted that it almost made him seasick – "as bad as a dose of ipecac."[9] (In other conversations, the Doctor frequently joked about the seasickness [and asthma] which made it difficult for him to travel [explaining some of his localism]: one famous if perhaps apocryphal story [attributed to Holmes by Freud, among others] has him very nauseous, walking the decks of a ship en route to London, when a lady introduces herself – "I have contributed to *The Atlantic Monthly*" – only to get the rejoinder, "Madam, I have contributed to the Atlantic daily." A very characteristic Holmesian joke: first, for the literalizing play on the interlocutor's words to form the retort, both an eruption from and an interruption of the dialogic speech context; second, for the light allusions to what Bakhtin would describe as the carnivalesque "grotesque body" often in the background of the Doctor's whimsical wordplay on anatomy and bodily functions; third, for the background quasi-medical sense that the only response to sickness, fear, or to one's passivity before oceanic gravity, is a therapeutics of laughter: verbal levity in conversation.)

On this day, though, as the Berkshire picnickers came down from the mountain to continue their talk around the dinner table, Duyck-inck noted that Holmes "said some of the best things and drew the whole company out by laying down some propositions on the superiority of Englishmen." This opening line was clearly aimed at Melville, and the former whaler took the bait, launching heatedly into a defense of the American climate, constitution, and genius. But more fireworks were set off when Holmes then reacted to these Young America effusions by suddenly changing his tune, now agreeing with Melville and in fact taking up his hyperbole only to develop it as, apparently with only a slight twinkle of irony crossing his straight face, he tried on him an invented "scientific" proof that Americans were growing stronger and larger at such a pace that in twenty years they might be sixteen feet tall: giants in intellect, giants in industry, giants in arts and letters. Perry Miller sees this seminal conversation, in this year so crucial to all of the writers present, as having finally brought Melville to the boiling point: first triggering his ambitious review of Hawthorne's works ("Hawthorne and His Mosses"), and then provoking the series of imaginative and metaphysical revisions which transformed that work which was then in progress, *Moby-Dick*.[10]

CONTRA-DICTION: AGREEING TO DISAGREE

Holmes felt that the sort of contrary spirit he displayed at this Berkshire picnic had its most electrifying effects among very diverse groups, or among people not well acquainted – though it would also then run the danger of being badly misunderstood, and thus provoking all-out war. But when he joined the Saturday Club, at the end of the decade, he would meet a group of interlocutors who took such puns and dialogic turns almost too much for granted. For that Club seemed to have been founded for the sake of such antithetical talk; its members were joined in their dedication to life, liberty, and the pursuit of contradiction. Noting the telling contrasts in character of the early Club members, E. P. Whipple maintained that, while most clubs might be based upon "mutual admiration," this was "a society formed on mutual repulsion," admission to which depended "rather on antipathy than sympathy." There were no bylaws or contracts to this unusual social "organization – or disorganization"; members apparently simply agreed to disagree.

It was ingeniously supposed that persons who looked on all questions of science, theology, and literature from different points of view would be persons who would enjoy one another's company once a month at a dinner table. Intellectual anarchy was proclaimed as the fundamental principle of this new organization, or rather disorganization; no man could be voted in who had not shown by his works this disagreement with those who were to be associated with him.

Whipple notes that occasional visitors to this Club scene could be as stunned or bewildered as some of those Berkshire picnickers. He describes one lively meeting, for example, which began when Motley's initial statement was immediately interrupted by Holmes, only to have Lowell then abruptly break in disagreeing with both men:

Still, in the incessant din of voices, every point made by one was replied to by another or ridiculed by a third, and was instantly followed by new statements, counter-statements, arguments and counter-arguments, hits and retorts, all germane to the matter . . . The other members of the Club looked on in mute wonder while witnessing these feats of intellectual and vocal gymnastics.

Tracing, in a very Holmesian vein, the attractions and repulsions and frictions of a series of such Club conversations, Whipple concludes with the by now familiar imagery of a social organism based upon the electrodynamics of an explosive wit: "the contact and collision of so many discordant minds produced a constant succession of electric sparks both of thought and wit." If in practice the Saturday Club was intellectually diverse but socially homogeneous (admitting only elite men), the theory of conversation outlined here is nonetheless very telling: in mid-century America, this leading club wants to see itself not as an enclave for like-minded familiars but as a continuation of the open-forum model developed in early coffeehouses; its talk is founded not upon pleasing agreement but upon "good-natured opposition," "the friendly collision" of intellects, "frolic hostilities of opinion . . . in the free play of wit and argument" – all the dynamic elements of interruption and vocal diversity that make the club a privileged forum for the mode of experimental, speculative, critical, free-thinking conversation so central to Doctor Holmes.[11]

While Whitman could contain contradiction as he contained multitudes –

> Do I contradict myself?
> Very well then I contradict myself,
> (I am large, I contain multitudes.)

– and Emerson could defend contradiction as basic to the dialectical structure of ongoing thought –

A foolish consistency is the hobgoblin of little minds, . . . Speak what you think now in hard words and to-morrow speak what to-morrow thinks in hard words again, though it contradict every thing you said to-day.

– Holmes simply celebrates it as basic to all of his everyday experience of dialogic verbal intercourse.[12] When the Divinity-Student asks how the Autocrat could write both poems praising wine and poems lamenting alcoholism (and we know that Holmes once, characteristically, submitted a high-spirited ode to wine to be read as the main toast at a Temperance Society meeting), the Professor replies, "Don't be 'consistent,' – but be simply *true*." He continues with an analogy to diamonds,

. . . the truest lives are those . . . with many facets answering to the many-planed aspects of the world about them . . . But a great many things may be made to appear contradictory, simply because they are partial views of a truth . . . (*CW*, II, 33–34)

Whether he is talking with Melville or with himself, then, Holmes' goal will be to break up the "single flat surface" of a seemingly solid old "Truth" through the back-and-forth movements of discourse; the closest we can come to a "whole view" of "Truth" is through the collection of "partial views" which makes up a conversation. In the endless give-and-take of his written table-talk, too, no assertion is ever final; each question opens into a multiplicity of possible answers; no statement can be put forth without immediately calling up its antithesis – or even several antitheses. For him, the "shock"-value of a statement is much more important than its truth-value. When conversation is a game of con-versions, any venture into diction plants the seed of its own contradiction. For even when the quixotic Poet wants to mount a direct attack upon contradiction, he soon finds his thoughts turning back upon themselves:

Come, now, – said I, – a man who contradicts himself in the course of two minutes must have a screw loose in his mental machinery. I never feel afraid that such a thing can happen to me, though it happens often enough when I turn a thought over suddenly, as you did that five-cent piece the other day, that it reads differently on its two sides. (*CW*, III, 90)

(Of course any regular at this breakfast-table club knows that in fact the Poet is anything but a model of consistency: his talk builds out of wild swings between what we might term the "manic" and "depres-sive" poles – sublime Joy and deathly Dejection – of romantic associationist Sensibility.) And Holmes everywhere celebrates this movement between oppositions, these "turns" between different "readings," as the prime generators of his talk and his thought.

Perhaps such a celebration is partly inevitable, just a rationaliza-tion for the uncontrollably centrifugal tendencies of a "mental machinery" which the Poet elsewhere describes as "in its nature discursive, erratic, subject to electric attractions and repulsions, *volage*" (*CW*, III, 107). But the Doctor is also as fundamentally com-mitted as Emerson is to a form of dialectical process: indeed while Emerson's essays (especially those from earlier in his career) often tend to move teleologically from one pole to another – from Nature to Spirit, from Fate to Free Will, from Quotation to Originality – the Doctor's talk is usually much less directional or conclusive, putting an even stronger stress on the value of a continual alternation between antitheses over any final, over-arching synthesis. Holmes might also beg to differ with those well-known Emerson words on contradiction – "Speak what you think now in hard words and to-morrow speak what to-morrow thinks in hard words again . . . though it contradict everything you said to-day" – for their stress on only one side of the interactive talk process, on the verbal inter-ventions of only one "self-reliant" self, on the importance of always saying what "*you* think" in an ongoing internal dialogue. The Doctor's conversation is at base an activity of the group, not a scene for self-assertion; one finds out what one thinks through participation in the turns of collective talk. And, for Holmes, if one's goal is not to stop the conversation but to start it, the "hard words" of Emerson's agonistic rhetoric are often less useful than the movements of a playful wit.

If, as Schlegel says, "Wit [*Witz*] is . . . a logical chemistry," the Doctor was well situated – as both a doctor and a writer, a material scientist and a material humorist – to suggest playful, experimental new "chemical" combinations or clashes between different sorts of people, between usually specialized discourses, between incommen-surable ideolects, or simply between the unlikely tenor and vehicle in a surprising extended metaphor.[13] Indeed his most basic writerly urge seems to develop out of a boyish scientific curiosity: he is always trying to rub two clichés together and see what sparks then begin to fly. (Bakhtin suggests the "carnival" relations of such a tendency in "wit" to develop explosive associations between usually opposed elements: the free contacts between diverse people during carnival festivities produce a fundamentally ambivalent holiday imagery of "carnival mésalliances" in which every thought or image appears only as it is paired with its dialogical opposite – high and low, fat and thin, light and grave, stupid and wise, youth and age, and so on.)[14] By tradition, *Witz* is figured as an unscrupulous marriage-broker, a travesty of a priest, constantly scheming to yoke together shocking new "family" relations, to marry opposites. Holmes was, in his social life as well as in his writing, a devious matchmaker in just this way. Like a child playing with a chemistry set, he was constantly setting up strange couplings – of "brilliance" and "dullness," "genius" and "character," or, most basically, of "levity" and "gravity" – which become highly charged by the resistances between their two opposed mental currents. The "collisions of discourse" in his carnivalesque conversations alternate between two fundamental tropics of thought: over and over again, enthusiasm meets criticism, house-breaking meets house-keeping, a rising inflation meets a sinking deflation, an extravagant, digressive, metaphoric literary sensibility meets the direct, mechanical, prosaic spirit of scientific analysis.

The dilettante Doctor extended the explosive spirit of these dialogic turns into all of the many fields of his interests. Rambling around within the grim laboratories of an emerging physicalist science, his wit could erupt as the "shattering of a retort" (to borrow the apt punning words of Freud) – in a humorous verbal give-and-take (rich in "retorts") which threatens at times to burst out of the test-tube ("retort") confines of such grave mechanism. Holmes remembers that even in his childhood, when he was first given a set of chemicals to play with, his first impulse was to try new mixtures and thus to cause a whole series of explosions – so that the smell of burning phosphorus still works for him as a "reagent" with some-thing of the effect of Proust's *madeleine*, always returning (as he says in a characteristic wordplay mocking both the associationist's labora-tory model of the mind and the Wordsworthian idealism opposing that model) "in a double sense 'trailing clouds of glory'" (*CW,* I, 75–76). This was the tenor of the Doctor's lifelong "conversation" with specialists in the scientific community. The wit of such talk, repeating the images of mechanistic science only to detonate them from within, shows us the "scientist" Holmes in his most character-istic position: as a naughty, impudent child hoping to upset or even to explode the grim adult voices of authority.

This man of *esprit*, especially of *mots d'esprit*, loved to play on the double senses of words, and also on the clashes between these senses from a number of complementary or contradictory discourses. And, contradicting the Master's warning about not "touching off squibs and crackers too near the powder-magazine," he was undeniably happiest when his remarks had an incendiary effect – even if this meant that he was always involved in heated controversy. In fact he was in such trouble all his life, figuring in extended debates with the Calvinist clergy (which reacted to him, in his words, as a "Nihilist incendiary," or, in the words of one witness, as "a sort of reincarna-tion of Voltaire"), with Young America, with all sorts of activist reformers, with homeopathic doctors, and even with the medical establishment.[15] The pinwheels of his combustive fun touch upon many of the most inflammatory topics of the day. His conversational pyrotechnics tend to throw all the cant and the received ideas of the Jacksonian era – the Age of Ideology, of partisanship, of dour dogmatism on all fronts – up into the air, to juggle with them, to view them from new perspectives, to ring the changes on their latent imagery, and thus to open up a whole range of questions and uncertainties beneath the veneer of Victorian certitude.

Like his persona, the genial country doctor in *Elsie Venner*, Holmes could suddenly "put on the glasses" of his medical gaze, stepping back from a parlor-room social event to observe the movements of the whole as a microcosm of the larger community. In fact, he often saw even the public debates in which he was involved both as large-scale conversations and as medical experiments, allowing him to measure reactive pressures in a profession or a culture the way he might measure the responses in any charged interpersonal conversation, by analyzing the verbal resistances to his interventions the way a "percussionist," or later a psychoanalyst, would. When he was engaged in a full-scale argument with Medical Society members, for instance, he offered this physician's diagnosis of that dialogic inter-action: "A loud outcry at a slight touch reveals a weak spot in a profession, as well as a patient" (*CW*, IX, vi).

But if conversation was, to the Doctor, the dynamic site for study of the attractions and repulsions of a "sentimental physics," he was certainly never the coldly curious, manipulative mad-scientist of a Hawthorne tale. He was in constant demand at functions throughout the greater Northeast for his gift as a catalyst: this Leyden jar could somehow build upon energizing oppositions which would leave a group warmer and more "charged" without being angry; usually the only explosions would be those of laughter, the only sparks would be those of newly active thought.

CHAPTER 5

A CONVERSATIONAL APPROACH TO TRUTH
The Doctor in dialogue with contemporary truth-sayers

[This truly intellectual banquet] . . . calls upon Truth, majestic
virgin! to get down from her pedestal and drop her academic
poses, and take a festive garland and the vacant place on the
medius lectus, – that carnival-shower of questions and replies and
comments, large axioms bowled over the mahogany like bomb-
shells from professional mortars, and explosive wit dropping its
trains of many-colored fire, and the mischief-making rain of
bon-bons pelting everybody that shows himself.
Holmes, The Autocrat of the Breakfast-Table

Some persons seem to think that absolute truth, in the form of
rigidly stated propositions, is all that conversation admits . . .
[But] conversation must have its partial truths, its embellished
truths, its exaggerated truths . . . One man who is a little too
literal can spoil the talk of a whole tableful of men of *esprit*.
Holmes, The Autocrat of the Breakfast-Table

Reports of the Doctor's social talk, then, keep returning to this basic
mystery: finally, we wonder, with Emerson, how did Holmes achieve
this special balance? How was he able to draw people out into
explosions that illuminate – without also sparking more destructive
fires?

Attempting to define a talk context making possible "interpenetrative" discussions between speakers representing divergent dogmas or
opposed visions, Holmes' table-talk papers give us a number of direct
lessons about how we are to respond to claims to "Truth" – or to
collisions of discourse between competing claims to "Truth" – in a
conversational setting, providing us with plenty of hints about how
we are to take the provocative assertions, the sudden reversals, and
the surprising hyperbole of many of the authoritative speakers at his
breakfast-table. He is always careful – as in the passage cited above
as epigraph for this chapter – to make clear that the "carnival-

showers" of his "explosive" talk-form are like but not like the "bomb-shells" used by professional warriors; the festival scene of his form of interruptive dialogue is meant to be like but not like – perhaps a moral equivalent of – a scene of actual fighting; the "free play of ideas" in his discussions is always seen to operate in a realm far removed from either the "free trade in ideas" of rough competition for dominance in the economic marketplace or from the brute conflicts of fatal force that decide differences of opinion on the battlefield. In fact fighting over the "large axioms" of Truth is always the main foil against which Holmes articulates his conversational ideal; "powder-keg" eruptions, from those unfamiliar with the art of interpenetrative, cross-cultural dialogue, are just what the "trains" of "multi-colored" talk must always avoid.

Mid-century America, though, torn by "culture wars" between hosts of dogmatists and Truth-sayers each seeking to sum up the world according to the fixed discourse of his or her church, institution, political party, or scientific discipline, was desperately in need of training in what Pratt terms the "art of the contact zone." Holmes' experimental efforts to open up a forum for some form of civil conversation between these separate, specialized voices can be seen as an important forerunner of efforts by twentieth-century philosophers coming out of various national traditions to define and defend the conception of a public forum for cross-cultural talk, and to show how such a talk context could suggest a new approach to monological discourses about or notions of Truth. Mikhail Bakhtin's vision of forms of "polyphonic" verbal interchange exploring "the dialogical nature of truth . . . counterposed to the *official* monologism which claims to possess the ready-made truth . . . and to the naive self-confidence of people who think that they . . . possess certain truths" – is founded in his analyses of the anti-authoritarian "jolly relativity" basic to the mixing of diverse voices in ancient traditions of banquet *symposia* or of folk carnival in the public square.[1] Jürgen Habermas gives another inflection to his speculations about "a conversational approach to 'Truth'," elaborating his ideal of criticism in the liberal, democratic "public sphere" with historical reference to what he sees as the new form of "unrestricted public discussion" that arose in the talk of clubs and coffeehouses in eighteenth-century England.[2] Taking a similar conception in quite different directions, Richard Rorty's advocacy of his ideal of a potential anti-foundationalist "conversation of the culture" – not advocating one Truth itself but serving as an arena for meetings between competing Truth-sayers – is developed in language revealing a strong awareness of the mid-nineteenth-century American roots of this tradition. Rorty's basic, systematic formulations about the philosophical import and uses of the conversation form might be helpful here as a frame for this chapter's exploration of Holmes' ideology of talk. What might it mean for "Truth" to "drop her academic poses, and take a festive garland and the vacant place . . . [amidst the] carnival-shower of questions and replies and comments" in multivoiced talk?

Rorty begins as Holmes does, by taking as his foil the sort of cultural overseer who dominates any conversation with his claims to adequate epistemological Truth: "The Platonic philosopher-king who knows what everybody else is really doing whether *they* know it or not" invokes a monolithic normalizing discourse which tends "to block the flow of conversation by presenting itself as offering the canonical vocabulary for discussion." In contrast to such a stance, and as a remedy for it, Rorty defines an alternative role for another sort of philosopher in quite a different sort of conversation. And here the locus also shifts, from the classroom, the church, or the lecture-room to a setting very familiar to Doctor Holmes: the nineteenth-century salon.

[The other role which the philosopher might play] is that of the informed dilettante, the polypragmatic, Socratic intermediary between various discourses. In his salon, so to speak, hermetic thinkers are charmed out of their self-enclosed practices. Disagreements between disciplines and discourses are compromised or transcended in the course of the conversation.[3]

If the foundationalist discourse of "reality" always moves toward monologue and a "final word" on every subject, the playful, exploratory dialogues of edifying, anti-foundationalist philosophy would work in just the opposite way: "The point of edifying philosophy is to keep the conversation going rather than to find the objective truth." In the hybrid texts of Rorty's "hermeneutic" philosophy as in Holmesian table-talk, the constructive arguments of the great systematic philosophers are then confronted by the reactive verbal forms of satire, parody, and aphorism; the rule-governed discourse of the hard sciences (the backbone of hard philosophy) must then enter into a dialogue with the playful, "soft" discourse of aesthetics. And the goal of such multivoiced interactions is never to merge these incommensurable discourses into one. Amidst this

Babel, one divergent language simply succeeds another, and for Rorty as for Holmes the only anchor amidst all of these oceanic fluctuations in "standards" is a plea for some sort of conversational "civility" – or the hope of bringing out through dialogue some areas of illuminating and "fruitful disagreement." Rorty writes that,

Hermeneutics sees the relations between various discourses as those of strands in a possible conversation, a conversation which presupposes no disciplinary matrix which unites the speakers, but where the hope of agreement is never lost so long as the conversation lasts. This hope is not a hope for the discovery of antecedently existing common ground, but *simply* hope for agreement, or, at least, for exciting and fruitful disagreement.

Both the overall model of such conversation and its particular resonances here (as in Rorty's later allusions to "the language of Henry and William James," or to "the subtle and polydimensional discourse of the drawing room") may serve as apt points of reference for a reading of Holmes' own sometimes surprising mid-century definitions of a conversational approach to Truth.[4]

THE USES OF PREJUDICE IN A REALM OF DOUBT

The Poet at the Breakfast-Table, a later and more self-conscious work in Holmes' table-talk series, offers some of the most direct and schematic expositions of the Doctor's ideas about the uses of talk. Holmes here divides the presiding role in two; his Poet character is clearly detached from the Imperial Self of this table's autocrat, the Master, so as to be able to keep up a running commentary on the "large axioms" of that speaker's blunt Johnsonian pronouncements. Throughout the book, then, the Poet uses the Master's talk as an object lesson, warning us of the difficulties in interpreting conversational discourse. He tells us, for instance, that he has come to enjoy "rubbing up against" the contrary discourses of the long-winded Master:

He stirs me up . . . because he has good solid prejudices, that one can rub against, and so get up and let off a superficial intellectual irritation, just as the cattle rub their backs against a rail . . . or their sides against an apple-tree . . . I think they begin rubbing in cold blood, and then, you know, *l'appétit vient en mangeant*, the more they rub the more they want to. This is the way to use your friend's prejudices. (*CW*, III, 6)

Though the Member of the Haouse heated up like a "powder-magazine" at the suggestions in the Master's frictional talk, the Poet establishes a natural, symbiotic relationship with him, with the same sort of "rubbing" against resistances that Emerson saw producing the "electricity" of wisdom. In talking as in boxing, it is not always necessary to fight "in cold blood"; the Doctor would want to recommend the benefits of intellectual exercise in simple mental sparring.

With his "opinions more or less original, valuable, probable, fanciful, fantastic, or whimsical, perhaps, now and then, which he promulgates at table somewhat in the tone of imperial edicts," the Master serves for the Poet not as an oracle or Truth-sayer but as a case study of prejudice (*CW,* III, 41). And when the Master himself admits that "There is one thing that I am His Imperial Majesty about, and that is my likes and dislikes," we have been prepared to recognize that his strong desire for solid standards on which to base judgment remains only that – a desire, not a solution but in fact a reflection of a general problem (*CW,* III, 71). The conversational setting of his talk allows us to place the Master's opinions by comparison to other prejudices and "private truths," and he only asks us to study his beliefs the way a pragmatist would study the doctrines of any religion: "I don't want you to believe anything I say; I only want you to try to see what makes me believe it" (*CW,* III, 309).

The central apostle at Holmes' supper, then, is not the sort of saint who would lay the foundations of a church but Thomas, the doubter whose role is to unsettle those foundations. The Master himself believes that "one man in a dozen ought to be born a skeptic" because "that was the proportion among the apostles" (*CW,* III, 205). And it is clearly that skeptical "experimental philosopher" among the saints who seems most representative of the talk at this table:

I suppose the life of every century has more or less special resemblance to that of some particular Apostle. I cannot help thinking this century has Thomas for its model." (*CW,* III, 194)

Whenever the Master does get too dogmatic, That Boy can always give him a shot with the pellet-gun, Ben Franklin can enter with broad winks and wise-cracks, offended opponents can disagree with the substance of his remarks, or the Poet will whisper to us in an aside, "I told you to look out for yourselves and not take for absolute truth everything the old Master of our table, or anybody else at it sees fit to utter" (*CW,* III, 267). One woman reader writes to the Poet that she has learned from these conversations to approach all questions as a radical skeptic. Comparing this table-talk to the disputes between Milton's loquacious fallen angels and to the arguments between free-thinkers at Goldsmith's club, she then summarizes the only doctrine that the Holmesian conversationalist can hold: "It seems to me all right that *at the proper time*, in the *proper place*, those who are less easily convinced than their neighbors should have the fullest liberty of calling into account all the opinions which others receive without question" (*CW*, III, 187–88). And in fact the Master's own creed, even as he defines it, seems mainly to be a negative one; his trains of opinion are based on the all-pervasive doubt fundamental to all Holmesian conversation. With typical assuredness, he declares that,

There is nothing I do not question. – I not only begin with the precept of Descartes, but I hold all of my opinions involving any chain of reasoning always open to revision. (*CW*, III, 148)

Of course the Poet confesses that he has to smile at this; he has been noting throughout how belligerent this autocrat can be in the face of any questioning of his hobbyhorses:

The old Master . . . is a dogmatist who lays down the law, *ex cathedra*, from the chair of his own personality . . . But if I found fault with him, . . . I should say that he holds and expresses definite opinions about matters that he could afford to leave open questions, or ask the judgment of others about. But I do not want to find fault with him. If he does not settle all the points he speaks of so authoritatively, he sets me thinking about them, and I like a man as a companion who is not afraid of a half-truth. (*CW*, III, 262)

How do we deal with such dogmatists? Once again, the Poet urges talking over fighting: rather than attack the Master's assertions "on the false side" out of a desire for "conversational victory," he likes to take them up "on the true side" and keep the process of thought going. But of course the Master is never a serious threat to the Poet, because something in the nature of ongoing conversation insures that the questions raised so assertively will always remain open and unsettled. Indeed, the republican, progressive dynamics of table-talk make the Master appear in his boardinghouse surroundings as a figure somewhat like Sir Roger de Coverley in the *Spectator* coffee-house – not as an active power but as a quaint relic of an old-world nobility whose time has passed. The Poet tolerates and even cherishes the stubborn Master as an amiable humorist, a last reflection of that dynasty of famous British talkers ("Samuel the First [Johnson], Samuel the Second [Coleridge], and Thomas [Carlyle], last of the

Dynasty") whose conversational style will soon be made extinct by the democratic and specialized spirit of talk in modern America: "for the conversational dogmatist on the imperial scale becomes every year more and more an impossibility" (*CW*, III, 262–63). And what really saves the Master, and distinguishes him from these English monologists, is our recognition that he is always more talker than truth-sayer. Finally, he is, as he says, more interested in questions than in answers. His speech does not stand solidly upon achieved certainties, but is always moving forward, exploring new territory; he does not converse about what he knows, but about what he does not know; he does not dictate to us, but rather speculates before us – trying to goad us into a reaction. The Poet notes that, at times, "he says some things peremptorily that he may inwardly debate with himself," and the Master admits that he often gets carried away with his hypotheses and ends up saying something he hadn't meant – for which he later feels sorry (*CW*, III, 262, 89). In these moments, he seems to use the breakfast-table as an arena in which to externalize his unresolved internal conversations: speaking provocatively for one "half-truth," he hopes to arouse interlocutors who will then give voice to the other half of the truth, or to another side of the issue. But in other lighter moods, when the Master does not say what he means, it is part of his ongoing campaign to promote his mode of hypothesis and irony against the demands of any monolithic Truth. Hoping to train readers new to such discourse, the Poet early on puts us on our guard about this aspect of the Master's talk:

There is a slight touch of satire in his discourse now and then, and an odd way of answering one that makes it hard to guess how much more or less he means than he seems to say. But he is honest, and always has a twinkle in his eye to put you on your guard when he does not mean to be taken quite literally. I think old Ben Franklin had just that look. (*CW*, III, 6)

BANISHING THE "FACTS" OF LAW, SCIENCE, AND THEOLOGY

Always worried – in each of his breakfast-table works – about the evident problems of reception for such talk, Holmes is then, like his Poet, constantly giving us lessons about how to receive its hypo-thetical, partial, soft "truths." And his main tactic here is to define his realm of "discourse" negatively, by defending himself against what it is not; his carnival of conversation is made possible by some crucial acts of linguistic exclusion. Through the ages, conversation has been the realm of the generalist and the dilettante, and the Doctor opens his breakfast-table series, in the *Autocrat*, by banishing the increasingly specialized discourses of the professions – including, of course, that of the orthodox church. (Of course the church at the time defined the problem differently: it erupted in irate reviews complaining bitterly not that Holmes ignored religious matters but, on the contrary, that he had dared to discuss them in a literary journal, using a non-theological language of everyday talk and a tone of "levity." If he mocked the cloistered, professional language of the theologians, the Doctor was still very much interested in religious topics.)[5] Both the Master and the Autocrat are themselves mono-logical promoters of dialogue, always concerned to distinguish their forms of conversational assertion from those of ideologues and Truth-sayers. It seems to the Autocrat that his realm is forever being threatened by two sorts of conversational "bully": the grave literalists and the grave dogmatists, both of whom tend to make every free-for-all into a fight.

In Holmes' table-talk, the figure of the scientist often stands as the scapegoat for both of these problem-cases. And here again the Doctor's approach is close to that of Rorty. Working within and against the discourse of twentieth-century Anglo-American phil-osophy, Rorty is especially concerned to defend the realm of spec-ulative, hypothetical conversation from the bullying language of scientific "fact." Like the Doctor, he warns that those who base their truth-claims on an appeal to the hardness of brute fact – "all this masochistic talk about hardness and directness" – are likely to adopt some of that metaphorical hardness and brutality in their conversa-tion. They are simply dictating the use of a vocabulary from one particular interpretive institution; and the supposed hardness of their scientific data may reflect more the social force of that institution than any force of physical reality:

The hardness of fact here is simply the hardness of agreements within a community about the consequences of an event. The same hardness prevails in morality or literary criticism if, and only if, the relevant community is equally firm about who loses and who wins.[6]

Holmes' Autocrat extends this figural sense of the "bullying habit of mind" associated with the language of the hard sciences. In his view, the fixed, monadic "facts" of the scientists tend, like theological doctrines, to encroach upon the airy levity of speculative dialogue:

Scientific knowledge, even in the most modest persons, has mingled with it a something which partakes of insolence. Absolute, peremptory facts are bullies, and those who keep company with them are apt to get a bullying habit of mind; – not of manners, perhaps; they may be soft and smooth, but the smile they carry has a quiet assertion in it, such as the Champion of the Heavy Weights, commonly the best-natured but not the most diffident of men, wears upon what he very inelegantly calls his "mug."

Scientists "think only in single file" while talk builds out of double-voices, double-meanings, and digression; their facts are too inflexible to respond to the clashes and collisions of opposing opinions in a "conversational approach to Truth." So even the speaker named the Autocrat is roused to attack the inherent belligerence in this "despotic way of thinking":

There is no elasticity in a mathematical fact; if you bring up against it, it never yields a hair's breadth; everything must go to pieces that comes in collision with it. What the mathematician knows being absolute, unconditional, incapable of suffering question, it should tend, in the nature of things, to breed a despotic way of thinking... Every probability – and most of our common, working beliefs are probabilities – is provided with *buffers* at both ends, which break the force of opposite opinions clashing against it; but scientific certainty has no spring in it, no courtesy, no possibility of yielding. (*CW*, 1, 55–56)

Even in the first paragraph of the first breakfast-table paper, the Autocrat announces his goal as the development in America of a literary sense, a way of "thinking in letters," which would explode out of the reigning mode – the mere calculation of facts and figures:

I was just going to say, when I was interrupted, that one of the many ways of classifying minds is under the heads of arithmetical and algebraical intellects. All economical and practical wisdom is an extension of the following arithmetical formula: $2 + 2 = 4$. Every philosophical proposition has the more general character of the expression $a + b = c$. We are mere operatives, empirics, and egotists, until we learn to think in letters instead of figures.

They all stared. There is a divinity student lately come among us to whom I commonly address remarks like the above... (*CW*, 1, 1)

This brief passage itself works to give us a loaded lesson about how this table-talk will always operate – and about what it might mean to "think in letters" rather than in empirical "facts." The Autocrat's topic, like Sterne's, will be the workings of the human mind – but most especially the *movements* of thought, as it works in words. From the first, we see that his study will develop as a series of analogies for mental operations (beginning with a comparison of our "heads" to the "heads" of these two mathematical categories). And we begin to sense what this "thinking in letters" might really involve: if we free ourselves from the exactitude and determinism of scientific formulae, we enter a realm of multiple interpretations and potential misunderstandings. The highlighted interruptions and incomprehensions of auditors (and perhaps the resulting laughter of readers) here mock the almost phrenological scientism of the entire attempt to classify minds so categorically – we note that the Autocrat admits that there are "many ways" of approaching these matters. So we are then launched into a realm of talk, of literary thinking and rethinking, which will involve bald directed assertions and quick denial, laughter, interruption, and a continual play on the multivalent, non-empirical properties of words (we get a hint of what to expect throughout this table-talk with the Autocrat's first plays on "heads," "thinking in letters," and then on the mock-Biblical tones announcing the arrival of the foil in the scene, that divinity–student "lately come among us").

But the site for such freewheeling improvisation and interaction seems always to be surrounded by hordes of fact-bearers. While the Autocrat works to keep the wheels of conversation turning, those arithmetical minds want to stop discussion dead in its tracks: their axiomatic "facts," he warns, are "intended to stop all debate, like the previous question in the General Court" (*CW*, 1, 28). Their voices can even break into the Autocrat's interior dialogues:

Some persons seem to think that absolute truth, in the form of rigidly stated propositions, is all that conversation admits . . . [But] conversation must have its partial truths, its embellished truths, its exaggerated truths . . . One man who is a little too literal can spoil the talk of a whole tableful of men of *esprit*. – "Yes," you say, "but who wants to hear fanciful people's nonsense? Put the facts to it, and then see where it is!" – . . . stick a fact into him like a stiletto. (*CW*, 1, 51–52)

The single Truth of the proposition here again meets the multiple truths of conversation – one more skirmish in a debate which continues throughout the Autocrat's papers. But bullying "facts" need to be warded off precisely because they tend to turn talking into fighting; they are associated with grave weapons of war – with stilettos or revolvers – inappropriate to the desired lightness of an unsettling war of words.

The men of facts wait their turn [during a discussion] in grim silence, with that slight tension about the nostrils which the consciousness of carrying a "settler" in the form of a fact or a revolver gives the individual thus armed. (*CW*, I, 142)

In one other early scene, the Autocrat erupts in talk full of the witty, multi-leveled "embellishments" of simile and metaphor sure to befuddle any Royal Society literalist, to utter his decree:

All generous minds have a horror of what are commonly called "facts." They are the brute beasts of the intellectual domain. Who does not know fellows that always have an ill-conditioned fact or two which they lead after them into decent company like so many bull-dogs, ready to let them slip at every ingenious suggestion, or convenient generalization, or pleasant fancy? I allow no "facts" at this table. What! Because bread is good and wholesome and necessary and nourishing, shall you thrust a crumb into my windpipe while I am talking? Do not these muscles of mine represent a hundred loaves of bread? and is not my thought the abstract of ten thousand of these crumbs of truth with which you would choke off my speech? (*CW*, I, 5)

Whether it is Necessary or True or useful or good or "good for you," the "bread" of such certainties simply does not mix with the breaking of bread in a breakfast-table symposium. The impulses of "discourse" are always at war with the truths of theology, of morality, of science, of political action, and even with the goal of a final, synthetic Truth in philosophy.

The Autocrat's own pronouncements, then, tend to work not as *doxa* – judgments based on the majority opinions of a culture or an institution – but as *para-doxa*: playing with and against received, majority opinion, drawing it out, exposing its contradictions, turning it back on itself for some self-reflection. He advances his own startling, exaggerated opinions not to settle matters but – to use one of his favorite words – to "unsettle" them. In the same way, when the Divinity Student wonders if certain subjects shouldn't be avoided in conversation with those of certain beliefs, the Professor remarks caustically on this "singular timidity on his part lest somebody should 'unsettle' somebody's faith, – as if faith did not require exercise as much as any other living thing, and were not all the better for a shaking up now and then" (*CW*, II, 294–95). This whimsically applied medical analogy reappears very often in the Doctor's defenses of his free-thinking and free-talking. Such a mechanistic view of the mind's operations, the desire to "give our mind's exercise" with unexpected shakes and turns, had been the premise of the Renaissance and late-Renaissance dialogic anthologies of scientific paradoxes which Holmes loved to collect and to read.[7] But his physicalist model of talk is explained with almost baroque elaborations on that base metaphor: our mental muscles cannot simply slave away endlessly in straight lines on single tasks; they must be let out once in awhile, for a holiday release of exercise in the open air. And our brains can then give our other organs a good shaking up: praising Boston as the brain of the American body politic, Little Boston tells us that,

There isn't a thing that was ever said or done in Boston, from pitching the tea overboard to the last ecclesiastical lie it tore into tatters and flung into the dock, that wasn't thought very indelicate by some fool or tyrant or bigot, and all the entrails of commercial and spiritual conservatism are twisted into colics, as often as this revolutionary brain of ours has a fit of thinking come over it. (*CW*, ii, 83–84)

This thinking proceeds not "in a straight line" but by "fits" and starts, and its "revolutionary" effects come about through the turns of talk. The Autocrat frequently urges the need to turn over the field of our ideas, up-rooting old ideas in order to plant new ones. Or, picking up Little Boston's imagery, he can celebrate the way that conversation serves to break up ruts on the highway of progressive thought. Indeed he takes as one model for his talk a water-sprinkler cleaning Boston streets, then imagining an important public role for his conversation as a "thought-sprinkler" forever washing away obstructions to free circulation on the culture's intellectual thoroughfares: "What would be the state of the highways of life, if we did not drive our *thought-sprinklers* through them with the valves open, sometimes ?" (*CW*, i, 27) The Poet too (certainly the same poet who gave us "The Deacon's Masterpiece; or, The Wonderful 'One-Hoss Shay'") gets very enthusiastic about the way a "hot thought" can "plough up those parallel ruts where the wagon trains of common ideas were jogging along in their regular sequences of association" (*CW*, i, 99).

When Holmes then extends *ad absurdam* current scientific proofs of the coming of an American Giant, or when he plays upon "making" metaphors to undercut the era's ideal of the "self-made man," he is clearly relishing the role of devil's advocate. Perhaps the most direct recognition of this stance is given by the Professor after he has surprised the boarders with a lengthy defense of the solemn meanings and uses of "wealth" and of "fashion": "I do not think there is much courage or originality in giving utterance to truths that everybody knows, but which get overlaid by conventional trumpery." Of course the danger here is that such shocking, exaggerated, hypothetical statements will be misconstrued by listeners or readers who do not understand that they emerge as contra-dictions, in a dialectical relation with other "truths." So the Professor appends a warning to his statements on "money" and "fashion," addressed to his "young friends" who might "be tempted to waste their substance on white kids . . . or to insist on becoming millionaires at once":

A remark which seems to contradict a universally current opinion is not generally to be taken "neat," but watered with the ideas of common sense and commonplace people. (*CW*, II, 151–52)

"TRUTH'S ETERNAL FLOW": TAKING THE *PARALLAX* OF THOUGHTS AND FEELINGS

Holmes is less interested in the flat statement of positions on issues than in the "mobility" of a play of ideas between these positions. "I find the great thing in this world is not so much where we stand, as in what direction we are moving," says the Autocrat at one point, taking the digressive tacks of a sailboat as an analogy to the turns of talk in his dialogues: "To reach the port of heaven, we must sail sometimes with the wind and sometimes against it . . ." (*CW*, I, 93). For the sentimental Poet, talking is most like sailing when his interlocutor is a woman. The air then seems to be charged by the "divine differences" of gender (somewhat as it is in conversations between different civilizations), and women are often seen to be the best barometers of the mercurial dynamics and shifting currents in these "vital interchanges of thought and feeling": one moment "microscopically intellectual" and the next warmly sympathetic, a female talker appears to be especially attuned to "the changes in temperature as the warm and cool currents of talk blow by turns." But before the Poet floats off too far in this nautical reverie, That Boy interrupts his private currents of thought, suddenly sending the table-talk in a different direction – and thus reminding us of the real dialectical import of such sailing analogies: ". . . the wind shifted all at once, and the talk had to come round on another tack, or at least fell off a point or two from its course" (*CW*, III, 95). Because in talk the currents are always changing, the temperature is always varying, the wind is always shifting, and one speaker-skipper is always being replaced by another, the final destination can never remain set for long.

Rather than concentrating on such finalities, then, Holmes focusses his attention on what he calls "truth's eternal flow" (*CW*, I, 147). For the process which was for the Poet an emotional roller-coaster is for the Master full of philosophical significance. Though the vitalism of this concept of Truth as an oceanic "flow" might not shock most nineteenth-century laymen, the idea that "no creed can be held to be a finality" is seen as a direct affront to theological verities.[8] The Master admits that in private many ministers make good conversational partners, and he is especially fond of those "good talkers" among the mid-century clergy who have learned the basic humbling lesson from their participation in the ever-turning tides of such daily verbal intercourse: "if he knows anything, [he] knows how little he knows." But too many ministers carry their priest-like, straightforward sermon form over into their talk, and their static public beliefs then leave them lagging behind in many discussions. They don't seem able to take new tacks to test the waters of progressive "currents" of public opinion, or to catch the force of new winds or new "spirit":

The old minister thinks he can hold to his old course, sailing right into the wind's eye of human nature, as straight as that famous old skipper John Bunyan; the young minister falls off three or four points and catches the breeze that left the old man's sails all shivering. By and by the congregation will get ahead of *him*, and then it must have a new skipper. (*CW*, III, 125)

The breakfast-table is a very liberal pulpit. The congregation involved in Holmes' table-talk is treated to a constant succession of ministers, whose diverse voices can be compared and contrasted in the atmosphere of absolute relativism inherent to the conversation form. Making a particularly nineteenth-century application of Pascal's comment that what is truth on one side of the Pyrenees is error on the other, the Doctor observes that the "most sacred terms . . . have entirely and radically different meanings in the minds of those who use them." Though they use these terms as though they were arithmetical counters, clergymen should notice in their interactions that "the figure 2 meant three for one man and five for another and twenty for a third." In a true conversation, though, they might recognize that they are using "variable terms," what the Autocrat called "thinking in letters"; the Master reports what one famous theologian said, summing up what he had learned in conversing with a dissenting brother: "Oh, I see, my dear sir, your *God* is my *Devil*" (*CW*, III, 184).

This lesson learned in theological disputes holds for talk in any realm. At the breakfast-table, each "text" opens up like Melville's *Moby-Dick* doubloon into a multiplicity of interpretations stated in a succession of diverse voices. When the Master gets out a nickel and asks That Boy to read both sides of it ("it's got two sides to it with different reading"), he is making a point about our ability to "read" other people – "That's it, that's it, – two sides to everybody, as there are to that piece of money" – and we have seen that the Poet later applies this lesson to the ongoing turns and the fluctuating "values" of all talk (*CW*, III, 81, 90). The tools of Newtonian optics also often enter the discussion to teach us about the relativity of perspectives and points of view in our relations with natural objects: Holmes had invented a stereoscope and built some bifocals out of his fascination with the interactions of the different visions of our two eyes, and his scientific speakers like to surprise us with comparisons of the same object viewed through a microscope, a telescope, and the human eye. When the focus shifts to the verbal form of any "observation," Holmes' conversations frequently turn, as we have noted, on debates about the validity of various dictionaries. And similar controversies arise about governmental or legal interpretation: in several table-talk passages we find that every speaker reads the Constitution according to the determinations of his own bodily and educational "constitution."

Talk will never bring such divergent views into complete agreement, but it may at least allow some illuminating mediation between warring truth-sayers. The Professor wants to serve in this way as an unattached mediator between ideologues; he points out that while Brown will always want to burn Smith or excommunicate him – simply because every "Smith is always a Smithite" – in a larger conversational perspective we must remember that "every man has a religious belief peculiar to himself," and that no single human subject can have possession of objective Truth: "the *Smithate* of truth must always differ from the *Brownate* of truth" (*CW*, II, 297). When the Gentleman Opposite scoffs at the Autocrat's use of the phrase "truth, as I understand truth" – accusing him of flying off into the ungrounded subjectivism of a Kantian "transcendentalist" when rock-solid "common sense" has proven quite "good enough for him" – the Autocrat can only reply: "Precisely so, my dear sir; common sense, *as you understand it*. We all have to assume a standard of judgment in our own minds, either of things or of people" (*CW,* I, 14). The movements of conversation tend to point up the arbitrariness and subjectivism in these assumed "standards." When the stern fundamentalist Lady in Black yells out her solution to all interpretative differences – "Go to the Bible!" – the Professor does just that. But he goes, for his "gloss" or "commentary" on her words, to an 1858 reading of the Bible, written by a Southern man, which finds in that Book the message that "trigamy" is the "remedy for existing social evils." Since this reading so clearly reflects the Southern roots and male desires of one particular reader, its proclamation of the need for a peculiar new institution is guaranteed to conflict with the beliefs of the orthodox Northern woman – especially at this time of great North–South differences in reading the meanings of the Constitution on the question of the institution of slavery. But it brings home forcefully the Professor's point: "what you bring away from the Bible depends to some extent on what you carry to it" (*CW,* II, 4–5). The Astronomer, who has often reminded us of the Copernican revolutions wrought by changes in optical perspective, also notes in his poem-manifesto that the Bible is built of not one but four gospels, competing stories which are then variously "read" by a wide diversity of readers (*CW,* III, 311).

Conversation never rests in one authoritative reading – whether of scientific "fact" or religious dogma – but offers instead multiple interpretive perspectives: North meets South, male meets female, the entomologist with his microscope meets the astronomer with his telescope, and "stories" told by clerics meet the common voices of laymen. This gives us, says the Professor, using one of his favorite optical metaphors,

the *parallax* of thought and feeling as they appear to the observers from two very different points of view. If you wish to get the distance of a heavenly body, you know that you must take two observations from remote points of the earth's orbit . . . To get the parallax of heavenly truths, you must take an observation from the position of the laity as well as of the clergy. (*CW,* II, 7)

Again, talking is a bit like sailing by the stars: we have to take our readings by comparing static Truths with those which are flowing. In the Holmesian set-piece cited as motto for this chapter, the talk at the

Autocrat's version of a philosophical *symposium* begins with a clear challenge to the idea that any pure, chaste, static, axiomatic Truth can stand outside the fluid, intoxicating, back-and-forth movements of spoken festival intercourse. ("This truly intellectual banquet . . . calls upon Truth, majestic virgin! to get down from her pedestal . . . and take the vacant place on the *medius lectus*, – that carnival-shower of questions and replies and comments . . .") Even within the indoor setting of an "intellectual banquet," then, we find that conversation is characterized by its flowing form and changing vessels; in another characteristic passage, the Autocrat describes the fluid nature of the opinions which arise out of specific speech occasions, out of that freewheeling, free-thinking "carnival-shower of questions and replies and comments," through a telling comparison to the special vessels (bowls without bases) used by the ancients to stimulate the discussions at their symposia:

How many of our most cherished beliefs are like those drinking-glasses of the ancient pattern, that serve us well so long as we keep them in hand, but spill all if we attempt to set them down! (*CW,* 1, 15)

Like these glasses, talk does away with "standards." The continual pouring of these intoxicating liquids is more important than their particular containers. But if we begin to take our assumed beliefs too seriously, or if we try to "set them down" as fixed, written moral laws, we may not be able to keep our tempers in hand, and will then spill out the sort of angry feelings certain to stop all dialogic flow.

Once more, the Autocrat is led here to stress the differences between the shifting opinions which emerge in conversation and the "facts" and formulae of mathematics. To him, talking is like playing *mora* – an interactive guessing game using numbers – and the point is not to force both sides into "agreement" on one victorious common ground or the other, but simply to find the highest common denominator between divergent positions. If we learn to "think in letters" (even to the point of playing upon the figural possibilities of arithmetical language), we will avoid petty, mechanical disputes about numbers:

I show my thought, another his; if they agree, well; if they differ, we find the largest common factor, if we can, but at any rate avoid disputing about remainders and fractions, which is to real talk what tuning an instrument is to playing on it. (*CW,* 1, 15)

This sense of conversation as an art rather than a science is invoked most strongly when Holmes is exploring ways to assure that

it will be "suggestive" rather than "argumentative": "Remember
that talking is one of the fine arts – the noblest, the most important,
and the most difficult, – and that its fluent harmonies may be spoiled
by the intrusion of a single harsh note" (*CW,* I, 52). The crucial
challenge in developing an "art" of interpenetrative dialogue across
differences while avoiding disputes is best defined by analogy to
music – especially to the playing of a many-stringed instrument like
the harp:

What are the great faults of conversation? . . . I will tell you what I have
found spoil more good talks than anything else; – long arguments on special
points between people who differ on the fundamental principles upon
which these points depend. No men can have satisfactory relations with
each other until they have agreed on certain *ultimata* of belief not to be
disturbed in ordinary conversation . . . Talking is like playing on the harp;
there is as much in laying the hand on the strings to stop their vibrations as
in twanging them to bring out their music. (*CW,* I, 10–11)

Like members of the Saturday Club, Holmesian talkers make
possible the free play of their experimental interactions by first
clearly agreeing to disagree about fundamental differences; like the
English and American speakers that Holmes' Professor imagines
preparing for a truly interpenetrative conversation between their
"two different civilizations," they cannot begin to share their
thoughts until they first "recognize what separates" them (*CW,* II, 35).

THE "BRAHMIN" AND THE "HUB": TWO CASE STUDIES IN THE READING OF HOLMES' CONVERSATIONAL TRUTHS

Holmes' speakers talk to raise questions, not to provide solid answers.
But over and over again boarders at the table are seen to take even
the most provocative assertions as answers, as "standards," as Poor
Richard maxims to be applied in action by all people to all of life.
The Autocrat can only stare icily when, after one of his witty praises
of the company of dull minds, a lady boarder reveals her own dull
limits (and then disproves his point) by taking him too literally and
too unilaterally: "Do not dull people bore you?" (*CW,* I, 6). And he
even sees a need to remind readers of the dialogic context of one of
his more virulent dismissals of all "facts" from the table:

[The above remark must be conditioned and qualified for the vulgar mind.
The reader will, of course, understand the precise amount of seasoning
which must be added to it before he adopts it as one of the axioms of his life.

The speaker disclaims all responsibility for its abuse in incompetent hands.] (*CW*, 1, 5)

But one phrase of enthusiastic listener response – the common ejaculation, after a nice aphorism or speech (even one's own), "That tells the whole story" – arouses the Autocrat's particular ire, as it reveals an unconscious tendency to side with the legalistic factual bullies against the most fundamental goal of conversation: it favors a synthetic resolution over the constant turns of ongoing talk.

"That tells the whole story" . . . is intended to stop all debate, like the previous question in the General Court. Only it doesn't; simply because "that" does not usually tell the whole, nor one half of the whole story. (*CW*, 1, 28)

Certainly a primary effect of all of these scenes showing up the slow-mindedness of certain scape-goated boarders and readers is a rhetorical one: it only heightens what was always a very active response from the rest of the audience. Like Sterne, Holmes invites a very intimate relationship with his readers – this is one function of this special sort of "conversational style" – and also reveals a deft mastery of their reactions. Like a jester, he divides his audience into different groups, flattering most readers with his winking recognition that they, at least, are not among those who have shown themselves to be priggish, prudish, censorious, literal-minded, or dull. Given the chance to join this charmed circle of select, sophisticated friends, the reader tends to be very eager to try to adopt the stances and language suggested to him in the asides of the ever-present host.

But the long history of uncomprehending responses to Holmes' complex conversational form suggests that Holmes' warnings against and examples of inappropriate readings were not simply standard tricks to flatter and attract an audience. Apparently in his day (as in ours) a realm of hypothetical discourse was very difficult to defend, and a "conversational approach to Truth" was novel (or archaic) enough to need continual reassertion and reenactment. Indeed it is unfortunate that the Doctor's mock warning-labels (his "directions for use") were not firmly affixed to some of his most controversial and influential conversational "words."

Though Holmes named the "Boston Brahmin," and though he gave Boston its lasting nickname as the "Hub," the way that these two coinages were so quickly taken up out of their ironic, dialogic contexts and applied as "Truths" antithetical to their initial point reflects in small scale a major problem with a great many overall readings of Holmes' works. Van Wyck Brooks noted this phenomenon, a strange momentum inherent in Holmes' imagery which seems almost to call for later misreadings: "He laid trains of thought that later became abuses, as the Boston mind developed under other conditions."[9] Like the similarly rhetorical, metaphorical, light-and-grave aphorisms of Nietzsche, the Doctor's conversational, hypothetical words have seemed fated to an almost instant reader use and abuse.

Holmes' first printed reference to Boston as the "Hub" comes in a long discussion in the sixth *Autocrat* paper – in a highly ironic context. Although the epigram may already have been well known, here it is introduced not by the Autocrat but by a stranger at the table, who interjects,

Boston State-House is the hub of the solar system. You couldn't pry that out of a Boston man if you had the tire of all creation straightened out for a crowbar.

This new speaker, or one modeled on him, reappears with a name and an insistent voice in the *Professor* papers, as Little Boston, the effusive deformed man who cannot yell a sentence without an exclamation point at its end, who turns any discussion around to his hobbyhorse enthusiasm for Boston, and whose mysterious dwarfism is finally diagnosed by the medically-inclined Professor as the fatal, physiological result (a somaticization) of a pathological provincialism: "It dwarfs the mind, I think, to feed it on any localism. The full stature of manhood is shrivelled – " (*CW,* II, 87). Little Boston, like Sir Roger de Coverley, is taken by the other boarders as an amiable humorist because his "whims and local prejudices" are so clearly a thing of the past; even Little Boston himself seems finally to recognize that Boston's cultural dominance in America is coming to an end, when on his deathbed he says, "My life is the dying pang of a worn-out race" (*CW,* II, 310, 301). So the speaker here is hardly an unambiguous defender of provincialism; in fact when he finally dies of his loud-but-amiable localism Little Boston has served as Holmes' clearest example of the limits of such narrow-mindedness.

The literal, mechanical imagery here picturing all creation by analogy to tires and crowbars – which places this hyperbolic "Hub" statement in the line of American tall-tales alongside the story of

Davy Crockett's unfreezing the cogs of the sunrise – also undercuts the seriousness of the "Hub" statement, as it develops from the base idea of planetary "gravity" which in Holmes always calls for the balance of a good laugh of "levity." And the entire passage had begun as a baring of the machinery of the Autocrat's form of aphoristic talk, with a self-reflexive analysis of the maxim form in general. The examples leading up to the "Hub" line proceed from a moralistic saying by Franklin in stages of increasing irreverence to "wise sayings" (like Motley's: "Give us the luxuries of life, and we will dispense with its necessaries") that are plainly shocking to some boarders (*CW*, 1, 125). Wisdom here gives way to wit, which seems to operate parasitically by playing off of wisdom – unsettling it from within.

There seems to be something inherently "provincial" in the very nature of the epigram: what this discussion points up is that "wise sayings" are indeed sayings, constructed by particular speakers on particular occasions for the promotion of their own particular (often provincial) interests. Such verbal performances must not be applied generally outside the realm of dialogic discourse as tools in the performance of life. The debate here focusses not on the definitive "Truth" of a maxim but on its literary qualities or its material worth; a few years after the first publication of *Bartlett's Quotations* (1855), the Autocrat admits that he is ambitious to create a saying surprising enough to be remembered and reprinted. (By the paper's end, though, even this deflating, materialistic emphasis is debunked when he admits that his famous Enlightenment comparison of the mind of a bigot to the pupil of an eye ("the more light you pour on it, the more it contracts") might not be original, and then launches into a pun-filled – "it is not proper," and so on – attack on the idea that a comparison or a maxim could be copyrighted and owned, that there could be a "private property in ideas" [*CW*, 1, 144–46].)

When the "Hub" line appears, then, we have been well prepared in many ways to be critical readers. And in fact even the Autocrat answers the line as a critical reader, stressing the aptness of "the satire in the remark" in subverting Boston pretensions. He then relativizes this sentiment by seeing the "Hub" phrases as but one word in a conversation of other assertions: the Boston booster had been initially provoked by the epigram, "Good Americans, when they die, go to Paris," which with its equation of heavenly and earthly cities had been intended to provoke the Divinity Student, but then the Autocrat adds to this list, "See Naples and then die," and a more general proposition of his own: "The axis of the earth sticks out visibly through the centre of each and every town or city" (*CW,* I, 124–26).

Conversation itself seems to work like a tire-iron, serving to pry people out of their spherical self-involvement. And cosmopolitan, endlessly discursive talk tends in just the opposite direction from the concentrated, definitive, and localist maxims surveyed here. The turns of talk operate most basically, then, as a challenge to any "provincialism" or "prejudice," a continual reenactment of the Copernican revolution, forcing each successive speaker to recognize the relative limits of his "standards" and "conceits." One Holmes poem describes the *Bildung* of a young asteroid which initially takes Boston's State-House for the sun, and begins to orbit around it, until Edison steps in with the warning, "You've made a mistake" (*DHB,* 128). And Holmes' anecdotes about his own education stress the transformations arising out of similar changes in optical perspective and planetary orbit: he describes several times the "shock" of a ten-cent peep through a telescope from the Boston Common to Venus as a truly revolutionary moment in his childhood, provoking a "vast and vague confusion of all my standards."

All my human sentiments, all my religious beliefs, all my conception of my relation in space for fractional rights in the universe, seemed to have undergone a change. (*AN,* 46)

But later in life Holmes would make such a difficult process of reorientation – a relativization of standards and an unsettling of gravitational fields – the very basis of his talk form, the movement fundamental to every turn in his cross-cultural conversations. The Doctor always remained fascinated by the comparison of different systems of measurement; he notes that discussions between Americans and Englishmen (as between Americans from different cities) will constantly run into difficulties in translating pounds into stones, or in using Boston State-House versus St. Paul's as a common standard of reference: "The difference in scale does not stop here: it runs through a greater part of the objects of thought and conversation." The point of such relativity is then once again brought home to Bostonian boosters: "We Boston people . . . have been in danger of thinking our local scale was the absolute one of excellence – forgetting that 212 Fahrenheit is but 100 Centigrade" (*DHB,* 99–101).

Several Holmes passages stress that the course of Truth is as full of change as the course of Empire. Each system of measurement holds only a temporary sway; even the State-House and the Bunker Hill Monument – those proud axes of the Bostonian universe – will eventually crumble into ruins. This is just the lesson that the speaker of any "Hub" maxim will face again and again as he participates in the ongoing motions of boardinghouse conversation: though each of us sometimes feels that we have a power of gravitational centrality, in fact none of us can take the sun's place at the center of the universe.

The "Hub" sentence could only be taken as an axiomatic Truth-claim or a chauvinistic localist slogan, then, if its conversational context were entirely ignored. Of course in day-to-day life the Doctor loved to repeat versions of this trademark line in other speech situations – as part of Lyceum talks or after-dinner speeches. But here again the word was clearly not intended as a "wise saying" which could "stop all debate"; it was not intended simply as a pat on the back for a Boston-based audience that already agreed with it; on the contrary, the "Hub" line apparently provoked its most electric effects outside of Boston's gravitational sway, among audiences from Kentucky to Maine who could take it as it was intended: as a challenge to lively, interpenetrative discussion between languages, regions, or "civilizations."

A briefer look at the context of another Holmes invention which also proved to have great sloganeering potential, the description of a "Brahmin caste of New England," can only help to elaborate this obvious but important lesson in "how to read Holmes." The first development of the Brahmin theme comes near the end of the *Autocrat*, again in a context of un-conventional conversational wit and wisdom. The Autocrat has just been praising the merits of dandies, which should be a hint that he is in one of his contrary moods. Certainly the summation of this lengthy point is at best back-handed, as it defends the dandy (earlier seen as a "very genteel idiot") in linguistic terms mainly as a sort of vacant expletive useful for keeping the conversation going –

Dandies are not good for much but they are good for something. They invent or keep in circulation those conversational blank checks or counters just spoken of, which intellectual capitalists may sometimes find it worth their while to borrow of them. (*CW*, 1, 257)

– but when he then turns to treatment of these "intellectual capitalists" the Autocrat's phrasing is even more ambiguous:

We are forming an aristocracy, as you may observe, in this country, – not a *gratiâ-Dei*, nor a *jure-divino* one – but a *de-facto* upper stratum of being, which floats over the turbid waves of common life like the iridescent film you may have seen spreading over the water about our wharves, – very splendid, though its origin may have been tar, tallow, train-oil, or other such unctuous commodities.

The "layers" imagery seems to have carried the speaker away from his initial point here, as it begins to dredge up ugly connotations of oily upward-mobility and dirty material mercantilism beneath the exaggerated moralisms and the glittering rainbow colors of this aristocracy's surface appearance. So the Autocrat has to start again, taking a new tack:

I say, then, we are forming an aristocracy; and, transitory as its individual life often is, it maintains itself tolerably, as a whole. Of course, money is its corner-stone. (*CW*, I, 259–60)

But this blunt formulation is at least as shocking – to factions all across the spectrum – as the last one. And that seems to be just what Holmes intended. First, of course, even raising the subject of an aristocracy in mid-century America constitutes a provocation to the huge majority in the party of the common man. Holmes seems to be at least as interested, though, in framing his points to shock those who consider themselves the cultural elite. No self-described leader could be too "unctuous" about his position after the unsettling reminder that it is not timeless but transitory (always requiring infusions of new, robust blood), and that it reflects not divine "election" or pure blood-lines or even innate taste and sensibility but only money (perhaps amassed through something as unseemly as the trade in oil) and the environmental influences that money can buy. Looking at American society with the unsentimental, realist's gaze of a clinical doctor (or of a naturalist novelist), Holmes observed the outlines of class forma-tions as undeniable, if unpleasant, natural facts:[10]

I think it is unpopular in this country to talk about gentlemen and gentlewomen. People are touchy about social distinctions, which no doubt are often invidious and quite arbitrary and accidental, but which it is impossible to avoid recognizing as facts of natural history. (*CW*, III, 57)

If it makes us squirm, all the more reason that we should make it the matter of our talk. Each time this "scientific" matter of social distinctions does enter into the realm of Holmesian talk, though, it is treated not with subtle logic and cool rationality but as the trigger to wild turns of inflammatory debate. The Master, for example, changes sides several times during one particularly heated, multivoiced exchange on the topic. While he opens with the bald assertion that "We have a native aristocracy, a superior race," later on he surprises the boarders when his example of such nobility is not city and school-bred but a sort of natural Billy Budd:

The last born nobleman I have seen, I saw this morning; he was pulling a rope that was fastened to a Maine schooner loaded with lumber. I should say he was about twenty years old, as fine a figure of a young man as you would ask to see, and with a regular Greek outline of countenance, waving hair, . . . The young fellow I saw this morning had on an old flannel shirt, a pair of trousers that meant hard work, and a cheap cloth cap pushed back on his head so as to let the large waves of hair struggle out over his forehead . . .

But then finally, worrying that he might be taken for "a labor-reform candidate for President," he veers sharply in the opposite direction (in imagery sharply opposed to the overall tendencies of Holmes' house-breaking imagery) to laud the environment of urban pavement over disease-ridden country soil, and a protected, indoor, "hot-house" human cultivation over any open-air rural learning: "The finest human fruit . . . are raised under glass." Here the Poet intervenes, suggesting that the Master intends "a metaphorical rather than a literal statement" (to which the Master cries out, "No, Sir!"), and later trying to calm us in our bewilderment at the strong, jerky movements of such rapid statement and counter-statement: "I do not believe the Master had said all he was going to say on this subject, and of course all these statements of his are more or less one-sided" (*CW,* III, 276–280).

DEFENDING THE REALM OF THE INTELLECTUAL

Of course the Master needn't have worried that we might take him for a Presidential candidate, since we can see that with his back-and-forth mind he wouldn't be able to toe a party line for more than a few consecutive sentences. And, clearly, Holmes' purpose in all discussions of "Brahminism" and "aristocracy," as in his use of the "Hub" maxim, is not to plead for his party line but to unsettle us in our own lines of thought, the same way that he wanted to "give an intellectual shake" to the head of the Divinity Student, or that he urged us to "shake up" our own faiths from time to time, or that he occasionally hoped to start us shaking with loud laughter (*CW*, i, 85; *CW*, ii, 295).

Holmes was always more a shaker than a mover. Like many of his peers from Harvard, he had closely followed the election of 1828, during his junior year, sensing its telling implications both for his personal future and for the future of the nation. Pitting a generalist intellectual (one of Holmes' own professors, John Quincy Adams) against a primitivist war hero (Andrew Jackson), the contest also developed in crass campaign tracts as a choice between action in the verbal realm and action on the battlefield:

> John Quincy Adams who can write
> And Andrew Jackson who can fight.[11]

Though often shrewdly couched in terms of a choice between democracy and aristocracy, this election became (especially in the rabidly anti-intellectual literature of Jackson's supporters) a referendum on the role of the intellectual in America.

In Holmes' view "intellect" lost that political battle, and he followed the dictate of the campaign's outcome by retiring forever from any active political engagement. But at the same time he seems in many ways to have accepted the terms of the 1828 election debate, and then to have gone on to refight that contest – in dialogue form, at the breakfast-table or in the dinner club – for the rest of his life. When raising again and again the questions of Boston's "Hub" centrality or of an American "aristocracy," the Doctor is not hoping finally to settle these issues, but on the contrary to use their continually unsettling shock-value to keep open a debate on the place of the intellectual – and thus to clear a space for the operations of intellect, since, for Holmes, debate *is* the place of the intellectual. Always denying any interest in action in the arena of politics and power, he began soon after his college years (with the first two experimental installments of "Autocrat" table-talk in 1831–32) to define an arena of conversational "discourse," modeled as a microcosm of movements in the political sphere but firmly separated from it, in which to celebrate and to enact the free play of ideas. This was to be an arena not for performative utterance but for speculative hypothesis and self-reflection. And while it certainly could still be a site for explosive, physical energies, this was to be an arena of verbal interaction: not for fighting but for thought.

In this atmosphere, it was only natural that Holmes and his cohort then led a major revival of interest in the conversation club – coming to see those centers of criticism as the "public sphere" most appropriate to their post-1828 situation. As Shields has shown, a long line of clubs in eighteenth-century England and America had defined a tradition of free talk deliberately separated from the operations of political or economic power, developing in conscious opposition to "prevailing civil myths," and thus often seen as a challenge to the political and religious order in their day:

Social clubs constituted havens of play and free conversation in which the sorts of expressions most troublesome to church and state could be voiced . . . In the second-story rooms of taverns and coffeehouses public opinion achieved its fullest scope of liberty by voicing criticism as wit . . . The playful indeterminacy of club conversation stood at odds with the solemnities of state, the dogmas of the church, the zeal of the sects, and the passions of the parties.[12]

In the same way, the mid-nineteenth-century talk club could seem to Holmes a haven for pleasurable or speculative discussion within a larger culture divided by political partisanship, theological gravity, and ideological rigidity. And while the dialogues at an institution like the Saturday Club – a talk group proud to proceed without by-laws or any written constitution, and proclaiming itself a "society based on mutual repulsion" and "intellectual anarchy" – would rarely treat political matters directly, in fact often developing as burlesques or travesties of actual legislative debate, this parodic "play politics" could make such a club a para-political forum helping to expand the scope of public opinion under the guise of light, witty verbal play.[13]

Holmes' written conversations, working to translate the dynamics of this sort of alternative talk arena into print, can then stand as crucial markers of a major nineteenth-century transformation in the role of the "Boston Brahmin" in American life. The humor of the *Autocrat* papers arises out of the contrast between an earlier leader like John Quincy Adams and the Autocrat; from Adams' vision of highly centralized institutions of national culture governed by men of intellect we move to the spectacle of a would-be despot who cannot even hold much sway as "carnival king" in the diminutive but highly decentralized realm of one breakfast-table. And the first chapter of Holmes' first novel, *Elsie Venner* (1861), "The Brahmin Caste of New

England," which first named the "Brahmin," also helps to define in its more straightforward prose the significant changes in this new situation. If, in the past, New England's secular priesthood had combined intellectual, political, and social leadership, by the time Holmes names the caste its representatives are no longer seen as both scholars and leaders: now the "Brahmin caste" is purely an "academic class," a community of "scholars," always pale-faced, white-linened, and often physically weak, defined by intellect alone. Distinct from Emerson's "American Scholar," Holmes' "Brahmin" is clearly disengaged from the operations of power, and more literally engaged in education (as a student or a teacher) – confining his activities to the realm of words.[14]

Like the realm of conversation, the realm in which the "Brahmin" moves is described mostly negatively: in the long "Brahmin" chapter of *Elsie Venner*, Holmes makes no mention of cultural leadership, of social power or authority, or of any form of action. (A long March 1856 letter from Emerson to Holmes, speculating on the "spiritual rank" and social situation of the now-marginal "scholar, [or disengaged man]" in mid-century America, suggests that Holmes and Emerson had been conducting an ongoing discussion on this vexed question, and also that Emerson's notions about the "American scholar," and about that scholar's necessary disengagement from irrational mass movements, may have had a significant impact on Holmes' later published description of the Boston "Brahmin.")[15] Holmes' "Brahmin Caste of New England" is clearly no race of rulers, no ruling class; and, in contrast to the table-talk about "aristocracy," the presentation in *Elsie Venner* does not involve money. We know, in fact, that Holmes later lamented that some readers had supposed he meant by the "Brahmin caste" a "bloated aristocracy." But Van Wyck Brooks reasons that,

Dr. Holmes was not to be blamed if other times brought other customs, if, in days to come, the Brahmans ceased to perform their function and, in proportion as they lost their vigor, advanced their worldly claims.[16]

The claims that Holmes does make for this new sort of "Brahmin" seem to be based on an important distinction between the new role of the "intellectual" and the traditional one of the "cleric." Indeed, the most famous modern definitions of these terms, given by Richard Hofstadter, are grounded in and very appropriate to the Doctor's transitional period. The Doctor's mid-nineteenth-century defense of an "academic class" amidst a "Bowie-Knife civilization" parallels Hofstadter's mid-twentieth-century defense, in *Anti-intellectualism in American Life* (1963), of an "intellectual class in America" against the background of 1950s know-nothingism. Holmes' writings can be seen as primary signs of a shift in the ideal of a "life of the mind" from that of a clerisy, close to society's assumptions, to that of an alienated avant-garde; from a model of end-oriented intellect in the service of power to disinterested intelligence with a goal of free speculation and criticism; from living off ideas to living for them. In Hofstadter's impressionistic formulation, an intellectual begins with the same calling to ideas that motivates the secular priesthood, but such potentially rigid "piety" is then balanced by "playfulness": a restless, mischievous delight in the play of ideas for its own sake. While the clerical mind may become constricted in the quest for certainty, in fanatical promotion of one external end or one "truth," the intellectual's skeptical play "turns answers into questions":

Whatever the intellectual is too certain of, if he is healthily playful, he begins to find unsatisfactory. The meaning of his intellectual life lies not in the possession of truth but in the quest for new uncertainties.

The resulting mental life is described as an ongoing interior dialogue between the poles of piety and playfulness, in very Holmesian terms:

It is, in fact, the ability to comprehend and express not only different but opposing points of view, to identify imaginatively with or even to embrace within oneself contrary feelings and ideas . . . The tensile strength of the thinker may be gauged by his ability to keep an equipoise between these two sides of his mind.[17]

We have seen that Holmes' table-talk references to an "aristocracy" at the nation's "Hub" have mainly a negative function, that of challenging consensus in a more corrosive version of the process Hofstadter describes as "turning answers into questions." Even Parrington recognizes this negative aspect of Holmes' definitions of Brahminism:

In his own special way, then, as a Brahmin of the Brahmins, Holmes was a rebel, a puller-down of worm-eaten structures, a freethinker rejoicing when free thought tossed a cargo of obsolete dogma into Boston Bay, or drew out a linchpin of some respectable social coach.[18]

But then, if Holmes' concept of "Brahminism," which emerges out of the back-and-forth, anti-foundational movements of his conversational context, is seen to have any more "positive" values, these too can be defined only in relation to that context. The only ground for this newly-defined "caste" is a very shifting, insubstantial one: the ground of "civil" conversation. And this realm seems to be governed only by one rule: that of "freedom of speech."

In *Elsie Venner*, the attributes of the "Brahmin" character Bernard and of his mentor Doctor Kittredge are indeed the attributes that we have seen associated with Holmes' conversation. Though he does enter the story with the advantages of pallor and education, Bernard (a medical student so strapped for funds he must interrupt his studies to work as a country schoolteacher) proves himself a "Brahmin" mainly by his ability to talk – or, to put it more exactly, to converse. For this doctor–confessor–psychologist hero does not speak just a single genteel language in a single tone: he is marked from early on by his special ability to understand a wide variety of professional and regional idioms, to be able to modulate his own language so as to engage easily with a range of interlocutors, and so to serve as a sort of moderator between the diverse dialects of limited, provincial speakers. We recognize his distinction immediately when he prevents a fight between country boys, mediating their dispute by translating between their private languages; the same gift helps him later, at the local parties which are the novel's highpoints, to work along with Doctor Kittredge to bring together the various warring theological and social factions in this small town. Against the backdrop of a deeply fragmented rural scene – a body politic divided by wars between social classes, races, churches, and chauvinistic boosters of each locality – Bernard enters to suggest the ideal alternative possibility of a cosmopolitan public man, without local or class or family affiliations, able to move comfortably among diverse strangers. But to develop this potential he will have to choose between two medical mentors: Kittredge, the country doctor, or the Professor, who narrates the novel from his comfortable position at a major medical school in the metropolitan center.

In contrast to the Professor, who is full of city smugness (a metropolitan version of provincialism), racial and class biases, academic pomposity, and absolutist opinions that he feels enable him to judge all the novel's actions from afar, Doctor Kittredge emerges as a doctor–talker epitomizing Holmes' conversational ideal: he is not chauvinistic, not always certain of his positions or diagnoses, and not detached in his judgments of others – as a medical practictioner engaged in a constant round of personal calls, his "sympathies" have been well "exercised by daily patient contact." And indeed most of this patient contact is conversational; some of the locals even suspect Doctor Kittredge does not "believe in medicine" (*CW*, v, 426), since he rarely prescribes drugs and instead uses talk (in one-on-one interviews or at larger dinner parties) as his main medium both for diagnosis and for therapy. The sympathetic Kittredge, a secular priest, has apparently become a rival or replacement for area churchmen through his verbal ministry to townspeople of every race and rank – even in fact serving as intimate minister to the ministers in a series of heartfelt dialogues with the heads of the local religious sects. Presenting a series of one-on-one interviews between the area's various "doctors" – heads of the Catholic, orthodox Calvinist, and liberal Protestant churches, as well as Doctor Kittredge – *Elsie Venner* tests the potential for "oceanic," interpenetrative conversation between persons of deeply opposed beliefs. And in each case the process of talk is meant to reveal that no beliefs are fixed, static, or final: each of these churchmen or doctors is seen to be in fact deeply uncertain, continually engaged in an anxious internal dialogue about his faith but unable to admit it. Opening the possibility of expression to such speculative thought, several of these conversations develop as true experiences of conversion, where the talkers are led to change their initial positions, or even sometimes seem to exchange positions with their interlocutor – as the Calvinist reveals his secular, humanitarian leanings, the Unitarian reveals his innermost desire for the security of Catholic ritual, and Kittredge himself reveals that in many ways his medical training has led him to Calvinist stances. (After one such exchange between two ministers, for example, the churchmen are bewildered by this transformational power in fluid, interpenetrative talk: "The younger minister was completely mystified. At every step he made towards the Doctor's recognized theological position, the Doctor took just one step towards his. They would cross each other soon at this rate, and might as well exchange pulpits" [*CW*, v, 258–59].) From this perspective, those who remain set in their unchangeable beliefs are seen as weak, childish, so traumatized they rush to "get rid of [their] liberty" through the seeming certainties of set rites and external symbols in religious orthodoxy, or of specific drugs and remedies in medicine. By contrast, the speculative intellectuals who are at the "front ranks of thought" break away from the "spiritual dictatorship" of the "propagandist ready with his bundle of finalities," and are seen as voyagers who dare to depart from protected ports for the "free thought and free speech" that takes place in the "round unwalled horizon of the open sea," giving themselves over to the difficult, uncertain freedom of ongoing, ever-changing talk that explores the flux of currents in the "ocean of thought" (*CW*, v, 252–54, 417).

Finally, the plot of *Elsie Venner* turns around the powers and limits of such conversation. The only suggestion of a potential positive cure for the mysterious problems of the novel's central female character, Elsie Venner, is a "talking cure": readers are led to believe that Elsie might find release from her inner demons either through intimate communication with Bernard, a possible lover, or through therapeutic dialogues with Doctor Kittredge. The situation is confusing because Holmes' flawed novel hints at a wild diversity of possible explanations and sources for Elsie's ailment, but, on one level, from the perspective of the medical conversationalist, Elsie's inhuman coldness and her snake-like lisp emerge primarily as symptoms of a fundamental defect in her abilities to speak, perhaps rooted in a lack of sympathetic intercourse with both parents in the "cold isolation" of her early childhood. Her core problem, then, is an exaggerated version of the problem that cripples so many people in this divided, uncommunicative region: we are told that she has "never shaped her inner life in words" so that her emotion might "open the gate for itself into the great community of human affections." As Sophy, her nanny and companion, explains: "she kin' o' got the way o' not talkin' much." So the only hope is that perhaps the arrival of the communicative Bernard or the sympathetic Doctor Kittredge (or later the nurse-like Helen) at her bedside will draw Elsie out into some cathartic self-expression (*CW*, v, 341–42, 419, 433). In the novel's muddled end, though, the possibilities for any sort of "talking cure" are left unexplored. After a last failed interview with Bernard (that shows her finally able to profess love, but then reveals that a cold, stumbling Bernard is unable to respond to such talk), an incurable Elsie takes to her deathbed – only to be further weakened when Bernard unknowingly sends her a bouquet that functions as a grave, fatal, non-verbal medical intervention: the bouquet given to Elsie turns out to be a natural potion or drug (like that given to Beatrice at the end of Hawthorne's "Rappacini's Daughter," or to Aylmer's wife in "The Birthmark") that eradicates the poison in her and erases the snake-mark on her neck but at the same time takes her life. Holmes' plot thus ends before Bernard's apprenticeship to

Kittredge is completed and he can imagine entering into genuine verbal intercourse with Elsie. (Indeed, in a disturbing last chapter we find that, soon after his final failed conversation with Elsie, Bernard falls back under the sway of the Professor, marrying "appropriately" into a rich family and giving up his dreams of serving needy patients of all classes to open up an exclusive city practice serving only wealthy clients.) *Elsie Venner* then leaves us with the sense that the conversational ideal it has developed is more suited to diagnosis of problems than to therapy – more a powerful vehicle for reflection and analysis than for action in the world.

Holmes, Rorty, and Habermas present parallel portraits of the talk-leader ideally suited to their conversational ideals. Indeed, when Habermas describes the emergence of a new sort of human character type suited to the new forum of free discussions in the "public sphere," he can seem to be uncovering the lineage of a figure like Bernard in *Elsie Venner*. Tracing the transmission of a form of "representative publicness" in the "culture of nobility" from the Christian knight through the humanistically cultivated Renaissance courtier, Habermas sees the English gentleman and the French *honnete homme* of the eighteenth century to be characterized (as Bernard is) by a "serene and eloquent sociability" which can be displayed publicly and can also have important uses in public life.[19] And when Rorty calls for the emergence of a new sort of philosopher whose abilities in conversation might help to charm "hermetic thinkers . . . out of their self-enclosed practices," and who might then serve as a "polypragmatic, Socratic intermediary between various discourses," his model too seems close to what Holmes was attempting to describe in Doctor Kittredge and Bernard. Holmes does not put the "Brahmin" Bernard forward out of an urge to stop the "currents" of social and intellectual change; both Bernard and Holmes aim in their talk, like the model philosophers in Rorty, to help "society as a whole break free from outworn vocabularies and attitudes, rather than to provide 'grounding' for the intuitions and customs of the present."[20]

Doctor Kittredge and the "Brahmin" Bernard personify Holmes' highest ideal for the breakfast-table and drawing room talk of the American mid-century: raising the hope that some larger verbal structure or forum will open up a liberating "conversation" between America's separate, specialized discourses. For Holmes as for Rorty, such non-disciplinary, non-directed dialogue does not put itself forward as a new authority but as the site for possible meetings between authoritative voices; and it is seen to be not static but progressive in its effects. If it is easy for us to understand how Rorty, faced with the unreflective scientism or absolutism of so many of the dominant discourses in twentieth-century America, can feel the need to revive or to defend the form of such an edifying "conversation of the culture," we will see in the next chapter that in Holmes' day, in the America of the 1830s to 1850s, the discovery of such a medium for thought, which might perform the social function that Dewey termed "breaking the crust of convention," could seem especially useful – really an urgent national need.

CHAPTER 6

CONVERSATION AND "THERAPEUTIC NIHILISM"
The Doctor in dialogue with contemporary medicine

> We are getting on towards the last part of this nineteenth century. What we have gained is not so much in positive knowledge . . . as it is in the freedom of discussion of every subject that comes within the range of observation and inference.
>
> Holmes, *The Poet at the Breakfast-Table*

"I know of no country in which there is so little independence of mind and real freedom of discussion as in America," wrote Tocqueville after his 1831–32 tour.[1] And the Doctor might well have been spurred on by a very similar sociological diagnosis as he began experimenting with his first two "Autocrat" conversations in these same years. In such an environment, the "Brahmin" playground of "conversation" could be seen to have a truly "edifying" role, opening up the possibility of a sort of "town meeting of the mind" (to use Carl Bode's description of the era's Lyceum ideal), and thus serving not as the site for a last stand of defense against change, but rather as a site *for* change — and as a training ground for the emergence of the first forms of new ideas and of new languages.

THE FORM OF CHANGE: THE SAGE IN AN "AGE OF UNCERTAINTY"

Conversation often seems to be the verbal form most appropriate to a transitional period. For if its "ironic" structure can seem to point blithely toward the future, operating as an engine of social and intellectual change, it must also be seen to reflect anxieties and confusions in the present, emerging as an almost inevitable response to such change. In 1884, looking back in bewilderment and wonder at the revolutionary changes which had occurred in almost every area of life during the mid-nineteenth century, Doctor Holmes characteristically finds (in the words cited above as motto for this

chapter) that the most fundamental advances did not involve quantitative increases in "positive knowledge" but rather a general expansion of the areas open to "freedom of discussion" – suggesting both
that such "freedom of discussion" might be seen as the ground which
makes possible any specific gains in "positive knowledge" and also
that this increasingly pervasive conversational debate and questioning develops something which is not only the complement of
"positive knowledge" but also in some ways its antithesis – a sort of
"negative knowledge." As it shakes the foundations of every solid old
"Truth," setting up collisions between the discourses of exclusive
dogmas, forcing unthinking ideologues to recognize that the ground
is shifting under their feet, the Doctor's explosive table-talk bares the
confused, anxious predicament of any honest thinker in his transitional period – a period we are now beginning to understand not as
an "age of equipoise" and self-satisfaction but as an "age of
uncertainty."[2] Indeed, the self-divided Holmes emerges as one of the
cultural figures most "representative" of this new sense of the era.
The period seemed to demand a very strange sort of cultural
spokesman – certainly not a fiery Truth-sayer or an insular apologist
or a defender of cultural coherences in the traditional mold of the
Victorian Sage.[3] A huge mid-century American readership made the
Atlantic a national publication and Holmes a national figure with
their overwhelming response not to the Autocrat's dogmatic pronouncements but to the overall dynamics of breakfast-table talk.
These multivoiced written conversations – with their tendency to
open every issue to a multiplicity of warring responses or to oscillate
endlessly between antithetical positions, and with their almost
pathological avoidance of univocal statements or of fixed standards
or of conclusions – speak very powerfully for the ambivalences of a
self-divided nation at a major turning-point in its cultural history.

For, although vociferous American boosters seemed to Tocqueville
to lack a forum for discussion of problems or minority positions, and
to be either unwilling or unable to admit the existence of dramatic
differences between their rival voices, the American mid-century was
not simply an age of buoyant, bumptious optimism or of complacent
Podsnappery. William R. Hutchison has described how internal
contradictions within American Victorian culture could give rise to
strong feelings of "cultural strain." Daniel Walker Howe has
suggested that many mid-century reformist projects developed out of
the desire to allay "secret doubts and confusions." And David

Grimsted writes that "recently several scholars have noted a strange disgust, uneasiness, and even terror with which Americans viewed their society in these years." At the same time that the country was rapidly becoming more diverse – with enormous territorial expansion, and enormous increases in population through several waves of immigration – new developments in the technology of transportation, communications, and industry were bringing these diverse elements into closer and more frequent contact. To Grimsted, it was the overwhelming speed of the succession of early nineteenth-century "revolutions" in thought and in social life, the now undeniable mobility of ideas as well as of people, that contributed to what he describes as a sort of schizophrenic "confidence-dread syndrome" characteristic of much American Victorian thought.[4]

William Ellery Channing, himself an emblem of one of the period's major ideological shifts as spokesman for the Unitarian revolt, remarked with awe upon the larger pattern and pace of historical change in America:

Our age has been marked by the suddenness, variety and stupendousness of its revolutions. The events of centuries have been crowded into a single life. Overwhelming changes have rushed upon one too rapidly to give us time to comprehend them.[5]

Doctor Holmes would not have been be able to comprehend these incomprehensible shifts any more than anyone else could, but he was – perhaps more than any other American author in the period – deeply concerned with and involved in these movements of change. His "polypragmatic," dilettantish spirit and his multiple careers had put him in touch with at least the outlines of revolutions and ruptures in a wide range of fast-developing fields: "How few things there are that do not change their whole aspect in the course of a single generation!" exclaims his bewildered Master in the 1870s (*CW*, III, 328). As a conversationalist, the Doctor made it his business to promote the latest theory, the abnormal new discourse that might unsettle the normal one; but if his works are then always involved with change, they are also obsessively worried about the topic – about the difficult questions raised by such unsettling movement.

At times the Doctor liked to appear in his public role as the Voice of Science, the sanguine annalist of technological progress. Near the end of his long life, which spanned almost the entire nineteenth century (1809–94), he imagines what he would have to say to

Dr. Thomas Young (who died in 1829) if that master doctor were to make a spectral visit to the Saturday Club in 1886:

I should tell him of the ocean steamers, the railroads that spread themselves like cobwebs over the civilized and half-civilized portions of the earth, the telegraph and the telephone, the phonograph and the spectroscope. I should hand him a paper with the morning news from London to read by the electric light, I should startle him with a friction match, I should amaze him with the incredible truths about anæsthesia, I should astonish him with the later conclusions of geology, I should dazzle him with the cell-doctrine, I should confound him with the revolutionary apocalypse of Darwinism. All this change in the aspects, position, beliefs, of humanity since the time of Dr. Young's death, the date of my own graduation from college! (*Our One Hundred Days in Europe, CW*, x, 2)

It is telling that the Doctor here sees Saturday Club conversation as the most appropriate forum for such a story, implying that the turns of that Club's talk made it somehow the medium for these "changes in the general condition of society and the advance in human knowledge" over the half century since Holmes' college days. And the Doctor, picturing himself in his usual role as an energetic, unstoppable speaker, gives us a nice sense of how such talk could make him the voice of the change: Holmes clearly likes to be able to burst upon a listener as if he were an "ambassador" from some foreign land, "clad in the grandeur of the new discoveries, inventions, ideas"; once again his talk is seen to provoke a sort of "culture shock" between two civilizations (British and American, past and present), with the collisions and sparks of this conversation now arising out of the nature of a subject matter which is itself startling, astonishing, dazzling, electric, explosive – even revolutionary.

Over his long life Holmes had the opportunity to write and rewrite prefaces to several new editions of his works, each one of course forcing recognition of the successive ascendancies of several generations among his readers – usually figured as the revolt of sons against fathers. He always used these occasions to try to tie his writings to the latest technological discoveries. Though he says he does not want his notes to "interrupt the current of the conversational narrative," the Doctor's 1882 Preface to the *Autocrat* has to bring us up to date on the latest extensions of electric power in the story of the world outside: electric lights now bring en-lightenment to our reading; the telegraph brings news from foreign scenes; and the telephone allows our "talk" to cover ever greater distances, so that now even two unlike cities can converse as though they were sitting at the breakfast-table.[6] (Holmes is also fascinated to report the stages of development of the bicycle, and predicts in his added notes that such frictionless movement will soon lead to everyday flights of "aerial swimming.")

But when the Doctor then touches upon the consequences of such dizzying developments for his own work in talk, the results are not seen to be so simply substantial or positive. The conclusion of his Preface vision of the "currents" of progress brings the matter home with understated suggestions of some shifty undercurrents here – intimations of the impermanence of all things.

All these [electric inventions] since 1857, and how much more than those changes in our everyday conditions! I can say without offense to-day that which called out the most angry feelings and the hardest language twenty-five years ago. I may doubt everything to-day if I do it civilly. (*CW*, i, vi)

Here, as in the comments from the *Poet* taken as the motto for this chapter, the Doctor recognizes that we have gained more in "freedom of discussion" than in any "positive knowledge," and that the process of such conversation then speaks for the all-pervasive skepticism which challenged the old solidities a quarter-century ago and which still serves to remind us that we live in a state of constant uncertainty.

Twenty-five years before, though, Holmes' explosive table-talk, throwing all fixed standards up into the air, had indeed called up a war of hard words, which resonated with arguments across the nation as the country approached civil war. While his written "conversations" seemed then to mirror the centrifugal chaos of conflicting opinions in a state of cultural *aporia*, Holmes was not so cheerful about such all-pervasive uncertainty: as the War commenced, he wrote to Motley in England of the "terrible uncertainty of everything – most of all, the uncertainty of the opinion of men, I had almost said of principles . . . you find all shades of opinion in our streets" (*DHB*, 50).

The late 1820s would have been the young Holmes' first moment of exposure to such unsettledness. The last two Founding Fathers, Jefferson and Adams, had died exactly fifty years after the Declaration of Independence on the same day, July 4, 1826, sending many journalists and orators into long laments about this sign of the loss of the last connection to the nation's roots. Then, in 1828, the same year that saw John Quincy Adams lose the Presidency (and Harvard students by implication lose their patrimony of national leadership), Holmes' father lost his church. This religious revolt remained for all of the Doctor's later life his fundamental model of change; but since he experienced it powerfully from both sides of the issue, it could only have aroused deep ambivalences. For just as the young man had himself turned to Unitarianism at Harvard, and had begun to assert himself as one of the ringleaders in the decidedly un-Calvinist drinking, smoking, and debating of the freethinking carnival that was undergraduate club life, the full implications of such prodigal digressions from the paternal path would suddenly have been brought home to him when the liberalizing currents in Cambridge came to focus on the inflexible figure of his own father, the orthodox Rev. Abdiel Holmes, who was finally forced by his parishioners to abandon his position at the First Church in Cambridge. Caught in a conflict between family loyalties and his own religious doubts, between sorrow at his father's "fiery trial" and exhilaration at the liberating movements which had begun at his "heretic college," young Holmes noted in a letter an unusual change in himself: "I am cross as a wild-cat sometimes." Like his friend Hawthorne, Holmes would then always be preoccupied with the double edge on the sword of change: while hailing a perpetual revolt of sons against fathers as the inevitable model for life progress, he would also return guiltily, obsessively, to meditate on the meanings of such revolt.[7]

HOLMES AND THE FRENCH REVOLUTIONS IN MEDICINE: THERAPEUTIC NIHILISM

But for Holmes this was only the first major turn – there were to be many other revolts following in this early pattern. The next major move was a literal uprooting, the voyage to Paris to begin two years of medical study in 1833. Edward Waldo Emerson's imagistic description of Holmes' unusual sort of "cultivation" rightly stresses the transplantations and uprootings which characterized his early formation: "the grafting of medicine onto a Puritan clerical stock, the re-potting into the Conservatory of Paris, the transplantation, after several years of vigorous culture, back to the native soil . . ."[8] And revolutions were very much in the air during the stay in Paris. Though his parents hoped he would defend himself against the wickedness of this French Vanity Fair, young Holmes eagerly sought out all levels of theater and cosmopolitan spectacle. In the soldier-ridden capital of King Louis-Phillipe (whose "revolution" of 1830 still needed much protection), the student also found his republican sympathies aroused, and in letters he could rise to a defense of what seemed for the moment a minority opinion: "If then a single principle first advocated, or best advocated by Robespierre, or St. Just, or Danton, or Marat, is found to be true, let it be advocated again . . ." On the left bank, Holmes might well have felt himself to be reliving the days before the French Revolution: dining with Lafayette on the Fourth of July, talking with agitated anti-government students and intellectuals over daily coffee at the Café Procope (the same café that had served earlier as a rallying place for Voltaire and Rousseau), protesting as one of his fellow-boarders was jailed for his political associations.[9]

Of course in Paris Holmes channeled most of his energy into long hours of medical study. But in medicine he became a committed participant in the most lively revolt of all: he had come to France to be among the first Americans to experience a movement that would revolutionize medical practice around the world – the birth of the "clinical method." Even Holmes' very first lecture series, in the fall of 1833, provided a dramatic introduction to the current war between the old and the new schools of French medicine. Students did not even have to move from their seats as they witnessed, in two juxtaposed lectures, a classic Holmesian "conversation" between diametrically opposed languages and ideologies. First came François Broussais, whose violent, bombastic verbal style reflected his position as representative of the older "heroic" medicine, which through the eighteenth century had posited visionary, holistic, monistic systems in diagnosis, usually advocating one cause and one cure for all ailments, and which then attempted to balance systemic tensions or humors through radical interventions such as purging, bleeding, or sweating. (Broussais was convinced that all disease was a version of gastro-enteritis, and his practice featured a lavish use of curative leeches.) But next came the man who would shortly succeed Broussais in the chair in Internal Pathology, Gabriel Andral. Holmes much preferred the chastened verbal style of this new "scientific" generation, and his Harvard training had already prepared him to be quickly won over to the newer viewpoint. Young Turk Andral was the eloquent voice for Pierre Charles Alexandre Louis, the modest clinician whose careful studies had forced the need for a medical "paradigm shift," and with whom the devoted Holmes would spend most of his time. Steeped in Newtonian science and British empirical philosophy, the party of Andral and Louis, "les Idéologues," urged a move away from extremely generalized systems to an extremely localized pathology, focussing closely on particular diseases and particular parts of the body. Their new instruments (percussion in 1808, the stethoscope in 1819, later the microscope, and a regularization of autopsy) opened up an unknown inner world of tissues and led to major discoveries in anatomy.

But the real thrust of their teaching was negative. Stressing the need for careful observation, new instruments to aid the senses, laboratory testing, and comprehensive "numerical" evaluation of therapies based on large samplings of patients at the new clinical research hospitals, Andral would point up the "imperfections" of present diagnoses and therapies, frankly admitting that doctors often worked in ignorance. Reporting the results of Louis' tests, or of his own microscopic examinations of the blood, Andral would be quietly pointing up Broussais' reliance on superstition and subjectivity, uncovering the cruelty of purgative methods which were now proven to have no positive effects. With their constant admissions of ignorance and error in the profession, their diagnostic optimism that went along with a strong pessimism about all current therapies, the new generation of medical men came to be called "therapeutic nihilists." For indeed, theirs was a very unsettling sort of revolution. If it cleared away the old myths and methods in preparation for later developments of "modern" medicine, the clinical method itself was purely transitional: it seemed to reduce all old cures to rubble while offering nothing positive as replacement.[10]

When Holmes returned to America in 1835, he quickly became the nation's leading spokesman for this radical new doctrine, applying it very broadly not only to medicine but to the many other areas of his expanding interests. His later work in a wide range of fields, certainly including his theory and practice of conversation, seems indeed to have been founded upon the very shaky ground of this "therapeutic nihilism."

As we survey, in this chapter and the next, the Doctor's work in two fields, medicine and psychology, we will see that the "nihilist" uncertainty inherent in his conversational approach to the current "standards" of these fields would lead him through an unceasing succession of intra-disciplinary revolts, while his most telling contributions to "positive knowledge" at each stage would then be informed by his central experience of conversational dynamics.

THE DOCTOR IN CONVERSATION WITH THE AMERICAN MEDICAL ESTABLISHMENT

The immediate effects of the theory of "therapeutic nihilism," as Holmes applied it in medicine, were mainly destructive – not likely to reinforce a self-righteous or secure sense of progress, not offering a very solid place on which to stand. The young man Calvinists would call a "moral parricide" for the way he abandoned his father's theology first used his Parisian clinical training to join in the general revolt against one of the leading figures of the Revolutionary generation and one of the Founding Fathers of American medicine, Doctor Benjamin Rush. Though he appreciated the important medical speculations of Cotton Mather, Holmes embarked with special fervor upon a lifelong series of attacks on Rush as the symbol of Enlightenment self-confidence. America's Broussais, Rush had declared that there is but one disease and one type of treatment; every malady was traceable to an excess or lack of nervous stimulation, and, since Rush distrusted natural powers of healing, each problem should then be treated through special sudden actions by a heroic doctor – usually with a single massive purging of the blood. (Rush had affirmed his willingness to take out as much as four-fifths of all the blood in a stricken body.) Playing maliciously on the eminent doctor's name, Holmes would suggest that Rush's obsession with nervous pressures could be traced to the "rush" of his own high-pressured blood and to the "rushing" of a Revolutionary spirit in the air – the Napoleonic sense that a violent cure could be found for any problem – which then led him to "rush" into intervention before he knew what he was doing. This "heroic" doctor then emerges as a model of the physician-figure who will reappear often throughout the writings of both Holmes and Hawthorne, a monomaniacal visionary carried away by his own invented cure, infected by a fanatical passion for his ultimate panacea, whose unnatural solution is finally revealed to have been the cause of rather than the cure for much human suffering.[11]

Of course Holmes takes Rush in part as a conveniently distant foil through which to attack the majority of physicians still using heroic techniques and massive drug-dosages in his own day. Rush may have influenced the American medical mind in its "self-confidence, its audacious handling of Nature, its impatience with her old-fashioned ways of taking time to get a sick man well," but Holmes knows that the heroic practice, with its trust in Art over Nature, also fits the temper of a Jacksonian nineteenth century:

How could a people which has a revolution once in four years, which has contrived the Bowie-knife and the revolver, which has chewed the juice out of all the superlatives in the language in Fourth of July orations, . . . which insists on sending out yachts and horses and boys to out-sail, out-run, out-fight, and checkmate all the rest of creation; how could such a people be content with any but "heroic" practice? (*CW*, IX, 192–93)

Stories of the exploits of mid-century frontier doctors like one Dr. Physick, famed for his daring cuts and his buckskin sutures, would resonate for Holmes with other aspects of imperial egoism and imperialist expansionism in America's "Bowie-knife civilization."[12]

   But here we begin to see some of the undersides of Holmes' "therapeutic nihilism." For now his lists of technological inventions are not cheerfully optimistic; and now his "revolutionary" medical theory places the Doctor in opposition to at least some forms of revolutionary action. The pure Parisian position, radically skeptical and disillusioning, promoting observation and management of the disease process rather than any intervention, in fact seems to operate for Holmes as a denial of the possibility of action. And the destructive energies of his attacks are not focussed solely on external objects; often they tend to turn back upon themselves, putting their speaker's entire profession into question. Whenever Holmes takes on Revolutionary doctors or frontier physicians or homeopaths or quacks, the thrust of his argument also often tends to undermine the stances of "regular" physicians and of their new-formed Medical Societies.[13] His early essay, "The Contagiousness of Puerperal Fever" (1843), though written in the hope that it would announce his entrance as a major voice in American medicine, develops the data of a Louis-style study of current therapy for childbed fever into a stirring melodrama, which builds to the conclusion that doctors themselves, blind to their own ignorance, have in these cases been dark "ministers of evil," carriers of the contagion they meant to cure, poisoning the purity of innumerable chambers of sacred maternity (*CW*, IX, 103–72). (It is interesting to see how, in the writing of this groundbreaking essay, Holmes' most significant, revolutionary insights once again emerge out of the dialogic interaction of his literary sensibilities and his medical training. Holmes may initially have been attracted to this complex and controversial medical topic because of his attachment to traditions of sentimental fiction which since the eighteenth century had seen maternal mortality as a central problem. Then, as the Doctor begins to develop his major conclusions here [strongly challenging the medical establishment], the "neutral" medical language and statistics of his clinical report seem suddenly to be interrupted by a reemergence of that mythic, melodramatic story, narrated in a charged, highly literary language which makes the scenes of endangered childbirth reverberate with metaphysical horrors. And for Holmes the prime horror resides neither in the disease itself nor in the carrier germs [whose existence he hypothesizes through literary speculation] but in the medical men who have been too arrogant to recognize their own role in spreading this fatal disease.) Though it won him his second Boylston prize at Harvard, and has since been widely reprinted as "one of the most important documents in American medicine," in its time this upstart essay won only virulent counterattack and censure from the medical establishment.[14] Already in this early medical writing, then, Holmes placed himself at the active center of highly polarized conversations within the medical community.

In the same way, Holmes' later speech, "Currents and Counter-Currents in Medical Science" (1860), though now hailed as "one of the finest statements ever written on the philosophy of medicine," earned a strong official disclaimer from the Massachusetts Medical Society as it rose from discussion of the errors of Rush, homeopaths, and quacks to a conclusion applied to the entire *materia medica*, in memorable phrases calling up the classically revolutionary gesture of the Boston tea-party:[15]

Presumptions are of vast importance in medicine, as in law. A man is presumed innocent until he is proved guilty. A medicine – that is, a noxious agent, like a blister, a seton, an emetic, or a cathartic – should always be presumed to be hurtful . . . If this presumption were established, and disease always assumed to be the innocent victim of circumstances, and not punishable by medicines, . . . we should not so frequently hear the remark . . . that, on the whole, more harm than good is done by medication . . . I firmly believe that if the whole materia medica, *as now used*, could be sunk to the bottom of the sea, it would be all the better for mankind, – and all the worse for the fishes. (*CW,* ix, 202–03)

Such a stand put even the former Dean of the Harvard Medical School in a very marginal position in mid-century America. Assuming the role of national spokesman for clinical nihilism, Holmes would try to frame the negative doctrine more positively and Romantically as a trust in Nature: what he (and others) termed "The Nature-Trusting Heresy." But the new name nonetheless reflects the fact that this position was indeed widely regarded as heretical.

His teacher Jacob Bigelow's article, "On Self-Limiting Diseases" (1835), had sought to refute the anti-Nature stance of Rush (who had written that "when the physician steps into the sick room, nature should be politely asked to step out") by describing the doctor's role as that of a "minister of nature," who does not attack a disease violently but observes it cautiously – caring for rather than curing the patient, and only helping the illness to run its course. Holmes saw this essay (which appeared in Boston just one year before Emerson's *Nature*) as a "bomb-shell," and became the most persistent agitator for its core suggestion of what Lewis Thomas describes as "one of the great subversive ideas in medicine": the idea that disease can result from the normal (or, as Holmes says above, "innocent") functioning of the body's own mechanisms for self-protection, with the corollary implication that the doctor's central task is not to eradicate the disease but to understand it.[16] But a host of critics quickly uncovered the more bomb-shell-like nihilism at the root of this self-described "faith." For though Holmes' stance became dominant in America by the 1850s, when he first returned from Paris he entered a strongly polarized situation. An angry New York physician could complain, in 1836, of a terribly morbid house-breaking tendency in the new materialist doctrines arriving from abroad:

The French have departed too much from the method of Sydenham and Hippocrates to make themselves good practitioners. They are tearing down the temple of medicine to lay its foundation anew . . . They lose more in Therapeutics than they gain by morbid anatomy – They are explaining how men die but not how to cure them.[17]

Brandishing that pejorative label "therapeutic nihilist," such critics pointed out that in undercutting the very foundations of allopathic practice this doctrine leaves the doctor, whether he is hopeful or pessimistic, as little more than a passive spectator on scenes of suffering.

While Holmes was probably correct in observing that active interventionist medicine had taken more lives than it had saved and hurt more people than it had helped (and, according to some historians, this remained the case until about 1950, when modern practice became in some cases a true life-saving activity), this was not the sort of message a practical-minded mid-century society, in the throes of a series of epidemics, wanted to hear.[18] This was no time to philosophize: uncontrollable outbreaks of cholera in the 1830s, 1840s, and 1860s, which threatened the lives and the security of all city dwellers, were also seriously threatening the position of all "regular" doctors in America. "Never before had the status of the American medical profession been as low," according to historian Charles Rosenberg. The failure of all heroic uses of laudanum, bleeding, electric shocks, ice water immersions or intravenous saline injections to stop the flow of the 1832 epidemic had done more than any clinical "nihilists" ever could to make doctors and the public aware of the limits of medical power and knowledge. But in this climate of doubt and confusion only "the intellectually ruthless in academic medicine," writes Rosenberg, were able to admit to such powerlessness: average practitioners had to try to do something; certainly their patients were showing a restless willingness to try anything – flocking to various irregular practioners and quacks in greatly increasing numbers.[19]

HOLMES' VERBAL AND CONVERSATIONAL CONTRIBUTIONS TO MEDICAL CHANGE

So, just as the medical "regulars" were attempting to shore up their ruins and establish themselves as specialized experts – with the first national organization, the American Medical Association, founded in 1848 – and just as Holmes was attempting to establish himself within this profession, the thrust of his writings nonetheless tended to tear down that temple, undercutting the distinctions between "regulars" and "irregulars," and highlighting the crisis of all medicine in this liminal moment before the birth of "modern" practice. ("The history of Medicine," he would bluntly assert in later writing, is " . . . a record of self-delusion" [*CW*, vii,172].) On the other hand, Holmes' Parisian training also gave him the experimental spirit to search for new solutions, leading him to discoveries which would point the way out of the impasse of this transitional phase. In the end, the momentum of his movement through several waves of small medical revolutions could turn on the clinical model itself, exposing some of its limits and opening up alternatives that are still being explored today.

The Doctor lived through "the introduction of pathology, histology, bacteriology, applied electricity, organic chemistry and modern surgery," according to Edgar M. Bick, always serving as "the whip which drove back the objectors and allowed the modern scientific concept of medicine to gain entrance."[20] After buying a cherished microscope in Paris, Holmes was years ahead of his time in introducing microscopy and histology in American medicine. With his special interest in optics, he also invented a stereoscope which allowed him to discover the phenomenon of "reflex vision" (the internal generation or transfer of impressions from one retina to the other).[21]

But the Doctor did not have the temperament of a true clinician; neither could he follow the bacteriological revolution of the post-1850 generation and devote himself to concentrated study in the laboratory. This meant that his "nihilist" pronouncements were all the more dizzyingly ungrounded, but also that he was freed to develop his major contributions to medicine, which would be not clinical but speculative: Holmes clearly worked best not in the realm of technology or of empirical study but in the realm of words. The 1843 essay on "The Contagiousness of Puerperal Fever," for example, anticipated the germ theory of disease that would only be proven fifteen years later by microscopists in the French laboratory of Pasteur. And the conclusions Holmes derived from his study – the need for sterilization and antisepsis – would only be scientifically advanced by Lister more than a quarter of a century later. But these breaks from the medical or scientific status quo, like the subversive vision here of "regular" doctors as potential "ministers of evil," arose in large part out of the play of the Doctor's speculative, mythical, and imagistic language rather than out of his clinical analyses of statistics. Indeed Holmes' central breakthrough here – his ability to conceive of a new, heterogenic model of disease transmission, in an important break from the dominant autogenic vision of the day – may well have been related to his theories of and extensive experience with conversation: for a conversationalist it would be only natural to see "communicability" – whether in the transmission of currents of feeling or of germs – as a dynamic interactive process. While an anti-contagionist like Charles Meigs would stress an atomistic individualism in urging that each patient and each illness is unique, a "private pestilence," for a clinician and conversationalist like Holmes disease is seen from a systematic or social perspective, as something that moves between people – thus opening a new focus on the possible movements of infection among larger groups in public life, and also on the dynamics of interactions between individual doctors and their patients. And here, as the Doctor developed, in language that sounded to medical "regulars" like something out of a medieval romance, an "animalcular" (germ) theory to challenge the overwhelming anticontagionism of his age, the effect was not simply "nihilist" destructiveness: by the later 1850s the most knowledgeable physicians came to think along these same lines, suspecting that perhaps cholera was contagious, and realizing that the only effective action to be taken against this epidemic would be quarantines and a public health stress on sanitation.[22]

The Doctor also made a verbal contribution to the chief American medical advance in the nineteenth century: present at the first 1846 experiments with the inhalation of ether to reduce pain in dental surgery, he gave this process its name, "anaesthesia," and then used his prominence as medical spokesman and educator to disseminate news of this humanitarian breakthrough rapidly throughout the country and the world.[23] So, while he was the leader of the Parisian party which "took away the old before there was anything new," and seemed to deny the possibility of any therapeutic medical action, Holmes was also involved in all of the major nineteenth-century discoveries – the concept of disease specificity, germ theory, the theory of infection, antisepsis, and anesthesia – which would overcome some of the major obstacles to and prepare the ground for the later development of new forms of medical intervention which might be less painful and more beneficial to patients.[24]

Holmes' writings and actions also often tended to work against any narrow specialization that might result from too strict an adherence to the clinical approach. Though he joined the AMA at its inception and often spoke for its members as one of the best-known physicians of his day, he certainly did not help the "regulars" to close their ranks or to claim sole possession of the mantle of authority. While the AMA was formed primarily to fight the "irregular" practices of homeopathy, and the Doctor contributed some of the most blistering (and amusing) attacks on the homeopaths – as in his "Homeopathy and its Kindred Delusions" – he could use such attacks to highlight central problems within regular medicine as well: he would, for example, point out that if the homeopaths' infinitesimal doses were bad, based upon a strange idolatry of drugs, at least they were less bad than the much larger doses of equally questionable drugs given by heroic, immoderate "professionals." And Holmes sparked a series of explosive, messy, and ugly debates in 1850 through his well-intentioned but finally muddled attempts, as Dean of the Harvard Medical School, to break tradition and open that exclusive and prestigious campus for the first time to three blacks and one woman student – making the 1850–51 academic year "one of the most controversial" in the Medical School's "two centuries of existence."[25] First, acting upon his ideal of diversity in the conversation of a community, he personally decided to allow Harriot K. Hunt to attend medical lectures, but then was forced to back down when confronted by an overwhelmingly hostile reaction from students, university overseers, and other faculty members. (She was simply asked to withdraw her application.) "Usually . . . the solitary advocate for women," observes Tilton, Holmes "was not prepared" in these fierce arguments "to fight for their rights."[26] Similarly, after the Doctor voted with the faculty majority to accept two black men as regular students, and decided on his own to admit a third – the formidable Martin Delany, already well known as a leading abolitionist, a rival of Frederick Douglass for leadership of the black community, and one of the fathers of black nationalism – the experiment created an immediate uproar among students and many professors. Again, faced with the outbreak of an extremely divisive public controversy, Holmes backed down, accepted the advice of his faculty, and dismissed the blacks after they had completed just one term at Harvard – leaving an intensely disappointed and further disaffected Delany just four months short of his prized degree. While Holmes' initial impulses here put him in the progressive vanguard – very few blacks had previously been admitted to any other American medical schools by this time, and the students Holmes accepted had been denied entry to many other, less prestigious, schools before they applied to the Doctor – he proved unable to stand up for his ideals when confronted by real-world political pressures. If he opened up a crucial conversation at Harvard, he "did not have the moral stamina," as Victor Ullman notes, to carry the day when the talk threatened to erupt into a fight, a power struggle with actual consequences.[27] Especially in his role as a Dean – fearful that the virulent public hostilities aroused in Boston just at this time by the Fugitive Slave Law might spill over into his academic realm and tear it apart – Holmes was not a political crusader. But this failed experiment in diversity at least did make it clear that the Doctor was not on the side of those seeking to protect the medical profession as an exclusive club for white male "regulars" only.[28]

Holmes also frequently lauded the skill and experience of humane nurses, asserting that the ideal practitioner of the future would be half-nurse and half-doctor. In fact, then, he took a lot from the "irregulars," often setting their voices and views in "conversation" with those of the "regulars" – and not always to the latters' advantage. Perhaps taking some cues from traditional lay healers, he filled the therapeutic gap created by clinical skepticism with a strong new emphasis on preventive medicine – promoting the central role of sound nutrition, fresh air, exercise, and amusing diversion from grim labors (a vision which would develop into a late nineteenth-century "gospel of relaxation"). In the same way, he would like what he found about the Thomsonians' populist crusades against specialization, and he felt that, in one way at least, the homeopaths' less painful, infinitesimal dosing was teaching people a fine lesson. Indeed it taught Holmes a few things, for reflection on those meaningless doses led him to early speculation on the "placebo effect," and to later work on the therapeutic importance of the psychological relationship between doctor and patient.

A CONVERSATIONAL APPROACH TO CARING AND CURING

The dynamics of this doctor–patient "conversation" became an area of major concern for Holmes. While Michel Foucault, in his studies of the birth of Parisian clinical approaches to disease and to madness, outlines an overall tendency moving from dialogue to monologue, from holistic, interactional, and verbal methods of diagnosis to purely localized and visual ones, Holmes shows that one could respond to the same clinical insights in just the opposite way: with a renewed attention to dialogue, and to the textures of the patients' spoken language.[29] With the Doctor's shift from curing to caring, verbal interaction in "talking exams" with patients became the main locus of medical operation, central to Holmes' new stress on humane treatment, on the "nursing" elements in medicine, on bedside manner, and in general on the psychological power involved in the therapeutic relationship.

All of this was probably only part of the natural reaction of a writer-doctor against the dry sterility and the pretensions to neutrality of the

new positivist, scientific medicine. Explaining to Agassiz why his
interests in poetry seemed to conflict with his ability to do concentrated physiological or laboratory research, the Doctor unleashed a
powerful unscientific metaphor – a figurative flight apparently taking
off to explore the implications of some actual experiments by Claude
Bernard – that vividly suggests some of the less savory and more
subjective elements at work in the empirical project:

> . . . I told him I liked to follow the workings of another mind through these
> minute teasing investigations, to see a relentless observer get hold of Nature
> and squeeze her until the sweat broke out all over her and Sphincters
> loosened – but I could not bring my own mind to it. He thought I should
> not be the poet he was pleased to consider me if I could.[30]

And the Doctor would find that, if the encounter between an
empirical scientist and his subject develops as an ugly power struggle
and rape, encounters between doctor and patient in a new medical
science based on this same empiricism could also then involve an
impersonal aggressiveness that was only more obvious and repellent
as the "subjects" of its treatment were human. According to
Foucault,

> The appearance of the clinic as a historical fact must be identified . . . by
> the minute but decisive change, whereby the question: 'What is the matter
> with you?', with which the eighteenth-century dialogue between doctor and
> patient began . . . was replaced by that other question: 'Where does it
> hurt?', in which we recognize the operations of the clinic and the principle
> of its entire discourse.[31]

As "what" is replaced by "where" and "you" is replaced by "it,"
verbal articulation gives way to a silent visual articulation of the
body. After the clinical revolution, a rushed, bureaucratic doctor
does not want the patient to tell a generalized, speculative story
about the origins of his problems, but just asks that he or she point
instrumentally to the local site of the symptom. Indeed near-sighted
concern with the objective "it" of the symptom – a particular pain in
a particular part – pushes the subjective "you" of the patient far into
the background. (Apparently German-based medical "nihilists" took
these tendencies even further than the French; valuing signs of illness
much more than his ill patients, one Viennese doctor could refuse
even pain-relieving remedies simply because they might distort the
revered symptoms, scoffing, "Treatment, treatment, that is nothing;
it's the diagnosis that we want.")[32] Though priding themselves on a

dry, neutral rationality, clinicians brought in a method incorporating new forms of institutionalized cruelty: the human standing before this medical gaze is carved up into muscles, nerves, and organs; in this reduced form, he is then manipulated only as a "specimen" for study in the larger cause of science; as part of the contract of this non-reciprocal situation, he is denied expression of what Foucault (in a flight of poetic prose) describes as "the whole dark underside of the body lined with endless unseeing dreams." Shryock too observes that in rejecting so completely all earlier holistic models of illness, the clinicians tended to lose interest in the body's generalized responses, and even in the patient as a person: "The subjective factors in illness . . . received less attention by clinicians during the nineteenth century than in any period before or after."[33]

But the Doctor was well situated to intervene at just these points with important criticisms of the clinical model. For his earliest medical mentor, Dr. James Jackson, had been especially attentive to the psychological importance of bedside manner: "The state of mind should be carefully observed," he says in one of his aphorisms, "and such means employed as will overcome the depressing passion." Holmes had noted the sentences in Jackson's *Advice to the Young Physician* prescribing levity in treatment, "Enter the sick room with grave demeanor. Then your patient will know you feel for him. But leave with a cheerful countenance, so the sick man will think his case is not too serious." (In *Elsie Venner*, Doctor Kittredge, attending to Elsie on her deathbed, goes on at length with similar advice about the handling of all the highly sensitive elements of bedside manner – facial expressions, general verbal tone, the major implications implied by minute changes in the phrasing of questions, and so on – as a warning both to physicians and to other sickroom counselors, such as clergymen.) In Paris, too, young Holmes had been impressed, as he followed Louis on his daily rounds, by that founding clinician's modest attentiveness to his patients.[34]

One of young Holmes' early humorous poems, "The Morning Visit," already clearly reflects his central concern with doctor–patient conversation, and criticizes the grave mechanism and impersonality of an emerging clinical style along exactly the lines of his later attacks on the experimental science of Agassiz:

> If the poor victim needs must be percussed,
> Don't make an anvil of his aching bust;

(Doctors exist within a hundred miles
Who thump a thorax as they'd hammer piles;)
....

So of your questions: don't in mercy try
To pump your patient absolutely dry;
He's not a mollusk squirming on a dish,
You're not Agassiz, and he's not a fish.   (*CW*, xii, 146)

Many of Holmes' later general table-talk discussions about the dynamic of conversation also develop at the same time this more specialized concern with doctor–patient dialogue. The Doctor had a peculiar sensitivity to these issues: he often warns that the daily intercourse between spouses or lovers (talk which opens us into intimacy through a "side-door" rather than through the more formal interactions at the "front-door" of our mental habitation) leaves both parties dangerously vulnerable, and that casual chatter with the wrong acquaintance on the street can thoroughly drain one's batteries. Along these same lines, the Autocrat points out that even a doctor using only words to treat his patients might easily overstep his bounds, becoming a Chillingworth whose cold, scientific curiosity or perhaps motiveless malignity lead him to abuse the great power in the confessor's role.

Taking very seriously the idea that doctors might replace the clergy as confessors in people's intimate lives, Holmes hopes that physicians will not simply repeat the mistakes of those earlier "conversationalists." The Professor takes as his text for the sixth chapter of his table-talk a blunt "clinical" observation made by the Poor Relation to the Divinity Student: "You don't look so dreadful poor in the face as you did a while back. Bloated some, I expect." Finding negative lessons here for all talkers, he goes on at greatest length in admonishments to clerics ("the common talk in sick rooms is of churchyards and sepulchres, and a kind of perpetual vivisection is forever carried on, upon the person of the miserable sufferer"), and to doctors ("'You have killed me,' said a patient once to a physician who had rashly told him he was incurable. He ought to have lived six months, but he was dead in six weeks"). Such lessons come frequently toward the end of *The Professor at the Breakfast-Table*; just as *Elsie Venner* concluded with scenes of talk around a dying Elsie, so much of the talk later in *The Professor* takes place around Little Boston, who is slowly passing away in his sickbed. While the Divinity Student is attacked for regressing into the priest's stance as he takes upon himself the role of a sermonizing Confessor, the Professor applauds the comforting, soft-voiced conversation of nurses and of women in general, who seem to him to reveal a real "genius for ministration" at these trying moments (*CW*, II, 130, 143–44, 274). In effusive passages taking up the era's "feminized" religion of woman, both the Poet and the Professor can even hail the "medicinal balms" of maternal nurses as Protestantism's answer to the Catholic Gospel of merciful Mary, and suggest that we worship and imitate the examples of such women in all of our social conversation: "There are Florence Nightingales of the ballroom, whom nothing can hold back from their errands of mercy" (*CW*, III, 311; II, 178, 140). But when the Professor returns from such sentiment to his more typical tones of skeptical levity, he can offer by way of contrast to such humane medical conversation burlesque portraits of characters like one Doctor Brainey, whose phrenology reflects the first primitive explorations of physiological localism, and whose exams then remind us by their pointed parody how far the dehumanized, non-verbal, clinical style of most doctor–patient interactions is from that humane ideal: "My first customer is a middle-aged man. I look at him, – ask him a question or two, so as to hear him talk. When I have got the hang of him, I ask him to sit down, and proceed to fumble [the bumps on] his skull" (*CW*, II, 201). (Arthur Conan Doyle – remembering the model diagnostic sessions which so impressed him when he was a student in a Scottish medical school – describes classic examples of this empirical, clinical style of medical interview as important influences on his writing. But while Doyle apparently later named his empiricist hero, Doctor Sherlock Holmes, at least partly after our Doctor Holmes, the American Doctor's actual conception of medical conversation was in many ways opposed to the clinical style of the detective. Indeed the Scottish model for Sherlock Holmes' dialogue form – with its impersonal, physicalist gaze and its one-way flow of information – stands as a perfect contrast to Holmes' ideal.)

Doctor Holmes was more able than most contemporary medical men to make these critiques of some clinical tendencies because he always kept one foot at the center of the clinical camp and the other foot quite far outside of it. While he espoused the Parisian theory of revolutionary skepticism, he was – as we have noted – little involved in actual clinical practice: he preferred activity in a multiplicity of other careers to a monastic life devoted to anatomical or statistical

research. As a writer, he was always attracted to the sort of speculation that the empiricists felt they had left behind; he loved to bring
back the clearly mythical, visionary imagery of ancient medical
history as the trigger to new thought; and his own irreducibly figural
language pointed up the metaphoricity of even the most "modern"
medical pronouncements.[35] For him, the clinicians' axiomatic belief
that diseases were objective realities was itself a metaphysical
assumption; the scientific invocation of the "facts" represented a
form of bullying which paralleled that of dogmatic theologians in
disrupting the currents of thought and of conversation. And, again, it
was in the application of his model of conversation to the realm of
medicine that the Doctor made some of his most radical departures
from the clinical approach. Some of these innovative and far-
reaching contributions are only now being recognized: Norman
Cousins, for example, introduces his popular 1979 book, *Anatomy of an
Illness as Perceived by the Patient*, which attacks excessive medical
interventionism with a repetition of the nihilists' arguments about
self-limiting diseases (and another slap at Benjamin Rush for killing
Washington), and which then goes on to advocate as positive steps
more humanitarian doctor–patient relationships and a therapeutic
use of conversation and laughter, with a telling admission: "I have a
missionary zeal about the medical writings of . . . Oliver Wendell
Holmes."[36] (Though Cousins looks to Holmes' therapeutics of
laughter and dialogue as a model for late-twentieth-century medicine, Holmes looked back to quirky carnivalesque writings of the
sixteenth century to find important models for these tendencies in his
own thought: in medicine as in literature, he was deeply influenced
by his reading of the French anti-clerical doctor-writer François
Rabelais. In Rabelais' edition of the *Hippocratic Novel* (1532), celebrated by Sterne and Bakhtin and one of the prized works in
Holmes' personal library, the Doctor would find an early version of
an empirical approach (anticipating clinical methods in its advocacy
of close observation, direct study of each patient, and its debunking
of old superstitions towards the goal of letting nature take its course
in disease: "laisser agir la nature") combined with a strong emphasis
on the therapeutic functions of laughter and relaxation. And the
Doctor was happy to credit the legend that Rabelais had written his
carnivalesque *Pantagruel*, with its bodily medical humor exploding out
of physicalist models, and with the wild verbal digressions of its
learned humor parodying the gravity of all fixed forms of ideological

discourse, for the solace of the sick.) And Holmes himself influenced generations of medical students, both in the nineteenth and twentieth centuries, with his missionary advocacy of the importance of dialogue and humor in a close, caring therapeutic relationship, and with his sometimes wild conjectures about psychosomatic aspects of illness – always approaching the relations of mind and body not through clinical localism but as part of a larger dynamic system, a system which could perhaps be most fruitfully conceived of as itself a form of internal "conversation."

But to explore this complex topic, as the Doctor's medical work here verges on speculations about mental movements and a holistic model of mind–body interactions, we must turn in the next chapter to a more complete history of Holmes' talk-based psychological insights and of his dialogic discussions with the psychiatric and neurological communities.

CHAPTER 7

THE SELF IN CONVERSATION

The Doctor in dialogue with contemporary psychology

> It is not easy, at the best, for two persons talking together to make the most of each other's thoughts, there are so many of them.
> [The company looked as if they wanted an explanation.]
> When John and Thomas, for instance, are talking together, it is natural enough that among the six there should be more or less confusion and misapprehension.
>
> Holmes, *The Autocrat of the Breakfast-Table*

In the field of psychology, too, Holmes began with French models only to go beyond them. But here, even more clearly than in his purely medical pursuits, the Doctor was always working dialogically on both sides of the issues, speaking on both sides of the arguments as they developed in a fast-changing discipline.

First, the Doctor would of course lend his voice to support what historians now describe as the "first great psychiatric revolution," inspired in France by Philippe Pinel, who, as administrator of hospitals for the Revolutionary government, in an early version of the clinical revolt, was said to have set madmen free of their chains, and thus set in motion an international process through which madhouses became asylums, madmen became mental patients, and mad-doctors became psychiatrists. Perhaps because Americans had been introduced early on to the work of an English advocate for such reforms, the Quaker Samuel Tuke, this change met little opposition on this side of the Atlantic. From 1820 to 1860, humane institutional care was the dominant trend in this field as in many others: with its mental hospitals, penitentiaries, almshouses, reformatories, and orphanages, the Jacksonian era was "the age of the asylum." By 1850, the "cult of asylum" had left at least every Northeastern state with its own insane asylum or asylum system.[1]

But, typically, when the Doctor later took up the theories which had been advanced by Pinel's disciples it was not to merge with the medical consensus but to use them for their shock-value when introduced into arguments in another field. His essay "Crime and Automatism," for example, advocates the French reforms suggested by the physiological psychology of Prosper Despine's 1868 *Psychologie Naturelle* (stressing the "rights of man," the "duties of society to criminals," the "limited responsibility" of a criminal for his mechanical "reflex actions," and the consequent value of rehabilitation by moral physicians over any "Truth" judgments or cruel "heroic" punishments from legal men) in order to raise difficult questions which might unsettle the harsh judgments of post-bellum America's increasingly conservative criminologists and justices. We get the sense that the Doctor is here engaged most directly in a pointed dialogue with his son, Oliver Wendell Holmes, Junior – who is at just this time applying himself feverishly to building the principles of judicial "certainty" which will ground his career in law (*CW*, VIII, 322–60).[2]

BREAKING OUT OF THE ASYLUM

At the same time, the Doctor's general questioning of "certainty" in authoritative judgment also led him to express great ambivalence toward the asylum movement. Occasional remarks indicate that he saw advantages to the old-fashioned method of home-care, which would allow a patient the continuation of a more normal "conversation" with family and world. And his burlesque 1861 *Atlantic* piece, "A Visit to the Asylum for Aged and Decayed Punsters," explodes every aspect of the asylum as part of its general carnivalization of all attempts at stable judgment.[3] Parodying the popular journalistic genre of the genteel tourist's visit to a "charitable institution," the Doctor finally shows that the gentleman-narrator is no more able to keep his distance from the contagious low punning contained here than are the asylum officials themselves. Recognizing that post-Pinel reformers had removed a system of external restraints only to try to force patients to internalize that system, while still keeping for themselves as "experts" the powers of moral supervision, judgment, and punishment, Holmes' pun-piece takes great pleasure in imagining a thorough disruption of the new scientific controls. The Superintendent's Rules and Regulations may try as usual to rationalize the day's activities with careful timetables, hoping to dictate even minor details of life, but "squibs and crackers" of wordplay always burst out before the required blessing at mealtime, *Joe Miller's Jest-Book* replaces the Bible for private meditation, and the *Index* of banished puns quickly becomes the most popular reading for inmate groups. Imposed categories break down when it proves impossible to separate "violent and unmanageable Puns and Punsters" from the others; classroom order dissolves when the prize student's name, Josselyn, sets everyone to "jostlin'"; and no Dictionary can clear up all this linguistic confusion – the house scholar erupts in a long series of puns based on both Worcester's and Webster's Dictionaries ("Don't you see that Webster *ers* in the words cent*er* and theat*er*? . . . Besides, Webster is a resurrectionist; he does not allow *u* to rest quietly in the *mould*"). In a mock-trial scene, attempt at judgment is foiled when the remark, "*Capital punishment!*" is mistaken as "*A capital pun is meant.*" And the asylum director has to admit that his own powers have been infected by the local disease. When we find out that his threat of a security cell is itself a "*sell*," a hoax, we realize that even punishment here can become a pun: as he says, "there is no pun-ishment provided . . ."

Though it is only a slight diversion, then, this typical Holmes carnival moment, built almost entirely out of anagrams, riddles, and puns, exploits the explosive potential in these short-circuits inherent in the material aspects of language to make some strong-felt and telling criticisms of the project of psychological reform. A spirit of "levity" can never be contained by an asylum monomania for sober "gravity"; deviant madness can never be contained, controlled, or isolated by a one-sided, normalizing reason: such "heroic" attempts at a cure for insanity will simply never work. What the Doctor most dislikes here – this urge to containment – is symbolized by the architecture of the asylum itself. Recognizing "moral architecture" as the major tool for their sort of rehabilitation, rationalist reformers had designed highly regular, repetitive, symmetrical, and immense institutional structures in the hope that this strong environmental impression would help to reorder and discipline the disturbed minds and lives of the inmates. But thick asylum walls functioned essentially to prevent conversation – whether it was conversation with the external world or with other inmates. With his climactic pun on the word "cell," the Doctor points up and mocks the concept of the thick-walled individual units which had been introduced in these utopian programs as part of the new stress on privacy and isolation.

Tocqueville in 1831 had compared the deathly silence of these asylum corridors to that in the catacombs, while Francis Wayland pointed out that the total individualism enforced in these institutions was contrary to man's essential "sociability." Within these silencing walls, only occasional interviews with the supervising doctor were allowed. And after Pinel or Tuke these infrequent medical conversations had little of the dialogic exchange about them: now talk was used mainly for observation or persuasive punishment, with the patient's part meant to involve only renunciation of his beliefs and of his private language. (Foucault notes, for example, that Leuret, a follower of Pinel, conducted his "dialogues" with inmates only while they were forced to stand in icy showers – which would give them a strong incentive to terminate the discussion quickly by agreeing with the doctor's advice.)[4] It is easy to understand, then, why Holmes would want to test the explosive forces of his hot-blooded "conversation" against the isolating walls of the asylum. And indeed life in his imaginary asylum becomes a sort of mad Tea-Party, with the private languages of diverse punsters forever mixing and colliding in a riotous celebration of at least the attempt at sociability. (We sense some disturbing rumblings below the surface of this Paradise of Punsters, though, as the uncontrollable linguistic disorder here touches upon the national disorder very much on all readers' minds in the month after South Carolina's secession from the Union: "Why is Douglas like the earth? . . . Because he was *flattened out at the polls!*" or "His grandfather was a *seize-Hessian-ist* in the Revolutionary War. By the way, I hear the *freeze-oil* doctrines don't go down at New Bedford.") This irrepressible conversation breaks down the walls usually erected between violent and non-violent inmates, and then dissolves the walls between doctors and patients, in a house-breaking movement which finally bursts out of the asylum architecture altogether. At the climax of this tour, as we approach the innermost cell for solitary confinement, our path gets less and less regular and rational, until we realize suddenly that this building-maze itself works as a sort of Escher-like architectural pun: the prison cell is a *sell*; so, at the interior of the interior of this asylum we find an exterior – the door to this final confining chamber turns out to be the other side of the same one through which we entered, and we open it this time to re-enter the wide world outside.

IN DIALOGUE WITH THE "SOMATIC STYLE"

After the Civil War, when interest shifted from the early-nineteenth-century psychiatry of institutional care (associated with Pinel) to later-nineteenth-century experimental psychology or neurology (associated with Charcot), the Doctor was again at the forefront of developments, keeping up with the "regulars" in their findings in the laboratories while also applying his literary sense to highly "irregular" and influential speculation for the future. If experimental psychology began in this country, according to current histories, in 1869, part of a sudden burst of interest which led to the founding of the *American Journal of Psychological Medicine* in 1870 and then to the establishment of the first professorships in "mental disease" in the early 1870s, it is surprising to find Holmes in his Harvard Phi Beta Kappa address for 1870, *Mechanism in Thought and Morals*, already both summarizing a wide variety of the latest findings in the field and attempting to evaluate the basic assumptions behind such new work. In a mixture of fact, speculation, and humor, the Doctor here set out to analyze in a provocative fashion the base metaphors of an emerging "somatic style" in medical science: the mechanistic images of the "train" of thought (with which he opens) and of the "telegraphic" mind. Asking his audience to wonder how far we can go in explaining "unconscious cerebration" as an automatic, autonomic system, a purely physiological "reflex action of the brain," he begins with a survey of diverse theories: ancient examples are juxtaposed with the new neurological studies of reflex action and brain lesions coming out of the advanced surgery and military psychiatry born during the Civil War; the tentative results of his own Harvard experiments in vision and a sort of electrochemical association are set in conversation with the most advanced French and German clinical discoveries following upon Broca's 1861 localization of the speech function through surgery on the third left frontal convolution of the brain.[5]

But the Doctor could never be simply a univocal advocate for the "latest" developments in any field. So, characteristically, we find that his *Mechanism* study itself builds as a dialogue – exploring ideas that Holmes' preface stresses are "open to discussion . . . and must expect to be disputed" (*CW*, VIII, vi). For while he is happy to use the new scientific models of hereditarian determinism as evidence in his ongoing arguments with theological and judicial visions of judgment, he seems to be much more divided in relation to debates within the medical–neurological community – and indeed self-division becomes the major theme of this work. Introducing his exploration with a motto chosen from his beloved Pascal – "Nous sommes automates autant qu'esprit" – the Doctor notifies us not to expect a linear scientific proof: his main theme will be a post-Calvinist version of the debate between fate and free will. Each of his surveyed research examples, then, serves as another variation on the study's over-arching philosophical theme – the definition of a dialogic model for mental process; each case study speaks its part in the age-old conversation between grave automatism and light *esprit*. (And, at the end here, as at the end of the parallel text, "Jonathan Edwards," the balance finally seems to tilt toward the urges of *esprit* – if only with vaguely Jamesian reminders of the importance of our "will to believe" in our own freedom.)

Throughout this ground-breaking essay, Holmes alternates between neuro-physiological (psychiatric) and verbal-rhetorical (psychoanalytic) conceptions of what he terms the "unconscious." At one moment, he can seem to see all mental motions as originating in one all-powerful, over-determining, "unseen" influence of somatic automatism: "The more we examine the mechanism of thought, the more we shall see that the automatic, unconscious action of the mind enters largely into all its processes" (*CW*, VIII, 284–85). In this mode, the Doctor can push his detailed, engineer's descriptions of the "machinery of consciousness" in "the underground workshop of thought" to the point that the brain seems simply the internalized forerunner of the scientific laboratory or the factory, and gears seem to squeal and smoke as they power all of our mental and emotional "drives" (*CW*, VIII, 274, 278).

But when Holmes then begins to elaborate on the contents of these "unseen" influences, they clearly build out of much more than just involuntary heartbeats, breath-patterns, or nerve and tissue structures: they can also involve eruptions of a whole range of "old prejudices," inherited beliefs, atavistic inhibitions, family and racial archetypes, childhood traumas, repressed sexual or professional desires, multiple personalities, and so on. (Holmes' general references here touch upon speculative topics, some of which he would probe in greater depth in the fictional form of his "medicated" novels: *Elsie Venner*, *A Mortal Antipathy*, and *The Guardian Angel*.) In the same way, when the Doctor turns to just-published research on aphasia (T. W.

Fisher, "Aphasia and the Physiology of Speech," *Boston Medical and Surgical Journal*, 22 September 1870), what interests him is not the possibility of a nuts-and-bolts localization of this or that speech function in this or that lobe of brain-matter; rather, he finds here (through a strange conjunction with the archaic theories of a Dr. Wigan) support for his emerging sense of the mind as a conversational interaction between two mobile, unlocalized, non-physiological, rhetorical "fields" – two tropics of the mind:

> The brain being a double organ, we naturally ask whether we can think with one side of it, as we can see with one eye; whether the two sides commonly work together; whether one side may not be healthy, and the other diseased; and what consequences may follow from these various conditions. This is the subject ingeniously treated by Dr. Wigan in his work on the duality of the mind. He maintains and illustrates by striking facts the independence of the two sides . . .
>   We have a field of vision: have we a field of thought? (*CW,* viii, 267–69)

THE COMMITTEE OF THE SELF

In the first rush of excitement at the discoveries of the new monistic "somatic style," Holmes could write essays on "The Mechanism of Vital Actions," "The Physiology of Walking," and indeed on "The Physiology of Versification." (The "Walking" piece describes the most basic form of human locomotion as a constant struggle against and use of the over-determining physical law of gravity – our forward mobility in life is always an attempt to delay a downward fall; the related study of "Versification" is a curious piece apparently attempting to shock belletrist readers with a quasi-mechanical explanation of prosody as "unconsciously" conditioned by the "organic rhythm" of the pendulum swings of those "time-keepers of the body" – the clockwork beats of our own breath, pulse, or muscular action – which places the Doctor somewhere between the organic poetics of a Whitman and the sometimes scientistic theories which would later emerge to support French experiments in *vers libre* [*CW,* viii, 261–321].)

But in the *Mechanism* lecture verbal action takes precedence over the actions of nerves, organs, or muscles. The most extended and most illuminating passages explore the workings of our "unconscious" not as they are opened up for static examination by the surgical scalpel, but as they manifest themselves dynamically in everyday speech: Holmes traces many examples of people orating, writing, arguing, conversing, or just talking to themselves. The "curious logomachy" of a Bakhtinian dialogue between two quarreling (or explosively conversing) women in a public square becomes our illustration of the "automatic, self-sustaining, continuous flow of thought"; the instant of an orator's inspiration is taken as the model of the "certain form of dialogue" which structures "the unconscious action of the mind" (*CW*, VIII, 290–91, 288). Moments from a few of the Doctor's many medical "talking exams" are brought forward as examples showing the need to study the "repetition compulsion" and other involuntary aspects of memory and language use; a poet's experience in composition makes vivid the related problems of unconscious plagiarism, suggesting that we often automatically repeat commonplaces from a cultural reservoir – or from our own memory bank of traumatic impressions.[6] Citing Descartes on the crucial meanings implied in every turn and slant of our handwriting, the Doctor urges a similarly minute "physiognomical" attention to the vocal inflections, emotional turns, and associations of imagery in diverse speakers. For examples of several talkers show that our minds are not only receivers but also transformers of images. Though the Lockean materialists tell us, writes Holmes, that the brain is "scarred and seamed with infinitesimal hieroglyphics," a reference to Daniel Webster reminds us that this writing need not be purely static or passively fated:

An idea in the brain is not an image carved in a marble slab . . . Shall the initials I carve in bark increase from year to year with the tree? and shall not my recorded thought develop into new forms and relations with the growing brain? Mr. Webster told one of our greatest scholars that he had to change the size of his hat every few years. His head grew larger as his intellect expanded. (*CW*, VIII, 289)

This mental growth often occurs when we are least conscious of it – as Holmes then reminds us with the carnivalesque vision of a drunken judge who "plants his ideas" organically before pronouncing decisions on the bench, by reducing his rational ideas into a sound-formed, internally-rhyming sort of jabberwocky mush, and thus beginning the sort of fertile, "unconscious" internal dialogue in which he becomes his own best interlocutor: "Ye see, I first read a' the pleadings; and then, after letting them wamble in my wame wi' the toddy two or three days, I gie my ain interlocutor" (*CW*, VIII, 290).

In his comical "Asylum" piece, the Doctor uses the verbal play of conversation to burst open closed asylum walls, and in *Mechanism* the serious scientist again calls upon the dialogic forces latent in conversation, this time to break apart the mechanistic laboratory model of the mind. As in the breakfast-table papers, Holmes here recalls his own experiences of social conversation to explain his ideas as to why we forget or mispronounce names, why we associate unlike things, or why we make revealing slips of the tongue.[7] Apparently we are ourselves built of diverse mental layers, always engaged in their own background dialogue, and often the promptings of one unconscious inner voice can interrupt or derail the train of thought in another more conscious one. *Déjà vu* would reflect such a disruption of our inner dialogue – the effect of a time lapse between two halves of the mind. (Already in the *Autocrat*, the Doctor had sought to explain *déjà vu* by speculating on "Dr. Wigan's doctrine of the brain's being a double organ, its hemispheres working together like the two eyes . . . the centre of perception being double" [*CW*, 1, 74]. And his invention of one form of stereoscope grew out of this conception of a radically doubled, decentered viewing subject, as the bifocal illusion of depth here builds out of each viewer's own internal fusion of two slightly different, partial images before his or her two eyes.)

Our dream-life, too, seems always to operate in this way. The *Mechanism* lecture, developing as the Doctor's most extended analysis of the divided self, and of a vision of mental process as fundamentally conversational, finds bipolarity in every element of the human constitution: we have two eyes, which see the world in paired images and paired, complementary colors; we have hearts which work through a collaboration of two interactive ventricles; we have right and left hands which have different talents and orientations; and, most important, we have a bicameral brain, housed in right and left chambers, which struggles toward judgment – like the house divided of our bicameral legislature – through the checks and balances of lengthy and sometimes angry debate.[8] In one of the most cited *Mechanism* passages, Holmes asks us to picture all of the interacting influences in the "underground workshop" of our thoughts – whether of sexual desires or of old prejudices – as the multiple voices of a House committee. And here again the two psychic economies – one involving brilliant, egoistic self-assertion, the other regulated by a more grave, repressive, and all-surveying moral power – are defined as differing internal economies of conversation:

We all have a double, who is wiser and better than we are, and who puts thoughts into our heads, and words into our mouths. Do we not all commune with our own hearts upon our beds? Do we not all divide ourselves, and go to buffets on questions of right and wrong, of wisdom and folly? Who or what is it that resolves the stately parliament of the day, with all its forms and conventionalities and pretences, and the great Me presiding, into the committee of the whole, with Conscience in the chair, that holds its solemn session through the watches of the night? (*CW*, VIII, 289)

In what seems here to suggest a weird mixture of the models of Webster, Whitman, Twain, and Freud, Holmes stages the self as a committee – with the chair always alternating between an "I," a "me," and sometimes even an "other me." And the "double" voice that arises to take the floor in our dream life is not always seen as the grave, introjected parental or social Conscience, returning to bring down any fountains of self-assertive wit. At least one *Mechanism* passage, describing the dialogic turns and interruptions between our conscious and "subconscious" mental layers, envisions a nighttime triumph for the voice of wit:

We not rarely find our personality doubled in our dreams, and do battle with ourselves, unconscious that we are our own antagonists. Dr. Johnson dreamed that he had a contest of wit with an opponent, and got the worst of it: of course he furnished the wit for both. (*CW*, VIII, 282–83)

As it elaborates upon the ramifications of such an approach to the dynamics of conversation, the *Mechanism* study shows Holmes moving along a path very similar to that traveled later by Freud and other American psychologists.[9] Turning away from individual anatomy and mechanistic physiology (and from the dangerous drugs in the medical pharmacy), with an increasing emphasis on the verbal realm and on the verbal interactions between doctor and patient; taking conversation as the laboratory for new sorts of experiments with the "associations" between words and the "associations" between people; following the Scottish rhetoricians and associationists in their internalization of rhetoric, thus using the "topics" of classical rhetoric to describe the mind's workings and to trace the "trains" of thought; and often carrying kinetic physiological models over in these new analyses of the energies and impulses in verbal fields: Holmes' diverse formative influences merged to lead naturally toward many specific insights, and toward a general perspective, that we might term "psychoanalytic."

While the operations of verbal symbols serve for Holmes to introduce a series of challenges to psychiatric orthodoxy, certainly (as we saw in Chapter Three) his vision of the dynamics of conversation is never totally divorced from the electro-dynamics of physics or physiology. His background in mechanistic medicine seems to be what distinguishes Holmes' highly metaphorical writing, and his clinical studies of metaphor, from the figurative writings of many contemporary Romantic symbolists. Concentrating on close analysis of active speech situations and on the material texture of words, he begins very early verbal studies of the involuntary aspects of language use: of the informing power of bodily pulses in our murmuring words; of the mechanical insistence of certain images and associations; of automatism in our compulsions to repeat phrases and to repeat patterns of interpersonal power relationships (as a form of transference) in conversational interactions with a variety of interlocutors. But while the Doctor in Holmes could thus speculate about the "physiology of versification," he finally tends, even in the scientistic *Mechanism* essay, not to see our verbal actions on the model of bodies and nerves but, in a reversal that is still very illuminating, to describe the relations between nerve-centers within the body, or between bodily processes and mental states, or between our various inner voices, on the verbal model of conversation.

As it verges on this tentative new vision based upon conversation, the *Mechanism* lecture becomes a dialogue about dialogue. Holmes is here writing out the drama of his own inner conversation, while also trying to envision some sort of conversation between the two warring aspects of a divided psychological community: Do the "somaticists" and "mentalists" have anything to say to each other? Could some sort of conversational common ground begin to suggest communications between their separate, narrow, professional languages? Of course, the Doctor cannot resolve these issues or force his dialogue toward a single synthetic conclusion – the debate between psychoanalysis and neurobiology is still going on in our day, with perhaps only diminished hopes for mutual comprehension or illumination.[10] But once again this essay finds Holmes attracted to and anticipating a moment of rupture or revolution within a polarized professional community, as he stages the multivoiced dialogue which would begin to erupt when, a few decades later, the paradigm of somatic orthodoxy began to be more broadly challenged.

Holmes ends *Mechanism* with the hope that his rambling speculations will furnish "hints for future study," and in this he was indeed very successful (*CW,* VIII, 309). Because the piece is structured as an unresolved debate, it would later serve as a helpful signpost to an important line of American psychologists who referred back to it as they faced what historian Nathan Hale, in his study of the beginnings of psychoanalysis in America, describes as the ground-breaking "crisis of the somatic style" – a crisis which would begin to emerge in Boston in the late 1870s, and finally erupt with full force in the period between 1895 and 1910.[11]

HOLMES AND THE CRISIS OF THE SOMATIC STYLE

Of course, the 1870 *Mechanism* lecture was given in the inaugural years of the "somatic style" (which Hale sees as having been dominant from 1870 to 1910) – a period in which the anatomy, physiology, and pathology of the "clinical style" became the basis for almost all study in psychiatry. De Broca's localization of the speech function in 1861, and the great numbers of neurological studies in American military psychiatry begun during the Civil War, had strengthened already existing tendencies to stress physical over verbal models, and surgery over doctor–patient conversation as the proper approach to any problem. But Holmes' meditations already begin to uncover some of the fundamental limitations of this neurological model, latent problems which would provoke the turn-of-the-century crisis. The new physicalist localism had led to the first brain surgery, and to the use of applied electricity to provoke reflex actions in nerves (making frogs' legs twitch or jump), but in many ways it was a step backward. The Doctor's wild juxtapositions of theories have the effect of recalling for his listeners many elements of previous psychology that were currently being ignored: the purist focus on anatomy and physiology was threatening to obscure older interests in the "psychosomatic" aspects of illnesses – the relations of mental states to bodily diseases; a near-sighted stress on localization would lead to a disregard for earlier holistic models of the interactive functioning of an organic mind-body system; a deterministic mech-anism challenged our sense of the workings of human volition, or personality, or mind, reducing these to the role of "ghosts" in the machine, mere reflectors of the causal actions of nerves.

Boston seems always to have been the center in America for those who have raised these sorts of questions about the "somatic style."

Hale notes that this city had a long tradition of intellectual generalists willing to formulate exploratory dissent; its lingering Transcendentalism and Unitarianism informed a strong interest in mental powers; like Vienna, it had long supported numerous asylums and elite hospitals for its great numbers of well-to-do, "nervous" invalids; and its many "irregular" medical theorists would also support extended speculation about mind cures (as promoted by Christian Scientists and others), hypnotism, suggestion, and other unusual psychical research. (It is not surprising, then, that Freud was invited to Clark University, in Worcester [near Boston], for his first series of American lectures.) Perhaps Holmes was drawing upon his city's long tradition in his Phi Beta Kappa address on "Mechanism";[12] certainly, with this speech and with his other psychological writings, he played a crucial part in the transmission of this general tendency to later generations in Boston and at Harvard, as he became a key early influence on the theorists of the "Boston School" who led the late-century development of an anti-somatic psychopathology.[13]

The Holmes passage that had the most documentable influence on the course of later psychoanalytical thought comes not in his scientific writings but in the *Autocrat* (though it appeared originally in an 1857–58 Lyceum lecture, "Our Second Selves"). Arising out of the Doctor's central experience of the confusions and misunderstandings inherent in conversation, this famous scene develops through a series of comical turns a conception of the self in its social relations, defined not in its spherical or self-reliant singularity but in its polymorphousness:

It is not easy, at the best, for two persons talking together to make the most of each other's thoughts, there are so many of them.
   [The company looked as if they wanted an explanation.]
   When John and Thomas, for instance, are talking together, it is natural enough that among the six there should be more or less confusion and misapprehension.
   [Our landlady turned pale; – no doubt she thought there was a screw loose in my intellects, – and that involved the probable loss of a boarder . . . A severe-looking person alluded . . . to Falstaff's nine men in buckram. Everybody looked up; I believe the old gentleman opposite was afraid I should seize the carving-knife; at any rate, he slid it to one side, as it were carelessly.]

Before the boarders decide his talk has finally led him over the edge, the Autocrat then quickly outlines his "theory of the three Johns." In any dialogue with Thomas, John will appear as the real John, John's ideal John, and Thomas' ideal John:

Of these, the least important, philosophically speaking, is the one that we have called the real person. No wonder two disputants often get angry, when there are six of them talking and listening all at the same time.

Just as he is making these remarks, though, the Autocrat is forced to confront another unexpected interruption; in the arena of actual table-talk, such "philosophical" points can be quickly countered or forgotten. Here, just as a basket of rare peaches that has been making its way around the table is about to be passed to the Autocrat, a boarder who happens himself to be named John makes "a very unphilosophical application" of the three Johns theory:

[. . . He appropriated the three (peaches) that remained in the basket, remarking that there was just one apiece for him. I convinced him that this practical inference was hasty and illogical, but in the meantime he had eaten the peaches.] (*CW*, 1, 52–54)

Some of the Autocrat's listeners will always react to his psychological or philosophical theories just as the Member of the Haouse does to the Master's statements at the beginning of the *Poet*: the idea of "interviewing oneself" shocks them; the resultant conception of the self as a disorganized committee in debate appears to them a serious threat to any solid sense of personal integrity. But for the literalist John the statement simply provides an opening for a fine retort. His eating the peaches here might remind us of Doctor Johnson's legendary gesture – kicking a rock – in pragmatic refutation of the philosophical ideas of Berkeley. For while the Autocrat here theorizes in monologue about the dialogues between multiple disputing personalities, all of the bracketed boarder reactions during his lecture enact his theme: they remind us how many truly "other" selves are always "talking and listening at the same time" at this breakfast-table; they show us how easily a train of talk can be derailed by wildly divergent private translations; and they suggest the violence that is ever latent in such "misapprehensions" and derailings. John's interruption then makes the classic Holmesian turn, as speculative philosophy meets pragmatic action, verbal inflation meets materialist deflation. If the Autocrat takes more than his share of the conversational pie, John may be on one level "convinced" by the theory, but in the meanwhile he will also be sure to take more than his share of the peaches.

Whimsical as it is, the conversational theory of the self put into play in carnivalesque passages like this from the *Autocrat* and *Mechanism* seems to have served as an important stimulus to later theorists as they began to mount a more serious, intraprofessional challenge to mechanistic models. Silas Weir Mitchell, though based in Philadelphia, had established early in his career a filial relationship with Holmes through an extended correspondence.[14] Although his mechanistic theories about "wear and tear" on the human body developed out of a misunderstanding of some of the Doctor's formulations about "mental fatigue," and his clinical observations were, as Hale notes, "sharply limited by the somatic style" (his omnibus diagnosis for most patients was neurological, involving weakening of the nerves), Mitchell appears to have been prodded by the example of Holmes to explore many issues and therapies which opened into new psychological terrain. Popularizing the concept of an office-based, mentalist psychotherapy, Mitchell centered his practice on the famous "rest cure" that implied some interaction between emotional–mental and physical states and also involved doctor–patient dialogue in a version of Holmes' "talking cure" – though in Mitchell's therapy these dialogues were much more authoritarian than the Doctor's, and were combined with extreme forms of isolating confinement. Fancying himself a doctor-writer very much in the Holmes mold, Mitchell produced psychological novels which, like the Doctor's, allowed him to delve into problems in irregular areas of abnormal psychology (split personalities, thwarted passions, and so on); the main character in his first novel was named Dr. Ezra Wendell. He also found that the writing of semi-fictional "conversation novels" liberated him to make some of his most intriguing speculations. One of these works, *Dr. North and His Friends*, a direct imitation of the *Autocrat* with a central character clearly modeled on Holmes, includes hypothetical asides on our verbal associations, on multiple personalities, on an "unconscious" building out of passional drives, and on anomalous case histories as it shows once again that the operations of the table-talk form can change our conception of the self, and that a very Holmesian humor can rise unexpectedly to unsettle "regular" medical certainties about our faculties of Will and Conscience, and about a unified and responsible personal identity. Dr. North's joke about the dilemma posed by the "crisis of the somatic style" at the turn of the century harks back quite explicitly to the "three Johns" passage in Holmes:

If I am two people, and one can pop up like a jack-in-the-box, I may be six people, and how can I be responsible for the love affairs of five? Have I six consciences?[15]

Morton Prince, the "Boston school" neurologist and leader in the advancement of American psychotherapy, also arrived at his most important contributions through an exploratory interest in the question of multiple personalities, or subconscious selves. And his 1885 argument for the power of human thoughts and feelings, accounting for suggestion and association through a rudimentary description of the activities of a "subconscious" – a foundational step in American psychotherapy – was based not only on recent French and British experiments but also on the still-familiar formulations of Holmes. (Hale remarks that, by 1890, "probably Janet's studies had made Holmes' idea seem relevant.") Prince suggested that words and images might have a seemingly irrational power over us because they operate "deep down in the lower strata of consciousness," in what Holmes had called the "second self" or "other fellow" – and that our mental life might indeed be made up of a number of dissociated "co-conscious" selves. Again, each critic of the "somatic style" stresses, as Holmes had, the linguistic elements in all diagnosis and therapy; for these therapists, the raw data about any disorder are always human speech and behavior – very local trains of thought which speak for general psychological problems. It was this verbal emphasis in Prince's practice and theory that led him to agree with Janet that most psychoneuroses were "mental" diseases of functional origin rather than problems localized in the nerves. After Prince had then been stimulated by the "chaos" that ensued following the breakdown of the somatic explanations for aphasia – ushering in a wave of more "dynamic" interpretations of the speech function – he finally found himself able to join European theorists who were rejecting the very foundations of the earlier, simplistic theories of physiological localization.[16]

But of all the leading American psychologists during the crisis years, William James was closest to the Doctor and his family: he was a lifelong friend of Oliver Wendell Holmes, Jr., and studied medicine under Holmes Senior. Like the Doctor, James began his career as a popularizing writer for the *Atlantic* and, even in his early articles, sought to question the materialist–physiological basis of contemporary theories of mental process. Through the later 1870s and 1880s, his preoccupations would be those that provoked Holmes' *Mechanism* lecture: a redefinition of reflex action, automatism, and the mechanism in mental habit, and a critique of localization theory. Facing this dilemma of determinism, James would try to define a subjectivity that is active rather than reactive, and a form of mental association that could be seen to operate at a level prior to that of the association between neurons. In codifying America's early conception of the unconscious, James pointed out that the discovery of the subconscious seriously upset previous notions of the self as a unity, operating in one-dimensional clarity about its motives. Many of the most powerful moments in his *Principles of Psychology* explore the interactions of the warring selves within us. Though he does not cite Holmes explicitly, as Prince and Mitchell had done, James certainly would have been well aware of the trajectory of the Doctor's medical-literary career, and of his theories of the self as a conversation between multiple personalities, when he began to develop his own elaborate descriptions of the complex inner life of the "social self."[17] In *Over the Teacups*, a retrospective breakfast-table work from 1890, the Doctor was happy to survey the new developments in psychology and find that his former student, William James, was carrying out studies that he himself had thought necessary – especially those about multiple personalities:

I have long ago noticed and referred to the fact of the stratification of the currents of thought in three layers, one over the other. I have recognized that where there are two individuals talking together there are really six personalities engaged in the conversation. But the distinct, separable, independent individualities, taking up conscious life one after the other, are brought out by Mr. James and the authorities to which he refers as I have not elsewhere seen them developed. (*CW*, IV, 166).

Holmes' biographer Tilton notes, about this passage, that, "The doctor's notions about 'I-My-Self & Co.' had passed out of the hands of the speculative poet into those of the scientific investigator."[18]

LAYERS OF THOUGHT

The Doctor himself, though, had used the wide-ranging and multi-vocal form of his other conversational works to probe and develop some of the further ramifications of his initial ideas about multiple personalities. *The Professor* takes as one of its main, recurring topics the study of this layering of our "currents of thought" – again as they manifest themselves in moments of social conversation. In chapter one, the Professor makes clear that the entire table-talk dialogue can be seen as a simulation of this process of one mind engaged in multivoiced thought: Little Boston and John must be allowed to interrupt, because they speak for "other" voices that can surge up within the Professor's train of thought and turn it in unexpected new directions. "Talk," says the Professor, "is only spading up the ground for crops of thought. I can't answer for what will turn up." To censor these rude or wild interruptions would be to limit oneself to the sterile monotone of a royal ego: "Better, I think, the hearty abandonment of oneself to the suggestions of the moment, at the risk of an occasional slip of the tongue . . . than the royal reputation of never saying anything foolish" (*CW,* II, 18). But the subconscious voices released in such slips of the tongue do not intervene simply to speak up for the "lower" impulses of childish whimsy, libidinal desire, or general anti-authoritarianism. Sometimes what erupts from a lower layer is simply a proper name that had been repressed or forgotten (*CW,* I, 134–35); at other moments a hidden voice might suddenly remind us of "an old dead sin laid away in a secret drawer of the soul . . . until it comes to life again and begins to stir in our consciousness" (*CW,* II, 91). Noting that, in parlor conversation, just when he has resolved not to touch upon a particularly hurtful point, it often becomes impossible for him to avoid unexpectedly blurting it out, the Professor wonders if this might be the symptom of some innate "torturing instinct" in his own personality, but finally explains that an unalterable "law of thought" always makes the surface layer of our conscious social talk very vulnerable to powerful undertows or interminglings with other verbal "streams" always flowing "underground" and autonomously as part of the dialogue of voices within us: "A thin film of politeness separates the unspoken and unspeakable current of thought from the stream of conversation. After a time one begins to soak through and mingle with the other" (*CW,* II, 95).

The Professor is full of examples of characters who find they are not in clear control of their speech, as foreign suggestions somehow seem to divert the currents of their thoughts. One young man is so happy with the success of his gallant remarks to a handsome woman that he falls into

a reverie, in which the old thoughts that were always hovering just outside the doors guarded by Common Sense, and watching for a chance to squeeze in, knowing perfectly well they would be ignominiously kicked out again as soon as Common Sense saw them, flocked in pellmell, – misty, fragmentary, vague, half-ashamed of themselves but still shouldering up against his inner consciousness, till it warmed with their contact.

When his castle of reason has been invaded by these naughty but warm-blooded animal-thoughts, he discovers how complex and contradictory the inner life can be: his initial self-gratification leads to the eruption of a series of archaic cultural and literary models that seem quickly to progress (or regress) through a history of male–female relations from complacency to desire to searing scenes of violent savagery that finally turn to threaten the dreamer himself. At this point, the Professor himself admits, "I am frightened when I find into what a labyrinth of human character and feeling I am winding" (*CW*, II, 88–89).

Some of the most intriguing of Holmes' speculations about the layering of our consciousness develop the suggestions in this love-reverie: as romantic desires can rub up against our rational discourse to induce a resurgence of ancestral voices (in this case with fragments from Hercules, John Wilkes, Cadenus, the Bible, and old ballads), so the lower layers are often seen to speak for long-buried "old thoughts." Holmes observes that, at some moments, just as we feel ourselves to be speaking with an Enlightenment freedom, "old prejudices" arising out of local and family history will emerge to "utter their magisterial veto" and block new thought. In such a scene, it is the grave voice of the forebears, and not the personal ego, which has the royal position and power; forcing us to repeat old patterns, this voice often cannot be repressed. In *The Varieties of Religious Experience*, William James had described a "subliminal conciousness" involving "whole systems of underground life, in the shape of memories of a painful sort which lead a parasitic existence buried outside of the primary fields of consciousness," and in 1890 he would make the important observation that the "subconscious selves" psychologists found speaking for these painful memories often seemed to possess social and cultural characteristics.[19] Such a vision was already central to Holmes' mid-century conception of mental layers in our "underground work-shop"; if the self exists as a conversation among diverse voices, this conversation often enacts an internal battle between rival cultural stereotypes. In the Doctor's view, each of our conversations also tends to reenact the dynamics of our specific family history, as we work out our emotional relationships to parental figures, or find ourselves unable to shake the "old prejudices" of ancestors from past centuries.

Chapter two of *The Professor* introduces the concept of thought as a conversation between at least three voices or mental layers that will preoccupy much of the ensuing talk, beginning with the blunt clarity of schematic assertion, but then moving into a series of loaded metaphorical elaborations that expose some of the fearful uncertainties inherent in this vision. First, a humorous scene of complex social chatter (like the "three Johns" passage from the *Autocrat*) leads to explicit semi-scientific characterizations of the three layers (which here sound very close to ego, id, and superego):

My thoughts flow in layers or strata, at least three deep. I follow a slow person's talk, and keep a perfectly clear under-current of my own beneath it. Under both runs obscurely a consciousness belonging to a third train of reflections, independent of the two others . . .

I observe that a deep layer of thought sometimes makes itself felt through the superincumbent strata, thus: – The usual single or double currents shall flow on, but there shall be an influence blending with them, disturbing them in an obscure way, until all at once I say, – Oh, there! I knew there was something troubling me, – and the thought which had been working through comes up to the surface clear, definite, and articulates itself, – a disagreeable duty, perhaps, or an unpleasant recollection.

Then, to explore this unadorned assertion, the Professor launches into two resonant extended metaphors which, while they seem to celebrate the liberating play of these multiple layers, also suggest grave limitations implied by this conception. Initially, we are led into a carnival scene, in which a three-ring circus is taken as the analogy for the three-layered mind:

. . . we may consider the mind, as it moves among thoughts or events, like a circus-rider whirling round with a great troop of horses. He can mount a fact or an idea, and guide it more or less completely, but he cannot stop it. So . . . he can stride two or three thoughts at once, but not break their steady walk, trot, or gallop. He can only take his foot from the saddle of one thought and put it on that of another.

– What is the saddle of a thought? Why, a word, of course. –

Twenty years after you have dismissed a thought, it suddenly wedges up to you through the press, as if it had been steadily galloping round and round all that time without a rider.

Once again our buried thoughts are imaged as animals: like the Common Sense castle-guard in the previously cited passage who finds vague bestial forms "shouldering up" to him, the rider here finds that even horses once dismissed will eventually come back "wedging up" to him. Emerson had worried that, "Things are in the saddle, and ride mankind," but Holmes seems to find a childlike joy in the idea that these Dionysian horses can really master their "rider." Horses conjure up a primal, sub-rational, bodily power; they provide the motive force for any movement in this circus, while the mind serves only as a guide. Indeed, these mobile animals can continue their automatic circulation even without a rider – as headless horses. What we see as willed thought, then, is actually but a series of momentary clown-like tricks (in a very limited, primitive sort of gymnastic act) done on the square backs of powerful, unstoppable, autonomous brutes.

The circus-scene offers an exhilarating liberation when its carnivalization of judgment is read in its dialogic context as an attack on Lockean psychology: this playful scene muddles and upsets any hope of keeping separate mental faculties neatly confined and compartmentalized; it mocks the basic Lockean desire to protect a clear rationality from all contaminating false associations. And the Professor makes such an attack explicit when he then offers, as a foil to the circus scene, a biting satire of academic modes of knowledge:

[One of this class of philosophers] exhibits an unfortunate truth, bandaged up so that it cannot stir hand or foot, – as helpless, apparently, and unable to take care of itself, as an Egyptian mummy. He then proceeds, with the air and method of a master, to take off the bandages. Nothing can be neater than the way in which he does it. But as he takes off layer after layer, the truth seems to grow smaller and smaller, and some of its outlines begin to look like something we have seen before. At last, when he has got them all off, and the truth struts out naked, we recognize it as a diminutive and familiar acquaintance whom we have known in the streets all our lives. The fact is, the philosopher has coaxed the truth into his study and put all those bandages on; of course it is not very hard for him to take them off. (*CW*, ii, 37–39)

The logical scientist works not with live, moving horses but with dead, tamed, static effigies; he avoids the emergence of new thought by working only with preconceived "truths"; he replaces the colorful, playful circus as an arena of discovery with the seriousness of an indoor study; instead of multi-leveled conversation, he gives us the monological humbug of a lecture; and, most relevant here, this sort of philosopher, in his obsession with the fixing of solid, immobile, "naked" truths, wants to do away with the multiple layerings which for Holmes constitute the true materials of active thought. In his own speculations as a psychologist, the Doctor would want to leave behind the scene of this sort of morbid, localizing anatomy class, as he begins to articulate a more dynamic, functional vision of the interactions of diverse forces in our conscious and subconscious mental life.

If *The Professor* concentrates on Holmes' conception of these inter-active mental layers – usually seen as a tripartite structure – *The Poet*, the Doctor's next table-talk work, focusses on description of the divided self – which is most often seen to function as a bipolar internal dialogue – as it attempts to confront the problems of judgment raised by this new approach to the mind's workings. The opening scene in the latter work, which we have already analyzed closely in Chapter Three of this study, finds the Member of the Haouse exploding in hysterical rage about lower-class revolutionaries coming to overthrow the rich, about government buildings being disordered and burned, about powder-kegs ready to ignite, and about a nightmare of his own hat being knocked off in a public humiliation – all of these outbursts reflecting an acute insight into some of the most unsettling tendencies inherent in psychological applications of the conversation model. The new sort of knowledge, which mocks the older academic vision of a mummified, rational "Truth," can also threaten to dethrone the ruling "ego," to under-mine the solid sense of a single, coherent self. What had triggered the Member here, after all, was simply the Master's introductory refer-ence to what had also been the point of departure for the Autocrat's dialogues: a casual reference to the idea of internal dialogue implied in the founding motto, "Every man his own Boswell":

The idea of a man's "interviewing" himself *is* rather odd, to be sure. But then that is what we are all of us doing every day. I talk half the time to find out my own thoughts, as a schoolboy turns his pockets inside out to see what is in them. (*CW*, III, 1)

To open out one's pockets is a far cry from burning down a State House – but then all of this converse has put the Member in a state of dream-like suggestibility. And in fact his wild dreams of congressional chaos work as the best illustrations of the Master's point: in our dreams as in our talk, we discover unknown new ideas, new fears and new drives, as we open ourselves to the multiple voices of interior dialogue.

But the table-talk in *The Poet* keeps returning to the Member's questions: if the self is a disorganized committee in debate, how can we ever arrive at a clear judgment on any issue? The Master interrupts a discussion of criminology with the observation that his self-division makes it hard for him to arrive at a final decision: "One side of me loves and hates; the other side of me judges, say rather pleads and suspends judgment" (*CW*, III, 227). He also warns That Boy, in a characteristic comment discussed earlier, that we should not be too hasty in evaluating people we meet; taking out a nickel, he prods the youth to observe that it can be read in two ways – "there ain't but one, but it's got two sides to it with different reading" – before finally observing that, indeed, there are "two sides to every-body, as there are to that piece of money" (*CW*, III, 81). Later, the Master admits that he often feels two voices within him arguing violently about what he should say in his parlor-room talk – "you know there are two of us, right and left, like a pair of shoes" – and that one of them (the "other I") can be impudent and abusive in its attacks on the refinement of the other:

That is a rather sensible fellow, that other chap we talk with, but an impudent whelp. I never got such abuse from any blackguard in my life as I have from that No. 2 of me, the one that answers the other's questions and makes the comments, and does what in demotic phrase is called the "sarsing."

And at this the Poet intervenes, to remark that he too often finds it hard to know how to value his own thoughts or the drafts of his poems, because his royal self in the Solomonic seat of judgment is always doubled by its alter ego the jester:

I have just such a fellow always with me, as wise as Solomon, if I would only heed him; but as insolent as Shimei, cursing, and throwing stones and dirt, and behaving as if he had the traditions of the "ape-like human being" born with him rather than civilized instincts. One does not have to be a king to know what it is to keep a king's jester. (*CW*, III, 206–07)

For Holmes, as for Freud, the new vision of the self is often described by analogy to a kingly court, and the story here is usually of a dethroning. But both the Master and the Poet seem surprisingly respectful of the bullying, jesting, youthful, lower-class, and animal-like "other fellows" who can force these revolts from within the civilized house of the "I." With their demotic "sarsing" and stone-throwing, these almost non-verbal elements can surge up to challenge and redirect the currents of verbal politeness and rationality, thus giving voice to a clownish levity always latent as a parasite within the court-life of this castle, always waiting in the wings to undercut the gravity of our magisterial pretensions.

Though they are both confirmed monologists, the Master and the Poet both also admit that their inner life operates as a dialogue. And the Master, though he often tries to fill the role of a Dr. Johnson and speak as an autocratic imperial self, in fact urges the benefits of having been soundly defeated at one point in the breakfast-table argument. In social conversation, another person, interrupting our stream of talk, can serve the same function as the jester "Shimei" within:

> Besides, there is a very curious sense of satisfaction in getting a fair chance to sneer at ourselves and scoff at our own pretensions. The first person of our dual consciousness has been smirking and rubbing his hands and felicitating himself on his innumerable superiorities, until we have grown a little tired of him. Then, when the other fellow, the critic, the cynic, the Shimei, who has been quiet, letting self-love and self-glorification have their perfect work, opens fire upon the first half of our personality and overwhelms it with that wonderful vocabulary of abuse of which he is the unrivalled master, there is no denying that he enjoys it immensely; and he is ourself for the moment, or at least the chief portion of ourself (the other half semi-retiring into a dim corner of semi-consciousness and cowering under the storm of sneers and contumely . . .), as, I say, the abusive fellow is the chief part of us for the time, and *he* likes to exercise his slanderous vocabulary, *we* on the whole enjoy a brief season of self-deprecation and self-scolding very heartily. (*CW*, III, 243)

Unlike the Member, the Master seems to have a strange relish for such self-humiliation, perhaps because he defines it as only a "brief season" of carnival revolt from the regular pattern, a way of releasing the "underground" forces in the workshop for the sort of fresh air and muscular "exercise" that can only strengthen what had become "tired" in the larger system. Certainly this kind of a holiday could promise a revitalization for the over-refined vocabulary of the "first person."

But Holmes himself was not always so sanguine about what might be released in such moments. His notes for *The Poet* show that he was considering as a talk topic his sense of being "Afraid of my own personality." And a letter to Mitchell from this period goes on at length about his means of dealing with "such a vicious and kicking brain as I have described my will as bestriding."[20] The Doctor knew from personal experience that, when the two halves of the walnut-shaped brain (as it is described in the *Mechanism* lecture) communicate with each other, the conversation is often as interruptive and multivoiced as any of his boardinghouse table-talks. Indeed, when these voices are interiorized – as they become ingrown, somatized – the debate can become even more charged, ill-mannered, and perhaps uncontrollable.

A crucial passage from Holmes' "Autobiographical Notes," mentioned earlier in another light, traces the roots of this conception of the dialogic self in his own personal history: the theory may have been informed by young Oliver's earliest experiences as a child in a divided household. Remembering himself as a boy torn and ambivalent in the face of an everyday domestic conversation always structured as a debate between the opposed voices of maternal "levity" and paternal "gravity," Holmes speculates that he then inevitably came to internalize the debate of these conflicting family voices as the base structure of his later social life, his literary life, and indeed of his dream life. And again he notes that the ongoing inner conversations of such a "double personality" are not always marked by parlor-room politeness.

Thus, though fond of society at times, I have always been good company to myself, either by day or night. The "I" and "me" of my double personality keep up endless dialogues . . . sometimes using very harsh language to each other. One of them, I am sorry to say, is very apt to be abusive and to treat the other like an idiot, with expressions which, if uttered, would make a very bad figure in these pages. (*AN*, 43)

The roots of Holmes' sense of the self as a bipolar household dialogue may be located not only in his childhood but also in his later life – in his busy participation in a series of Boston clubs and parties. The great diversity of the social occasions on Holmes' calendar would call for the sort of grace that Byron celebrated as "mobility": the ability to transform oneself like a chameleon to suit a great variety of interlocutors in a great variety of settings. The social whirl seems to impose its own fragmentation of the personality; performers on the social stage must develop a large repertoire of roles and learn to speak in many voices; they must develop the consciousness of what William James calls a "social self" – and this is just what Holmes is describing in the "three Johns" passage and his other psychological speculations arising out of his experiences of a life in talk.

In the field of psychology as in medicine, then, the Doctor's stress on the conversation form put him in what might best be called a conversational relationship with professional orthodoxy, as he debated the discipline's assumptions and pushed its limits restlessly through successive developments over a good part of the nineteenth century. And as his arguments are often advanced in conversational form, so his own speculative theories often involve applications of the base model of conversation. Dialogue can serve negatively (like the "therapeutic nihilism" of the medical clinic) to help challenge and demolish antiquated notions, but, especially in psychology, conversation can also serve as the basis for more positive advances. We have seen how, for Holmes, the talk form could stimulate exploratory new descriptions of the mind's functioning; talk was also, though, central to his hopes for a new, more effective mental therapy.

THE "TALKING CURE": OPENING AN INTERCOURSE WITH THE WORLD

In Part Three we will take a closer look at Doctor Holmes' central reliance upon doctor–patient dialogue in his actual medical practice, as we trace reports on the progress of his "talking exams" with Melville and Hawthorne. But we might note here that even in his literary works the basic plot often revolves around a doctor's attempts to engage other suffering characters in diagnostic and therapeutic conversation. As Van Wyck Brooks noted, Holmes' medical "mission" was to bring people out in talk, to get them quite literally to ex-press the hidden or repressed "layers" of their thoughts.[21] After a long discussion of somatization (explaining how one can read people's unverbalized thoughts in their actions or "body language"), the Autocrat bursts out with an expression of what we have seen as perhaps his most basic belief:

Sometimes it becomes almost a physical necessity to talk out what is in the mind . . . It is very bad to have thoughts and feelings, which were meant to come out in talk, *strike in*, as they say of some complaints that ought to show outwardly. (*CW*, 1, 134)

This belief is put to a severe test in the Doctor's first "medicated

novel," *Elsie Venner*, but finally it seems that the disease of Elsie's mind
has its source in an early-life disruption of full familial contact and
communication, and the only possible hope for her care or cure is
contact with a doctor-friend whose conversational abilities and
bedside manner can help her to "shape her inner life in words" and
at least to try to open her heart into "the community of human
affections" (*CW*, v, 341–42, 418). A difficult, serious case like this
reminds us that not every "talking exam" can be an instant "talking
cure"; Holmes did not share the early optimism of William James,
who could write of the psychologists' new therapies: "Alter or abolish
by suggestion these unconscious memories, and the patient immediately gets well."[22] But even if Elsie Venner's case reminds us that talk
is not always an instant therapy, the novel nonetheless concludes by
observing a series of verbal counselors at Elsie's deathbed – comparing the effectiveness of the talk modes of various religious figures,
the sensitive nurse Helen, and Doctor Kittredge, whose clinical focus
on observing and managing the disease goes along with a counseling
relationship with a patient he knows will soon die – stressing the
value of intimate conversational sessions for their role in diagnosis
(based upon the textures, rhythms, and imagery of the patient's story)
and in all humane care.

The overall plot of *The Professor* parallels the turns in the Doctor's
life at the end of the 1850s, as it narrates the Professor's movement
away from medicine towards a talk-based psychology. The only
ongoing story that carries us through this breakfast-table chatter
involves the Professor's many attempts to get at the "secrets" of
several other boarders – especially those of Little Boston and the
Young Woman. Part psychoanalyst and part detective, he is always
going through people's drawers and diaries, and snooping in their
rooms – often begging questions about the sort of cold, prying
scientific curiosity that tends to trespass upon all privacy – but his
main access to secrets comes through conversation. Talk is his
"dynamometer," he tells us, as he tests for nervous or explosive
reactions to probing remarks which are explicitly used as catalysts in
these quasi-chemical "experiments" (CW, ii, 93, 96). Surveying
people's belongings, he is very aware that everyday objects can carry
the most resonant mysteries, and the strongly material aspect of his
verbal emphasis is revealed in his several close-up analyses of his
subjects' dialects, handwriting, and freeform doodles. The shift to a
more psychological, interior concern here leads to a change in

conversational mode at the book's end: as we move away from the more public breakfast-table to one sick man's room (the bedroom of a dying man, Little Boston), we also move from multivoiced repartee to a series of more intimate, one-on-one encounters. Then, in these deathbed scenes, the Professor only pretends to take the patient's pulse while he surveys the room for symptomatic evidence: his new science puts the doctor at the bedside rather than in the clinic, and leads him to neglect physiological–anatomical data while stressing signs of mental life. Recognizing that he has no "heroic" power to save the man's life, he turns to the psychological aspects of the case, and begins extended analysis of the broken sentences and free associations of the patient's self-expression. The heightened confessional tone of these final moments speaks for Holmes' serious hope that new conversation-oriented doctors might take over the minister's role to become confessors listening to people's private problems. Like *Elsie Venner*, this table-talk book then concludes with a comparative discussion of the bedside manner of clergymen, female nurses, and the coldly curious Professor.

The alliance of a detached, scientific doctor and a loving female nurse that is highlighted in *Elsie Venner* and *The Professor* also emerges as the final saving formula in a late novelistic case study by Holmes, *A Mortal Antipathy*, which follows the curing of a young man forced into total isolation by his incapacitating fear of women. All of the characters in this "medicated novel" share the same goal: to "worm" the secret out of this beautiful hermit, to draw him out in conversation. Whether they are nasty small-town gossips, prying interview journalists, or flirtatious young girls, each of the novel's characters then work out of the central Holmesian impulse most clearly expressed by the town's Dr. Butts:

He could not look upon this young man, living a life of unwholesome solitude, without a natural desire to do all that his science and his knowledge of human nature could help him to do towards bringing him into healthy relations with the world about him. (*CW*, VIII, 87)

With his increasing stress on these uses of the "talking exam," Holmes might well be taken as an early voice in the movement toward what Philip Rieff terms the modern "therapeutic culture." But the examples above show that the main goal of the Doctor's medical conversations was just the opposite of the "therapeutic" involution feared by Rieff. Unlike the conversations of twentieth-

century psychoanalysis which, according to Rieff, have come to
sanction a narcissistic self-scrutiny that isolates the patient in an
endless fascination with the labyrinthine nuances of his private
problem, talk here was meant to bring the patient out of morbid
introspection, promoting the dying eighteenth-century ideal of the
"Public Man" against the tendencies of an increasingly privatized
mid-century society.[23]

Part Three of this study elaborates upon these general conversational
goals. Exploring the cultural, familial, and psychological sources of
the Doctor's sense of conversation as a dynamic bipolar alternation
between the voices of gravity and levity (Chapter Eight), or between
impulses to house-keeping and house-breaking (Chapter Nine), this
analysis of "The Two Poles of Conversation" attempts to develop a
fuller sense of what is involved for Holmes in these two "tropics of
thought." Then, tracing the Doctor's "talking exams" with
Hawthorne and Melville, and studying his literary works in their
"conversation" with grave house-keeping plots and images in Sterne,
Dickens, Hawthorne, and Melville, the following chapters show how
the explosive tendencies in Holmes' characteristic talk form could be
seen to operate as a force bringing a speaker, an interlocutor, a
patient, or a reader out of his or her walled-in self – helping, in
Hawthorne's phrase, to re-open an intercourse with the world.

The two poles of conversation

CHAPTER 8

THE BIPOLAR DYNAMICS OF HOLMES'
HOUSEHOLD DIALOGUES
Levity and Gravity

Just as the eye seeks to refresh itself by resting on neutral tints
after looking at brilliant colors, the mind turns from the glare of
intellectual brilliancy to the solace of gentle dulness; the tranquillizing green of the sweet human qualities, which do not
make us shade our eyes like the spangles of conversational
gymnasts and *figurantes*.
>   Holmes, *Mechanism in Thought and Morals*

What is this transient upward movement, which gives us the
glitter and the rainbow, to that unsleeping, all-present force of
gravity?   Holmes, *The Professor at the Breakfast-Table*

In an early review of what he rightly sensed would be Holmes' major
literary work, *The Autocrat of the Breakfast-Table,* James Russell Lowell
celebrated the dizzying effects of the many turns, shifts, and clashes
basic to the Doctor's strange new verbal form as a "universal
Catherine-wheeling of fun and fancy." And indeed initially Holmes'
table-talk does often seem to spin wildly out of control, sending out
sparks and speeches in all directions, spiralling far from any central
point or voice with an irrepressible centrifugal force, dispersing any
attempt at sober signification into a carnival of jabberwocky mush,
so that even more private moments of calm internal discussion
develop along the lines of a three-ring circus – or of the unending,
disorderly proceedings of a multivoiced committee in debate. It may
be, Lowell continues, that with his conversational free-play Holmes
has invented a "new kind of rocket" that can "*stay up* against all laws
of gravity."

After a more extended look, though, we begin to discern the
outlines of repeating patterns which structure the seeming disorder
of this dialogic free flight. First of all, the Doctor's vision is always
resolutely bipolar: if his dialogues take the form of a disorderly
congressional committee in debate, for Holmes that committee

always continues a bipolar argument between two parties in a bicameral legislature, which itself stands as a figure of the bicameral mind; the mind is then related to a physiological system which is itself doubled in all of its functions and parts; and if a particular verbal exchange sends out sparks like a Roman Candle, for Holmes that is the successful result of a charged electrodynamic contact between two voices representing two opposed poles of thought: "I have often noticed," the Autocrat tells us, in one of his primary examples, "that a hopelessly dull discourse acts *inductively*, as electricians would say, in developing strong mental currents" (*CW*, 1, 29). The "alternating currents" driving the two-stroke engine of this sort of antithetical conversation are sparked, at each particular moment of contact or interruption, by confrontations between two "polarized" discourses. Though his boardinghouse may at times seem to be exploding in a chaotic, multivoiced free-for-all, then, the turns of talk at Holmes' table are always structured by an underlying logic of continual alternation between opposed voices and stances. In fact Holmes' dialogues most often develop as a series of bipolar couplings: over and over again, "brilliance" meets "dullness," "genius" converses with "character," a rising rhetoric of enthusiasm confronts a deflating scepticism, powerful centrifugal tendencies must always work with and against the resistances of ever-present centripetal force, and so on. And many of these moments of antithetical interchange can be seen to develop as particular versions of or variations upon one dynamic coupling which becomes paradigmatic in Holmes' work: the bipolar dialogue between the voices of "levity" and "gravity."

The Autocrat provides a clarifying introduction to Holmes' sense of the workings of such a dynamic levity–gravity system in conversation when his most enthusiastic speech rising in flights of fancy to describe "truly intellectual" table-talk as a "carnival-shower" of "explosive wit" is brought down by one of John's typically blunt interruptions. Here he finally recognizes that at this table, as in the natural world, the movements of life and thought are organized by a law of continual alternation: conversational brilliance must always meet its match in nonverbal dullness; high-flying levity must always coexist with and confront the downward forces of gravity. Opening a speculative dialogue between rhetorical theory and natural science, exploring possible parallels between the movements of our words in talk and the movements of water, the Autocrat then observes that, just as surely as the "mighty fountain-column springs into the air," so must it soon be pulled back down to the level of the sea (*CW*, 1, 64–65). Like the comic conversation in the "Laughing Gas" chapter of *Mary Poppins* that makes Uncle Albert's tea-table literally fly up into the air – until serious thoughts suddenly intrude to bring it crashing back down to the ground – the light, winged talk at the Autocrat's breakfast-table continues to turn through successive confrontations with the downward force of weightier voices.[1] And by the end of his review of the *Autocrat*, Lowell comes to similar recognitions: the Doctor's "Catherine-wheeling" wit is not purely light; its high-flying brilliance does not simply defy "all laws of gravity," but in fact emerges out of a "perpetual" interplay with many "grave" issues in contemporary thought; its "wanton zigzags" and digressive tacks work in relation to "more regular" thought and to deeper gravitational patterns guiding the stars and sea-tides; finally, then, this is a "humor whose base is seriousness." To understand Holmes' "levity," Lowell tells us, we must come to understand it in its constant cohabitation with these forces of "gravity."[2]

LEVITY AND GRAVITY IN NINETEENTH-CENTURY THOUGHT: A STERNE TRADITION IN AMERICA

Such notions about the dynamic interrelations between "levity" and "gravity" – based upon such seemingly whimsical play upon the multiple resonances of each of these key terms – were certainly not unique to Lowell and Holmes. Indeed they reflect a habit of thought widely shared in the culture of Victorian America – a habit of thought especially evident and important as it was explored as a literary topos by a long line of self-conscious English and American writers throughout the nineteenth century. But this overarching bipolar vision of life and thought as a dynamic system, a continual struggle between the opposing, quasi-physical forces of "levity" and "gravity," was not confined in application only to the realm of literature. For many nineteenth-century Americans, "levity" and "gravity" were key terms expressing connections between the era's dominant conceptions in literature, science, and theology. In his literary and his scientific writings, Holmes both works with and plays upon this widely-shared habit of Victorian thought; his table-talk writings, structured as perpetual reenactments of the oppositions basic to the "levity"–"gravity" system, both reflect and reflect upon this paradigm basic to the mid-century vision.

Joel Black's "The Second Fall" provides a rich, helpful, schematic overview of the many possible applications of this nexus of thought in nineteenth-century culture, offering comprehensive historical research into the terms "gravity" and "levity" as they have been developed through long traditions of use as key figures in rhetorical theory, theology, and natural science. Though Black's study began as an inquiry into the workings of Thomas Pynchon's *Gravity's Rainbow*, and though he then locates the roots of this system of thought in theories of classical rhetoric and ancient science, his analysis finally concentrates on the period of the fullest development of such thinking: the late eighteenth and early nineteenth centuries, that awkward transitional moment in which Enlightenment Reason and science collided or merged with the alternative models of an early Romanticism. Surveying Romantic Irony in a wide range of litera- ture produced in England and in Germany in this era, Black finds that these works often develop as bipolar struggles between two interrelated forces or voices: inflation confronts deflation, disorder confronts order, enthusiasm confronts criticism, and, in what is for Black the most fundamental opposition, levity confronts gravity. In Sterne, Byron, Jean-Paul Richter, and Friedrich Schlegel, Black sees the levity–gravity interaction operating on at least three levels, elaborating a complex system of thought which describes relations between the seemingly diverse fields of literature, science, and theology.[3] And this tradition of thought continued to develop in Victorian America, so that even in Holmes' world "levity" and "gravity" would serve as key terms defining the poles of ongoing debates in all three fields.

In theology, the moral seriousness of the "grave" vision is founded on a universalizing application of the doctrine of the Fall – levity here would come to be associated with irresponsible deviations from an orthodox morality based upon the sense of Man's original sin. But the serious, realistic worldview of modern physical science is also founded on its own law of the fall: a law of nature, the law of gravity. In a post-Newtonian world obsessed with the idea that a single law of gravitation might control all natural motions, levity or "levitation" would involve rising movements and urges toward physical lightness which work against the inexorable forces making us heavy, pulling things downward. (In mid-nineteenth-century America, scientists were still debating the problems raised by studies like William Whewell's "Demonstration that All Matter is Heavy," while an alternative scientific tradition continued to try to define a second force of "levitation" that would counterbalance the monolithic system of gravity. Schopenhauer, for example, apparently drew inspiration from a school of nineteenth-century plant physiology that found a variable and disorganized "vitality" in organic growth and opposed this to the invariable determinism of inorganic gravity. And Priestley, working out of and against Lavoisier's researches on oxygen, searched for a "levitative fluid" he called "phlogistan." This "nitrous air," a light "laughing gas" and an anesthetic, was seen not as a positive element but as a negative quantity, a principle of combustion, and an inversion of gravity – offering once again the vision of a natural "subtance which might possess levity.")[4] A "grave" minister in the era could, though, find that the new science of gravity meshed well with the theology of the Fall, and might then invoke an over-arching vision of "gravity" by taking up the position of post-Newtonian physical science – the sense that all material things are heavy and tend downwards – as simply a worldly illustration of the moral–ethical lessons to be drawn from man's original Fall. For minds educated in both the "gravity" of Protestant theology and the "gravity" of Newtonian science, the apple of Adam's Fall could often be analogically associated with the apple said to have fallen at Newton's feet. To take a founding American example very much on Doctor Holmes' mind: Jonathan Edwards, whose powerful formulations brought Newtonian physics to bear upon the theology of the Fall, identifies innate sin with the physical weight of the human body in its state of constant peril, defining a universe of Calvinist gravity which can offer no counterbalancing sense of any physical or spiritual forces for "levity," no upward movement to lighten the heavy Bunyan-like "burthen" upon mortal flesh :

Your wickedness makes you as it were heavy as lead, and to tend with great weight and pressure towards hell; and if God should let you go, you would immediately sink and swiftly descend and plunge into the bottomless gulf.[5]

The intellectual oppositions embodied in the levity–gravity system also affect the dynamics of literary form, and writers in this tradition, interested in exploring this habit of thought – especially those who, like the Doctor, come out of a background in traditional theology or have a strong training in contemporary science – often seek to counterbalance or to test perceived problems in the models of theological or scientific gravity through their experiments in verbal modes of "levity." In the rhetorical tradition, the voice of "gravity" requires a heavy seriousness of tone versus light frivolity or "levity," and prescribes a straightforward narrative form proceeding as directly as possible to the point or moral or conclusion. "Levity" in the verbal realm involves all the literary elements that work against a grave, scholarly-clerical, straightforward narration: strong urges to digression which resist the moralist's or theologian's emphasis on any structuring end; an uncontrolled metaphoricity which might threaten the plain style advocated by both Royal Society scientists or Puritan rhetoricians; and an irrepressible "lightness" of tone which might seem to mock the "heavy" voices of moral seriousness or psychological depression. Most basically, then, literary "levity" involves straying from the point – or not taking the point seriously. From the point of view of grave rhetoricians, though, verbal digression (straying from the straight and narrow of literary order) is equated with moral transgression (straying from the straight and narrow of the dominant moral order).

But it is important to stress that in the thought about this levity–gravity interaction neither pole or voice or force is ever seen to exist in isolation; in this quasi-physicalist vision of a dynamic bipolar system, each voice needs the other, each gains its charge only through opposition to the other – it is only when the two poles are in contact that the vital sparks begin to fly. In Byron or in the German Romantics, the model here is very often astrophysical: the planets, we are told, stay in their orbits by always pushing forward away from the sun, staying up as the mysterious eccentric force of their digressive, centrifugal, wandering "levity" balances the tension of a centering, centripetal pull – the universal law of gravity. The central sun and the orbiting planet must work together; both forces are necessary in this system. In Sterne's *Tristram Shandy* – perhaps the paradigmatic literary work in this levity–gravity tradition – the eccentric turns of endless digressions make the novel seem to float like a flying machine, a "lighter-than-air indirigible," but, as Sigurd Burckhardt points out, this verbal levity has to be seen to interact with and explode out of strong forces of gravity – out of concerns with literal seriousness, with physical heaviness, and with the theological Fall. In "*Tristram Shandy*'s Law of Gravity," Burckhardt writes:

We must read Sterne much more literally – i.e., corporeally – than has commonly been done; we are sure to miss his meaning if we smile too quickly at his "irony" . . . Sterne's final joke is again and again that he is not joking.

To follow the movements of literary imagery "corporeally" means, for Burckhardt, to ground our readings of such digressive humor in the "gravity" of both Protestant theology and Newtonian science, so as to restore "to the word 'gravity' the physical weight and concreteness which we too readily vaporise into the evanescence of an idea."[6]

Friedrich Schlegel, looking back to Sterne's example as he codified and promoted the mode of self-conscious writing that he termed Romantic (or Socratic) irony, celebrates the ambiguities of the lightness of tone here, while also stressing, as Burkardt does, the interpretive problems posed by this line of works centrally defined by their hovering between the poles of levity and gravity. In the *Lyceum* fragment taken as motto for this book, he predicts that the "harmonious bores" will always be at a loss when confronted with the Romantic ironist's "union of *savoir-vivre* and the scientific spirit" which makes everything "playful and serious" at the same time. Faced with hybrid writings bringing together science and humor, blending grave analysis and effervescent wit, readers might well "fluctuate endlessly between belief and disbelief until they get dizzy and take what is meant as a joke seriously and what is meant seriously as a joke."[7] This aphorism neatly captures the dilemma of any reader of Holmes' table-talk works. And if we would begin to reread Holmes, we would do well to keep Burckhardt's and Schlegel's warnings about such interpretive difficulties in mind. For the Doctor's work springs to new and more complex life – its flights of levity more explosive, and its burden of gravity more material – when we recognize his place in this tradition of Romantic irony, in the line of Sterne's scientific humor, and in his relations with the associated works of Lichtenberg and Diderot.

Most authors in the English and European tradition defined by Black looked back quite consciously to Sterne as their most important forebear, and Sterne is in many ways – in his intellectual concerns as well as in his literary form – the author closest to Holmes. (At least one contemporary reviewer hailed Holmes as the "American Sterne.")[8] The Doctor was also very clear about his sense of himself as speaking for a much-neglected but ongoing Sterne tradition in America. This Sterne tradition has indeed been much neglected in American literary history. But Holmes' writings remind us that the canonized works of the American Renaissance – dominated by an extreme moral seriousness – arose in conversation with contemporary American voices of literary levity; that the Organicist notions of American Romanticism developed through interactions with native developments of an alternative Romantic Irony; and that the heritage of American Puritanism in this era worked in dialogue with an inheritance from the literature and thought of eighteenth-century England and Europe. Jay Fliegelman has pointed out that, in fact, Sterne's *Tristram Shandy* became one of the nation's most popular works as soon as it was published in eighteenth-century America. Sterne's plots, like those of many other works surveyed by Black, play out the dynamics of Lockean pedagogy in their oscillations between the levity of a schoolchild's truancy and the gravity of the narrow path set by his teachers and parents. Perhaps because this basic Lockean plot was so central to the concerns of the "truant" Revolutionary Republic, then, Sterne began as an author with an important American heritage.[9] And Holmes can help us to see how a line of philosophic comedy coming out of Sterne could continue as an important voice in the nineteenth century. Literary historians have too often limited the scope of Sterne's relevance in America by attributing to his influence only raucous, schoolboy burlesques (such as those in the early work of Irving) or effete male sentimentalism (as seen in the later writings of Irving, or in D. G. Mitchell). But in Holmes we find the convergence of intellectual and writerly interests which allows a continuation of Sterne's scientific humor and also of some of the literary experimentation related to Sterne's foundational play on the levity–gravity opposition.

LEVITY–GRAVITY "COUPLINGS" IN HOLMES' TABLE-TALK

But how would this English or European tradition of thought and writing – centering upon dynamic alternations between levity and gravity – play itself out in the specific local circumstances of mid-nineteenth-century America?

In the case of Holmes, a bipolar hovering between the voices or stances of levity and gravity can be seen to characterize both the moment-by-moment alternations between paired speakers in many of the key passages of his table-talk writings and also the broad outlines of his career – as that develops in a wide range of fields. Holmes was a word-juggler who could, like Sterne, seem to throw the whole universe up into the air in an exquisite flying motion; but he was also a Newtonian scientist centrally concerned with the operations and meanings of a scientific system founded upon the law of gravitation. His sprightly verbal pyrotechnics must always be seen against a background of rapid contemporary developments in heavy mechanistic technology; the "soft objects" of his aesthetic play always come up against (and often threaten to unsettle) the rigorous rules developed to control or describe the "hard objects" of hard science. If, as Lowell observes, in his medical career Holmes "suffered by giving evidence of too much wit," that wit was certainly never divorced from the serious concerns of the medical profession; the levity of the Doctor's scientific humor explodes scientific gravity from within, erupting out of contradictions in mechanistic models of the universe or of the mind, pushing Newtonian or Lockean physicalist arguments *ad absurdam*, to their hilarious breaking points.[10] Similarly, in the social world, the jokes and paradoxes that made Holmes so famous worked to send up the cant and moral seriousness of the Age of Jackson, an "Age of Ideology," but they gain their force from within that censorious climate. (In the boardinghouse setting, the voice of the Doctor's humor is always seen to be surrounded by "a pessimistic tribe of Pooh-Poohs," a society of Chicken Littles – people who extend their view of gravity even into the most distant skies and so, when they lift their heads to the heavens, can only conceive of them falling.) A jester in what he saw as a dour, depressive and repressive era, the Doctor advanced the causes of conversational pleasure, carnival laughter, cheerfulness, and the Rise of Man against a repressive work ethic enforcing the limits of scarcity economics in all walks of life, against a cruel interventionist medicine and physiological psychiatry, and most determinedly against the grave old-school Calvinist "Inquisitors" whose doctrines of original sin and human iniquity – the Fall of Man – dominated the America of his youth. As one 1895 reviewer noted in retrospect, "No writer did more in his generation to soften the harshness of the Puritan temper, or to disperse . . . the chilling gloom of its austere rule."[11] In fact Holmes saw Calvinism in its American manifestations as the cause or model of all other forms of restrictive "gravity" in his day. In Christian journals and vituperative sermons, outraged orthodox voices answered the statements in Holmes' table-talk pieces point by point, after each number. But while it was the Doctor's general "levity" that made him perhaps the prime enemy for many retreating Calvinists through the mid-century – the *Christian Examiner*, for example, was shocked above all by the formal and tonal "levity" of his treatment of theological topics – Holmes did not find the weight of this heritage easy to escape: he returned obsessively throughout his life to a central concern with the "grave" topics of crime and sin, and to scientific, naturalistic revisions or translations of all that had been included under the earlier doctrine of the Fall.[12]

On a more local level, many of the turns in the talk of Holmes' breakfast-table dialogues play out in small scale this same sort of symbiotic interaction between light voices and grave ones. In Sterne's *Tristram Shandy*, conversations in the Shandy household always develop as a story of "diametrically opposed temperaments, perpetual misunderstandings, and mutual devotion."[13] As he structures the interactions between speakers at his breakfast-table, Holmes is constantly presenting us with levity–gravity couplings operating very much along the same lines – in which the paired voices collide, interrupt one another, but also work together as part of a larger system, sharing unspoken sympathies or affinities – as though such Victorian "marriages-of-opposites" were an irreducible building-block in his mental universe, the primary structure out of which any more complex combinative form must be built.

At the end of *The Professor at the Breakfast-Table*, for example, the Professor directly confronts the problem of marriage, giving us a prescription which he says is based on his own relation with his wife: "A person of [flighty, brilliant] *genius* should marry a person of [even-tempered, dull] *character*." Preparing here for the unlikely engagement of two of the other characters at his boardinghouse breakfast-table – announcing the nuptials of brilliant, artistically gifted Iris and the solid-but-"plain" Marylander – the Professor recalls that the flighty gift of gab that has made him famous always needed the conversational balance of his wife's even-tempered quietness. When he then surprises his listeners by launching into one of his periodic praises of "dull people," what emerges is an archetypal image of the levity–gravity dialectic as a fundamental household structure:

How we all like the spirting up of a fountain, seemingly against the law that makes water everywhere slide, roll, leap, tumble headlong, to get as low as the earth will let it! That is genius. But what is this transient upward movement, which gives us the glitter and the rainbow, to that unsleeping, all-present force of gravity, the same yesterday, to-day, and forever, (if the universe be eternal,) – the great outspread hand of God himself, forcing all things down into their places, and keeping them there? Such, in smaller proportion, is the force of character to the fitful movements of genius, as they are or have been linked to each other in many a household. (*CW*, II, 287–89)

We can imagine some of these compact Victorian homes almost bursting with the effort to contain the energies released by the collisions of such strong physical forces. Here again marriage is seen as a household conversation between dynamic natural polarities: between an airy, rising fountain and a downward-flowing sea; between the lawless explosions of a human aesthetic urge to freedom and a physical law that merges the scientific and theological senses of *gravitas*.

Perhaps the strain of the Professor's effort here to close his book with a properly grave marital union, to turn from many chapters full of the brain's "glittering" intellectual gymnastics to the sentimental demands of the heart, to argue against his own usual position at the breakfast-table and in the household, betrays itself in some of the harsher language that makes the stubborn status quo of gravity sound in this description a bit like a prison – "forcing all things down into their places, and keeping them there." But he then quickly shifts to another analogy developing the same image of ships at sea that we saw the Autocrat use to describe the "zig-zag" movements of Holmes' witty and interruptive writing. The "gay-pennoned" tall ship of genius (its colorful masts rising up from the ocean like those fountain bursts do) is majestic as she swims against the tide, says the Professor, but we know that she is also strongly affected by the pull of ocean currents; she will need a solid tug-boat as spouse to navigate "all the tides of circumstance." Then continuing on the smaller scale of his well-known hobby, the Professor notes that although he enjoys the muscular thrill of sculling upstream against a current, there is also much to be said for the opposite mode of passivity before the river's natural flow. (When he then amplifies his argument for the rule of gravity over the waters of the household with a picture of himself in his scull, lying in the "black cradle in which I love to let the great mother rock me" [*CW*, II, 289–90], the phrase resonates strongly with the opening of the Whitman poem which was first published later in the same month as this last number of *The Professor* [December 1859], the introductory line of which in a later revision became the poem's title: "Out of the Cradle Endlessly Rocking.")[14]

Of course Holmes did not feel the tidal force of this "dull" gravity only in his own home life; and he would never see it in isolation from its electrodynamic opposite. For the Doctor, almost every human relation seems to build out of "sympathetic" repulsions and attractions between matched, magnetic pairs; to him, all couples seem to interact like our familiar table-top toys, those black and white dog-magnets that orbit around each other in strange and sometimes hilarious ways. This tendency to see all verbal exchanges on the pattern of a bipolar household dialogue between the voices of white levity and black gravity explains, for example, Holmes' curious one-paragraph treatment of the Emerson–Carlyle correspondence in his biography of the Transcendentalist poet:

The two writers reveal themselves as being in strong sympathy with each other, in spite of a radical difference in temperament and entirely opposite views of life. The hatred of unreality was uppermost with Carlyle; the love of what is real and genuine with Emerson. The old moralists, the weeping and the laughing philosophers, find their counterparts in every thinking community. Carlyle did not weep, but he scolded; Emerson did not laugh, but in his gravest moments there was a smile waiting for the cloud to pass from his forehead. The Duet they chanted was a Miserere with a Te Deum for its Antiphon; a *De Profundis* answered by a *Sursum Corda*. "The ground of my existence is black as death," says Carlyle. "Come and live with me a year," says Emerson, "and . . . one of these years . . . I will come and dwell with you."[15]

If all thinking is a communal effort, every "thinking community" will then divide the dialogical process of its mental life between the archetypal antitheses which the founding doctor, Hippocrates, defines in Burton's *Anatomy of Melancholy*: it must contain the complementary humors of both Heraclitus and Democritus. And here the grave Calvinist frowner and the sweet, loving Transcendentalist smiler reveal the strong "sympathetic" attractions which can underlie such a polar opposition. Holmes shows that their antiphonal duet – at least as he sets up the conversation – leads naturally to thoughts of a sort of "marriage." Indeed, the dynamic relation of these two correspondent voices – needing each other, wanting to balance each other in a household coexistence – can stand as the clearest paradigm of Holmes' idea of bipolar marriage.

As a telling indication of the centrality of this marriage ideal – based upon the vision of affinities between the opposed voices of levity and gravity – to Holmes' table-talk works, we might note that many contemporary readers apparently used *The Autocrat* as their "courting book." The dynamic of levity–gravity "coupling" here was probably of special relevance for Samuel Clemens (Mark Twain), as he marked his copy of this "courting book" for Olivia Langdon in 1869–70. *The Autocrat* became the favorite book in common between these unlikely lovers; after their marriage they kept it in the tin box that held all of their love letters. Holmes' table-talk works could serve as perfect "conversation-pieces" between partners of such different backgrounds; indeed, for Twain and "Livy," *The Autocrat* seems to have become a symbol of their relationship, speaking for both of their voices, and for the dynamic interactions between them. What developed as the "game" or drama of the unlikely relation between Twain and his future wife – between his humor and her seriousness, his irreverence and her orthodoxy, his bohemian improprieties and her genteel respectability – took its schematic shape in the margins of Holmes' book, and on the pattern of levity–gravity interaction basic to the relations between the paired talkers at Holmes' breakfast-table. Twain's chosen love was a model of the culture's conventional notions of gravity: she was a product of the upper-class social order which frowned upon drinking, smoking, and swearing; she would scold and correct Clemens, sending him Biblical texts and sermons in the hope that he might become a Christian believer; and she disapproved of humorists in general, often finding it hard to grasp Sam's jokes. But through the mediation of Holmes' written conversations, Twain could instruct Livy in literary levity – "That is a joke, my literal Livy," was his patient annotation in the margins of one breakfast-table passage – and she could learn to take up her role as editor, critic, the muse-as-censor of her bad boy's blasphemies and bad taste, the serious straight man required as resistance in the creation of his humor, the planetary center from which he could digress as "prodigal" but around which he turned – in a word, she learned her position in what James Cox aptly terms Twain's "comic dialectic": as gravity to his levity. Livy was, in Twain's favorite nickname for her, his "dear little Gravity"; he encouraged what he called her "gentle gravities" at the same time that he laughed at them, and he seems to have relished the way in which his romance followed so closely the culturally defined bipolar pattern.[16] (It is not surprising, then, that many of Twain's comic writings also develop as some of the era's clearest epitomes of this levity–gravity dialectic: in "The Notorious Jumping Frog of Calaveras County," the humorous, digressive tale about the "levitations" of a gravity-defying frog gains its charge as it works in explosive opposition to the forces of literary, theological, and scientific gravity that finally bring the frog down; and "The Facts Concerning the Recent Carnival of Crime in Connecticut" presents a picture of the narrator's inner life as a difficult, wounding internal debate between the voices of levity and gravity that is literalized in the rising and falling movements of an externalized Conscience.)[17]

If in his visions of household life Holmes sees light wit necessarily coupled with a heavy partner, in other defenses of dullness this complementary companionship develops not only in relation to the Victorian thematics of marriage, but also as a model of many literary interactions – as an image of the different sorts of temporary pairings of reader and writer, or of speaker and listener, in the "households" of the breakfast-table or of the church. Here the electrodynamic movements of levity and gravity reflect more clearly two polarities of literary style.

Holmes' dynamic model of conversation leads him frequently to voice concern about the underside of this vision – to worry about the dangers or discomforts of energy drainage (sometimes seen almost as vampirism) which can occur in any interpersonal contact that is not charged by a sympathetic affinity. Too much parlor-room contact with "men of *esprit*" can drain one's battery of vital energies, warns the Autocrat. Of course the boardinghouse victims of the Autocrat's own Ancient Mariner monologues probably know this only too well by now, but he nonetheless leaps ahead to expand upon his witty attack on wit with a series of overt and covert similes and metaphors. Trying on the ill-fitting dullard's mask of a work-ethic maxim-moralist, he admonishes us to be sure to balance the electrically "jolting" shocks of contact with our brilliant friends against the negative charge that comes with rubbing against our duller ones: the "dazzling" light of combustive sensibilities must alternate with a cooler, calmer darkness; the "jerkiness" of artifically-ordered digressive talk (like the "fitful movements" of the fountains of genius in the *Professor* passage cited earlier) must work in dialogue with reminders of the "natural order" of things:

There are men of *esprit* who are excessively exhausting to some people. They are the talkers who have what may be called *jerky* minds. Their thoughts do not run in the natural order of sequence. They say bright things on all possible subjects, but their zigzags rack you to death. After a jolting half-hour with one of these jerky companions, talking with a dull friend affords great relief. It is like taking the cat in your lap after holding a squirrel.

What a comfort a dull but kindly person is, to be sure, at times! A ground-glass shade over a gas-lamp does not bring more solace to our dazzled eyes than such a one to our minds. (*CW*, i, 6)

This Autocratic set piece does snare one gullible listener who reveals her own limits by taking it too literally as a statement of permanent, one-sided belief: "Do not dull people bore you?" she asks. But this speech is not simply an ironic joke intended to draw out the dullards at the table. The same paradox appears again as Doctor Holmes tries to work himself up for his most serious attempt at sustained analysis of what he saw as the ultimate "grave" topic – "mechanism" – near the beginning of his lecture, *Mechanism in Thought and Morals*. This passage can serve as a revealing example of the complex rhetorical movements involved as the Doctor works out his literary–scientific conception of the "naturalness" of dialogic turns from brilliance to dullness, or from levity to gravity:

Just as the eye seeks to refresh itself by resting on neutral tints after looking at brilliant colors, the mind turns from the glare of intellectual brilliancy to the solace of gentle dulness; the tranquillizing green of the sweet human qualities, which do not make us shade our eyes like the spangles of conversational gymnasts and *figurantes*. (*CW*, viii, 268–69)

Here, when the Doctor returns to the levity–gravity topos in the context of a scientific study of the "underground workshop of thought," what is seen elsewhere as a dialogue involving the multiple voices of a household now becomes a conversation between two mental modes; what could be a description of an external, everyday parlor-room interaction might also be seen to take place between the two halves of one walnut-shaped brain. Perhaps the "tranquillizing green" side is more clearly chained to the autonomic pulses of the heart (with workings more clearly related to the laws which make weights fall and rivers flow downward to the sea), and perhaps the other tends to erupt in the freer, fountain-like movements of "brilliant" intellectual gymnastics, but most important here is the way in which each of these trains of thought is seen to influence the other's

tracks. The model for this interaction is once again astrophysical –
based on the orbits of digressive planets around their strong, gravitational center. In the Doctor's view here, the involuntary bodily
system, which he calls the "unconscious," exerts a powerful gravitational force on the flights of our conscious "talking thought": these
invisible physiological motions "make their influence felt . . . just as
the unseen planets sway the movements of those which are watched
and mapped by the astronomer" (*CW,* VIII, 282).

But, as we saw in Chapter Seven, throughout the *Mechanism* essay
Holmes oscillates between physiological and rhetorical conceptions
of what he is defining as the "unconscious." If at times, as above, he
wants to be a "Newton of the Mind," defining laws of mental gravity
originating in the over-determining bodily system, at other times he
explores the topic more in the liberating light of "brilliant" figural
talking and writing.[18] In fact, underlying this discussion of the
dialogic relations between bright and dull colors and between bright
and dull modes of talking is a dialogic relation embedded in the very
form of the Doctor's sentence; the most characteristic passages in
Holmes' writing, like this one, gain their charge as they contain
within themselves a collision between two opposed modes of discourse – here the Doctor's words, building out of an internalized
dialogue between figurative and literal "voices," enact their subject:
the dialogue between literary levity and scientific gravity. While the
description of our need to turn our eyes from bright colors to gentle
green is spoken in the voice of Holmes the serious scientist, here
again the defense of dullness (as a balance to those seductive *figurantes*)
comes in a well-honed aphorism, with a highly *figural* working out of
multi-leveled analogies between the operations of vision and of
intelligence (an intelligence which seems mainly to be defined by the
evidence of elaborate rhetorical figuration). The effect of Holmes'
uses of "science" is often such a witty yoking of "fact" and "figure";
here he is pleased to revive the fossilized metaphors of "light" in our
usually loose talk about "brilliance," "dullness," the rhetorical
"colors," and so on. But the result is not a one-way literalization of
all metaphors; the contamination of realms is mutual – fact and
figure, gravity and levity, always maintain a complex dialogue here.
If on the one hand these rhetorical figures are made to conform to
materialist common sense, suggesting the applicability of grave
mechanistic laws to the involuntary motions of the mind, on the
other hand the facts of dull science also clearly begin to take on, by

the end of the passage above, some rather sprightly metaphorical colors. Holmes' self-reflexive plays upon literary figures then have a lightening effect upon his scientific facts; these commonplace observations appear in a very different "light" when we reread them as allegories of figuration. So, even in its literary form, this passage enacts its theme: a continual alternation between dullness and brilliance. It seems that thought can never be reduced to one "color"; "flowers" can turn first up toward the light, and then away from it. Preparing for his play on light imagery in this passage, Holmes has already reminded us that colors in fact always appear as complements: each time we confront the sensation of "red" we instantly call up as well a closed-eye, virtual image of "green." So the "turns" described here – from brilliancy to that shady, pastoral green – seem not to depend simply on accidents of external circumstance, but to be movements somehow inherent within the bipolar constitution of each pair of eyes, or of each human mind.

When he is not writing science or presiding over the serious, melodramatic endings of one of his books, Holmes feels freer to be more of a fountain-like *man of esprit* himself. Certainly in the Doctor's literary works the levity–gravity alternation does not always end with a victory for the grounding forces of scientific law. And in many other conversational couplings of dull and witty speaker and listener, the Doctor is far from reverent to the bores.

One important church scene in the *Autocrat* epitomizes Holmes' sense of the functioning of levity–gravity couplings in any dialogic verbal interaction – and shows how these polarized oppositions can operate on many levels at once. Explaining that he often does his best thinking while attending Sunday services, the Autocrat develops a "reverential" defense of his preacher's dullness that has a strong backhand twist to it. Here the grave sermonizer is put in the same position as the "unseen planets" of the "unconscious" in the *Mechanism* passage discussed earlier: serving as a sort of bodily "unconscious" to the many-layered mind of the witty, restless listener, the preacher's words provide an unceasing background drone to other more lively "mental currents." This time, though, the interactions of brilliance and dullness are seen not as planetary, but, in a related scientific imagery, as electrodynamic – as the contact between two poles in a system of alternating conversational currents:

I have often noticed . . . that a hopelessly dull discourse acts *inductively*, as electricians would say, in developing strong mental currents. I am ashamed to think with what accompaniments and *fioriture* I have sometimes followed the droning of a heavy speaker, – not willingly, – for my habit is reverential, – . . . (*CW*, I, 29)[19]

Imagining the interrelations of dancing wit and "heavy" speech here then leads the Autocrat into another of his virtuoso extended analogies – this one taking the bipolar levity–gravity topos to define the interactions between two literary modes:

If you ever saw a crow with a king-bird after him, you will get an image of a dull speaker and a lively listener. The bird in sable plumage flaps heavily along his straight-forward course, while the other sails round him, over him, under him, leaves him, comes back again, tweaks out a black feather, shoots away once more, never losing sight of him, and finally reaches the crow's perch at the same time the crow does, having cut a perfect labyrinth of loops and knots and spirals while the slow fowl was painfully working from one end of his straight line to the other. (*CW*, I, 29–30)

Like a fountain, like a fireworks rocket, like a wayward planet, the Autocrat sees himself here in constant airy flight, doing centrifugal arabesques behind the backs of the dour speakers of his day, always hovering around contemporary dogma but refusing to alight.[20] At least in its name, the kingbird seems to represent a more colorful, courtly verbal style against the common Puritan plainness of both the professional garments and the rhetorical "clothing" associated with a country-based clergyman. But the kingbird is not over-civilized; it flies with a youthful spirit, while the slow, heavy "old crow" seems barely able to get off the ground. The crucial difference, though, is in the form of their flights, as the Autocrat contrasts the digressive tendencies of his levity with the "straightforward course" of the grave black fowl. The syntax of the long last sentence dramatizes the contrast: it begins and ends with repetitive framing clauses that are naturalistically and grammatically straightforward – perfect models of "gravity" in literary form – but its expansive middle section erupts in a flight of unparallel dependent clauses that mimes the jerky, zig-zag movement of this playful sort of hummingbird.

As the somber Calvinist crow here clearly represents "gravity" in its moral and theological stance as well as in its physical weight and in the boring, mechanical logic of its sermon style, the Autocrat's digressions can threaten a "truancy" from the straight-and-narrow path in dogmatic substance as well as from the "straight-forward" literary form. That is why this is one of the many Autocrat statements that provokes an immediate electrical sensation at the breakfast-table: a virulent negative response and "secession" from the censors on one side of the room. But these sparks only prove once again the Autocrat's point that a weak battery – as in those who would attempt quickly to ground this flight of fancy – can be flash-charged "inductively" if it comes into contact with a strong current from the opposite electrodynamic pole.

In fact, though, the structure of the Autocrat's statement is not so one-sided as it may have seemed to those over-hasty censors. Certainly this metaphorical excursus has allowed a few pestering "tweaks" that might ruffle the feathers of the church – with those references to heavy flapping, to basic dullness, to the "slow fowl," and to the word "painful." (In the essay on "Jonathan Edwards," Holmes explains that the word "painful" was given its indicative new meaning by the Puritans, who changed its original connotation of "taking" pains to the new sense of "causing" pain.) And the basic conception here is undeniably disruptive of the dour old clerical order. First, the very idea of envisioning a sermon as a dialogue transforms the closed, monological, "preaching" form into an open conversation, thus stressing the fundamental and active role of the lay listeners over that of the church's professional elite of speakers. Then the idea of seeing this church conversation on the model of a battery, introducing the naturalistic electrical system as an explana-tion of meeting-house dynamics, itself yokes opposites together to shocking effect. But finally we must recognize that the Autocrat does not leave the church; he does not begin to speak on his own; he continues to figure himself as a listener and a dependent member within the congregation. Here again the model remains bipolar: like the suns and planets in the works of Byron or Richter, the crow and kingbird in this passage define two alternate and interrelated trajec-tories of flight; after each "hovering" loop-the-loop the prodigal kingbird comes back down to rejoin the crow in his slow, burdened pilgrim's progress. The witty, orbiting bird is never free of the dull fowl's over-determining planetary "influence"; after all the tacks and indirections, both end on the same perch at the same time. The kingbird's progress in this church scene is like that of the sailing ship in another of the Autocrat's familiar analogies, which, for all of its "devious" tacks, will still orient itself to the ocean's gravitational tides, and towards the final port: "To reach the port of heaven, we must sail sometimes with the wind and sometimes against it" (*CW*, 1, 93).[21]

In the terms of natural ecology, the dialogic interaction of the crow and kingbird here is pictured as a symbiotic "household" of host and parasite. In the Autocrat's musical terms, wit offers but a series of "variations" on a solemn traditional theme; its sprung rhythms will still depend on the orthodox cadences of that "hereditary instrument" always droning as a memorial echo in the background. The situation calls up an image used frequently by Holmes to describe the predicament of poetic "sensibility": the kingbird here might be said to be singing in a cage. And as his flight is framed by the crow's, so the "levity" of the Autocrat's literary impulses is seen to explode out from within the "grave" frames of sermon-logic and solid church walls. The glosses of this very "writerly" listener here still never wholly depart from the grounding text of the preacher's words.

Holmes' telling self-portrait as a parasite within the host traditions and discourses of his day – here most particularly within the received tradition of Calvinism – speaks for strongly ambivalent tendencies: the scene can be read as revolutionary or as deeply conservative, depending on whether we accent the power of levity in the flight or that of gravity in the frame. Holmes himself, though, often liked to imagine that the light, hyperactive wingbeats of that little kingbird could send wind-waves carrying some quite weighty repercussions.

CHAPTER 9

HOLMES' HOUSE DIVIDED
House-Keeping and House-Breaking

The process is like that of respiration . . . New ideas act upon society as oxygen does on the body, attacking its errors, which pass away from the lists of human beliefs, and strengthening the new truth which is building in its place.

Holmes, "Autobiographical Notes"

Build thee more stately mansions, O my soul,
   As the swift seasons roll!
   Leave thy low-vaulted past!
Let each new temple, nobler than the last,
Shut thee from heaven with a dome more vast,
   Till thou at length art free,
Leaving thine outgrown shell by life's unresting sea.

Holmes, "The Chambered Nautilus"

Thought about the church brings out some of Holmes' deepest ambivalences – as we have just seen in the *Autocrat* passage about the interwoven flights of crow and kingbird. And as we turn to other passages throughout his writings, we find that the same polarities which emerge in external relations to make a sermon seem to develop as a symbiotic household dialogue between speaker and listener can also operate internally, so that the process of all thought can be described as a dynamically unstable "marriage" between light and grave voices, and any possibility for personal change or growth – in the intellect, the emotions, or even in the bodily system – can only be imagined as emerging out of dialogical interrelations between light, airy, kingbird-like wingbeats and the solid, fixed, framing walls of the church or family home. In this chapter, we will see how the Doctor's uses of and plays upon the culture's conventional notions of a levity–gravity opposition – and his senses of the larger implications of each of these polar terms – were grounded in extended meditation on the pattern of his personal experience as a child growing up in a divided household: a family life that placed the young boy at the center of an ongoing dialogue between his mother's "levity" and his father's "gravity." We will then see how, for Holmes, the dynamic effects of the levity–gravity dialogue can often come to be figured as alternate responses to that original household model: voices of levity are most frequently associated with imagery expressing "house-breaking" urges to rise up and explode out of framing walls; voices of gravity, on the other hand, are usually associated with opposed "house-keeping" movements tending to build up heavy walls and to reinforce their constraining power.

LEVITY–GRAVITY DIALOGUE IN YOUNG HOLMES' DIVIDED HOUSEHOLD

At the end of *The Poet*, when the Master is preparing to wrap up the last chapter of the last book in the original breakfast-table series, the boarders jokingly deflate a "sense of some impending event" when he promises to let them in on a "secret" that he says sums up the meaning of his entire "literary life." The boarders of course don't pay attention because they have been disappointed too often – the Master and the Professor and the Autocrat are always running into interruptions or digressions whenever they have promised to pin down "the great end of life" in convenient maxim form. It is something like waiting for Coleridge (another long-winded, mono-logical theorist of the bipolar) finally to define the Imagination in his *Biographia Literaria*. Since his universe seems characterized by its lack of synthesis, the Master finds it hard to roll it all up decisively into a ball. But this time, perhaps without knowing it himself, he surprises us. The long retrospect on his life now allows a new insight into the painfully ambivalent pattern of his childhood progress, and the Master is able to offer a revealing formula ironically defining his identity as an unresolved battle for "mastery." It seems that, since early childhood, he has carried inside himself the deep structure of a divided household:

I did not know then that two strains of blood were striving in me for mastery, – two! twenty, perhaps, – twenty thousand, for aught I know, – but represented to me by two, – paternal and maternal. Blind forces in themselves; shaping thoughts as they shaped features and battled for the moulding of constitution and the mingling of temperament. (*CW*, III, 320)

This cryptic speculation bursts out as somewhat of a non-sequitur even within the usual idiosyncratic logic of the Master's free-associative table-talk; but the context of the remarks gives us a clearer idea of the large range of impulses seen to be involved in either the "paternal" or the "maternal" "strains" of this internalized family quarrel. Basically, the Master has been describing his literary life as a counter-balance to the theological and cultural inheritance of old church traditions. The urges of literary expression must always meet those of repression; and even at the pre-verbal level somatic tensions between these two "blind forces" can leave the body, as well as the mind, painfully torn. Elaborating his vision of a bald, schematic split between new talk and old books, new and old cultures, new and old selves – in a series of oppositions that will culminate in the description of that archetypal struggle between maternal and paternal strains of blood for "mastery" of the young boy's constitution – the Master pictures his childhood as having been achingly divided, with each new thought rising (like the flight of the kingbird around the black crow) only to meet the physical resistances of received belief:

Many things that I have said in my ripe days have been aching in my soul since I was a mere child. I say aching, because they conflicted with many of my inherited beliefs, or rather traditions. (*CW*, III, 319–20)

Like a Montaigne, the Master is less interested in any static inherited identity that might have existed before his written self-portraits than in the self that emerges through or is created by his books; he has only grown as he has "essayed" new ideas and new selves in an active verbal process, as he has given verbal form to each "aching" latent impulse. This literary process, then, involves not only discovery of the new but also release from the old. ("All uttered thought . . . is of the nature of an excretion," was the Professor's formulation of this view [*CW*, I, 196].) And, characteristically, the Master here defines the action of verbal expression by analogy to the dynamic economy of bodily energies: it dissolves the blocks to free circulation, expels ("gets rid of") masses of useless matter, and thus lightens the load of pent-up pressure.

Generally, the writing that has allowed him to "unburden" himself seems to develop in an airy, upward movement against the downward pull of an oppressive weight of tradition. And the tendencies implied in the covert metaphors of this psycho-physiological language become much more explicit two paragraphs later, when the Master's mercurial mind suddenly leaps for comparison to an entirely new scene – now focussing all of these musings in a meditation on the flight of a passenger balloon. Here the internal, physiological tensions between new verbal expression and old beliefs, and the dialectical strivings between maternal and paternal blood, both come to be clearly associated with the most classic image of the levity–gravity topos. The overall pattern of his literary career, says the Master, has been that of a floating airship: a dynamic bipolar alternation between forces that rise and those that fall, a balancing of the opposed impulses of balloon and ballast:

[As a writer] I have got rid of something my mind could not keep to itself and rise as it was meant to into higher regions. I saw the aeronauts the other day emptying from the bags some of the sand that served as ballast. It glistened a moment in the sunlight as a slender shower, and then was lost and seen no more as it scattered itself unnoticed. But the airship rose higher as the sand was poured out, and so it seems to me I have felt myself getting above the mists and clouds whenever I have lightened myself of some portion of the mental ballast I have carried with me. (*CW*, III, 319–20)

Of course the Master will not let himself get too carried away with what Van Wyck Brooks saw as the lightening tendencies in verbal expression. He quickly adds here that, like Lowell's rocket, the airship in flight may amount only to a short-lived brilliance, a fountain-like scattering shower that soon "pours out" all its fuel and contents as it heads for "oblivion." And in paragraphs immediately following this enthusiastic flight scene, he stops to develop the more fearful possibilities of formless dissolution latent in some of these phrases: "is seen no more as it scattered itself unnoticed." The Master then gives as examples of his most satisfying writings paradoxical passages which undercut this balloon-rise, in fact mining the antithetical vein of gravity. Now taking up the voice of science, he notes that though trains, steamships, and hot-air balloons *seem* to speak for a continual progress built on radical breaks from the past, in fact "there is no new thing under the sun." This is a favorite theme of the Autocrat, the Professor, the Poet, as well as of the Master: the unconscious repetition of the old within the new. Along these lines, the Master follows his exhilarating image of an airship's liberating rise – and of the release in throwing off that heavy mental baggage – with several plodding pages analyzing examples of the stubborn, cyclical recurrences of the weight of tradition. After following his flight, then, we are brought back down to earth with a jolting thud.

This passage of the Master's talk is certainly complex – approaching its important "secrets" by a train of zigzags, leaps, paradoxes, and antitheses. But we might begin to get a sense that there is a method to these meanderings when we compare them to central passages in Holmes' "Autobiographical Notes" – passages which proceed through a remarkably similar sequence of associations in describing the details of Holmes' childhood education, filling in the Master's picture of a household built around a levity–gravity opposition between maternal and paternal forces. Holmes' father, the "Notes" tell us, was an Orthodox clergyman and "the grandson of an Orthodox deacon," who thus inherited his thorough belief in the "harsh" "doctrines of Calvinism." His mother, on the other hand, represented a contrary inheritance of wealth and social position: she "was a lady bred in an entirely different atmosphere from that of the straight-laced puritanism" (*AN*, 37). Ann Douglas describes such a household dynamic as the defining pattern that shaped the lives of a whole generation of genteel or sentimentalist writers in the mid-century: Irving, Willis, Mitchell, Curtis, Clark, Longfellow, Lowell, Tuckerman, and Warner, as well as Holmes. Feeling belittled as light idlers by stern, orthodox fathers, they each saw themselves as following their mothers in adopting a sunnier creed and moving into literary writing.[1] But, in Holmes' vision, every picture we are given of the household interactions of his father and mother resolves itself into one fundamental pattern, along the lines of a specifically Calvinist distinction between "gravity" and "levity."

Though the "Notes" describe the Reverend Abdiel Holmes as a kind and gentle man, his background led him to take the most austerely orthodox position within what the Professor calls "the graver profession" (*CW*, II, 113). Raised in old-fashioned Connecticut, and educated at Yale, the bastion of the Puritan faith, Abdiel insisted on giving his children a rigorous Calvinist training that permeated all aspects of home life. At the "sober family board" of the "quiet clergyman," the Holmes children would hear endless "gloomy" lessons about the "Fall of Man" (*AN*, 51, 50, 46). Their father dictated the family reading of the 107 questions and answers of the shorter Westminster catechism, requiring the childrens' frequent repetition of the doctrines about original sin and infant depravity:

. . . we learned nominally that we were a set of little fallen wretches, exposed to the wrath of God by the fact of that existence which we could not help. (*AN*, 38)

The older, irreverent Doctor remembers, too, that the textbook of such New England households, the *New England Primer*, attempted to inscribe these grave lessons into each foundational element of the child's language, teaching him repeatedly to associate with the letter "A," for example, the "monstrous absurdity": "In Adam's fall/ We sinnéd all" (*AN*, 45).

In the Puritan home, the Sabbath was a day of special gloom, as the decorum of silence and inactivity (such a special strain on this hyper-active, hyper-talkative youngster) was rigidly enforced. And the minister's son would hear at least two sermons every Sunday, afterwards listening in on the many visits from other clergymen callers. When we realize how much church talk young Oliver heard on these days, it is easy to understand how, as we saw earlier, in the *Autocrat* he could come to see the sermon-voice as a sort of "hereditary instrument" always droning on in the background; how as a kingbird he could fade in and out of those sermons without losing his place; and why, in the *Mechanism* study, he sees the voice of Calvinist gravity as part of his "mental ballast," as one of the "old prejudices" or "family memories" that will always have a strong force in the "unconscious," holding a planetary sway over the upward flights of new thought.

While as a child Oliver was exposed to a diverse range of theological positions (hearing visitors to the house, guest speakers at his father's First Church in Cambridge, and usually accompanying his father for exchange visits to other pastorates in the wider Boston area), his father became over the years more and more staunchly identified with one very rigid, extreme stance within this spectrum of voices: that of the orthodox purist. If the child found himself naturally attracted to those clergymen "who had a cheerful look and smile in spite of its being the Sabbath day," his father was allied with "others of sad and solemn mien, whose presence lent additional gloom to the Puritan solemnity" (*AN*, 38). Too often his father's Sunday visitors were men

smitten with the Sabbath paralysis which came from the rod of Moses and killed out their natural spirits, and was apt to make them – to childhood – dreary and repulsive. (*AN*, 35)

As Holmes here continues with endless elaborations of these caricatural distinctions – between the smilers and the frowners – we sense more and more clearly the outlines of a larger complex of theological issues: the contemporary debate between levity and gravity as it emerges into a child's consciousness. While Oliver warmed immediately to the "benignant smile" of Unitarian Harvard's genial President Kirkland, he knew that his father was closer to the visitors of "sour aspect"; for, despite his kind heart, Abdiel's theology placed him in the grave line of Jonathan Edwards, whose view of children as "vipers, and worse than vipers" was a rude shock to the sensitive youngster (*AN*, 38–39). If Oliver preferred the new "class" of preachers like Henry Ward Beecher who spoke on a conversational model as "living men to living men," his father was a good friend of Lyman Beecher, Henry's father, and listened only to the voice of that older class of preachers, those who spoke in admonishing tones as "dying men to dying men" (*AN*, 38).

And as the diverse voices of liberal theology grew stronger in Cambridge, Abdiel's tolerance and listening range narrowed in embattled reaction. Before he could expose Oliver to Harvard, the "heretic college," he sent him for a year to rigid Andover, in a vain attempt (as Tilton puts it in a half-apt medical phrase) "to have him inoculated with orthodoxy."[2] Then, from 1826 to 1829, while Oliver was revelling in the free range of conversation in all the clubs, debates, and carnivals at Harvard, Abdiel suddenly decided to silence the doctrinal dialogue in his Cambridge pulpit – ending his policy of "liberal" exchanges with guest speakers from a multiplicity of doctrinal schools, and instead following Lyman Beecher in instituting an "exclusive" policy of opening the church only to exhortations from Orthodox Calvinists, with fiery Lyman Beecher himself as a frequent visitor. This stand made Abdiel Holmes the center of theological controversy in Cambridge for several years. After a year of uneasiness with this unrelenting and univocal series of dour divines, Abdiel's parishioners formally requested a return to "liberal" exchanges – to include even the Unitarians. When he stood firm, the parish and town were forced into a long intramural struggle, finally, during Oliver's senior year at Harvard, resulting in Abdiel's removal from the pulpit. Revealing a deep division within church walls between clergy and laymen, this struggle also opened outward with a ripple effect to expose an intense parallel debate within the walls of many Cambridge households: many families, notes one

biographer, were here "split into opposing camps," and one parish-
ioner wrote, describing the effects of this Abdiel Holmes affair, that
now "husband is against wife and mother is against daughter, as it
were."[3]

Reverend Holmes' removal was thus a sign of the revolutionary
times for many New England parishioners and for many divided
households – and the moment clearly and permanently marked his
son Oliver's thought. In small scale, it presented a telling symbolic
model of republican revolt against patriarchal authority, which
would naturally "hit home" to a young man just taking his first giant
steps into the revels and riot of the world-upside-down at Harvard,
just graduating into manhood, just beginning to make a name for
himself – with a fame based on just the sort of "levity" that his father
so opposed. To find his father suddenly stripped of his former
position, at this transitional moment in his own life, would naturally
prove a shock to this sensitive adolescent, understandably leaving
him with deep strains of anxiety and guilt. Through his later life,
Doctor Holmes would become a progressive voice for change who
nonetheless, very much like his contemporary Hawthorne, always
harbored strongly ambivalent feelings about the filial revolt implied
in any revolution.

But if Abdiel wanted his parishioners to hear only one voice in the
church, he could never so silence the daily dialogue that his children
heard at home. Oliver's mother, Sarah Wendell Holmes, was an
irrepressible voice for levity in all aspects of family life. She had
grown up in religiously liberal Boston and Cambridge rather than
Connecticut, and her ancestors were not clergymen but wealthy
landowners, merchants, and even a doctor. While Abdiel labored
alone among the scholarly volumes in his study, his wife's main joy
was sociability, in any pleasant group activities that allowed free play
to her steady stream of witty chatter. As biographer Tilton writes,

Lightheartedness came to her more easily than to her husband and infected
her children. Her daughters turned into village belles; her sons, into wits.[4]

This smiling mother would dispel any puritanical gloom in the home
by bringing dancing masters to town to teach the children the latest
movements, often reciting romantic and sentimental poetry and
always urging the cause of expressive music. A Holmes poem –
explicitly contrasting his mother's aesthetic play to his father's

theological gravity – records one triumph of her lightheartedness, the moment when (following the Romantic fashion) she had a piano installed in the house:

> . . . the father asked for quiet in his grave paternal way,
> But the mother hushed the tumult with the words, "Now, Mary, play."
>
> ("Opening the Piano," *CW*, ii, 73)

In fact the specific terms "gravity" and "levity" were apparently most likely to be invoked in Calvinist debates about music. While Abdiel had grave misgivings about the "light and unhallowed airs" to which some church hymns were being set, his wife Sarah was an avid supporter of the new music. It was probably her influence that led to young Oliver's early habits of constant whistling and singing, to his hobby of flute-playing, and later in old age to his classically comic attempts at the violin. Even at a very early age, in an act of impulsive self-assertion that may have shocked his father, little Oliver whittled himself a flute on which he would play without stop, everything from the Irish melodies of Tom Moore, some of his mother's favorites, to the hymns of Isaac Watts. If the flute which became his childhood trademark seems (as a symbol of the "poetic") to anticipate Holmes' later interests in verse, his habit of mixing light airs with hymns here also anticipates the sort of kingbird levity with which the witty Autocrat will add musical *fioriture* to the steady drone of a sermon. The introduction of such music into church solemnities represented, to Orthodox Calvinists like Abdiel Holmes, the most direct and dangerous threat of "levity." Even Watts – with his pleasing, optimistic poetry replacing Jehovah's Old Testament harshness with benevolence; with his Lockean pedagogy allowing at least some freedom of educational exploration and rational theological inquiry to the prodigal child not seen as innately depraved; and with his central role in the shift from the strict patriarchal family to a new affectional model of man as loving son to both his earthly and heavenly fathers – was a subject of much discussion among the orthodox in the era, which is probably why Doctor Holmes so often mentions Watts as having been a childhood favorite.[5] It was only after a long campaign by young Oliver and his mother, and after much inner struggle, that Abdiel had finally consented to allow Watts' hymns in his church. Even then, as he gave out the new hymnals, he spoke in grave tones of his concern about such aesthetic "levity": "Let none regard these sacred songs as mere entertainment.

Above all, let none perform with levity." But as the biographer who cites or paraphrases this admonishment then notes, "There was small doubt that Oliver, up in his room, performed with levity."[6]

And there was no doubt that Oliver was infected with his mother's light frivolity in other ways too. He was very much like her in many of his traits: mother and son were both unusually tiny (especially in contrast to Abdiel's big, broad-shouldered build) and she always said that this made them quick, energetic, busy – they were both always buzzing like hummingbirds from one project to another around the house. Like his mother, Oliver was also almost pathologically talkative, a chatterbox who would continue to bubble cheerfully with new stories or jokes no matter how often he was shushed by his father or by teachers. Sociability was for both of them the greatest need, and it would be held up by Doctor Holmes as his greatest value.[7] The "Notes" and other Holmes recollections also suggest that young Oliver was – like his mother – often playfully mischievous. He was caught several times smoking cigars behind the barn (anticipating his great joy later in life in the convivial smoking and drinking of his active club life). And one biographer speculates that it was "the Wendell heritage . . . that had impelled him" at age seven to drag his younger brother John with him in playing hooky to attend the town's last public hanging (an early indication of his taste for colorful mixed crowds and spectacle that would lead to a life-long fascination with carnivals, circuses, burlesque houses, humbug "museums," lyceum lectures – and to a general love for the theater which would become another subject of long, bitter debate between Oliver and his father).[8]

This was just the sort of infectious attitude to "entertainment" and "levity" that Reverend Holmes saw endangering church services; his wife and son were happy with new hymnal music – and they did not seem appalled as parishioners began to arrive in church wearing their finest gay bonnets, as if going to a show. As one Holmes-family biographer summarizes this problem, "Abdiel Holmes was troubled; neither punishment nor prayer made his boy look sternly on solemn things." Throughout Oliver's life, and especially as he embarked on a serious profession, Abdiel continued to warn his son about his "frivolity": though the quips and puns of his humorous poems might win foolish applause at public readings, they were certainly not suitable for a grave physician and might actually harm his reputation.[9] Other paternal figures throughout Holmes' life agreed with

Abdiel. For Dr. Jackson, Oliver's medical mentor at Harvard, levity was his student's most distinctive humor – and his clearest drawback: a letter introducing Oliver to his son in Europe warned, "Do not mind his apparent frivolity."[10] And indeed many early Holmes patients were apparently put off by this breezy wit who seemed unable to take himself, his profession, or their complaints very seriously; his only reaction to the report of an illness might come with the wordplay of one of his anti-maxims: "be grateful for small fevers."[11] (This may be one reason why Doctor Holmes soon shifted mainly to medical education – and to his famously witty lectures.) But Holmes' frivolity only seemed to increase as he grew older: he came to be known as "The Laughing Doctor"; and it was his "levity of tone" that so especially outraged orthodox readers of his break-fast-table treatments of theology.[12]

Generally, then, when writing as an older man looking back on his life with a desire to mythologize certain special childhood events, to see in these everyday details the emergence of a deep pattern of larger significance for his later life, the Doctor would return again and again to scenes of direct confrontation between levity and seriousness. His autobiographical sketches often highlight the moments of his most frequent childhood sin: it seems Oliver was always laughing at the wrong time. Such convulsive outbursts of levity came apparently as a spontaneous and instinctual defense against Calvinist gravity. The "Notes," for example, are especially proud to single out one such scene as an early indication of an emerging independent character. Family history has it, he says, that even when forced while almost a babe to listen to "one of the most distinguished leaders of the Orthodox party," he had laughed out loud in the Meeting-house, struck by the hellfire speaker's pained grimaces – and that later that day he had contrived somehow to upset that same preacher's inkstand in an unconscious, prankish revolt that, he jokes, "left a very black spot in my memory" (*AN*, 35–36).

The recurrence of these sorts of scenes in Holmes seems to suggest that, like the dark doctors who were found in the "Contagiousness" essay to be carrying a deadly and highly communicable puerperal pestilence every time they invaded a scene of childbirth, these grave Calvinist frowners can induce an almost chemical reaction of resistance every time they approach a healthy, happy child. The Autocrat, for example, jokes that the "chilling look" of one divine (said to be preparing himself "for that smileless eternity" by "banishing . . . all joyousness from [his] countenance") could communicate an instantly contagious illness even while he is simply saying hello:

I have sometimes begun to sneeze on the spot, and gone home with a violent cold, dating from that instant. I don't doubt he would cut a kitten's tail off, if he caught her playing with it. (*CW*, i, 92–93)

And amplifying that defense of child's play in another of these levity–gravity confrontations, Holmes tells us in the *Professor* that the forced long faces of Calvinist visitors to his father's home often sent him into inexplicable and uncontrollable fits, here not of sneezing, but of laughter. Apparently the young Oliver thought that, with such unnatural expressions, these guests must be clown virtuosos showing off their repertoire of funny faces (*CW*, ii, 231). Like Yorick in *Tristram Shandy*, who cites Rochefoucauld's maxim defining "gravity" as "a mysterious carriage of the body to cover the defects of the mind," Holmes is happy at each of these moments to make light of the stern faces of these clergymen, shifting into a deflating medical humor which removes all spiritual content from their gestures, takes their frowns as mere physical ticks, and then often willfully misreads these outward signs of straight-laced orthodoxy as crookedness, discovering inner conflicts and somatized tensions behind the Calvinist's grave physiological contortions:[13]

Another [Orthodox clergyman] had a twist in his mouth that knocked a benediction out of shape, and proved afterwards to have a twist in his morals of a still more formidable character. (*AN*, 35–36)

A VITAL LEVITY IN CREATIVE READING

On the one hand, there is a determinist fatality built into this physiological approach to the development of ideas: if young Oliver's father's ideas are "blind forces" in the blood which can be seen to have "shaped features and battled for the moulding of the constitution" (as the Master said in the passage which introduces this chapter), then there seems to be little the boy can do to prevent the eventual warping of his own face and body along the same lines as those of these grimacing clerics. But on the other hand the early discovery of this ability to re-read or mis-read or re-"figure" the received signs or texts or faces in his Calvinist milieu is also seen in Holmes' "Notes" as the major liberating turn of his childhood –

perhaps offering a literary way out of the bind of physiological determinism.

Of course, the boy's levity will always necessarily remain reactive, in a parasitic relation to the givens of grave books and ideas; during the education of his years in the family home, his only available roles are those of reader or of listener – in the face of words received from others. But Holmes soon found that reading can operate as a very active form of reception – as it does in the kingbird–crow passage about the Autocrat's creative uses of the listener's position at church sermons. This mode of "writerly" reading might open for the child in a closed Calvinist household the possibility of a new interpretive freedom. Almost every domestic scene in the "Religion" section of the "Notes" describes his household life as built out of a series of gravity–levity pairings like that in the *Autocrat* between the preacher-crow and the parishioner-kingbird: again and again, we meet dialogic household interactions between text and reader, between speaker and listener, between dogmatic writers trying to frame our lives (with their *doxa*) and a lively audience using reading as retort to escape that frame (creating *para-doxa*).

Holmes always supported the perhaps un-American value of a childhood spent knocking around among books, and the "Notes" make clear how central a role books had as influences on his early development. But it is also clear that his father's scholarly library – containing only one piece of secular fiction, and strictly censored for the children – though large, could seem to a playful child very grave (a burden literally too "heavy") and very narrow:

[My father's library] was very largely theological so that I was walled-in by solemn folios making the shelves bend under the load of sacred learning.[14]

The curious and wily child, though, developed a number of strategies for reading his way out of this walled-in home situation. Heathen that he was, he had, he says, "a kind of Indian sagacity in the discovery of contraband reading," and he soon knew how to find all the "green patches among the deserts" of his father's dull and expurgated collection (*AN*, 41). The boy also found other uses for these books, often building fortresses out of them – thus reshaping the study walls, felt to be penning him in, to make new houses built on the forms of his own more romantic fantasies of adventure.[15]

He learned, too, more importantly, how to read against the grain of a text: he lists, as "one of the books that most influenced me,"

Scott's Family Bible, but then admits that he was *not* influenced "in the direction the author intended" – on the contrary, Scott woke the boy up to the "enormities" of the Calvinist creed about the Fall of Man (*AN*, 42). Holmes then continues with a long list of all the writings that he read and opposes: pietistic biographies of sickly, devout children which seemed less apt for wholesome, growing, full-blooded youth than the new children's books which were more imaginative, adventurous, and lighter-handed in their moralism; Wigglesworth's poem, "The Day of Doom," on infant depravity; Saurin's sermons, which Oliver remembers his "father placing in [his] hands"; and so on. Many of these works seemed designed, as part of their very reading experience, to imprison the youthful reader in their construction of the world, closing around him like the high, heavy walls of books in Reverend Holmes' study. The *New England Primer*, for example, hopes to write Adam's fall into the very building blocks of the child's language – but Oliver rejects this imposition; Jonathan Edwards' treatise on "Freedom of the Will" ties the reader's will up "hand and foot in the logical propositions which he knots inextricably about them," and yet we have only to lay down the book "to feel as if there was something left free after all" (*CW*, viii, 376); similarly, *The Pilgrim's Progress*, which "represents the universe as a trap which catches most of the human vermin that have its bait dangled before them," itself has a trapping effect which "captivates" its readers – but Holmes grants its power only as a work of wonderful fancy and imagination, thus interpreting its moral elements against Bunyan's intention:

[Bunyan's work] made the system, of which it was the exponent, more unreasonable and more repulsive, instead of rendering it more attractive. (*AN*, 42–43)

When we realize that Holmes' "Notes" on his religious upbringing build mainly as a sketchy elaboration of a theory of critical reading, several extended passages which at first sight may have seemed digressive interruptions gain a new relevance: they help us to see how this active, dialogic relation to received texts might operate, and where it might lead. The "Religion" notes end, for example, with recognition of a general alliance with the goals of the Higher Criticism which had been ironizing all interpretation of the Bible by questioning the historical facticity of its figures, and studying its "legend" as a human construct. Here again, as in the descriptions of

Reverend Holmes' library, the received theological writings are seen as a wall, but now Holmes imagines the possibility of a mode of reading that could take that solid-seeming barrier apart – and then rebuild it again in new form:

The great Truths in our sacred legends are the stones laid in a cement of human errors. The object of what is called the higher criticism, which is only another phrase for *honest* criticism, is to pick out the mortar from between the stones, – to get the errors from between the truths which are embedded in them. The stones will remain, for the eternal laws of gravity are the basis of their stability. (*AN*, 46–47)

As Yvor Winters has pointed out, Holmes always remained strongly addicted to the Puritan habit of allegory.[16] Here, in a movement very much parallel to that in his well-known *Autocrat* allegory of the rock (which extends Puritan domestic symbolism to describe an Enlightenment attack on the clergy, as a "rock" is lifted and dark insects scatter from the "light" [*CW*, 1, 111–13]), Holmes offers the paradox of a figural statement of the need for a naturalistic, "factual" reading of all figures. In both cases, the basic goal is to open up the closed world of the churchmen, to make the "rock" of the church less of a private, walled-in cloister. But the historicist or scientific Higher Criticism is not adopted as a monolithic truth to replace the clergy's interpretation; taken as a single absolute, such science would only leave us facing a more formidable and restrictive wall, and "laws of gravity" which might be even more absolute. So Holmes, characteristically, would stress the initial wall-breaking power of such new interpretations over the force of any final reconstruction. He seems to welcome the new Criticism mainly as it may serve to make our reading a dialogue between possible "constructions" of the text (or of the wall). The effect may be what the Professor calls a "depolarizing" of the Biblical imagery, a translation of the old stories into new terms that somehow diffuse the magnetic charges of superstition and habit which have become associated with the received version. But the new reading-as-translation here would not be completely revolutionary: rather than reduce the wall to rubble, it would simply leave a more natural, refurbished "dry wall" in its place; not denying the weight of the old stones, it would simply reinterpret the forces of theological Gravity in terms of Newton's scientific "law."

The "Notes" mention another approach to a "science of religion" that might also open univocal readings of the Bible to dialogue: "the comparative study of creeds" (*AN*, 43). Long before comparative religion became institutionalized in America, Holmes was one of its strong advocates, reading widely in Indian and Oriental thought – in fact in 1879 he was one of the enthusiastic sponsors of an extremely popular study of Buddha's life, *Light in Asia*. This wide-ranging reading was undertaken not so much in search of new belief as to provide new perspectives on Calvinist and Christian doctrine, and to promote pragmatic study of the reasons for and the effects of religious belief. (William James, who studied with Holmes and was a close friend of his son, would later develop solid studies following the sort of comparatist impulses that the Doctor only touches upon in scattered passages.)

Though he welcomed the liberating new readings of such sciences, Holmes himself did not have the temperament for thorough, systematic, concentrated scientific study; he could never stick to any one subject, one interpretation, or one voice for very long. And this literary idiosyncrasy apparently emerged as a telling trait even in his early childhood – as young Oliver began to develop the one set of reading habits that was truly his own. When the "Notes" digress into seemingly trivial recollections about these reading habits, about Holmes' everyday experiences with books, what begins simply as a self-mocking memory of boyhood idleness and of an inability to sit still finally emerges as one of the most illuminating moments in the entire portrait: in retrospect, these early bad habits seem to set a fundamental pattern of personal style, laying the groundwork both for the Doctor's lifelong practice of writerly reading and for the special mode of aphoristic, digressive, and allusive writing that comes out of such reading:

I read few books through. I remember writing on the last page of one that I had successfully mastered, *perlegi*, with the sense that it was a great triumph to have read quite through a volume of such size. But I have always read *in* books rather than *through* them, and always with more profit from the books I read *in* than the books I read *through*; for when I set out to read *through* a book, I always felt that I had a task before me, but when I read *in* a book it was the page or the paragraph that I wanted, and which left its impression and became a part of my intellectual furniture . . . Besides, I have myself written a great many books, – . . . (*AN*, 40–41, italics and ellipses in original)

Certainly this boy's bad habits are in tune with the times: with Poe's "doctrine of intensity" in the short form, leading him to read even epic works as a series of extractable lyrics; with the reader's aesthetic of this age of anthologies, perhaps epitomized in the 1855 appearance of *Bartlett's Quotations*. But Holmes is not interested in a practical man's quick read to extract a book's useful essence – quite the contrary; and unlike the submissive sentimentalists of this retrospective era, he does not want to stock his memory with past commonplaces out of deference to a bygone golden age of the heroic fathers. The goal of this reading, rather, is a certain independence from the received texts; it would open a way for the belated reader in this transitional period to begin to turn those old texts to his own uses. In contrast to the sort of grave reading which sees each book as a dense, imposing monolith and applies a work ethic to make long immersion in each book a duty and a plodding task, young Oliver discovers an alternative which is light, playful, irresponsible – and indeed childish.[17] (Such a mode of response to the "anxiety of influence" is quite different from the High Seriousness of Harold Bloom's "strong misprision"; it seems most closely related to eighteenth-century forerunners of that Romantic stance.)[18] Following the urges of desire rather than those of duty, this child-reader still accepts a place "in" the old books, but he does not allow them to frame his activity completely, cover-to-cover. The reader need not accept the narrative architecture of a given tome; he need not be walled in by the book's covers. To the child-reader, a book may have more than one point of entry, and more than one exit.

Like the "aristocratic" or "writerly" reader in Roland Barthes, Young Oliver "draws the text out of its internal chronology," and his very unscientific method of cutting texts up or starring special fragments and phrasings may then serve as it does for Barthes to unsettle any "singular, theological meaning" dictated by that "tutor text," with liberating tentatives towards a plurality of possible interpretations.[19] While the Higher Criticism may help Holmes here, in picking out special stones from the artificially mortared walls of received books, this mercurial reader will not want to open things up only to close them in a new way; rather than simply accepting or rejecting a text, he will try each stone-fragment in multiple new settings, placing it into mosaic-dialogues with other texts, other critical voices. Such re-use of found phrasings as part of the shifting arrangements of his own intellectual "furniture" makes this reader less a consumer than a producer of texts – so it is not surprising that at the end of the passage Holmes makes an elliptical leap from the topic of his childhood reading habits to that of his adult work in writing. And from this we can gather that this writing will share something of that youthful style of reading: it seems likely that it will build as a sort of *bricolage*, assembling received discourses in new combinations; and it will likely share the essential digressiveness of that reading mode, hovering like a butterfly between readerly allusions – never resting long in any one interpretive or creative stance.

For Barthes, a reader's "systematic use of digression" serves to "interrupt . . . any ideology of totality" in the tutor text, and the same effect seems to be inherent in the approach of Holmes-student.[20] Picking up *Pilgrim's Progress* in this way, for example, would put Oliver-the-reader in the role of a prodigal always digressing from the pilgrim's predestined path, thrilling to the fantasy or adventure of individual scenes as they are bracketed off from the moral, theological, and literary end-terms of the full narrative, taking the story's images as tropes for his own imaginative uses without reference to the allegorical resolution which should reveal the true Christian meaning in each of these images as types. In this schematic view, there are two basic roles for the reader: that of the reader-pilgrim, or that of the reader-prodigal. In one mode the student-reader should adopt the traits of a mule (or any beast of burden), accepting the heavy "burthen" of the narrative order and ideology as his given task, ploddingly advancing with it along well-worn one-directional ruts. In the other mode, he is like a quick-moving bird who alights on a scene or image only briefly before buzzing off with his morsel, in a back-and-forth flight that seems to mock the size and weight of the host-text. And whatever the animal analogies that are used, this same opposition recurs frequently in Holmes. We have met such a pair of opposites already: the kingbird's lively digressive listening found its polar contrast within the bird world in the mode of the clerical crow. And in the "Notes" Holmes defines two readerly responses to the tutor texts of Calvinism along similar lines, by distinguishing the rides of two sorts of horse:

The effect of Calvinist training on different natures varies very much. The majority take the creed as a horse takes his collar; it slips by his ears, over his neck, he hardly knows how, but he finds himself in harness, and jogs along as his fathers and forefathers had done before him . . . Here and there a stronger-minded one revolts with the whole strength of his nature from the inherited servitude of his ancestry, and gets rid of the whole harness before he is at peace with himself. A few shreds may hold to him . . . (*AN*, 42)

The sense of unrestrained revolt here may be uncharacteristic of Holmes – and we note that he quickly remembers the "few shreds" as an honest afterthought. But the explosive attack on Calvinism as a carriage "train" harnessing blindered beasts of burden along a one-way "highway of thought" recurs very often in the Doctor's writings – most famously with the explosion of the "One-Hoss Shay" ("The Deacon's Masterpiece," *CW*, 1, 252–56). And in at least one other passage, from *A Mortal Antipathy*, the image of a rolling, unreined horse emerges out of a discussion of literary form very similar to that in the "Notes": here the wild, disporting animal is opposed to the work-horse drudge as an analogy to the way that a playful, extravagant, writerly digressiveness is opposed to the long, painful, beginning-to-end progress of serious narrative (*CW*, vii, 28). But the "Notes" description of this unharnessing revolt also gives us a strong and very apt sense for a crucial household issue behind all of the discussions of a child's reading-as-resistance: the given texts are received as an "inherited servitude" from the student's "fathers and forefathers."

The paragraph that begins with Holmes' discussion of his liberating habit of "reading *in*" all books then ends with a long description of the source of these books: his father's library. So the pictures of what he calls his "mental library," full of the "intellectual furniture" gleaned from his light, writerly reading, are meant to serve as a defensive preparation for and contrast to our entrance into the very material presence of Abdiel Holmes' study. Holmes' seemingly quixotic and childish desire simply to avoid entrapment between the covers of epic tomes is thus related to a more serious and understandable desire to avoid entrapment within the four walls of the family library. His mode of active reading implies an active model of the mind, which might free the memory from pure repetition of external influences, and which might allow him to select and reorder the raw materials of the given library so as to "furnish" and structure the "library" inside his head along very different lines.

The central scene in the "Notes," so important to Holmes that he describes it twice, in detail, in the brief space of this ten-page essay, clearly situates his early childhood discovery of this active or antithetical reading within the larger household pattern of parental interactions, and suggests that mother and son were silent accomplices in the effort to break out of a grave readerly entrapment. The family's ritual rehearsal of the Westminster Catechism (one of the

most highly scripted forms of question-and-answer exchange) apparently involved for young Oliver a strongly ambivalent complex of
tendencies to both obedience and revolt. Following the wishes of her
husband, Mrs. Holmes each time "sobered her pleasant countenance" to hear the recital of these central articles of faith. But Oliver
repeated the programmatic words only "nominally":

Much of its language was mere jargon in my ears, – I got no coherent idea
from the doctrine of transmitted sinfulness, and the phrases of "adoption,"
"justification," and "sanctification" had as little meaning for me as the
syllable by the aid of which we counted ourselves "out" in our games. (*AN*,
38–39)

Of course in some ways Reverend Holmes here got all he could
ask for: from his early years on, Oliver could rattle off both the
longer and the shorter Catechisms almost in his sleep. Even if the
doctrines here remain a mere sequence of sounds, like those of the
"Pledge of Allegiance" as repeated by today's public-school children,
they must still in this process inevitably become part of the speaker's
lifelong mental baggage, his automatic verbal unconscious. But if
paternal decree thus succeeded in making the grave Catechism (like
the dull crow's sermon) the background drone framing all household
activity, Oliver's musical mother seems also to have allowed a wide
latitude for kingbird-like "variations and *fioriture*" on that given
theme. She was clearly only going through the motions when she
adopted her Calvinist frown, and her son apparently did the same
in mouthing the text. As he did when responding with laughter to
the grimaces of visiting clergymen, so Oliver here diminishes the
Calvinist "figures" by taking them absolutely literally, as pure sounds
divorced from any authorial intention or symbolic meaning. The
effect is a carnivalization of the Assembly's ideology of Judgment.
Manipulated as mere objects, the ritual words can be exploded from
within. Emptied of any sense of necessity or of physical motivation,
dour Calvinist faces and phrases can come to seem funny and fun.
The Catechism can here be turned upside down, to emerge as a sing-
song children's game – where Election seems to become simply a
matter of "counting out" some of the players. So, in the setting of this
sort of dialogic reading, even simple repetition can open the univocally serious and pious official doctrine of the Fall to unsettling
possibilities of disparagement and profanation in a free play of

ambivalent laughter; the "face" of saturnalian levity can peek out as the other side of the "figures" of gravity.[21]

But although Holmes tells us, "I do not think we believed a word of it . . . An instinct was working in me which could not be choked out by the dogmas of the Assembly's Catechism," throughout his life he nonetheless continued to inhabit the Catechism, working parodically or parasitically within its frame (*AN*, 38). Indeed much of his mature writing seems to develop both in its images and themes as an extension of these first youthful experiments in the mode of active reading. For example, one of Holmes' most controversial Lyceum lectures, "The Chief End of Man," for the season 1858–59, was an unorthodox lay sermon which provoked a flood of criticism as it ironically glossed a text from the Westminster Catechism.[22]

These childhood scenes of mother and son repeating the Catechism under paternal direction serve as an epitome of all the discussions of reading in the "Notes," and help us to see the place of these strategies of mischievous misreading within the dynamics of Holmes' divided household. For the Catechism ritual puts young Oliver in a classic "double bind" that is not easily resolved. Gregory Bateson has defined the "double bind" as a dialogical or self-contradictory system of communication within the family household which makes every statement between parent and child operate as a multi-leveled message built of conflicting impulses – and which then may be reflected in an inner dialogue of multiple voices which develops within the schizophrenic child. Applied unscientifically, this communications model seems particularly apt as a description of Holmes' household reading situation here, where the Catechism words between mother and son become the medium for a complex meta-communication speaking both for filial obedience and for revolt.[23] And indeed the "Notes" survey of the theological controversies of Holmes' early years, and of their resonances in the dialogical relations between his mother and his father, concludes (in a passage cited earlier, but which can now be understood more fully as it arises out of a family history) with the recognition that for him the debate will never cease: undecided and torn, the child will come to internalize the verbal conflicts around him so that all of his thought proceeds as an ongoing interior conversation between diverse voices:

Thus, though fond of society at times, I have always been good company to myself, either by day or night. The "I" and the "me" of my double personality keep up endless dialogues, as is, I suppose, the case with most people, – sometimes using very harsh language to each other. One of them, I am sorry to say, is very apt to be abusive and to treat the other like an idiot, with expressions which, if uttered, would make a very bad figure in these pages. (*AN*, 43)

LEVITY–GRAVITY DIALOGUE IN THE PROCESS OF BREATHING: BODILY MODELS FOR CHANGE

We can easily understand why, when such a man turns to writing, he will find the domestic dialogue to be the most suitable and attractive form. Even if, for the reading public, he might have to tone down some of the expressions of his inner voices, his best and most characteristic pages will still be clearly patterned after those endless dialogues of "I" and "me." It will be only natural that Holmes' most innovative and interesting contributions – in medicine as in literature – will develop out of his idiosyncratic new approaches to conversation. In the same way, it seems that the internal divisions of this "double personality," which lead him to see even the self as a small society, made Holmes a classically "social" person with a lifelong attraction for converse and company. For at night, or whenever he did find himself alone, and so would be forced to play out these "endless dialogues" in solitude, the experience could apparently be very tense and painful.

As the "Notes" describe it, this inner conflict between "I" and "me" works on visceral and verbal levels. For, paradoxically, Holmes the social butterfly was in many ways a very internal man. With the same movement that we saw in the Master's final statement in *The Poet*, the "Notes" first see the era's theological debates as operating within the family household, then see that household debate as operating within the individual psyche, and finally see that psychic debate as operating in the psycho-physiological tensions and strains of the body. And this conflict seems only to gain in force as it is internalized. Although Holmes is typically jocular about it, his description makes clear that the dialogue of these voices – as they become somatized – can become rude and charged. We saw that Holmes experienced the Catechism readings in this same way, as a vaguely physiological battle between a rising "instinct" and oppressive "dogmas" that would "choke [it] out"; and this scene was paralleled by the very physical revolt of the horse bucking against his harness restraint. Then, as the outer world seems divided into two camps distinguished by the bodily marks of their smiling or frowning faces, so the inner life of the child develops as a struggle between two models of internal physical deportment – between the visceral habits and postures associated with levity or with gravity.

Like many in this age of "sentimental religion," Holmes most often approaches theological problems through the eyes of the child, examining doctrines not for their truth value but for their effect as influences on a youth's sensitive mind and growing body. When theology is thus subsumed under the aegis of childrearing, the medical psychologist's analysis will tend to focus on the physical results of a belief – as though studying the healthful or harmful effects of a foreign substance ingested into the body. Sunday School children's books, for example, with their pious, melancholy child-heroes always in the process of dying, can be quickly dismissed as an unhealthy, stifling influence on the growth of a rosy-cheeked child full of natural energy. And the *New England Primer*'s ideas about Adam's fall threaten seriously to break a cog in the mental machinery, arousing an angry response from the voice of medicine:

Doctrines like that, introduced into the machinery of a young intelligence, break the springs, poison the fountains, dwarf the development, ruin the harmony, disorganize the normal mechanism of the thinking powers. (*AN*, 45)

But in some ways the doctor's view of the bodily repercussion's of "gravity" is not so different from the orthodox clerical one. The theological doctrine that the child must be punished for the sins of his first parent is here translated by a medical doctrine that the child will suffer for his actual father's errors in child-rearing; the concern simply shifts from the problem of an inheritance of the Fall to that of an inheritance of the theology of the Fall. Either way the inheritance is seen to leave deep mental and organic marks; either way the gravity of verbal and genetic repetition places heavy weights on the developing constitution. The Doctor's view here, in fact, seems to build on a residue of the American Calvinist ideas of declension which see the workings of "gravity" in the spiritual and genetic downward flow from generation to generation.

So America's mid-nineteenth-century apostle of scientific progress and of the Rise of Man, then, can often sound like a Cotton Mather in his obsession with the psychological difficulties of a break with the grave tradition of his Puritan predecessors. Each time young Oliver repeats the *Primer* rhymes or the Catechism, the verbal struggle is paralleled by a visceral one: on the one hand his father's doctrinal influence threatens to crush or to realign the rising "springs" of his mental machinery; but, on the other hand, the son will be torn by deep guilt for any failures of repetition, for any waywardness from the filial-pietistic path. Paradoxically, the deviations which seemed an ever-present temptation to Mather require for Holmes the necessary but harrowing ordeal of a lifelong struggle. If for the associationist the vulnerable child-mind is passive before its environmental influences, any fundamental change of mind is hard to imagine. It is difficult to avoid repeating the past when it has become ingrained habit, even a bodily stance. Though Holmes also posits the existence of a vague rising "instinct" that cannot accept the dogma as it is handed down, it must require a crippling effort to shake the mental train out of these deep physiological ruts.

The associationist Doctor is not the only one who stresses the bodily repercussions of Calvinist theology. This physicalist sense seems in fact to be central to the orthodox position as well – which helps to explain the enormous hold it could have over a child's heart and mind, and why young Oliver could feel this "gravity" first as a sort of somatic ache. Yorick was on to something when he defined gravity as "a mysterious carriage of the body"; this "gravity" is also the "burthen" on the shoulders of Bunyan's Christian, that heavy millstone which so obsessed the daily thought of Hawthorne. And it is the main thrusting force in the universe of Jonathan Edwards, whose synthesis of Newtonian physics and Calvinist theology made possible his powerfully literal sermon imagery identifying innate sin with the physical weight of the human body: "Your wickedness makes you as it were heavy as lead."[24] The same law of "gravity" would form the basis both for Abdiel Holmes' theology and for his avid hobby interest in writing the *Annals* of American science. It is the effect of this whole oppressive system that young Oliver is attacking when he mocks the frowning faces of his father's friends; the carriage of the body, the neck, the back, the mouth – all betray the strains of "gravity" as a way of life.

And certainly the son of an orthodox minister would not be likely to escape these same influences. The "Notes" vividly describe the physical ingestion and "incorporation" of Calvinist ideas:

Born near the beginning of the century, my mind was early impregnated with beliefs which, in the minds of those whom I consider the best thinkers of the present, are utterly extinct, and replaced by newer thought. (*AN*, 44)

Despite his rationalist's sense that, in an evolutionary view of intellectual history, these beliefs are doomed to "extinction," Holmes' psychology makes it difficult to explain the practical process that makes such evolutionary change possible. Doctrines become stubbornly irrational habits when they impregnate the mind of a well-trained child; like food, an idea seems to enter into an organism's very circulation, thus intimately working to shape the body's future growth:

The doctrine of the fallen race was incorporated into the food of the New England child as truly as the Indian corn, on which he was fed, entered into the composition of his bones and muscles . . . The doctrine of the Fall of Man, and all connected with it, was not only wrought into the intellectual constitution of a New England child, coloring his existence as madder stains the bones of animals whose food contains it, but it entered into his whole conception of the universe. (*AN*, 44–45)

This is one Holmes version of an argument common in the era: while many were bemoaning in general terms the poverty of the American "soil" and cultural environment for the growth of native artists, complaining of the new country's lack of past or external models for creative work, the Doctor sees the soil as all too loaded and the past as all too present – in fact as a mental block to new efforts. To him, the "New England doctrine" is the specific element in the "soil" of the intellectual environment which inhibits new growth in the American mind.

Once inscribed into the boy's very bones, as part of every muscular movement and each reflex of the mental machine, the conception of the Fall will certainly resist transformation. Holmes' description of the effect of his lifelong internal conflict with these stubborn early influences – as it becomes a costly, crippling wrestling match between opposed aspects of the self – then culminates in his most intimate and incisive picture of what seems indeed to have been the pattern of his life:

No child can overcome these early impressions without doing violence to the whole mental and moral machinery of his being. He may conquer them in after years, but the wrenches and strains which his victory cost him leave him a cripple as compared with a child trained in sound and reasonable beliefs. (*AN*, 39–40)

The Master says that he could only recognize the pattern of his life's progress – that internal debate between paternal and maternal strains of blood – from the vantage point of ripe old age; and Holmes in the autobiographical "Notes" tells us that he was well beyond "the comparatively immature age of threescore years and ten" before he could "analyze the effect of these conflicting agencies" in himself (*AN*, 40). But finally, after all his emphasis on the strong verbal and visceral influences of paternal gravity, Holmes in his late-life visions offers an overall life model attempting to reconcile the awareness of such constraining conservative forces with the undeniable thrust of an opposing "mighty impulse" of levity, of evolutionary change. For no matter how wrenching and violent it is, the Doctor recognizes and in fact wants to celebrate continual intellectual progress – in individuals as in nations. Young Oliver himself, after all, grew out of his inheritance to become one of his age's major spokesmen for "that mighty impulse which carries the generation to which we belong far away from the landmark of its predecessors" (*AN*, 40).

Like the Master's, Holmes' illustrations of this vision of an oceanic current of progress are chemical – the changing shape of a lump of alum rock gradually dissolving in a test-tube here apparently suggesting something of the way the old "stones" of Calvinist mental blocks can dissolve or change shape (*AN*, 40) – or physiological:

The process of extricating ourselves from those early influences which we are bound to outgrow is a very slow and difficult one. It is illustrated by the phenomenon of waste and repair in the physical system. (*AN*, 43)

But the main thrust of all of these scientific models (as in the Master's vision of two warring strains of blood) is to reassert the fundamental role of dialogue, to recognize an alternation of opposing polarities as the base dynamic on almost every level of human life-process, and thus to explain change and progress as a counterbalance to the heavy solidities of the status quo. For these models simply expand the range of the levity–gravity interaction which we have seen elaborated in so many household scenes between Holmes' mother and father, suggesting by analogy the ways in which the poles of such a dialogue can function both internally (with the formation of new tissues in the body) and in the outer world (with the formation of new ideas in the intellectual history of an age).

REVOLUTION IN RESPIRATION

Many nineteenth-century thinkers would see in the growth of each individual a small-scale enactment of the intellectual growth of his age or of all mankind. Since the Doctor's life in fact spanned almost the entire nineteenth century, 1809–94, he would find it hard to avoid comparing his personal progress with that of nineteenth-century America as a whole. But Holmes' analogical thinking in his autobiographical "Notes" goes so far as to see each breath in a person's body as a microcosmic reflection of the larger dialectical pattern of ideational change in the entire "body politic." In the following key passage, he is explaining further the difficulty we have in getting rid of our early impressions, and that he himself had in emerging from the Calvinist cocoon to keep pace with the dizzying developments across America:

The process is like that of respiration. The oxygen taken into the system preys upon its effete material, which is carried out by exhalation and secretion, at the same time that it adds the vivifying element to the forming tissues. New ideas act upon society as oxygen does on the body, attacking its errors, which pass away from the lists of human beliefs, and strengthening the new truth which is building in its place. (*AN*, 43–44)

Hegel, in a highly indicative paragraph from the "Preface" to his *Phenomenology*, invokes a cluster of imagery very similar to that we have been tracing in Holmes' "Notes" to see in the educational *Bildung* of the individual a type of the progress of universal Spirit, to see the literal birth of a single child as analogue to the birth of a new age arising out of the French Revolution, and then to see this large-scale movement of radical separation from the inherited world of the parents as a process beginning with an eruption of the dialectic within the household, emerging with the dissolving power of "spirit" in the child's first breath:

It is surely not difficult to see that our time is a time of birth and transition to a new period. The spirit has broken with what was hitherto the world of its existence and imagination and is about to submerge all this in the past; it is at work giving itself a new form. To be sure, the spirit is never at rest but always engaged in ever progressing motion. But just as in the case of a child the first breath it draws after long silent nourishment terminates the gradualness of the merely quantitative progression – a qualitative leap – and now the child is born, so, too, the spirit that educates itself matures slowly and quietly toward the new form, dissolving one particle of the edifice of its previous world after the other . . . This gradual crumbling which did not alter the physiognomy of the whole is interrupted by the break of day that, like lightning, all at once reveals the edifice of the new world.[25]

For Holmes as for Hegel, breathing is a veiled physiological model of revolution, with airy oxygen acting out a sort of somatic saturnalia as it disrupts or dissolves the obstructive blocks of heavy, decadent bodily tissue. The Doctor's play on the words "pass away from the lists of human beliefs" suggests that the "lists" of beliefs are not so much dry catalogues as they are arenas of a violent combat, so that oxygen is put in the role of a young warrior storming the barricades with the goal of opening arterial flow in the city as in the body, and so that the "passing away" of "effete material" into that excretory flow also becomes the medical–political euphemism for its final destruction in this purge.

Breathing becomes a central dynamic image throughout the Doctor's writings – the process of respiration preoccupies him just as the process of vision preoccupies Emerson. Holmes' lifelong problems with severe asthma seem to have made him very conscious of the process of breathing – and led him to see it not as an autonomic bodily function but as a willed action, a process involving constant struggle between opposing physical forces. In *A Mortal Antipathy* one of the Doctor's characters describes breathing, typically, as a "rising and falling" movement requiring endless "toil" to "lift the bars of the cage, in which his breathing organs are confined, to save himself from asphyxia" (*CW*, VII, 261–62). And if respiration here is seen as analogous to ventilating a room or breaking out of a prison, Holmes frequently calls up this form of airy action when treating his central theme: the determining powers of environment and heredity. When such questions of heredity come up in the opening pages of Holmes' biography of Emerson, for example, the Doctor is happy to be able to quote Emerson himself on the power of a child's breath: "Some qualities [Nature] carefully fixes and transmits, but some, and those the finer, she exhales with the breath of the individual, as too costly to perpetuate" (*RWE* 2). The physiological model here leads Emerson to an unusual accent on the positive value of the "finer" inherited racial and familial characteristics – with individual development seen mainly as destruction and loss. But here again, as in Hegel, it is the child's breath which brings the potential to dissolve the old solidities, to serve the impulses of a rising "spirit." For better or for worse, each breath we take works to help us break out of the confines of the given body, to break out of the house of our fathers.

In his exploration of the revolutionary potential in breath in the "Notes" passage cited above – where "new ideas" are seen to "act upon society as oxygen does on the body" – Holmes finally shies away from some of these radical implications in a characteristic way,

with an interjected statement that goes against the grain of everything in the "Notes" but which helps to make clearer what is at stake
for him in this vision of dialectical oppositions within bodily process:

It is fortunate for our civilization that our early impressions are got rid of
with such difficulty. The conservative principle is always (except at brief
intervals) largely in excess of the destructive and renewing tendencies which
go hand in hand with the task of improving society. (*AN*, 43)

As he developed his sense of these progressive potentialities in
physiological functions, Holmes could often feel a need to reassert
the power of a restraining counterforce. His essay on "Jonathan
Edwards," for example, ends its meditation on free will versus
hereditary fate by exploring analogies between the functioning of
bodily organs and of cultural "organisms," concluding with the same
ambivalence voiced in the "Notes": "what we want in the religious
and in the political organisms is just the kind of vital change which
takes place in our bodies, – interstitial disintegration and reintegra-
tion." And the last sentence of this essay then leaves us with a
warning about the house-breaking powers that may be unleashed
through the dynamic movements of this organic system. If the forces
of "disintegration" are not balanced by movements of "reintegra-
tion," the somatic revolts which clear out arterial passages and free
us from old dogma might finally destroy the frames of all temples:
"the mighty explosives with which the growth of knowledge has
furnished us should be used rather to clear the path for those who
come after us than to shatter the roofs which have long protected and
still protect so many of our humble and trusting fellow-creatures"
(*CW*, VIII, 401). The Doctor concludes a review of Herbert Spencer
with the same admonition: "interstitial renovation" must involve
resistances to change as well as progressive forces which "carry
away" effete matter and effete ideas (*Autocrat's Miscellany*, 285).

If these dialogic flip-flops in Holmes' stance indicate his unresolved
ambivalence in the face of these two tendencies, his inability to
choose one side or the other, they also lead him to continue to
explore the ramifications of each "principle," and to recognize the
workings of both poles in himself and in his world. Respiration is one
of the most basic physiological examples one could choose of a
bipolar process: in this most common act, we all alternately inhale
and exhale. And as the Doctor describes it, the internal results of this

breathing involve the organism in a classic struggle between levity and gravity – with the light forces of oxygen meeting up against the solid weight of body tissue, and then slowly tending to dissolve vulnerable matter and carry it off into the air. As in the Master's analogy to the flight of a hot-air balloon ("I have got rid of something my mind could not keep to itself and rise as it was meant to into higher regions" [*CW*, III, 320–21]), the oxygen here is associated with a dynamic operation which (in the same idiom which again literalizes ex-pression as a form of excretion) "gets rid of . . . early impressions" to allow both the rise of new personal impulses and by extension the general rise of modern man. As the writer-aeronaut lightens himself of his "mental ballast" by showering sandbags into the sky, so the movement of oxygen works to disperse stony blocks into fine particles which can then "pass away."

"THE HEART REFUSES TO BE IMPRISONED": HOLMES, EMERSON, AND HEGEL ON BILDUNG IN THE BLOODSTREAM

Though Holmes may sometimes find his own suggestions unsettling, the "Notes" image of a respiratory dialogue works as a model of continual change, implying an ongoing struggle between the new and the old, the airy and the solid, the destructive and the conservative. And the goal in each of these interactions is always (for the alum-rock dissolving in the test-tube as for the "effete" tissue "preyed upon" by new air) to dissolve fixities, to open a free flow despite the obstacles of physical and mental "blocks," to contribute (even on the level of arterial circulation) to the flow of progressive currents. From such passages we can see that Holmes' thought would be permeated by the nineteenth-century ideal of constant and cumulative advances in science, that he would see this collective progress as analogous to the growth of a single person's mind, and that he would be especially interested in the moments of scientific revolution which open a field to new paradigms. As they did for the writer–scientist Gaston Bachelard, these concerns would converge for Holmes in the vision of a sort of "psychoanalysis of the sciences," which would seek to isolate the elements (usually over-determining patterns latent in unconscious reliance upon certain fixed mental images) in normal science that might become "mental blocks" to further exploration.[26] By pointing out these obstacles, an analyst like Holmes or Bachelard would hope to free the group scientific mind from its fixations and thus to free up the "circulation" of ideas and the progress of general knowledge. Even outside the sciences, Holmes' lifelong preoccupation with the role of "prejudice" and "habit" in his own thinking – "prejudices" involving racial or political ramifications, as well as epistemological ones – led him to much meditation of the means of dissolving such obstacles to healthy mental flow and to happy social life. (We have seen that many of the Holmes phrases frequently excerpted by critics to illustrate his "Brahmin" prejudices or Bostonian provincialism are often in fact intended to foreground those views, to begin to analyze them, to mock them, and finally to help root them out – and that such attacks on "prejudice" and "habit" are in fact fundamental to both the themes and the rhetorical form of the Doctor's conception of conversation.)

Holmes' primary obsession with "getting rid of" his father's Calvinism led him to a general model of the thinking process which would impel him to challenge his "constitutional" "conservative principle" in many areas of life. With the dialogical pattern outlined here – this version of *Bildung* in the bloodstream – the Doctor's quirky, witty empiricism brings him close to what he might elsewhere describe as the "foggy" realm of German metaphysics, into the Hegelian world which "is never at rest but always engaged in ever present motion." Here no idea is solid or static; each belief rises out of an evolutionary struggle that also dooms it to future "extinction." Even the "new truth" (a strange, revealing formulation) that the Doctor finds forming itself in the bodily tissues and in the "lists of human beliefs" will stand only as the most recent voice in an ongoing debate – a debate that will soon bring forward other voices to put that "truth" in question. So the momentum of the logic by which Holmes envisions his break with the inheritance of Calvinism can at times bring him very close to the most progressive stance of his friend Emerson. In fact, Emerson's essay "Circles" develops very much along the lines of Holmes' "Notes": in Emerson as in Holmes, the classic vision of a form of nonsynthetic verbal dialogue (analyzed earlier in this study) is seen to begin with the first stirrings of a process of dynamic debate in the circulation of the blood:

But the heart refuses to be imprisoned; in its first and narrowest pulses, it already tends outward with a vast force, and to immense and innumerable expansions.

Every ultimate fact is only the first of a new series . . . There is no outside, no enclosing wall, no circumference to us. The man finishes his story. . . Lo! on the other side rises also a man . . . Then already is our first speaker not man, but only a first speaker. . . In the thought of tomorrow there is a power to upheave all thy creed, all the creeds, all the literatures of the nations, and marshal thee to a heaven which no epic dream has yet depicted.[27]

The Doctor might well be wary of following the blithe enthusiasm with which his Saturday Club partner extends their shared conversational impulses, celebrating the most radical house-breaking possibilities inherent in the form. Emerson saw that the "conversation" that begins in the domestic household tends to explode out of it. Beginning in childhood with a simple unsettling of paternal impressions that "haunt" the mind, emerging in an arterial alternation between centripetal and centrifugal movements of our blood, and then forming itself in a social life of constant struggle between parlor-room speakers, the dialogic movement described by Emerson soon begins to rattle the furniture in that Victorian frame, to unsettle scientific facts and religious creeds, and finally expands outward with an up-heaving motion of destruction and renewal that reaches even to Heaven.

For both Holmes and Hegel the organic analogy of bodily growth diffuses such implications of a revolutionary rupture in the dialectical process, giving it the shape of a simple, natural evolution. But Holmes' phrases, as we have seen, carry resonances which remind us that there will be "brief intervals" when the "destructive tendencies" in breathing must overwhelm the conservative order. And the previously cited passage from Hegel's "Preface" to the *Phenomenology* (full of background allusions to the French Revolution) clearly marks the "lightning"-like "breaks" when gradualism ends with a sudden "leap" into the "new world." Both thus recognize that the organic world itself can develop through radical movements of differentiation and separation. First conjured by the image of a child's respiration, Hegel's scenes of revolt are all based on the idea that a slow, incremental quantitative progress can eventually lead to qualitative differences – even simple bodily nourishment (nursing) can bring about the birth of something completely new. Similarly, even if young Oliver felt that he was born with the Calvinist idea of the Fall flowing into his blood by direct descent, and incorporated into his daily food, Holmes' physiological model also recognizes the equally primary operation of a liberating educational "nurture" – a form of nourishment which can alter the forms of "Nature." In fact, then, the body is far from static: the Doctor's anatomy lectures often stop to digress in wonder about the fact that we are built upon change, that our cells are constantly dying and being replaced, and that this demanding process depends upon good nurture. And our body is certainly not monolithic. We have seen that Holmes always brings out the doubleness in our physiological "nature": the brain has two chambers, the heart has paired ventricles, the two eyes receive the world in complementary colors, the blood contains a struggle between paternal and maternal strains, and respiration involves a battle between oxygen and the solid tissues.

It is the fundamental bipolarity of this model which gives it its revolutionary potential, and which brings out a side of Holmes too often ignored – an aspect of his thought which links him to the nineteenth-century visions of radical change seen in Hegel and Emerson. If, in the paternal–maternal household as in the body, any preferred scene of "origins" seems not to be unitary but to be irreducibly bipolar, attention shifts away from concern with the unity of any beginning or end to concentration of the effects of dialectical process. And this evolutionary process will build out of differences rather than upon simple repetition, working not simply as a quantitative unfolding of possibilities latent in the first Form but through leaps between qualitatively new forms which are seen to burst out of the old frames, only to pass away in their turn. If each form (*Bild*) here emerges out of and so contains within itself a formative dynamic (*Bildung*) of destruction and differentiation as well as of construction, an overview of the process will envision not a single expanding Form but a series of forms – each one framing the bipolar elements which will lead to further dialectical development.

In more concrete terms, if we follow the many threads of household imagery in each of these passages from Hegel, Emerson, and Holmes, we find that the overall plan in each case involves not one expanding house but a progressive movement through a series of houses – each one framing the two poles of an explosive and vital conversation. In the previously cited passage from Hegel's "Preface" to the *Phenomenology*, the child's first breath typifies microcosmically the continual progress of an expanding "spirit" which dissolves its successive material frames, so that the birth-scene paragraph ends with a generalized revolutionary imagery of crumbling "walls," dissolving "edifices," and changing "physiognomies." In his essay

"Circles," Emerson stresses over and over the expansive power in dialogue that always leads it to break out of domestic frames or constraints. These expanding conversations, then, serve throughout the essay as the clearest models of what Emerson sees as a universal system of ever-enlarging circumferences. This growth will find itself housed in bigger and bigger shells, each time again growing to explode the walls of its previous formal limit. "Every spirit builds itself a house, and beyond its house a world; and beyond its world, a heaven . . . Build, therefore, your own world," was the very telling motto at the end of Emerson's "Nature."[28]

With this nexus of ideas so pervasively in the air, it is not surprising that Holmes' "Notes" on his childhood should be permeated, as we have seen, by a similar imagery of dissolving rocks and breaking walls – whether these obstructions are seen as the stone fences of Biblical legend, the full-freighted shelves of the paternal library, the alum-rock in the test-tube, the mental "blocks" to new thought, or the obstacles to the flow of arterial circulation. In fact the first and earliest childhood scene given in the "Notes" pictures birth as a paradigmatic rupture – again by analogy to a bird breaking out of its shell: "When the chick first emerges from the shell, the Creator's studio in which he was organized and shaped, it is a very little world with which he finds himself in relation." Like Hegel's child, and unlike the timid marsupial that Holmes sees clinging to its maternal pouch, this curious, wayward chick is soon repeating that initial gesture of its birth to expand that "little world" by small increments – "first the nest, then the hen-coop, by and by the barnyard with occasional predatory incursions into the neighbor's garden . . ." – thus serving as a model for the child's educational progress which opens out of drawers to closets, from small rooms to large houses to fenced yards, and then into a series of ever-larger frames in the outer world:

The low room of the old house – the little patch called the front yard – . . . the back yard with its wood-house, its carriage-house, its barn, and . . . I could see the vast expanse of the Common . . . – the immeasurably distant hills of the horizon, and the infinite of space in which these gigantic figures were projected . . . I felt my way into the creation beyond. (*AN*, 29–30)

This quasi-Emersonian vision of human growth as a continual enlargement of optical horizons, repeated often in Holmes' writings, leads quickly here from the confines of Oliver's first "atmospheric existence" to the largest airy expanses – with the extreme "shock" of the boy's first telescopic view of the planet Venus.

Jolted by this confrontation with Venus as with a mirror-image of his own life (since he knows that Venus' size makes it a twin of the Earth), young Oliver first feels a "vast and vague confusion of all [his] standards," but then learns to take the planetary "transit" as a model for the trajectory of his own *Bildung*. Like Jean-Paul Richter, who in his novels and pedagogical theories often described education in terms of planetary flight, Holmes develops from this sighting of Venus the "educational theory [which] is the basis of my working creed": an orbiting planet seems to deny the dogma of the "Fall of Man," as it is not only falling according to the "laws of gravity" but also continually rising; it is not only consuming its organic "fuel" but also always renewing those life-forms; it calls up for human observers a vastness which breaks the frames of Biblical measures of space and historical time. And the phases of Oliver's reactions here show that he has indeed learned the "lesson" of this planetary movement, internalizing the bipolar process seen operating in Venus' flight: first drawn up and out into an airy infinite that threatens to dissolve all solid standards, the boy's mind then returns to the ground of his old house and his old planet – but with a new recognition of the expansive forces at work even within those limited frames, forces which make the planet Earth seem not a material prison but a progressive, developing "educational institution" (*AN*, 45–46).

"BUILD THEE MORE STATELY MANSIONS": HOUSE-KEEPING AND HOUSE-BREAKING IN DIALOGUE AT HOLMES' TABLE

We find these same dual tendencies of mind informing (and complicating) much of Holmes' thought about houses. For if the dynamic dialectic of mobility and fixity, of airy centrifugal expansion and solid centripetal contraction, of destructive change and conservative stasis seems to be built in to the child's early home life, his parents' conversations, his education and his play, and even into the formation of his body, it is not difficult to imagine that the pattern of what we have been calling the household dialogue would assert itself in the architectural meditations of the mature man as he plots the course of his later years. He will tend to see his progress, and that of the world, as a movement which breaks walls and builds new ones, not simply expanding out of a still natal center by building successive additions onto the parental home but in fact moving away from that unipolar point of origin through a series of such framed centers, a series of new dwellings.

Indeed, the house becomes the image underlying Holmes' thought on a wide range of issues. But his thought about the house builds out of a tension between two strongly opposed approaches to that house form: between impulses to "house-keeping" and to "house-breaking." If even Emerson pauses during the spiraling progress of his "Circles" essay to recognize a pole of fixity within the general flux – "[yet] this incessant movement and progression which all things partake could never become sensible to us but by contrast to some principle of fixture or stability"[29] – Holmes' thinking will certainly be divided between these two poles. For while the household dialogue described in his "Notes" contains powerful urges toward revolutionary Emersonian flights, it also recognizes the opposing pull of a gravitational force descending from Jonathan Edwards. And Holmes' attitudes towards the house image in his other writings then reflect this ambivalence in wild oscillations between what the "Notes" describe as "destructive" tendencies and the "conservative principle."

Holmes would always love to return imaginatively – with a proto-Proustian impulse evident in all his works – to the scenes of his youth, always carefully associating each memory trace with a precise drawer or corner in a particular room, or with a special position in a specific household niche. The yellow "gambrel-roofed" house celebrated in so many of his writings thus came to serve as a memory theater. (Even in this era, the "arts of memory" often used the mental image of a succession of rooms as the architectural "storehouse" in which to arrange and keep a large number of discrete scenes or elements for ready recollection.) The remembered structure of this first parental home seems to offer Holmes some assurance that the material marks of his personal identity will be retained, its overall frame providing a model of psychological integration. For the ancient tradition linking the topography of domestic architecture to the *topoi* of verbal memory merges neatly here with a mechanical Lockean model of the mind as a "dark room," a storehouse lined with regular cabinets rationally organizing sensations – in this case the environmental influences of the early childhood home – into clear and distinct categories. Even in his serious psychological studies, Holmes' metaphorical flights often take to the furthest limit the age's commonplace image of the mind as a house, whimsically distinguishing the mental "faculties" of conscience, will, rationality, the unconscious, and so on, by analogy to the habitual operations on separate "floors" of the home: descending from the haunted attic to private bedrooms, from sociable public spheres down to the vital but also potentially subversive forces half-buried in the "underground workshop" of the cellar. When we see that for Holmes every aspect of domestic architecture thus carries a strong psychological charge, that every place in the house is also a mental "place" loaded with associations, it is easy to understand the fixated repetitiveness of his returns to that formative scene and the fanatical care with which he locates his every move within it. As he sends himself sleep-walking through the rooms of his memory theater, he is seeking to save precious details from the threat of airy "oblivion" (ominously mentioned as an effect of the light flight of the Master's hot-air balloon); to preserve the childhood house is to preserve the forms of identity – indeed to preserve the ordering frame of the mind.

This strong house-keeping instinct received its first brutal shock when young Oliver and his family were forced to leave the "gambrel-roofed" house; and even as an adult Holmes would be traumatized when the house itself was later razed. In fact a version of the same trauma would recur as he faced the necessity of each change of housing in his long life. Even if the moves only involved the geographical and cultural shock of a shift from one Cambridge neighborhood to another (the Doctor was remarkably faithful to his birthplace), he would find each evacuation unsettling, and each would provoke long, deep thoughts that he could not help but share in his writings. (Faithful readers of the breakfast-table papers and novels could and did chronicle Holmes' every reluctant change of address – as each was reported at length in these writings as a landmark event.) In his personal experience, then, Holmes would often find himself clinging like a marsupial to his enclosing pouch.

But if one side of Holmes thus values the security, stability, and solidity of the house, in other moments he could speak as a radical "house-breaker." Throughout his career, he writes eloquently and at great length about the need to leave familiar houses, to remodel old houses, even to destroy old houses completely. (In fact the Doctor was apparently an active supporter of some of the major Boston redevelopment schemes of his day; he did not stand in the way of such "progress" – and even worked for the plan which eliminated parts of his favorite old Cambridge neighborhoods to create the Back Bay.)[30] The Autocrat consciously appropriates the Puritan language of conversion to make a well-known, witty maxim out of Holmes' current anxieties about leaving a familiar house:

We die out of houses just as we die out of our bodies. . . . Men sicken of houses until at last they quit them, as the soul leaves its body when it is tired of its infirmities. The body has been called "the house we live in"; the house is quite as much the body we live in. (*CW,* I, 241)

This is a secularized version of the point that Holmes' ancestor Anne Bradstreet made in her poem "Upon the Burning of Our House": we must wean ourselves of attachments to our mortal frames; our souls must always be ready to move on. The narrator in *A Mortal Antipathy* returns to a long meditation on that Autocratic saying when he treats the final destruction of Holmes' old "gambrel-roofed" birthplace; but even after pages of sentimental reminiscences he is able to agree that, yes, we must die out of our houses, and he finally musters the levity to admit that, "The slaughter of the Old Gambrel-roofed House was . . . a case of justifiable domicide" (*CW,* VII, 23). The Professor also glosses the Autocrat's idea when he is able to note very cheerfully about another forced move that, as soon as we are reconciled to a change, we suddenly find ourselves impatient with and weary of the old home: our

thoughts and affections, each one of them packing its little bundle of circumstances, have quitted their several chambers and nooks and migrated to the new home, long before its apartments are ready to receive their bodily tenant.

This model of transplantation both soothes our contemplation of death – when we will finally "die . . . to all earthly lodgings" – and stands as the example of a most dynamic approach to life. To change a habitation forces us to change our old habits; and even imagining these uprootings and moves brings about what is for the Professor the most important transformation: "the change from the clinging to the present to the welcoming of the future" (*CW,* II, 275–77).

Such celebrations of transplantation, uprooting, and mobility are seen by Holmes both as basic to the dynamic movements of his conversation form and as particularly appropriate for American life. It is "a most un-American weakness," says the Professor, for a man "to think it necessary to hang about his birthplace all his days." One should feel little urge to "cling" to the maternal nest in such a modern and fluid society, for "the apron-strings of an American mother are made of India-rubber" (*CW,* II, 285). Holmes pays homage to the early American founders of this tradition of mobility in the poem "Robinson of Leyden," which celebrates the Pilgrims (rather than the Puritans) for their association with continual removals and ocean voyages (and their link to the waters of a "living fountain" of wisdom which "overflows" the wall-like obstacles of "Luther's dike or Calvin's dam"). These founders had "no home," but lived only as eternal exiles in the fluid environment of boats moving upon the sea (*CW,* II, 174). This recurring oceanic imagery is also explored by the Autocrat, especially in the table-talk installment that leads up to his poem, "The Chambered Nautilus." And here too the idea of our home as a boat, ever-mobile in the face of winds and surf, leads to maxims about the need to leave old haunts and old friends: "for grow we must, [even] if we outgrow all that we love" (*CW,* I, 93).

Several of the sloganeers at the Doctor's breakfast-table pick up this advocacy of oceanic mobility and fluidity over any attempt to set up fixed walls or obstacles. "The old-world order of things," says the Professor,

is an arrangement of locks and canals, where everything depends on keeping the gates shut, and so holding the upper waters at their level; but the system under which a young republican American is born trusts the whole unimpeded tide of life to the great elemental influences . . . (*CW,* II, 295)

After the Professor's similar introductory speech in which he imagines himself breaking out of the confining walls of his house like a "red-cap" revolutionary breaking down the "barricades," Little Boston is moved to the first of his familiar orations hailing Boston as the great place for "cracking things up," for pulling down turnpikes and roadblocks in favor of a freer flow on the highways of thought (*CW,* II, 14–17). The Master's related motto is "don't fence me in," as he attacks those who favor specialization or professionalization over generalized knowledge, those who favor a Narrow rather than a Broad Church, and so on – always relying upon the fundamental imagery of a breaking down of walls or of private, narrow "fences." We soon notice that these movements are everywhere in the Doctor's writings – his characters tend always to turn their pockets inside out, open up closets, open doors, break down walls, uncover caches, or, often, to imagine the complete destruction of a house. And these house-breaking impulses seem to operate as inherent forces within the conversation form itself – which is intended to enforce a sort of transplantation or up-rooting with each change of speaker, and which should thus work to bring interlocutors out of themselves, and out of their provincial spheres.

While much of the Doctor's writing is set in the Victorian drawing room, and is thus quite naturally dominated by the common drawing-room topic of the house, this setting and subject matter do not in Holmes' case necessarily imply a Last Stand for the "Fireside" coherences or the status quo, a retreat from diversity, an attempt to define a "separate sphere" insulated from the social and physical currents of the larger world. A preoccupation with the image of the house does not necessarily make the Autocrat an American Podsnap, or an Uncle Toby – always trying to "fortify" the walls of his mind against new influences. For we have seen that in the Autocrat's conception, the house is not privatized, static, or unipolar. This was an era which often figured its largest concerns in architectural imagery. Writers like Catherine Beecher had begun to define the "domestic economy" as a microcosm containing, with its ventilated air and channeled heat, the great currents of energy in the larger physical world; Beecher would not be surprised at the Professor's picture of dynamic household battles between fountains of levity and the oceanic currents of gravity.[31] In a nation obsessed with the family model of national politics, the "House Divided" naturally became in 1858 Lincoln's telling image of the dangers in America's regional differences, and writers on the politics within the family in this period could also rally around this same house image: in 1840 the conservative Heman Humphrey warned that increasing conflicts between paternal and maternal authority in the American home threatened to dissolve the basis of family union: "your house being 'divided against itself cannot stand'."[32] In mid-century America, then, the house could often serve as a model for thinking about a whole range of contemporary cultural problems, and could be seen to contain a whole range of possible flashpoints for Holmesian fireworks at the breakfast-table.

Holmes' table-talks are often modeled on the mid-century domestic conversation he knew so well, and so often dwell on the characteristically minor domestic topics: the fashion in summer housing, the talk of the town about interior alterations, problems of the domestic economy, chatter about the security and intimacy of the quiet home sphere, and so on. But Holmes then finds within the surface imagery and rhetorical structure of his era's everyday verbal converse the symptoms of deeper problems, and the appropriate form for the literary exploration of these problems. Resetting exchanges of prim, fashion-magazine banalities as mock philosophic dialogues, discovering complex threads of metaphor amidst the complacencies of the parlor, Holmes seems to want always to test the limits of the domestic form. A lifelong concern with issues related to houses, house-frames, and households is behind his witty wordplays upon the fashionable talk of domesticity; he takes this fashioning and refashioning very seriously.

One set piece in the *Autocrat*, for example, begins as chatter about the best location for a summer residence, but ends with a complete unsettling of any form of "domestication." The final imagined setting describes the ur-scene for Holmes' meditation about houses, as the fragile domestic frame is contrasted with the impersonal infinite of the ocean:

Yet I should love to have a little box by the seashore. I should love to gaze out on the wild feline element from a front window of my own, just as I should love to look on a caged panther, and see it stretch its shining length, and then curl over and lap its smooth sides, and by-and-by begin to lash itself into rage and show its white teeth and spring at its bars . . .

The exaggeratedly proper, fussy, even precious writing here clashes dramatically with the topic of savage outdoor life. This speaker seems a caricature of small, dry, cowardly gentility – in many ways the larger scene makes him seem an early Prufrock. And like Prufrock, who finds himself faced with the sensual movements of a metaphoric, cat-like "yellow fog" outside his window panes, this indoor man finds himself gazing at a shifting form – as the passage continues it becomes a cat, a panther, a mermaid, a siren, a metronome music box – which seems especially threatening in the sudden emotional turns which seem to be projections of the speaker's own repressed urges. The delicate style accents the littleness of the "little box," stressing the desire for some protective frame in that "front window," and the domestic need to assert personal identity and ownership through such containers – "of my own." But the theme of the larger passage has been the relativity of standards and measures, and this picture of the "little box" then moves to a second stage (imagining the ocean with an "inward eye" rather than with the detachment provided by the window-frame) that immerses us in the measures of the sea:

. . . who does not love to shuffle off time and its concerns at intervals, – to forget who is President and who is Governor, what race he belongs to, what language he speaks, which golden-headed nail of the firmament his particular planetary system is hung upon, and listen to the great liquid metronome as it beats its solemn measure, steadily swinging when the solo or duet of human life began, and to swing again just as steadily after the human chorus has died out and man is a fossil on its shores. (*CW*, 1, 264–65)

From the indoor "chambers of memory" we here move to what Prufrock would later call the "chambers of the sea." Now all that was associated with the fixed house-frame is lost in flux: local culture and national government, racial identity, language. As the firmament itself becomes infirm, even the planetary system becomes a mere provincial measure – the gravitational center is seen simply as another domestic conceit, like the nail on which one hangs picture frames in that "little box." Our measures of space and time are relativized by this apocalyptic musical measure, which speaks for the evolutionary movements that will eventually make all human houses and bodies mere empty fossils carried by the ocean flow.

A similar movement occurs in another *Autocrat* passage, which describes an eternal war between the forces of Nature and of Civilization, but then accepts and even applauds what is described as a lower-class, revolutionary invasion of Boston by armies of weeds and grasses. Something in nature does not love a wall: these plants begin by cracking pavements, eroding columns, and finally leave us with the prospective vision of even the Boston State-House (often taken by Holmes as the symbol of his own identity, and the very "hub" of his "solar system") returning to the ground in ruins (*CW*, 1, 273–74). But of course at other moments this house-breaking movement is not so grave. One topic of parlor-room chit-chat is a comparison of the forms of "hospitality" in different parts of the world: "The shade of a palm-tree serves an African for a hut; his dwelling is all door and no walls; everybody can come in. To make a morning call on an Esquimaux acquaintance, one must creep through a long tunnel; his house is all walls and no door." Here again the contrast pits open, wall-less structures against closed ones. But now the Autocrat is in a summer mood, and so is more than ready to recognize the limits of his own "little box": "Once in a while . . . one may realize . . . by a sudden extension in his sphere of conciousness, how closely he is shut up for the most part." Inspired by the wall-lessness of the African example, he begins to allow far-off sounds to invade his private sphere: locusts from the nearby tree, baby's screams, tinmen pounding, horses stamping in the public square. If the house structure had at other moments offered a model of Lockean hierarchical organization, that order now breaks down – smells mix with sights, animals mix with humans, voices of babes and workers mix with those of refined talkers in the parlor. Even the windows that might have stood for intellectual detachment seem to be caught up irrationally in the animation of this stifling day, and begin to "gape, like the mouths of panting dogs." Finally, recognizing that the private house has become a sort of public souk, the Autocrat expresses his urge to

stroll into the market in natural costume, – buy a watermelon for a halfpenny, – split it, and scoop out the middle, – sit down in one half of the empty rind, clap the other on one's head, and feast upon the pulp. (*CW*, 1, 302–03)

Preferring the vitality of the market to the Lockean dark room, the Autocrat here replaces the proper and solid Victorian house-frame with the mushy, natural rind of a melon, thus taking the basic hot-weather impulse to open windows to its carnival limits.

Perhaps the clearest overall vision of the movements of Holmes' house-breaking comes in his most successful serious poem, "The Chambered Nautilus." Beginning as a meditation on the spiral-shaped mollusk that develops by constantly breaking the restrictive walls of each "outgrown shell," leaving "the past year's dwelling for the new," this poem finally rises to find here an Emersonian model of all human progress: "Build thee more stately mansions, O my soul" (*CW*, 1, 97–98). The Nautilus offers a perfect example of what we have seen as Holmes' sense of a dialectic movement in nature: it works in the larger world just as respiration works within the body; it shows how the domestic interior can become the central arena for the actions of a millennial progress. Once again the model is founded in bipolar interactions: first, between the house-box and its oceanic environment; secondly, between the shell-walls (which protect the creature from wind and water) and the airy gases which fill these

walls (which make that interior a flotation chamber to give the
Nautilus its potential buoyancy). The dialogue that rises from within
this natural form is thus a classic household alternation between
levity and gravity: the spiraling movements of airy expansion tending
to break the hard forms of each successive bodily container. As we
then look at the larger cross-section of a Nautilus shell, the spiraling
progress of this house-breaking growth seems to represent a force for
levitation against the falling tides of gravitational nature in "life's
unresting sea."

Holmes' choice of topic here was probably inspired by Saturday
Club and Harvard debates between Asa Gray and Louis Agassiz
contrasting the Darwinian model with various other Christian and
Romantic versions of evolution. Holmes and Emerson would listen in
on such discussions with great interest; in fact Emerson could bring
such discussions together with his early interest in natural sciences to
frame his dialectical vision very much along the lines of Holmes'
poem, using the image of a shellfish changing its house: the growth of
man's thought may be likened to that of a shellfish, he writes, "which
crawls out of its beautiful but stony case, because it no longer admits
of growth, and slowly forms itself a new house."[33] But it does not
seem that Holmes' "Nautilus" finally aims to take any firm stance in
this controversy about evolution; his poem works more as what
Bachelard, in his study of commonplaces about shells as a subset of
human ideas about houses, calls "a vast dream of shells."[34] The goal
of such dreams of the inhabited shell (as in the eighteenth-century
evolutionary tables of J. B. Robinet) is often most generally to convert
what could be the image of a shut-in life, of an exteriority that is
limiting, into an image of ongoing progress. Very often this progress
is then seen, as it is by Holmes, also as a vaguely Christian emblem of
resurrection: to die out of one shell is to expand into renewed life in
the next. But the end of Holmes' vision is unclear. The Nautilus'
motive force seems to come from within, not from any divine
overseeing power; the series of bodily "temples," and of church
structures and religious creeds, work only to "shut" the Nautilus
"from heaven"; and its eventual death does not seem to be celebrated
as an apocalyptic marriage of natural and divine forms, or a return
to Paradise.

But if the final synthesis here cannot be known or imagined,
Holmes' main interest is in the continual alternation of antitheses.
His poem is not a celebration of the final resting place, but a call to

action: human life, like the sea, should be "unresting." In the last stanza, even when the last mansion has dissolved into the waves, and the soul seems to have died out of its mortal coil forever, what arouses the poet is not that final merger but the grandeur of the process of house-building and house-breaking: "Build thee more stately mansions, O my soul." Each "temple" that we build is seen as a "little box" in comparison to the ongoing chaos of the sea; and while we must build houses as part of our rising life process, no house can be more than a temporary and limited frame. For each new thought, we must break out of the prison of a former preconception. But this house-breaking ideal arises out of a dual recognition: we need house-frames, while at the same time we must always break out of them; we have an inner buoyancy, but we must also recognize the natural law of gravity. "The Chambered Nautilus" finally leaves us, then, not with any one system but with the vision of an infinite progression of systems, or, in the Doctor's more characteristic domestic imagery, not with any one house but with the vision of an infinite succession of houses.

CHAPTER 10

"CUTTING OFF THE COMMUNICATION":
FIXATIONS AND FALLS FOR THE WALLED-IN SELF

Holmes in dialogue with Sterne, Dickens, and Melville

Wemmick's house was a little wooden cottage in the midst of plots of garden, and the top of it was cut out and painted like a battery mounted with guns.

....

"That's a real flagstaff, you see," said Wemmick, "and on Sundays I run up a real flag. Then look here. After I have crossed this bridge, I hoist it up – so – and cut off the communication."
Charles Dickens, *Great Expectations*

Holmes' vision of this fundamental process of dialogic alternations between impulses of "house-keeping" and "house-breaking" did not arise solely out of his private preoccupations and personal history; on the contrary, it was developed quite self-consciously as a pointed elaboration upon habits of thought widely shared in mid-century culture. Indeed, the Doctor's interest in the wall-breaking powers of levity can be seen to have emerged out of and been shaped by his desire to open up a dialogue with the works of a line of English comic writers – most notably Sterne and Dickens – who had explored in classic, caricatural form the implications of the contemporary urge to "fortification" of the self or of the domestic sphere. And Holmes' fascination with the house-breaking potential inherent in the movements of multivoiced conversation also formed the basis of his ongoing dialogue – continued in casual talk at social meetings, in intimate medical interviews, or in written works – with some of the leading American literary voices of the day, as we will see here in following his relations with Melville and Hawthorne. In Sterne, Dickens, Melville, and Hawthorne, as in Holmes, one central plot movement always pits walls against words; whatever its origins, the main goal of a wall-building impulse is to block the flow of household dialogue – to "cut off the communication." Again and again, the house-keeping urge is associated with a heavy weight of gravity, and the main threat to its order is a house-breaking levity which threatens to erupt in any turn of human conversation.

Uncle Toby in *Tristram Shandy* and Mr. Wemmick in *Great Expectations*, two of the most famous "house-keepers" in English literature, might serve as the most useful reference points for our readings here, helping to define in extreme form some of the central impulses involved in this one pole of Holmes' architectural thought. Certainly these two characters would have been prime reference points in the Doctor's own mind, since they figure so importantly in the fictional worlds that he made the models for his own, and since these eccentrics play out a classic predicament in the English traditions of philosophic and amiable humor that so strongly inform Holmes' own comic sensibility.

Following his hobby-horse to construct every imaginable sort of fortification in his private garden, Sterne's eccentric Uncle Toby becomes a parody of the eighteenth-century scientist or mechanician with his innocent faith in projects and devices and his complete mistrust of language. Redesigning his tiny cottage as a Disney-style fantasy imitation of a Gothic fortress, Dickens' Wemmick stands as the ultimate caricature of his age's desire to make domestic and business life into "separate spheres." Tracing the progress of each of these comic characters' distinct trains of thought, in their idiosyncratic enthusiasms for the "fortification" of the domestic sphere, we can see how the Lockean philosophical preoccupations of the eighteenth century – the urge to isolate and insulate the impressionable mind from the invasion of random external influences, and to "fortify" or frame that inner mind in a rational order as protection from the vagaries of irrational verbal associations – come in the mid-nineteenth century to inform everyday household practices on many levels. In the later period the impulse led to the desire to set off all aspects of private home-life (the realm of hypersensitive women, of impressionable children being educated under their influence, and of tired working men who return to be refreshed by this scene) as a "separate sphere" protected from any commerce with the corrupt outer world of public business. The commonplace desire was here, then, to make the Victorian home (and thus the Victorian mind) an impregnable Castle.

But if Sterne and Dickens provide multi-leveled insights into such obsessions with the building and reinforcement of architectural

frames, their caricatures (like many we have seen in Holmes) also
reduce the impulse to its most absurd forms, uncovering a basic
paradox in such monomania: when the desire for fixity becomes a
fixation, what seemed a solution can itself be revealed as the core
problem. In fact, while both Wemmick and Toby develop elaborate
schemes to cut off all conversation with the outer world, to quaran-
tine the self from any communication as though from a "communicable" disease, they clearly nonetheless build their fortifications on the
image of that outer world. Even within their strongly-defended
interiors, both characters bear the deeply-impressed marks of the
exterior influences they mean to deny. As Wemmick seeks to avoid
the memory of his workdays at Newgate Prison by making his home
into a prison-like "Castle," so Toby seeks to avoid the memory of his
wound at the siege of Namur by making his home a heavily fortified
battleground and his mental life a compulsive reenactment of that
original siege.

MELVILLE'S "CHIMNEY" CONFRONTS HOLMES' HOUSE-BREAKING CONVERSATION

Melville's short story "I and My Chimney" shows how these house-
keeping impulses could play themselves out in nineteenth-century
America – in specific opposition to the house-breaking tendencies of
Doctor Holmes' mode of conversation. The narrator of Melville's
tale, who barricades himself behind the brickwork in his family home
and refuses to "surrender" the hypertrophied and still-swelling
chimney to his wife and daughters, is clearly a descendant of
Wemmick and especially of Uncle Toby. Though this man's bodily
problem seems the inverse of Toby's, his psychological wound clearly
involves the same "place." Defending the exaggerated fireplace to
compensate for some real or imagined phallic injury, displacing all
his energy onto that reified stone shaft, this narrator is paralyzed by
his topological fixation, rendered as immobile as the stoneworks he
wants to protect. And the resultant inflation of his imperial ego, the
private "I" of the story title, though it seems to satisfy him, also
makes the narrator a caricature of the era's pipesmoking literary
bachelors – it seems to make him impotent. Such an unnatural
expansion of one element of the household architecture leaves little
room for anything else; in fact, it actually destroys the household
around it. Like the "effete" tissue matter that Holmes saw building

up as a solid obstacle to needed bodily flow, the chimney in Melville's story grows to block any "circulation" in the house. The "sour and unsocial" narrator's chimney cramps his wife's movements, keeps her and her "eggs" away, and inhibits any attempts to expand out of this stony, thick-walled atomism into more public forms of "conversation."

It seems strikingly appropriate, then, that the proto-psychoanalytic specialist in "mental architecture," called in by the wife to deal with this extreme case of pathological "house-keeping," should be clearly modeled on Doctor Holmes himself. (Several critics have identified the Mr. Scribe of the story as Holmes, since the story seems to be based on the several occasions in June 1855 when Mrs. Melville finally convinced her husband to consult with their Berkshire neighbor, Dr. Holmes, about his mysterious and protracted, seemingly psychosomatic, illness.)[1]

Melville seems to have sensed the larger implications of the Doctor's impulse to "house-breaking" in psychological spheres. He associates Mr. Scribe with the "surgical operation" which brings part of the chimney into the open air, with the sort of bourgeois "architectural reformer" who wants only "to destroy . . . old-fashioned houses," following the latest fashions in interior remodeling to open up communicating passageways and entries that had previously been blocked by the swollen chimney.[2] In fact, carrying on in this way, Mr. Scribe seems to threaten to break down, subdivide, or even "remove" the central shaft itself. The narrator knows that Mr. Scribe, when he senses that the chimney may conceal an inner "reserved space, hermetically closed," containing hidden secrets passed down in the family through the house, will never stand for such enclosures; he will soon be "bursting open" the secret recess at the "heart of the house" (*HM*, 176, 179–80, 188). We see that, most generally, in all of his plans, Mr. Scribe wants to open up public spaces within this private realm, to construct parlors to accommodate what he might call conversational "coming out" parties bringing many new guests into the house. For all of these architectural changes are allied with Mr. Scribe's basic goal: the promotion of household conversation.

Because what he really wants is to set back in motion the dynamic process of household dialogue, Mr. Scribe's main tool in all of this "house-breaking" is verbal. His passageways would open the home to sugary, feminized fops like the "exquisite . . . of superfine discourse" who pleases the women in the pantry, and from there lead to a whole range of disturbing conversational intrusions on the narrator in his silent fort. And the technique of Mr. Scribe's treatment of the narrator (a technique of analysis through genial conversation that Holmes used with many patients, notably Hawthorne) seems to operate mainly through talk – but through a form of talk which this patient resents as a prying invasion, the verbal equivalent of "that wall-breaking wish of Momus" to "break into [the human] breast" (*HM*, 174, 188).

To the hyper-privatized narrator, the cold curiosity of such dialogical surgery verges on what Hawthorne would call an unpardonable sin against the human heart. But the analyst's goal here is not the forcing of any single confession, or the uncovering of any one localized secret chamber; rather he hopes (probably in vain) to stimulate a general revival of the household dialogue that the chimney fortification had grown to block, to set back in interaction the familiar poles of conversation: between the autocratic "king of the house" and the more democratic diversity of other family voices; between the conservative man obsessed with all old things and the young, energetic, progressive wife always changing with the latest fashions. Indeed, Holmes' actual visits with Melville seem to have consisted mainly of long conversations, in which the Doctor would prescribe freer dialogue within the family, while also suggesting that Melville get out of the house, for recreation and later (when the paralyzing depression continued) for a trip to the Holy Land. Of course, neither of these men was as one-dimensional in his architectural thought as Melville's story suggests. But the tale's illuminating ironies should nonetheless help to shake up our stereotyped notions about Holmes: for here we find the "Fireside Poet" (supposed defender of the indoor realm with its conservative coherences and safe stasis) advocating the bursting open of an established hearth, and the supposedly provincial Boston-bound Doctor then preaching the related gospel of travel to the author we know as the manly, radical, and adventurous travel-writer and whaler.

Sterne seems to suggest a similar diagnosis and prescription in the case of his Uncle Toby. But a fertile, house-breaking conversation seems to be just what Toby is incapable of. Like the giant chimney arising to take over the house in Melville's tale, huge battlement walls rise up in Toby's domestic scene to block the flow of any household dialogue. The fortress-home that Trim and Toby erect to seal their garden finally emerges as a classic model of the barren household: its sterile closure (meant to keep out infectious influences, and to avoid sexual confusion in the "unsteady uses of words") condemns them to a permanent bachelorhood (*TS*, 86).

Though as a soldier he had been the attacker, Toby gave up early on in his failed efforts with homemade "projectiles" to concentrate on defensive works. It was a decisive shift, for by the book's end he seems in need of explosives to allow him some escape from his expanding mental fortress. And of course his related failures in each attempt to build a bridge symbolize his lack of constructive interactions with the world. Walls can only separate and divide; stones can only build reified, static works; in order to make connections between ideas, or to get meanings across between people, Toby needs a bridging language; he needs to face the difficulties of addressed utterance, to shoot some words out into the world and then follow their wayward passage through dialogues between speaker and interpreter.

Of course it is impossible completely to avoid such verbal interaction. But since Toby's purism has left him unprepared, he is often vulnerable to the Widow Wadman's advances, as she forces him into conversation. Putting the worst face on the mischievous games, passional impulses, and misunderstandings inherent in the use of words, the Widow's talk returns incessantly to Toby's sore spots, and shatters his fragile Edenic illusions every time. But, as Sigurd Burckhardt comments, in the very phrases of Lockean pedagogy: if he had been cast out of the Fortress earlier in his life, it might have proven for Toby a Fortunate Fall into sounder and more realistic moral development.

. . . since language is by its very nature communicative and transitive, it cannot fashion itself into a self-contained little world like Uncle Toby's, a world which has its purity in simply being. It must venture forth, entrust itself to the Mrs. Wadmans; it must mean.

....

And so, as soon as the peace of Utrecht breaks out and compels Toby to break out of his artificial world into the real one of discourse and communion, the world in which marriages are made and children begotten, the artfully managed purity is destroyed, the ambiguity which it tried to overcome by exclusion has its revenge.[3]

Linking the movement of verbal dialogue (seen on the affectional model of a fertilizing, bipolar household conversation) to the explosion of a hermetically-sealed artificial construct, and to the necessary progress of a prodigal as he breaks out of a parental home to continue his own educational growth in the conversation of the larger world, Burckhardt's reading of Sterne here is very close to the reading we might expect from "America's Sterne," Doctor Holmes.

Burckhardt's perspective can also help us to see how in Sterne, as in Holmes, the impulses of house-keeping and house-breaking may operate as a household dialogue between gravity and levity. Like many conservative house-keepers, stubbornly holding on to their ancient home frames, Toby in his fort seems to be dominated by a continual looming sense of gravity: he is surrounded by heavy things that are constantly falling. To Burckhardt, his case emerges as the clearest epitome of "the very corporeal gravity which orders Sterne's strange universe."[4] Built out of a monomaniacal desire to exclude the memory of an original fall (we are told that Toby's groin injury was due not to the projectile force of the stone that hit him, but more "owing to the gravity of the stone itself" [*TS*, 79]), Toby's stronghold will paradoxically be haunted by one fixed idea: an always impending fall. This is how the excluded ambiguity gets its revenge.

Like Melville's fixated narrator in "I and My Chimney," Toby develops as a comic-book illustration of the Holmesian lessons that the attempt to hide a secret can add to its pressure and weight as mental ballast, and that lack of verbal expression can exaggerate the force of an internal or somatic impression. As the Doctor warns us,

Sometimes it becomes almost a physical necessity to talk out what is in the mind . . . It is very bad to have thoughts and feelings, which were meant to come out in talk, *strike in*, as they say of some complaints that ought to show outwardly. (*CW*, i, 134)

When such mounting physical pressure is blocked, with no outlet for conversational release, its hiding "place" can swell to monstrous size. And, in Toby's universe, when the weight of the resulting fortifications then "strikes in" psychosomatically, it seems always to strike in one "place" in the body. As Burckhardt observes, "A messy fatality attends the falling bodies of the novel [rocks, sash windows, chestnuts] . . . They always land on the genitals."[5] Trying to deny the Fall in one sense, Toby's mechanical cures only perpetuate the law of the fall in another sense. Seeking refuge in a garden laboratory for "pure" science, surrounded by controllable technological devices, he should not be surprised that things still fall, and that they fall on the body; among these engines the only law is that of physical gravity. Constructing high fences around his second Eden, Toby is nonetheless surprised by sin, brought down by the invasions of a wounding, fallen language. Finally, Burckhardt sees Sterne suggesting that the way "to heal the wound which the law of the fall has made," to tap an upward movement of levity that can explode from within gravity, is to venture forth into the realm of words and wit, where falling forces enter into a dynamic dialogue that seems itself to rise: "We would not be flying except that someone had the wit to discover that air is heavy."[6]

GRAVITY AND THE ELIMINATION OF CONVERSATION: ARCHITECTURAL INTROVERSION IN DICKENS

If Toby's physicalist purism was finally dominated by the law of the Fall, so, in *Great Expectations*, Wemmick's retreat into technological tinkering is dominated by mechanical regularization: the "law" of the office. And the life within Wemmick's little enclave, like that in Toby's garden, clearly comes to be dominated by protectionist, outward-directed gestures of exclusion. The cannons are the only really functional elements here, and the gun-fire ceremony shakes the very foundations of this fragile china-glass and stage-set realm. With such a mania for wall-building defensiveness, Wemmick's Castle seems in fact to be slowly shrinking, confining and constricting all movement and growth within. Dry-rot is beginning to set in as a sign of the need for circulating ventilation and, tellingly, hearing seems to have atrophied with the total lack of verbal communication within these walls.

While Wemmick has moved one step ahead of Toby in perfecting construction of a bridge, his one-way drawbridge nonetheless epitomizes the goal shared by both of these eccentrics in their drive to architectural introversion: the elimination of conversation. As he proudly hoists up his bridge, Wemmick voices the hope that it will symbolically "cut off the communication"; and while he intends by this gesture simply to fence off the outer world, we see that in fact his life inside the Castle reflects this denial of communication in its denial of words.[7] Because the Aged Parent is (revealingly) very deaf – he has permanently hoisted his personal drawbridge – most of the time life in Wemmick's silent garden bower proceeds as it did on Toby's lawn: through exaggerated gestures, reverent nods, preset messages on crazy mechanical flip-cards, and wordless military rituals.

Dickens' picture of this wordless, walled-in Walworth life here certainly gives us a wonderfully rich and clear insight into the predicament of the "house-keeper" in Holmes' age, and a strong reminder of the limitations inherent in this stubborn Victorian urge to protect the Fortress-Home. Wemmick epitomizes the mid-century mode of thought that Holmesian conversation is meant to unsettle. Though the Doctor's talk form might seem to Wemmick, to the narrator of Melville's "I and My Chimney," or to Uncle Toby to involve a fearful form of verbal "surgery," a prying invasion of the private sphere, for Holmes the process of dialogic alternations between voices always speaks for a tendency diametrically opposed to that expressed by Wemmick's raised drawbridge or Toby's failed bridge projects, working to shake the foundations of the house-keeping urge, to clear away obstacles to free intercourse, and so to open up verbal bridges and passageways for commerce between self, home, and world. As we will see in the next chapter, these basic oppositions between walls and words were played out in their fullest complexity during the lifelong dialogue between Holmes and Nathaniel Hawthorne.

BREAKING THE HOUSE OF ROMANCE
Holmes in dialogue with Hawthorne

It is as clear to me as sunshine . . . that the greatest possible
stumbling-blocks in the path of human happiness and improvement, are these heaps of bricks, and stones, . . . which men
painfully contrive for their own torment, and call them house
and home! The soul needs air; a wide sweep and frequent
change of it . . . There is no such unwholesome atmosphere as
that of an old home, rendered poisonous by one's defunct
forefathers and relatives! I speak of what I know! There is a
certain house within my familiar recollection . . .

I could never draw cheerful breath there! . . . And it were a
relief to me, if that house could be torn down, or burnt up, and
so the earth be rid of it . . . For, Sir, the farther I get away from
it, the more does the joy, the lightsome freshness, the heart-leap
. . . come back to me . . . a great weight being off my mind.

What we call real estate – the solid ground to build a house
on – is the broad foundation on which nearly all the guilt of this
world rests.   Nathaniel Hawthorne, *The House of the Seven Gables*

> But who is he whose massive frame belies
> The maiden shyness of his downcast eyes?
> Who broods in silence till, by questions pressed,
> Some answer struggles from his laboring breast?
> An artist meant to dwell apart,
> Locked in his studio with a human heart.
>   Holmes, "At the Saturday Club"

Throughout the period of their major literary productivity, Doctor
Holmes and Nathaniel Hawthorne were engaged in an intense and
intimate dialogue with one another – a dialogue of great shaping
significance in the lives and writings of both men. Certainly, for
Holmes, Hawthorne served as a key interlocutor, emerging in many
ways as the Doctor's psychological and spiritual double, a powerfully

provocative voice-in-resistance, a gravitational center for his mean-dering, dialogical thought.

These very different men were often in close contact. As two of the leading Boston-based writers frequently called upon to join other authors at gatherings organized by the publisher Fields, as two of the major contributors to the *Atlantic* often brought together for working meetings by editor Lowell, as table-mates through many years of Saturday Club conversations, as close neighbors in the small Berk-shire town of Pittsfield (during a key period for Hawthorne's writing), as doctor and patient (during crucial periods for Hawthorne's physical and mental health), and as attentive readers of each others' works, Holmes and Hawthorne kept their fingers on each other's pulses throughout the mid-century, each following the other's pro-gress with extremely close attention. (Indeed, Holmes was so im-pressed and fascinated by the mystery of Hawthorne – his personality, his writings, and the trajectory of his career – that on Hawthorne's death he urged the novelist's family to give him permission to write the first Hawthorne biography. But Sophia Hawthorne objected strongly to the Doctor's project. In her view, such a prying invasion, a medical "case history" probing for the most intimate psychological details and perhaps revealing them with no sense of the sanctity of the human heart, would completely violate the spirit of the very introverted, secretive novelist. How could the Doctor – like Melville's Mr. Scribe seemingly lacking any sense of privacy – hope to narrate the story of this intensely private man?)

But if the depressed, reclusive novelist (especially so in his later years, those of his closest dealings with Holmes) and the gay, sociable, loquacious humorist might at first seem an unlikely pairing, they nonetheless apparently continued in their many meetings to work through the turns of an especially charged ongoing conversation, spurring each other on by speaking as alter-images in polar oppo-sition on a wide range of shared concerns. Like Holmes, Hawthorne was centrally preoccupied with the problematic but necessary inter-action between light and heavy approaches to life – and with the continual alternation between "merry" and somber aspects of American thought. And he was especially close to Doctor Holmes in his obsession with two major, interrelated themes associated with the pole of "gravity": the heavy, inescapable burden inherited as the legacy of Puritanism in the American psyche and in American culture; and the moral implications of new developments in science and medicine – especially in the mechanistic pseudo-sciences verging on spiritual and psychological matters. Like the Doctor – who also served as Hawthorne's personal physician for occasional "talking exams" – Hawthorne would focus again and again in his fictions on the figure of the doctor, testing a vision of the medical doctor as "moral physician" and as a model for the artist, and anxiously exploring the powerful dynamics of doctor–patient relations. Working in conversation with one another, then, Holmes and Hawthorne could use each other as sounding boards as they played out and explored key aspects of the bipolar system of thought they shared. The dialogue of these doubles would always turn on the antitheses basic to the writings of both authors, alternating between the voices of introverted gravity and extroverted levity, house-keeping and house-breaking. For, as we will see, in Hawthorne as in Holmes the opposition between gravity and levity is often figured as an opposition between house-keeping and house-breaking – and both of these bipolar interactions are seen as fundamentally related to opposing movements in conversation.

Hawthorne was a strange and strangely compelling interlocutor. We have seen how many of his writings – such as "The Minister's Black Veil," "Rappaccini's Daughter," and *The Scarlet Letter* – speak both for a deep fascination with the possibility of direct self-revelation in face-to-face talk, with a form of conversational intercourse that might bring about a full marriage of minds, and, on the other hand, for an incapacitating fear of self-loss in such powerfully intimate verbal interaction. Throughout his life, he worried about the difficulty of combining warm sympathy and sociability with what he saw as the chilling isolation inherent in the writer's lonely craft. And these intellectual and imaginative preoccupations seemed to express themselves in Hawthorne's characteristic position of reserve in everyday conversation. But Hawthorne's author friends also found that this internal man's mysterious silences and withdrawals made him in fact a surprisingly powerful presence in talk. Emerson observed that, while Hawthorne's reserve finally made full dialogic exchange with him impossible, it nonetheless also gave him a remarkable power to draw others out into streams of self-disclosive talk: "It was easy to talk with him, – there were no barriers, – only, he said so little, that I talked too much, and stopped only because, as he gave no indications, I feared to exceed." Melville found himself similarly "drawn out" by Hawthorne's "sociable silences" into especially intense, ambitious discussions. Something in Hawthorne seemed to offer the possibility of a profound verbal "friendship" – but then when his conversational partner had taken the invitation and talked himself out on a limb, he would find that Hawthorne had withdrawn, leaving him in dialogue only with himself. Like the uncommunicative Bartleby, Hawthorne could provoke his interlocutors into the sort of exploratory internal conversation that leads to self-revelation and then – as it follows the dialogic turns inherent in this verbal form – into self-criticism. Richard Brodhead sums up the situation very well: "Hawthorne's reserve commonly made others feel that he was looking for them to initiate a relation. But then, when he failed to join in the exchange he seemed to invite, he made others feel embarrassed at their own sociability."[1]

In his own efforts at dialogue with Hawthorne, Doctor Holmes seems to have been happy to take up a role as advocate of sociability and conversation (as he did with Melville), feeling drawn to the sad, silent, and frequently sick Hawthorne and fussing over him, hoping by humor or by easy entreaty to draw him out of himself, to help him make light of his heavy problems, to open him to some intercourse with the world – or, in more Holmesian terms, to join the Club. Shortly after the publication of *Elsie Venner* and *The Marble Faun* (novels paired and compared by many readers of the day), when the reclusive Hawthorne made one of his increasingly rare visits among the company at the publisher Fields' lively breakfast-table, the Doctor was obviously very pleased simply to see him getting out of the house. But the meeting, as remembered by hostess Annie Fields, then develops into what might be a scene from the life of Bartleby. (Indeed, in all of their dialogic interactions, Holmes and Hawthorne seem to play out the opposing roles defined by Melville in "Bartleby," that "Story of Wall Street" – full of dividing and confining walls – which develops the social, political, psychological, and even metaphysical opposition between the narrator and Bartleby as most fundamentally an opposition between two attitudes toward conversation.) At the Fields' breakfast-table, Holmes throws out the first probing aphorism – "A long while ago, I said Rome or Reason; now I am half inclined to say Rome or Renan" – and then turns suddenly to Hawthorne:

"By the way, I would write a new novel if you were not in the field, Mr.

Hawthorne." "I am not," said Hawthorne; "and I wish you would do it." There was a moment's silence. Holmes said quickly, "I wish you would come to the club oftener." "I should like to," said Hawthorne, "but I can't drink." "Neither can I." "Well, but I can't eat." "Nevertheless we should like to see you." "But I can't talk either." After which there was a shout of laughter. Then said Holmes, "You can listen, though; and I wish you would come."[2]

Most likely aware of Hawthorne's very deep feelings of both attraction and repulsion to the Church of Rome (to which two of his daughters would convert to become nuns), the chatterbox Doctor sets up the antitheses of what was for both of them an explosive inner dialogue, hoping to draw out this rare visitor either in heartfelt intellectual discussion or in "shouts of laughter" as the serious issues lose their contours to the pure witty surface play of sound similarities – Rome or Reason, Rome or Renan – dancing along here almost without "rhyme or reason."[3] But Hawthorne does not take the bait so easily. Like the "Bartleby" narrator, the Doctor here must wonder: what does a friend or analyst do with an interlocutor slowly disappearing before his eyes, an underground man who only speaks to deny his ability to talk, whose only impulse is introverted retreat as he thus strips himself, one by one, of each facet of his public, expressive presence? No writing, no drinking, no eating, no talking, no hearing: clearly soon this figure will no longer even be "seen." But Holmes' concern here is founded neither on complacent misunderstanding nor on cold medical curiosity; it reflects a strong-felt recognition of fundamental likeness: in their writings, these two are always very much, as the Doctor lightly notes, in the same "field."

MEDICAL ROMANCE

Because they were indeed so often drawn to exploration of the same "field" of fundamental issues and images, Holmes and Hawthorne continued their dialogic interaction in their writings as well as in their social relations. Many of their essays and fictions can be seen to develop as paired works – written in response to one another, and often building upon the other's specific imagery, either to elaborate upon it or to develop it in an alternative direction. Taylor Stoehr shows, for instance, how Hawthorne was deeply marked by Holmes' essay on "Homeopathy": both men joined their fascination for such pseudo-sciences with sceptical debunking of them; both denied the material pharmacology of homeopathy but learned from its popular success to stress the psychological functions of medicine – the placebo effect in drugging, and the verbal power and authority of the doctor; and both were led by such insights to radical criticisms of the drug-dependent "heroic" medical establishment – if Holmes' essay sees homeopaths as quacks, it also suggests that allopaths can become barbaric witch-doctors. Though the Doctor's partisan tract upset Hawthorne's in-laws (the Peabody family physician published an angry reply) and mocked one of Hawthorne's early friends (for a poem on Perkins' tractors), Hawthorne seems nonetheless to have sided with the Doctor in this case. And in fact, in his own classic reworkings of these same complex medical themes – for example, in "The Birthmark," published several months after the appearance of Holmes' essay – Hawthorne seems to be mining the depths of some of the suggestive case history details found in the Doctor's piece: the ideas of a drugged perfume and of a poisonous, globed vaccine; the idea of "testing" such new drugs on family and friends; the idea of a facial blemish falsely cured by a persuasive quack; and the general background sense of the dangers of wizard doctors hurting those they would help.

In his turn, as the passage of Holmes–Hawthorne table-talk cited above shows, when the Doctor began writing his "medicated novels" in the 1860s and 1870s, he saw himself entering a "field" already defined quite specifically by Hawthorne. The first of Holmes' attempts at such fiction, *Elsie Venner*, for example, was immediately recognized by contemporary readers as a twin (or double) to Hawthorne's "Transformation" (*The Marble Faun*), but it even more clearly develops out of and responds to scenes and symbols from several early Hawthorne stories – especially "The Birthmark" and "Rappaccini's Daughter." Exploring the possibility of translating grave moral–theological questions into the terms of medical–physiological science, working in a hybrid fictional mode that combines vestigial traces of Romance magic and myth with Naturalistic realism, *Elsie Venner* centers on the case of a young woman of exceptional beauty and power – like Beatrice in "Rappaccini's Daughter," reared in an unhealthy way by a doting but distant father – who is associated with Eve in the garden and who, after she is marked at birth by snakes, develops a mysterious affinity for plants and animals, channeling much of her erotic–emotional energy into intimate relations with non-human beings. Infected by something poisonous in Nature, she is taken as a secular figure for original sin – blocked by an accident of birth from entering into sympathetic attachments with other humans. Becoming (again like Beatrice) a subject of fascination and repulsion for a group of male physicians and church doctors who surround her, Elsie establishes a special hold over one young male medical student, Bernard (a close relative of Giovanni in Hawthorne's tale). Unlike Hawthorne, though, Holmes pulls up short in exploration of this young male's role in the drama – avoiding speculation about the possibility that some of the poison here may have its source in his own conflicted fantasies about Elsie, or in the cold scientist's inability to love – and closes off the expected plot of Bernard being drawn into a romantic relation with the female figure of Romance. Though much of the novel had raised the hope that Elsie might find a release in therapeutic conversation with Bernard that would help her achieve one oft-repeated Hawthornian goal – shaping her emotions into language so as to open "the gate . . . into the great community of human affections" (*CW*, v, 419) – in the end the young doctor simply cannot deal with her disease, so he cuts off verbal communication with her and instead retreats to an impersonal, perfectionist cure found in the medical pharmacy: a bouquet he has delivered to Elsie turns out, without his consciously knowing it, to be the antidote to her poison. But if Bernard's gift cures Elsie, eradicating the snake's mark, it also kills her; as in Hawthorne, making the love object pure also makes the love object die, because the poison was very much a part of her nature. Holmes diverges from the Hawthornian plot in his emphases at this end, though. He does not concentrate on the loss of a life or of a human relationship here; and for him the lesson is less about the doctors' failures than about a clarifying recognition of the limits of human powers of curative magic or art – a provocative materialist revision of Hawthorne's themes of sin and human responsibility. But by this time in fact both writers could claim equal share in these mutually-developed themes: as Stoehr notes, "Hawthorne's own interests in the physiology of sin and the psychology of guilt were . . . close to Holmes'."[4]

Exploring such questions, both writers often turned to medical fictions to study with much ambivalence the role of the doctor as a moral physician – in his relation both to the older clergy he replaces and to the aspiring younger authors to whom he also seems close kin. And both were centrally preoccupied with doctor–patient relations –

with the potent and perhaps dangerous magnetic power exerted in the dialogic intercourse they saw as the scene of any cure. But as timid, hesitant, self-conscious transitional figures, Holmes and Hawthorne also both tend to accent the dangers of the old ministrations rather than to herald any miraculous new cure; they are both concerned with the moment when confession becomes a forced violation; they both return again and again to admonishing scenes in which perfectionist, heroic doctors repeat the sins of the Puritan fathers as necromancers infecting their healthy patients with the germs of death.

This last theme begins early in Holmes, in his first serious medical essay (on "The Contagiousness of Puerperal Fever," written 1836–38), which develops as a Gothic horror tale condemning dangerous "medicine men" who, working to eradicate an external "evil" without recognizing that they themselves may be the source of the problem, travel from one sacrosanct childbed to another as carriers of the deadly pestilence of puerperal fever. And it is also a lifelong theme in Hawthorne, already outlined in its most basic form in a very early story, "The Haunted Quack" (published in an 1831 giftbook alongside one of Holmes' earliest signed poems), which builds out of recognition of central facts constantly stressed by the Doctor (and which remained sadly true until well into the twentieth century): interventionist doctors – selling useless drugs to make a profit out of sickness – actually cause more pain and death than they prevent; these doctors keep no one out of the grave and in fact put many people there before their time. In "The Haunted Quack," as in his last tales, Hawthorne studies (as an allegory of his own writing career) the case of a young riverboat confidence man whose quack "art" in inventing an elixir of eternal life seems to link him with the sins of witchcraft and with the "horrid crime" of a woman's death – leading him finally to the Holmesian gesture of throwing his entire pharmacy into the river. So Hawthorne, like Holmes, would stress throughout his writing career the fact that the medical cure can become a deadly torture, and that the scientist's most highly developed "elixirs of life" can also be the deadliest of poisons.

In the 1850s and early 1860s, when public confidence in and respect for the medical profession was at one of its lowest points ever in America, Doctor Holmes turned more and more to literary activity (or to medical practice that was mainly verbal – to diagnostic conversations, medicated novels, and public lectures), while

Hawthorne began a series of unfinished romances all obsessively exploring the failures of medicine (*The Dolliver Romance, Septimus Felton, Doctor Grimshawe's Secret*). At this point, though, arising out of this shared predicament and these shared insights, the verbal modes and strategies in the parallel medical romances of Holmes and Hawthorne also diverge markedly to reflect their very different personalities and stances. While one finds himself increasingly isolated within the walls of a Romance world denying "conversation," the other develops a "house-breaking" conversational approach (to medicine as well as to fiction) which, for all its benefits, also finally seems to deny him access to any transformative Romance power.

Hawthorne, like the grave doctors in his spare, private allegorical fictions, came to feel that his art, with its basis in solitude, had developed at the expense of his more genial nature, bringing with it a fatal incapacity for the warmth of human "conversation." But he also continued to yearn for the emergence of what he calls a "physician of moral diseases," a sort of minister (or miracle-working priest) who can offer through his special, secret arts absolutions or cures. He seems to identify his art with that of the doctors whose dangerous magic he must explore fully before a final renunciation. Paradoxically, on the other hand, it is the Doctor who finds it easier to renounce completely the black arts of both fictional romancer and medical necromancer. If Hawthorne seems at times to share the homeopathic desire that some cure be found, a clinician like Holmes works only to explode all past cures; while Hawthorne retains a lifelong fascination with the hubris of past quacks and visionaries, Holmes always warns against such irrational superstitions: to him, "the history of Medicine [is] . . . a record of self-delusion" (*CW*, VII, 172). As part of a thoroughgoing Protestant "disenchantment of the world," with a naturalism that banishes magical practices from medicine as it does the supernatural from religion, and with a related republicanism challenging the specialized knowledge of professional clerics or of doctors, Holmes, like the doctor personae in his talky, rambling, open-form novels, accepts severe limitations on man's curative powers – thus at the same time limiting his ability for sustained fiction.[5] Almost the only positive power and value left to the "therapeutic nihilist" is that of open, social conversation. And in *Elsie Venner,* as we have seen, it becomes clear that such talk, while useful as a diagnostic tool and as a comfort to the stricken, cannot save the patient from a fatal disease. But in other situations Holmes nonetheless continues to hold out the limited hope that the same explosive, effervescent dialogic process that allows him to take apart old beliefs, old cures, old fictions, and old fixations may also offer some distance from the self, some lightening of the burden of a grave inner humor, and some opening into vivifying, affective intercourse with the diverse human community.

WORDS VERSUS WALLS

In his social encounters with Hawthorne, the Doctor often found his efforts at this sort of lightening, bridging conversation running up against a firm resistance in the walls of secrecy and silence surrounding his fellow novelist. But, at the same time, what brings these two opposed voices together in such interactions, and charges as well as challenges their efforts at talk, is always a shared, underlying fascination with just these opposed movements in conversation. Like Holmes, Hawthorne explored the dynamics of intimate verbal interaction through a lifetime of writing – most memorably in the fearfully intimate exchanges of words and breath between Giovanni and Beatrice in "Rappacini's Daughter," or the dangerously confidential doctor–patient dialogues between Chillingworth and Dimmesdale in *The Scarlet Letter* – often focussing his explorations of such verbal intercourse on oppositions between walls and words: figuring the dynamic tendencies associated with the voices of gravity and levity as movements of house-keeping and house-breaking.

From the very beginning of his literary career, Hawthorne defined his special predicament as a writer through this imagery of houses and walls. In the early letters in which he began to form his mythic self-image, he pictured himself becoming mysteriously walled-in in a Romance "dungeon" cut off from human interaction, and so trapped in a double-bind: on the one hand, as several prefaces make clear, every word he produces will be part of a struggle to break down these walls and "open up an intercourse with the world"; on the other hand, each effort at writing also tends to reinforce the power of the Romance witchcraft that created those confining walls in the first place.[6]

The doom of this dividedness is the prime subject in one of the most important of Hawthorne's "sketch" prefaces: "The Custom-House" is built around rapid alternations between these two polar extremes of house-keeping and house-breaking – an immobilizing "home-feeling with the past" or a homeless, placeless, progressive mobility – developed in related Holmesian terms as a dialogue about the value of "transplantation." In Holmes' table-talk works, "transplantation" is a frequent topic for vigorous argument – and it also then emerges as a key movement seen to be inherent in the very form of his multivoiced, interruptive conversation. In *The Professor,* for example, thought of his own attachment to his childhood house leads the Professor to a strong speech attacking the nomadic tendencies of the "mechanical and migratory" American race, which lead too many youths to leave behind the homes of their parents:

But the plants that come up every year in the same place . . . give me the liveliest home-feeling. Close to our ancient gambrel-roofed house is the dwelling of pleasant old Neighbor Walrus . . . It is a rare privilege in our nomadic state to find the home of one's childhood and its immediate neighborhood thus unchanged. Many born poets, I am afraid, flower poorly in song, or not at all, because they have been too often transplanted. (*CW,* II, 247–48)

But then, characteristically, something in the nature of house-breaking talk seems to lead the Professor suddenly to turn on himself in another intervention during the same dialogue, now arguing strongly for the antithesis of such "home-feeling." This time, after a disquisition on the grafting and replanting of pears, he launches suddenly into a stirring defense of the need to assure the same sort of fertile match between young people and their environment:

Just at the period of adolescence, the mind often suddenly begins to come into flower and to set its fruit. Then it is that many young natures, having exhausted the spiritual soil round them of all it contains of the elements they demand, wither away, undeveloped and uncoloured, unless they are transplanted. (*CW,* II, 243)

Holmes' conversation, then, tends always to turn on – or to overturn – any assertions of fixed localism. To put it in his astrophysical terms: not even Boston is truly the "hub" of the universe.

But when Hawthorne's narrator writes, in "The Custom-House," that he cannot leave his native Salem because it seems to him "the inevitable centre of the universe," he finds it hard either to celebrate this gravitational attraction or to laugh about it.[7] The telling word in his version is "inevitable." While he admits that "the connection which has become an unhealthy one, should at last be severed," each time he tries to fly from his home town, he tells us, some strange "doom" or primal "spell" soon brings him orbiting back (12–13). And the undeniable physical force that draws him to return to Salem for his new job in the Custom-House has as its mental equivalent a "repetition compulsion": his thoughts seem inevitably to turn and return about the central family scene of those seventeenth-century courthouses. This homing instinct, then, reflects the downward pull of a "gravity" that is both physical and spiritual; staying in the same place as his ancestors, Hawthorne resigns himself to his place in the family line and to his implication in the family sins.

In a sudden reversal, though, the ongoing process of the Custom-House world surprises Hawthorne's narrator out of this fatalism, and his sketch – paralleling the alternations between voices in Holmesian talk – turns at its end from the voice of grave house-keeping to an extreme form of house-breaking levity. When the revolutionary movement of an election means that he loses his job, the narrator suddenly pictures himself as a homeless, eternally wandering, Whitmanian democratic spirit, forever breaking out of the atomizing confines of the private household, of fenced-in private property, of the single political party, or even of the limiting frame of personal identity, to merge with the largest and most boundless of communities, with

a tendency to roam, at will, in that broad and quiet field where all mankind may meet, rather than confine himself to those narrow paths where brethren of the same household must diverge from one another... (35–36)

Concluding with surprising eruptions of manic verbal wit and a marked emphasis on the gestures of uprooting, severing, cutting off, disconnection, transporting and transplanting, the "Custom-House" sketch leaves us with images of American transience, of a nation always on the move, of a mobile people in mobile homes – with no time to look back to the land-based, settled world of the aristocratic family or to their Puritan past. And this movement finally propels the narrator himself out of his Romance confinement in Salem: "Henceforth [my old native town] ceases to be a reality of my life. I am a citizen of somewhere else" (37).

In its rapid alternation between these two polar voices of house-keeping and house-breaking, "The Custom-House" actually seems more appropriate as a preface to *The House of the Seven Gables* than to *The Scarlet Letter*. For *Seven Gables* turns on just these antitheses, recognizing in them two dynamic poles dividing American thought as the nation entered a crucial period of transition. Developing as an anthology of possible approaches to domestic architecture, *Seven Gables* collects the entire spectrum of mid-nineteenth-century stances and then sets the classic statements of these stances in dialogue, playing out their psychological and social implications very schematically and in great detail. Here the two warring families representing the two "sides" defined by the divisive gesture of house-building – those inside and those outside of its walls; those forever contained by the manse and those excluded from it; the possessing–possessed and the dispossessed – find their fates somehow built into the structure of a single house. And the main question for both the Pyncheons and the Maules becomes: how does one get out of this house?

As a sign of his infirmity, Clifford oscillates wildly between diametrically opposed positions on the question. At first an archetypal house-keeper, he insists on remaining confined in the family manse even though this clearly weakens him mentally and physically, but when he does finally cross the threshold of his "arched window" and break out of the house, abruptly released from inner darkness into outer sunshine and from the stifling house "atmosphere" to a rush of fresh "air," this former "inveterate conservative" erupts into long speeches presenting a bald epitome of all revolutionary mid-century arguments against the gravity of house-keeping:

It is as clear to me as sunshine . . . that the greatest possible stumbling-blocks in the path of human happiness and improvement, are these heaps of bricks, and stones . . . which men painfully contrive for their own torment, and call them house and home! The soul needs air; a wide sweep and frequent change of it . . . There is no such unwholesome atmosphere as that of an old home, rendered poisonous by one's defunct forefathers and relatives! I speak of what I know! There is a certain house within my recollection . . .

. . . I could never draw cheerful breath there! . . . And it were a relief to me, if that house could be torn down, or burnt up, and so the earth be rid of it.

. . . What we call real estate – the solid ground to build a house on – is the broad foundation on which nearly all the guilt of this world rests.[8]

If Clifford's house-breaking here is limited as a fragile man's momentary mania, a one-day revolutionary saturnalia after years of confined conservatism, Holgrave stands as the novel's example of the way in which such a vision of progressive house-breaking can become the solid basis of an entire life. He eats "no solid food"; he has no permanent country and no permanent vocation; he is the mobile new individualist, "homeless," "digressive," forever "putting off one exterior, and snatching up another, to be soon shifted for a third" (76, 153). And Holgrave makes most explicit the architectural imagery that forms the foundation of all of his reformist theories as he rises to a Holmesian or Emersonian vision of life in a succession of eternally-changing houses:

> We live in Dead Men's houses . . . But we shall live to see the day, I trust, when no man shall build his house for posterity. . . If each generation were allowed and expected to build its own houses, that simple change . . . would imply almost every reform which society is now suffering for. (159)

Referring specifically to Colonel Pyncheon's "inordinate desire to plant and endow a family," Holgrave then makes the classic appeal for the necessity of continual uprooting and transplantation – for the renewal of human blood as well as for the genetic renewal of plants and animals:

> To plant a family! This idea is at the bottom of most of the wrong and mischief which men do. The truth is, that, once in every half-century, at longest, a family should be merged into the great, obscure mass of humanity, and forget all about its ancestors. (160)

So, for Holgrave as for Clifford, the new "theory" of house-breaking leads to an exhilarated, exclamatory rise at the thought of a literal and figurative breaking of the vessels, a democratic blending of the blood-streams, an emergence from patrician seclusion into a Whitmanian "merge" with the oceanic flow.

Though Hawthorne's deeply divided novel is largely taken up with swings between the extreme positions of Clifford and Holgrave, it ends with attempts at reconciliation of these antitheses through the mediating figure of Phoebe. Throughout the book, Phoebe is seen as a mobile character continually crossing static thresholds, moving ever closer to marrying the realms of gravity and levity, of darkness and daylight. Finally, advocating a modified house-breaking, she twice repeats, "Let us throw open the doors" – to uncover her family's dark secrets and defuse their power – and then teaches Holgrave to repeat her words: "Let us open the door at once," he finally agrees (262–64). But now, under the influence of his love for Phoebe, that previously lawless nomad prepares for marriage and a return to the fold with concluding images of happy house-keeping – "hereafter it will be my lot . . . to build a house for another generation" – surprising us with his desire to construct the new family seat out of solid stone, "thus giving that impression of permanence, which I consider essential to the happiness of any one moment" (264, 271).

But while the dialogical antitheses of *Seven Gables* do find their bald, schematic resolution here, many readers find Hawthorne's work much more vital and convincing in its description of the oscillations of the ongoing dialogue than in its neat, artificial conclusion to the argument. Like Holmes', Hawthorne's most characteristic writing develops out of a continual process of wild swings between the progressive vision of a Holgrave and the conservative self-imprisonment of a Clifford – or between the manic and the depressive aspects of Clifford's dual personality – alternating between the voices of light house-keeping and grave house-breaking to define these positions, explore their ramifications, and probe their weaknesses from within. The bipolar dialogues of irony sparkle with vitalist life in one writer and bristle with a heavy, scathing, unsatisfied sarcasm in the other, but both Holmes and Hawthorne finally find themselves in the position of a Clifford: as mid-century Americans hesitating on the threshold between two very different worlds, they are deeply ambivalent, deeply uncertain, deeply self-divided.

A FINAL "TALKING EXAM"

All of these concerns shared by Holmes and Hawthorne – revolving around medicine and romance, levity and gravity, house-keeping and house-breaking – were epitomized with dramatic clarity in their final meeting. A very apt endpoint for their long-intertwined paths, this last conversation might have been a scene from one of the two novelist's own works. In 1864 it had become clear that Hawthorne's health was failing seriously, but because of his medical pessimism he stubbornly refused to consult any doctor. Finally, though, to placate his pleading wife, he agreed to see Doctor Holmes. So the Doctor arrived for this interview, as he had for his consultation at Melville's home, as a concession to the wife of the household. But Hawthorne's choice of Holmes over the homeopaths favored by the Peabody family also suggests his recognition that this Doctor shared his basic stance on medical issues. Indeed these deep similarities, this shared therapeutic skepticism or nihilism, put Holmes in a very difficult position for this "talking exam." The two authors who had been so obsessed with medical themes and who had written so much about the doctor–patient interaction were finally forced gingerly to play out such a scene between themselves – in the face of a very serious illness.

Characteristically, the exam was not physical but psychological: the two men simply got out of the house for some fresh air, exercise, and conversation during a half-hour stroll on a Boston street. And Holmes had already sketched his diagnosis even before they met. Reporting on this "talking exam" in an *Atlantic* essay, he directs readers to his previous, unsigned 1860 *Atlantic* review of *The Marble Faun* that analyzes Hawthorne's spirit as unbalanced by one over-riding humor: unrelenting melancholy, or morbid depression, expressed symptomatically in a marked withdrawal from social relations. Hawthorne is seen as an "austere Puritan preacher" who overlooks mercy and grace for the rigid code of Puritan Law, and who thus closes himself and his novels off from "Addison's contentment and sweet and kindly spirit."[9] Hawthorne of course had written much the same things about himself. At their last consultation, knowing that Holmes shared his interest in the relation of spiritual diseases to physical ones, Hawthorne apparently expanded on his greatest anxiety and one of his best-kept secrets: the fear that his excessive, debilitating self-scrutiny and his current bodily deterioration might lead him to complete insanity.[10]

But if they shared such speculations, neither of them had any solutions to the questions raised. Holmes' diagnosis was based on the movement of conversation, and this conversation also offered his only tentative hope for recovery. Conversation with this friend and patient, though, had always been a special challenge. A late Holmes poem takes up the mythic self-image that Hawthorne had presented in his work, recalling the "great Romancer" as a stern, veiled minister or as an Essex wizard centrally defined by his characteristic role in the Saturday Club talk:

> But who is he whose massive frame belies
> The maiden shyness of his downcast eyes?
> Who broods in silence till, by questions pressed,
> Some answer struggles from his laboring breast?
> An artist meant to dwell apart,
> Locked in his studio with a human heart . . .
>
> ("At the Saturday Club," *CW*, XIII, 269–71)

The same grave humor that keeps the writer locked in and framed by the house of Romance forces him to dwell apart from society, isolated from its daily intercourse. But Holmes reports that at their last meeting, even when Hawthorne's despondency was clearly threatening his life, he could only repeat once more the conversational pattern that had become familiar; even as a physician in a "talking exam," the Doctor can only try again to press a few questions at the maidenly introvert:

With all his obvious depression, there was no failing noticeable in his conversational powers. There was the same backwardness and hesitancy which in his best days it was hard for him to overcome, so that talking with him was almost like love-making, and his shy, beautiful soul had to be wooed from its bashful pudency like an unschooled maiden (98).[11]

As modest as Uncle Toby, dwelling apart within his own silent walls, and forced out of those fortifications only by someone with the talkative persistence of a Widow Wadman, Hawthorne is confronted here by a completely different vision of verbal intercourse – by a household model that cannot help but see dialogue as affective, passional, interactive.

But the Doctor would not push his talk so far as to violate his patient's secret heart. Unlike the early Freud, he does not see such dialogue as "verbal surgery." In fact, he clearly shares Hawthorne's scruples here, favoring a friendly, discursive, two-way exchange over any imposition of one-sided medical authority or any directed series of leading questions. He is centrally aware that his patient does not want to have his "infirmities dragged out of [him] by the roots in an exhaustive series of cross-questionings and harassing physical explorations," and he notes again that the talking exam must not attempt to duplicate the percussionist's anatomical one: "it was not my duty to sound all the jarring chords of his sensitive organism" (98). Here Holmes' report emphasizes a key theme he has often stressed in his table-talk works, novels, or medical lectures: while his clinician's training frequently gives the doctor a sad ability to recognize and note the clear physical signs of serious disease or impending death in a patient, his dialogues with that patient must remain indirect and quite carefully limited. "Rather than condemning him to a forlorn self-knowledge such as masters of the art of diagnosis sometimes rashly substitute for the ignorance which is comparative happiness" (98), writes Holmes in his report on the meeting with Hawthorne, the goal in medical conversation should be to avoid unnecessary revelation of the depressing diagnosis, and then simply to try to take the patient's mind off his illness so that he will remain alive longer, hopefully and happily extending his last days.

Thus, the difficult, delicate situation that Holmes had described in many literary scenes – around Elsie's deathbed in *Elsie Venner*, or around Little Boston's deathbed in *The Professor* (*CW*, II, 254–82) – played itself out again in his "talking exam" with Hawthorne. In this particular case, though, Holmes found Hawthorne already gravely resigned to his own death, and knew immediately that such grave resignation would only make that prognosis more certain. (Privately, just after the exam, the Doctor wrote letters to the novelist's concerned friends, notifying them in characteristically imagistic, mythic, unscientific language, that "the shark's tooth is upon him."[12]) So, with this fatal acceptance unspoken in the background, the medical conversation could dispense with diagnosis and turn from curing to caring – serving what was for Holmes one of its main functions: as a sort of verbal anesthetic. Indeed, the Doctor who gave "anaesthesia" its name seems to envision an anesthetic function in much of his talk – especially in its medical uses: against a backdrop of death, disease, and grave fatality, light, digressive conversation must always avoid direct recognition of the end.

But Holmes' *Atlantic* report on the short talk with Hawthorne is very indicative of the Doctor's modest hopes for such medical "conversation." On every level, the novelist's introversion here meets a nursing urge founded in sociability – seeking to draw him out of his seclusion. Because the Doctor's therapeutic conversation was meant to serve as a tool promoting the eighteenth-century ideal of the "public man" in the face of an emerging "atomistic individualism" in nineteenth-century America, it tended in just the opposite direction from the talking exams of twentieth-century psychoanalysis which, at least according to critics like Philip Rieff, have come to encourage a narcissistic self-involvement that finally isolates the patient in endless returns to the original, traumatizing scene. In this way, the Holmes interview with Hawthorne has its parallel in his late novel *A Mortal Antipathy*, which focusses on a young man, in many respects a very close image of Hawthorne, whose medical problem is pathological self-seclusion. The way out of this predicament, it seems, is simply to try to open up a conversation with the larger world. A whole series of townspeople – from gossips to flirts to journalists to the local physician – seem to stand waiting to urge this isolato back into human circulation. Doctor Butts, the small town's wise medical counselor, then neatly sums up the perspective and the conversational goals of the Holmesian physician in a verbal encounter with such a retiring subject:

He could not look upon this young man, living a life of unwholesome solitude, without the natural desire to do all that his science and his knowledge of human nature could help him to do towards bringing him into healthy relations with the world about him. (*CW,* vii, 87)

When Holmes met Hawthorne for their last talk, the friendly "exam" did not confine itself to a lab or a study, but instead was structured around a rambling city walk. Thus as a verbal form this "talking exam" was not static or framed but moved out into the world, containing in microcosm all the elements of a healthy life that the Doctor could endorse as essential elements of preventive medicine and of what he called the "Nature Cure": recreation (getting out of the house); relaxation (to counter the era's grave work ethic); travel (during this city walk Holmes apparently added his voice to those of others urging Hawthorne to take the ill-fated trip with Ticknor – during which the sick man, Ticknor, suddenly had to become a nurse as his supposedly healthy companion, Hawthorne, fell ill and then died); fresh air and exercise; good food and drink; and above all the stimulant of good fellowship.

This social spirit extends to the Doctor's attitude toward drugs. Referring to the scene from *The Dolliver Romance* which he reprints at the end of his report and obituary on Hawthorne, Holmes notes that during their last conversation he offered the novelist no "infallible panacea of my own distillation" but only "familiar palliatives . . . a few cheering words and the prescription of a not ungrateful sedative and cordial or two" (98). In a private letter describing the exam in more detail, he also recalls that as the two strolled past a nearby pharmacy, he "treated [Hawthorne] to simple medicines as we treat each other to ice cream."[13] While this drug-store side-trip seems to have been a joking effort to break the ice of a mutual nervousness about doctors and drugs – clearly this was no wizard threatening with fatal potions, no mesmerist or Chillingworth prying with his magnetic talk – it also reveals something about what Holmes valued more positively in medicine. Though he clearly has little faith in curative drugs, he seems to see some role for the calming placebo and for the pain-killing sedative. But most important for the Doctor is the convivial atmosphere of this drug-taking: the sort of good-

humored talk and toasting that turns the pharmacy into a club and
the drugs into festive and "familiar" food and drink; the party feeling
that makes treatments into surprise "treats"; the childlike playfulness
that allows these two to make light both of pretentious medicines and
of portentous illness. And this sort of conversational treatment
involves no authoritarian force-feeding of drugs, of questions, or of
answers; this is meant to be a mutual affair in which the two "treat
each other." Holmes brings out the close heart-ties at the root of the
already archaic word "cordial," and sees these alcoholic "spirits"
working to invigorate and raise the spirits of a patient's depressed
heart, not in any hermetic enclosure but within the community of
"familiar" feeling – as part of a cheering meal with family and
friends.

This is why, in his report on Hawthorne's death, Holmes can fully
endorse the vision of *The Dolliver Romance*, where Doctor Dolliver's
inherited "cordial" has the same "bitter taste" that has led many
past Dolliver patients to their deaths – the taste of that first Eden
apple – and carries the Puritan medical emblem: a Brazen Serpent.
And he is happy to find Hawthorne here preparing to renounce such
fatal night-time potions for the more natural, familial, daytime
medicine offered by the small grand-daughter, whose nursing simply
trusts to the healing power of love in human relations as she leans to
"kiss it and make it better." (Again, this sort of archaic medicine
stresses the heart-ties at the root of any "cordial.") Holmes had
always wished that Hawthorne would develop more fully the potential of his Pearl and Phoebe, young cheerful household spirits who
seem able to nurse older melancholics towards a healthier vision.
Finally, he hopes that in the unfinished *Dolliver* Hawthorne has
imagined an Aylmer or a Chillingworth figure who can learn from
his playful young grandchild – this time named Pansie. He also hopes
that Hawthorne has himself learned with Doctor Dolliver that even
if he could find, amidst the drugs of the poisonous pharmacy, an
elixir of eternal youth, this embalming miracle-medicine would only
take him out of life's natural cycles and wall him off from Pansie –
with her "true cordial" and her true youth. Reprinting the only
completed *Dolliver* chapter as part of his obituary notice, Holmes
notes that here the Doctor learns to laugh with a benign humor at his
Puritan desire for the supernatural and at his own inevitable mortal
fall. Though the novel was unfinished and their final consultation
was brief, both encouraged Holmes in his belief that the final position

of Doctor Dolliver reflected that of Hawthorne himself. Eight days after their last brief meeting, though, Hawthorne was dead, and Doctor Holmes was called to serve as one of the pall-bearers at his funeral.

PART FOUR

Closing the conversation

CHAPTER 12

CONCLUSIONS
Holmes Senior in dialogue with Holmes Junior

> The highest conversation is the statement of conclusions.
> Oliver Wendell Holmes, Junior, "Books"

Rather than simply summarizing here what we have said earlier in this study about Doctor Holmes in the conversation of his antebellum American culture, it might be most useful, in this brief conclusion, to take a step outside of the Doctor's social circles and out of his era, as a way of beginning to situate and to evaluate his achievements, to get some sense of the larger ramifications of his conversational ideal. We do not have to look further than Holmes' own household to find a perfect foil, for his son was a writer who developed out of and in reaction to the Doctor's verbal world. The distinctive literary style and stance of Justice Holmes – which made him one of the most representative voices of postbellum America – arose out of a strained lifelong "conversation" with his father, a conversation reflecting fundamental differences about the workings of conversation. If Doctor Holmes always urged the opening of conversation, we will see that Justice Holmes, while he grew up within the conversation defined by his father, finally became preoccupied with "the statement of conclusions," and thus developed a series of new strategies for closing this conversation.

Perhaps we have lost an important sense of how difficult it must have been for an extraordinarily ambitious young man to grow up in mid-nineteenth-century Boston – or anywhere in mid-century America – with the name of Oliver Wendell Holmes, Junior. How could he possibly live up to or live down such a household name? How could he make a name for himself? Because Justice Holmes finally succeeded against these odds, because he so successfully usurped the name of his father and erased the Junior from his own, many of us today have forgotten what Holmes Senior represented in antebellum America, or even that he represented anything at all. But if we thus underestimate Doctor Holmes' national reputation and his important contributions in a wide range of fields, we will necessarily fail to recognize crucial factors in the intellectual development of his son.

For if Holmes Junior was finally able to forge an identity for himself as a "Representative Man" epitomizing many of the movements of American culture after the Civil War, his engagement in these large-scale intellectual transformations seems to have been stimulated and informed by a long private history of psychological battles: Holmes Junior could draw upon, be frustrated by, analyze, and often then revolt against a father who stood – in the eyes of his city, of much of the culture at large, and certainly of his son – as one of the figures most truly "representative" of the antebellum Northeast. The father of modern American law was the son of the mid-century's best-known doctor – one of the fathers of modern American medicine. But, as we have seen, Doctor Holmes could never be confined to accomplishment within one narrow profession. If his son emerged from the war as one of the first determinedly "scientific" specialists, Holmes Senior was one of the last of the true generalists, campaigning in every possible forum against increasing specialization among lawyers, clergymen, scientists, and doctors, while himself contributing significantly to contemporary debates in medicine, psychology, law, natural science, and theology, as well as in literature.

The connecting thread, tying together all of the Doctor's multiple professional activities, his literary and medical work, and his social life, was always his interest in the base model of "conversation." And his successes in written and spoken conversation were what made the Doctor a universally-recognized "representative" of Boston culture at the moment of its highest flowering. Holmes Junior would certainly have shared his contemporaries' identification of his father's conversation with the "conversation of the culture" in antebellum New England, even as he remained much less readily pious, much more ambivalent, toward his father, toward that culture, and toward that model of conversation. Developing a profound insight into the larger ramifications of this conversational form, Holmes Junior came to see it less as representative of a cultural flowering than as symptomatic of a deep cultural failure. We can then read his sudden "conversion" during the Civil War to what he called "the soldier's faith against the doubts of civil life" as an attempt to find a way out of the predicament of his father's talk form.[1]

Holmes Senior was a man of questions, and while Holmes Junior meditated as deeply as anyone on these received questions, his greatest impulse was to find solid answers to them. If the Doctor's mode of conversation poses central problems of authority, of interpretive certainty, the Justice's rush to solve these problems reflects the most basic "felt necessity" of the post-war generation: the rush to judgment.

CONVERSATION AND THE PROBLEM OF AUTHORITY

Holmes Junior inherited from his father the family's strong concern with literary style – the sense that one could and should combine one's specialized professional activities with a broad knowledge of literature and a strong interest in writing. And each of the Holmeses then carried this sense for literary style into his social life – developing that mysterious quality of charisma or personal style that makes a common man a "character," and makes his daily life a performance to be observed and recorded by hosts of surrounding Boswells. With his motto, "Every man his own Boswell," Doctor Holmes made clear his desire to become the Doctor Johnson of America – a figure whose blunt or brilliantly witty off-the-cuff opinions would form the talk of the town and of the nation. This sense of life as an ongoing verbal performance – as a carnival of talk – pervaded not only all of Holmes Senior's public activities but also the Holmes household life, as the Doctor engaged even his young children in a conversational free-for-all at the dinner table – offering an extra helping of marmalade as prize for the cleverest remark at each meal.[2] And the father also seized every chance to introduce his children to the wide world of public life, taking them out often to fairs, carnivals, circuses, museums, and performances of high or low theater. Justice Holmes' legendary – perhaps because somewhat incongruous – tastes for popular theater and burlesques, for witty free-thinking conversation, for playful pranks, for cigar-smoking and the occasional drink clearly derive from his early life with his hypersociable father. Like his father, Holmes Junior also found his best aphorisms and retorts, sparked in these festival moments, quickly becoming the matter of myth – so that now, in several admirers' collections, anecdotes containing the Justice's table-talk and spontaneous general opinions are often printed alongside excerpts from his legal opinions, as both sorts of opinion are apparently given an equal weight by the power of his personal authority.[3]

By a triumph of personal style, each of the Holmeses thrust himself onto the public stage to become a symbolic, larger-than-life character in the national consciousness – a representative of his age. Holmes Senior transformed himself and made his place in American mythology almost overnight when, in 1857, he introduced and became identified with his popular persona: the "Autocrat of the Breakfast-Table." Holmes Junior began his life with physiognomical features remarkably similar to those of his father, but the Civil War gave him his new face and figure: as a telling symbol of his liminal transformation during the war, Junior sprouted the oversized, bristling cavalryman's mustache – a military mask standing as the visible mark of his emerging ideological difference from his father – which became his lifelong trademark as he earned his own public place in the American pantheon: a walking daguerreotype out of the nation's past, the "Yankee from Olympus."[4]

The pontificating Autocrat and the mustachioed Yankee warrior: each Holmes stood in his day as a central figure of authority. But the differences in their achieved personae then speak for a major transformation in attitudes toward such authority between antebellum and postbellum generations. Both Yankee and Autocrat are opinion-makers, but the judge will offer his legal opinions as *doxa* – judgments based not on any absolute truth but on the majority opinion of his culture or institution – while the Autocrat's pronouncements tend to work as *para-doxa* : always playing with and against received, majority opinion, drawing it out, exposing its contradictions, turning it back on itself for some self-reflection. If the Yankee's opinions are meant to settle matters, the Autocrat's opinions unsettle things – we have seen that "unsettle" becomes one of Holmes Senior's favorite words. His startling, exaggerated opinions are intended to start conversation rather than – like the Yankee's – to stop it.

The Autocrat stands, then, as a very strange sort of Victorian sage. And the Yankee may well have been shaped in his role as sage of the postbellum era by his uneasiness and exasperation with the perceived limits of his father's Autocrat character. If Holmes Junior sought the grave voice of cultural authority, his Doctor father had founded a secular priesthood (that of the Boston "Brahmins") with a very different tone. The light, airy verbal fireworks of the Autocrat's levity erupt in explosive opposition to antebellum voices of literary, theological, or scientific gravity, promoting the free play of ideas against excessive moral seriousness, Shandyan digressiveness against a literary decorum of plain directness, the Rise of Man against a Calvinist stress on man's original Fall, and the rising, centrifugal movements of "levitation" against the downward-tending force for concentration in Newton's gravitational law. If Doctor Holmes became an early spokesman in medicine for the "gospel of relaxation" and for the therapeutic uses of laughter, advocating exercise, play, and holidays as relief from the oppressive rigidities of work discipline and a heavy Puritan conscience, Holmes Junior apparently felt by the end of the century that such therapeutic levity had won too unbalanced a victory. He then emerged as one of the main spokesmen for the "cult of the strenuous life," urging the application of martial discipline and willpower as his own remedies against a dissipating frivolity and ease, against what historian Jackson Lears describes as a modern sense of "weightlessness."[5]

What would threaten the Yankee most here, though, is not any single competing "gospel" or "cult" or any single opinion, but the overall rhetorical setting in which those opinions arise: the Autocrat shows what happens to cultural authority when it enters the arena of conversation. The Doctor's most fundamental joke, reflected in the title and in the basic structure of his first table-talk work, *The Autocrat of the Breakfast-Table*, is that even in the reduced realm of one small boardinghouse breakfast-table, the movement of multivocal conversation can upset any attempt to assert an omnipotent, Old-World, autocratic authority. We have seen that the turns of talk at Holmes Senior's breakfast-table operate as a sort of perpetual revolution, insuring that each attempt to monopolize the floor or to control the flow of talk will soon be unsettled by explosive outbursts from the loud, diverse crowd of surrounding voices. Even the Autocrat himself, though he may desire to reign as a centralizing dictator, becomes just one of a succession of "carnival kings" – he expands upon his enthusiasms each time only to be then mocked and dethroned by the interruptive rabble.

We have seen that Holmes Senior in fact celebrates not a cultural totalization imposed by a ruling Boston Brahmin but rather the vitalizing multiplicity of boardinghouse voices. And this dynamic talk form stressing interruption and vocal diversity seems to bring with it

a serious challenge to the solidity of any certain axioms or authoritative judgments. The Doctor's model of the "truly intellectual
banquet," once again, holds up

> that carnival shower of questions and replies and comments, large axioms
> bowled over the table like bomb-shells from professional mortars, and
> explosive wit dropping its trains of many-coloured fire, and the mischief-
> making rain of *bons-bons* pelting everybody that shows himself, . . . (*CW*, 1,
> 64)

We can imagine this as the household scene into which Holmes
Junior was born, and which he would try to escape as a warrior and
then as a judge. For Junior might recognize dark undercurrents
within such celebrations of dialogical play. The Justice who became
obsessed with the search for legal "certainty" in judicial decision
making would find in such conversation the ultimate image of
antebellum uncertainty, relativism, and indecision: the model of
cultural authority in crisis.

CONVERSATION AND THE CARNIVALIZATION OF JUDGMENT

In the face of this "carnival-shower of questions and replies," a
Justice's reflex might well be to want to judge between these
conflicting claims, but the Doctor's conversations always operate on
many levels as what we have called here a "carnivalization of
judgment." First, on the most basic level, the breakfast-table divided
becomes Holmes Senior's model of a mind divided: a model that
undercuts any sense of a unitary, stable identity which could stand
outside the multivoiced committee-of-the-self and resolve its internal
disputes. We have seen that Doctor Holmes makes a great deal of the
fact that we have a bicameral brain, housed in right and left
chambers, which struggles toward judgment – like the house-divided
of our bicameral legislatures – through the checks and balances of
lengthy and sometimes angry debate.[6] And, in its most characteristic
scenes or recurring "plots," the Doctor's table-talk is constantly
putting before us pictures of committees that can't decide, debates
that never end, mock trials that end only by overturning or judging
the judge, and so on.[7]

   If there is a point to all of this comic misrule, it is part of the
Doctor's lifelong crusade against overcertain judgment. Doctors
should not rush into diagnoses or heroic cures. Magistrates and

clergymen should not be too quick to bring their fellow men before the "tribunal of their private judgement" – either as saints or as sinners. The representative passage that makes this point sets the unsettling skepticism inherent in free conversation as a direct challenge to such rigid positions: "all persons who proclaim a belief which passes judgement on their neighbours must be ready to have it 'unsettled', that is, questioned, at all times and by anybody." When this all-questioning corrosive power of conversation is then pushed to its extreme limits – under Holmes Senior's banner of the "freedom of ideas" – the movement clearly threatens to undermine much of the authority most basic to legal interpretation: "If to question everything be unlawful and dangerous, we had better undeclare our independence at once; for what the Declaration means is the right to question everything, even the Truth of its fundamental proposition" (*CW*, II, 302, 295). Holmes then goes even further to accent the complete subjectivism and relativism implied by his notion of the talk form. If Brown and Smith each have a belief which would dictate that the other be burned at the stake, he asks, how do we decide between their claims? We cannot, answers Holmes' Professor: humans have no access to absolute "Truth" – and "the *Smithate* of Truth will always differ from the *Brownate* of Truth" (*CW*, II, 302, 295, 297). The only hope is that some larger, intersubjective conversational structure might serve here as an alternative to one-sided judgment, drawing both Smith and Brown out of themselves to sense the limits of their provincial beliefs and private laws, and so to stop judging each other and acting on those judgments – to begin, most simply, to try to talk, with only the "law" of "civility" to guide their verbal interaction.

In his nonconversational scientific essays of the 1870s, the Doctor became preoccupied with these problems of subjectivism and judgment.[8] We get the sense that Holmes Senior is here engaged in a dialogue with his son – who in these years is applying himself feverishly to determining the basic principles that will guide his later career in law. At the same time that Holmes Junior is preparing his legal breakthrough – a rejection of "mental facts" in favor of "external acts" toward the goal of judicial "certainty" – the father is probing further into the subjective and internal questions that highlight the uncertainty of all judgment.

Exploring new mechanistic and deterministic models of human psychology, the Doctor often conflates contemporary justices with

Puritan divines for their tendency to punish those they see as fated (or genetically programmed) to do evil. The Doctor always opposes "Oriental" government and worship – despotism based wholly on external acts and mechanical forms, related to the wrathful God of "Justice" presented by Jonathan Edwards – to an "Occidental" model of mild, humane laws that respect the inner nature of individuals – a model related to visions of a smiling, forgiving form of heavenly ruler. This Western Sovereign has duties toward man and respects the rights of his created beings just the way a Western sovereign government must: "we are called upon to assert the rights and dignity of our humanity, if it were only that our worship might be worthy the acceptance of a wise and magnanimous Sovereign" ("Mechanism," *CW*, VIII, 309). So, while Holmes Junior is developing the legal thought that will put a great new stress on the subordination of all subjects to the all-powerful sovereign state, his father is harking back to earlier ideals of the "rights of man." Rather than debate the "forfeits of criminals to society," Holmes Senior here joins humanitarian philosophers and philanthropists who are concerned with "the duties of society to criminals" ("Crime," *CW*, VIII, 328).

And while the Doctor is fascinated by examples in the new criminal psychology of Elsie Venner-like "moral monsters" who seem to be genetically programmed for crime, he does not think such cases should be judged in the legal system. The law, he writes – in phrases not likely to have pleased his son – is "mechanical," a "coarse tool" fitted only for "expediency"; its punishments are like the harsh treatments attempted by "heroic" doctors: trying homeopathically to cure pain with pain, an eye for an eye, legal men only add to the general suffering in the universe: "We hang men for our convenience or safety; sometimes shoot them for revenge" ("Mechanism," *CW*, VIII, 306–07). Justice Holmes, on the other hand, would come to believe that orderly community must be based on the sacred violence of human "sacrifices." While agreeing with his father that we cannot judge an insane man to be immoral, he would nonetheless feel certain in judging the man's acts in terms of their social effects, and then opt for penalties of death, life imprisonment, or sterilization for the good of the state. These harsh responses are sometimes seen by legal historians as extensions of Holmes Senior's positions in his novel *Elsie Venner* and elsewhere, but in fact the Doctor's views are in general diametrically opposed to those of his son.[9] He uses these anomalous cases to challenge judgment, to unsettle it, and thus to

urge greater consideration of internal causes and then more forgive-
ness for human frailties. Rehabilitation by moral physicians should
replace the judgments of legal men. Even later in the 1870s, the
Doctor is still at least tentatively advocating an application in the
judicial realm of the French psychiatric reforms coming out of the
experiments of Philippe Pinel: "We are to have done with gibbets
and fetters, then, for the most desperate offenders, and are to
substitute moral hospitals. We are to give up the idea of punishment
for these unfortunates and institute palliative and curative treatment" ("Crime," *CW*, VIII, 346).

To the end, the Doctor remains deeply divided as to the solutions
to these questions (which is why his conclusions are still phrased as
paradoxes, and put in the mouths of others), and his essays become
most digressive and conversational at their conclusions, just as they
must face these issues of judgment. But the hypotheses that are aired
here nonetheless build as strong, unsettling challenges to any voices
of legalistic certainty. From the new French thought, the Doctor feels
that the "magistrate should learn something which will cause him to
think more leniently of the unhappy creatures whom he is compelled
to sentence; the divine may be led to reconsider his traditional
formula of human nature ("Crime," *CW*, VIII, 349). And Holmes
Senior ends his most sustained study of contemporary criminology,
"Crime and Automatism," with a characteristically anti-authoritarian admonishment turning the tables on those judges who inflict
the "gravest penalties" for seeming "sins": "if [sin] were in court the
prisoner might not rarely sit in judgment on the magistrate"
("Crime," *CW*, VIII, 360).

Of course Holmes Senior never comes to a firm stand on these
serious, nagging issues; his primary verbal mode is not the conclusive
essay but the ongoing process of table-talk. But these questions of
judgment are always latent in every moment of the Doctor's table-
talk works – though here the problem is not studied theoretically but
enacted dramatically. In the endless give-and-take of the Doctor's
table-talk, no assertion is ever final, each question opens into a
multiplicity of possible interpretations, no statement can be put forth
without immediately calling up its antithesis – or several antitheses.
And while this chaos may be exhilarating on one level, to a Holmes
Junior it might also stand as a troubling picture not only of a mind
divided or of a boardinghouse divided but of a nation divided.

Lecturing each other at cross purposes in private, specialized languages or in different regional dialects, the table-talkers at the Doctor's Giant National Breakfast-Table (with its "legs in every Atlantic and inland city, – legs in California and Oregon . . . legs everywhere, like a millipede or a banian-tree") are unable even to agree about which dictionary to use to clear up their perpetual misunderstandings.[10] And certainly the Autocrat is no help in resolving the mounting tensions. So, as we have seen, the breakfast-table realm he rules over develops as a matchbox caricature of the United States Congress in these years just before the war, with differences in regional languages emerging as fundamentally incommensurable modes of interpretation. The Autocrat here finds himself in a comic version of the predicament of Daniel Webster, faced with "revolts" and "secessions" but unable to dictate any interpretive unity amidst this carnival of diverse voices.

But how could mid-century Americans respond to these images of a breakdown in the "conversation of the culture"? Some would search for the final word in a definitive dictionary; some would seek one unshakable reading of the Constitution; some would propose an Academy of American English; some, in an effort to structure the passions of parliamentary debate, would formalize Robert's Rules of Order; and some – like Holmes Junior – would find their answer by breaking out of the verbal realm with all of its problems of knowing and interpreting, leaving behind the drawing room and the debating-hall for the new setting of the battlefield, and then finding there a new model of conflict and resolution in the operations of physical force – in the active Judgment of the Civil War.

DRAWING ROOM TO BATTLEFIELD: FROM THE "FREE PLAY OF IDEAS" TO "FREE TRADE IN IDEAS"

The relation of Holmes Senior and Holmes Junior, then, develops in many ways as an "inner civil war." First, this father and son were always quite openly involved in a difficult intrafamilial struggle – a household civil war that apparently came to a head, and to some resolution, during the son's participation in the nation's Civil War. Holmes Junior seems, perhaps because of his rush to resolve the problems posed by his father's conversational stance, to have become possessed by an internalized image of that war experience – an image which dominated much of his later thinking and writing. Like an Uncle Toby, he came to live every day as a reenactment of this inner civil war – marking the anniversaries of each wound, reliving each battle, applying the basic martial lessons. This image of war replaces Holmes Senior or antebellum Harvard as a central figure in the young man's mind, taking its place next to the Constitution as the text for his future legal thinking. The extralegal precedent of martial law becomes for him the model for interpretation of civil law.[11] And armed struggle can now also serve as a new model for literary form, an alternative to the pre-war polite conversation epitomized by his father. Active conflict – a fight to the death – suggests to Holmes Junior a pragmatic way out of the uncertainty and relativism of an unending war of words; the strenuous life of battlefield action comes as a cure for the indoor idleness of drawing-room life.

Finally, what begins here as a private intrafamilial struggle develops as a very neat case study of what George Fredrickson describes in *The Inner Civil War*, a struggle and conversion that was taking place among a great many Northern intellectuals during the war years. One of the turning points in Fredrickson's study comes in a letter from John Lothrop Motley to Holmes Senior about Holmes Junior – taking the war's effect on the young soldier as a sign of a general militarization of the culture: "The young poet, philosopher, artist has become a man, *robustus acri militia puer* . . . When a whole community suddenly transforms itself into an army . . . what a change must be made in the national character."[12] The tone of war-fever excitement here is curious, since in this latest sign of the times Doctor Holmes whether conscious of it or not – would be reading the death sentence of his pre-war form of life. The most significant element in this youth's initiation into a new authoritative manhood seems to be a change in his attitude toward writing and thinking – a movement away from poetry and philosophy. And Fredrickson sees Holmes Junior's shift here as indeed "representative": the experience of military heroism and discipline within a hierarchical organization would teach many a gentleman-intellectual a new respect for institutions, for law and order, and for the role of a central state power.

While Holmes Senior had been seated onstage next to Emerson as he gave his speech "The American Scholar," had been inspired by it to venture himself into this new intellectual profession of lecturing, and had later hailed that speech as America's "intellectual Declaration of Independence," Holmes Junior would come during the war to shed what Fredrickson calls "the whole Emersonian style of intellectuality" for a new model of specialized professionalization – that of the "soldier-intellectual."[13] We shift here, in Richard Hofstadter's terms, from the realm of the "intellectual" – involving a fundamentally conversational model of thought that relishes contradictions, questions, and the "play of the mind for its own sake" – to what he terms the clerical "intellect": the goal-oriented mind in the service of institutional or state power.[14] (Late in life, Justice Holmes quipped that his epitaph should read: "Here lies the supple tool of power.")[15] While before the war Holmes Junior had seemed to be following in his father's footsteps as a dreamy student with that earlier period's characteristic "Problem of Vocation," after the war he would – just as Motley predicted – quickly give up his dabbling in philosophy and poetry, applying himself with new martial spirit to specialized study of the law. If Holmes Senior had named and defined the "Boston Brahmin" as a member of an "academic class" completely removed from political or social leadership – part of a quirky attempt to define some role for the speculative intellect that had become so marginalized in Jacksonian America – Holmes Junior leads a new generation that would carry the banner of the "Brahmin" onto the public stage, abandoning the academic cloister as part of an effort to reassert an activist role for the patrician class as professional experts within public institutions.

But Holmes Junior's war experience did not provoke a complete abandonment of writing. Rather his wartime conversion involved crucial transformations in his literary goals and style. Again, Holmes Junior's progress in this regard seems to epitomize that of a generation. Edmund Wilson's *Patriotic Gore*, a study of the effect of the Civil War on American literature, takes Holmes Junior as one of its most representative figures. His last two chapters summarize the overall change – "the chastening of American prose style" – and then illustrate that change with a final close examination of the writings of Justice Holmes. Concentrating on stylistic marks more than on overall rhetorical structure, Wilson attributes Holmes Junior's much-noted verbal qualities – austerity, grim concentration, a tough terseness – to the influences on him of wartime leaders like Grant and Lincoln, who in crisis had to be verbally decisive, to bark out their orders and judgments, to convince and direct in a "language of responsibility." There is certainly a war-time violence to Holmes Junior's oft-repeated self-admonishments to be, in his own use of words, like the Lincoln described by Wilson, "direct and cogent, to try to hit the nails on the head."[16] His motto for writing – one must have "an instinct for the jugular" – alludes to his having himself been shot in the neck at Antietam (with the bullet just missing his own jugular vein); it speaks for the unflinching anatomical accuracy sought in this new mode of "realism"; and it captures the Justice's desire to give writing and thinking some of the decisiveness of war – questions are resolved when one alternative shoots and "kills off" another in an arena of action and force.[17] This motto also implies that ideas battle for survival with the "instincts" of animals guarding their territories and their own lives: even if, as Holmes notes, "we do not know what we are talking about" much of the time, "we do know that a certain complex of energies can wag its tail and another can make syllogisms." And we also know that "a dog will fight for its bone."[18]

Holmes Junior would take up these models of military command as part of his personal effort to release himself from his father's purely verbal world. He came to feel that his hypersociable father had wasted too much valuable energy, letting himself be "largely distracted into easy talk and occasional verse," and for that reason had never produced a truly "great work." After long exposure to a paternal voice marked by a fountainlike lightness and diffusion, the Justice would become, in Wilson's apt phrase, a "real concentrator of thought."[19] Much of Doctor Holmes' humor centered on the human tendency he often displayed himself: the inability to stop talking. We have seen that he was fascinated by the phenomenon of the conversational autocrat, like Coleridge, who threatened to turn any dialogue into monologue. Holmes Junior did not want to speak in this atmosphere of timeless ease – with hours for vision and revision. Even if there were no present crisis, he would pretend there was one. He learned to stand up while writing his opinions in an effort to make himself come right to the point. While indirection works as the central dynamic of Holmes Senior's conversational style – as one voice is interrupted by another or as any Autocratic monologist finds his train of thought wildly derailed by metaphors driven more by the vehicle than the tenor – Holmes Junior develops, in contrast, an obsession with directness of expression. And if the Doctor had an easy fluency that allowed him to go on and on, playing with the old-fashioned long periods of the day, the Justice always had to work to chisel out his words and sentences: they march along to abrupt conclusions; they do not flow actively but take the form of blunt declarative assertions. Most often these statements are built around the verb "to be": "I believe that the struggle for life is the order of the world"; "I do think that man at present is a predatory animal"; "I used to say, when I was young, that truth was the majority vote of that nation that could lick all others"; the Constitution "is an experiment, as all life is an experiment"; "The life of the law is not logic; it is experience."[20] These are definitions, autocratic edicts, or clearly marked statements of firm personal belief intended to distinguish by fiat what is from what is not.

Finally, though, the difference between the pre-war and post-war American literary styles of Holmes Senior and Junior is not simply a contrast between long periods and short periods, or between metaphoric "floweriness" and a "chastened" plain style. For certainly the Doctor too could be blunt: his talk is a continual coining of pointed aphorisms; a great number of his sayings have passed into the nation's treasury of "anonymous" household words; and certainly the endless flow of these witty maxims and anti-maxims around the family table would have been a primary influence on the development of Holmes Junior's aphoristic style. But even the shortest sayings of this father and son are worlds apart in their effect. The Doctor's aphorisms tend to be jokes and riddles, turning back upon themselves in the grand manner as they undercut their own truth value. But while the Doctor mocks the moral maxim, the Justice works to hone lasting "jewels five words long" which will become memorable parts of the legal tradition or even take their place among the proverbial sayings of wisdom literature.[21] If the Doctor's statements are often extreme, this is because they are intended to trigger new thought or to spark further discussion; when the Justice's aphorisms are extreme, it is in the hope that they will put an authoritative end to all discussion.

Fundamentally, then, what Holmes Junior develops in the war is a powerful and all-pervasive "sense of an ending." He wants to end sentences, straightening out any digressions at the insistence of an end-oriented grammar. And he also wants to end questions or conversations: his letters and his legal opinions are famously lacking in reasoning or reasons; they simply hit us with the answers. (Yosal Rogat estimates that, in average length, Holmes wrote probably the shortest opinions in the history of the Supreme Court.)[22] When he does find himself faced with a situation or a predicament in which he is unable personally to pronounce judgment, he will then usually make a very certain declaration about the limits of human knowledge before leaving us with an appeal to a Higher Court: the familiar vision of Judgment, an abdication before the greatest ends of all – the ends of history, or even the apocalyptic end of time.

Richard Rorty's basic distinction between two approaches to conversation may be useful here. We have observed earlier that when Rorty opposes those who want to close conversations to those who seek to continue them, the latter model, opening the possibility of a utopian "conversation of a culture," often seems very close to that of Doctor Holmes. For Rorty too defines an alternative position for the philosopher who would speak from the floor of the drawing room rather than from the lectern of a school or church, not as a monological specialist dealing in definitive truths and hard facts but as a conversationalist-generalist-dilettante who might serve to moderate discussions between diverse specialists or dogmatists, bringing all the culture's voices together in a realm where the only common ground is civility, the only agreement is about a hope for future agreement, the sole desire is to keep the conversation going. And Rorty would defend the airy levity of speculative, hypothetical dialogue just as Holmes Senior does, by banishing hard scientific "facts" or fixed "Truths" and always distinguishing this realm of discourse from that of action.[23]

We have seen that the Doctor is constantly defending himself against conversational bullies who come toting the legalistic "facts" which are "intended to stop all debate, like the previous question in the General Court" (*CW*, I, 28). Such "facts" invade the realm of light, unsettled conversational give-and-take as grave "settlers" – always associated with knives, revolvers, attack dogs, or other such weapons of war. The bearers of such "facts" threaten to replace the turns of well-polarized talk with a battlefield finality: "The men of facts wait their turn [during a discussion] in grim silence, with that slight tension about the nostrils which the consciousness of carrying a 'settler' in the form of a fact or a revolver gives the individual thus armed" (*CW*, I, 142). So the Doctor is always concerned to stress the differences between conversational and applied truth:

Some persons seem to think that absolute truth, in the form of rigidly stated propositions, is all that conversation admits . . . [But] conversation must have its partial truths, its embellished truths, its exaggerated truths . . . One man who is a little too literal can spoil the talk of a whole tableful of men of *esprit*. (*CW*, I, 51–52)

Holmes Junior, on the other hand, represents the opposite approach to talk. As a legal specialist and judge, his job will be to "stop all debate," his interest will be in "rigidly stated propositions," and his own sentences will inevitably work as performative utterances that make things happen in the public sphere – a Justice's sentences are active in the sense that they "sentence" other people. The first sentence of Holmes Junior's first published college essay seems to predict his later developments in this regard. The self-serious piece begins, "The highest conversation is the statement of conclusions."[24] Later in life, the Justice distinguished judicial opinions from the opinions expressed in social conversation by distinguishing the battle-field or the marketplace or the court-room from the drawing room:

I know of no true measure of men except the total of human energy which they embody. . . The final test of this energy is battle in some form – actual war – the crush of Arctic ice – the fight for mastery in the market or the court . . . It is one thing to utter a happy phrase from a protected cloister; another to think under fire – to think for action upon which great interests depend.[25]

Holmes Junior would point out that the genteel conversational ideal of a Rorty or a Doctor Holmes would be impossible if applied in a real world where voices are unequal and the most powerful ones would soon silence all the rest. In the transition from Holmes Senior to Holmes Junior, we have a perfect case study of what happens to the ideal of a "free play of ideas" in the site of a battleground or a marketplace. The Justice's "free trade in ideas," based on these latter models of conflict, involves a violent struggle: the survival of the fittest. While Holmes Junior can occasionally envision a role for the Constitution in keeping open the "conversation of the culture" – "The Constitution is made for people of fundamentally differing views" – more often he seems to feel that law in fact does not enter the scene until this conversation – now seen as a battle to the death – is over, until the play of ideas has been settled by the play of force: "Law embodies beliefs that have triumphed in the battle of ideas and have translated themselves into action."[26]

The attraction of this conflictual model is clear: it opens the possibility of a resolution to multivoiced dialogue. So while Holmes Junior always retained the philosophical skepticism of his father, this did not lead him to be at all uncertain in judgment. During his war experiences he seems to have developed what he describes in "Natural Law" as "the desire to have an absolute guide."[27] His early labors on *The Common Law* provided him with a general theory – a firm set of propositions – which he could apply to all questions he later faced. Rogat notes that *The Common Law*, reflecting Holmes' "constant search for the authentic voice of the sovereign," allowed the Justice to write forceful and succinct opinions in later years, as it made possible the "efficiency" of deciding through ideological "blinders." Holmes Junior was, in Rogat's estimation, "the least hesitant of men": "It is difficult to think of anyone who expressed fewer qualifications or occupied fewer half-way positions . . . He may have said that nothing was true once and for all, but on any particular occasion in making any particular decision he was convinced he was right."[28] If this judgment is accurate, it defines the most crucial shift in writerly stance between Holmes Senior and Holmes Junior. And many admirers of the Justice's writings would agree with this assessment: as his friend Francis Biddle wryly observed, "He distrusted affirmations . . . yet . . . made them with an oversimplification that was only partially concealed by the form of witty aphorism which they usually took."[29] It is the Justice's success in achieving this mysterious quality – in becoming a voice of authority – that continues to be the source of his undeniable attraction both to legal theorists and to general readers.

Edmund Wilson noted a general tendency Holmes Junior shared with other writers of the war generation: they "give the impression of speaking with certainty; yet what seems to be certainty is often mere rigidity. It is a costume, a uniform, still worn after the crisis no longer decrees it."[30] But what was it in the war experience that could serve as the model for such writerly authority? Many decades after the war had ended, Holmes Junior offered one overall explanation in his Memorial Day speech, "The Soldier's Faith."

In 1895, the year after his father's death, Holmes Junior returned to Harvard with a summation of what appeared to him in retrospect to have been the "divine" "message" of the Civil War. The Justice speaks in "The Soldier's Faith" as one who has been "touched with fire": a soldier's life under gunfire gives him an agnostic's version of a Pentecostal inspiration, and his testimonial has the form of a conversion narrative. We are urged in unusually purple prose and in poetry to move from doubt to faith, but the faith here is strangely modern and hollow: the Civil War hero wants to promote "the soldier's faith against the doubts of civil life." As a young soldier, he may have gone to war with an abolitionist's belief in a militant Puritan God of

Judgment, but the sordid scenes of battle then stripped him of belief in any absolute causes. Only one faith and one fierce Calvinist vision of Judgment do remain intact through the fight: a "blind belief" in the need for belief and in war as an end in itself; a religiously tinged "cult of strenuous life." If he marched South singing the millennial "Battle Hymn of the Republic" – "Mine eyes have seen the glory of the coming of the Lord/ . . . His Truth goes marching on" – this young soldier came back having transferred his faith from the fully revealed ("mine eyes have seen") Truth of the Lord to a blind process of military assertion; what is left as a Truth here is simply the "marching on." God speaks in verse in the Justice's post-war oration, then, only through violent victories: "I am the Will of God/ I am the Sword."[31]

This conversion narrative was probably intended to shock its Harvard audience, for it defines the turning to this new form of "faith" through a series of contrasts with Holmes Junior's childhood life in Cambridge and at Harvard – as a turn away from the world of his all-doubting father. The most immediately noticeable contrast is in literary style. In a creaky chivalric prose (reflecting the Justice's interest in the late-nineteenth-century revival of Sir Walter Scott, and a related interest in the contemporary literature of medieval chivalry and gentleman crusaders – especially in the works of Charles Eliot Norton – which had captivated him during his fighting days), Holmes urges a thorough break from the domestic literature of parlor conversations, and from "the literature of . . . American humor" with its "individualist negations . . . revolting at discipline."[32]

And if the literature of martial action suggests a way out of endless domestic talk, for Holmes Junior this movement reflects a personal change as well. His speech makes clear that the move away from Cambridge and out of his family's parlor was experienced as an initiation: the turn from doubt to faith is also a turn from childhood to maturity. Holmes Junior had asserted repeatedly in his letters home late in the war that "I started in this thing as a boy – I am now a man."[33] In "The Soldier's Faith" he stresses that war seems suddenly to convert young recruits into old men. In fact war itself is personified as an old man, a wise man, a "teacher" who takes the place formerly held by the father and by Harvard. But by sitting "at that master's feet," the soldier becomes himself a patriarch. The Justice refers to his childhood memories of Revolutionary War soldiers, "white-haired" men who had been the cultural heroes of his youth; he implies that the Civil War seems to have had the same effect on him – making him one of those white-haired men. And indeed he did emerge from the war to speak and write from then on with the authority of experienced old age.

While all children make some such transition to adulthood, it is easy to understand why there might be an exaggerated, even violent, insistence on the importance of such a transition in a child whose own father seemed to him never to have achieved adult authority. The child is father to the man: Wordsworth's phrase, taken literally, captures the relation between the 5'3" tall Holmes Senior and his 6'3" son. The Doctor, a youthful, frivolous prankster seemingly incapable of seriousness, kept his boyish appearance almost all of his long life. In his yearly class-day poems for his Harvard Class of 1829, Holmes Senior continued to refer to his generation as "the boys" even when they were all in their seventies or eighties – always noting with amazement that although they have all become judges, teachers, and doctors, they are all still "just boys."[34] And Holmes Senior's breakfast-table writings often celebrate the triumph of naughty youths over grave patriarchs or experts, in general unsettling any certain authority while putting nothing positive in its place. A classic member of what George Forgie calls "the post-heroic generation, . . . a generation of sons," the Doctor never had the opportunity to be heroically active in either the Revolutionary War or the Civil War.[35] But in his own day he mocked the heroics of the "Bowie-knife civilization" developing in the West and in America's other imperialist adventures and spent much of his energy attacking the "heroism" of the American forefathers – whether that of Calvinist divines and judges or of interventionist doctors like Benjamin Rush, who reflect the Revolutionary era's urge to "rush" into every situation with painful "heroic" cures.

But if the Doctor revolted against the authority and heroism of the nation's fathers, his son in "The Soldier's Faith" then revolts against him for his lack of authority and heroism – or, in the terms of the speech, for his lack of "faith." The Civil War helped Holmes Junior to define a new form of heroism for a new age – a heroism involving neither individual effort nor outstanding action but mainly the ability to become a cog in a large, disciplined machine, to accept one's place as a single soldier in the unknowable movements of a huge army. This is a heroism not of leadership but of obedience, a heroism of

"blind belief." And Holmes Junior's new stress on the word "blindness" here helps us to understand the use of this special vision of
heroism. It offers a way out of doubt and skepticism, a way out of
questions about knowledge and interpretation, a way of acting in
uncertainty.

While in "The Path of Law" Holmes Junior takes a rationalist
Enlightenment position to attack "blind imitation" or the "blind
guess" based on received legal precedents, the irrationalist argument
of "The Soldier's Faith" turns to "blindness" as a positive value. The
speech opens with the epic-heroic image of a blind man playing a
flute, but then narrows the import of that image as it applauds military
action based on "blind belief." And in the most famous passage in the
speech, Holmes Junior mentions "blindess" (or "not seeing") twice
as part of his solution to the dangers of a paralyzing skepticism:

> I do not know what is true. I do not know the meaning of the universe. But
> in the midst of doubt, in the collapse of creeds, there is one thing I do not
> doubt, and that no man who lives in the same world with most of us can
> doubt, and that is that the faith is true and adorable which leads a soldier to
> throw away his life in obedience to a blindly accepted duty, in a cause which
> he little understands, in a plan of campaign of which he has no notion,
> under tactics of which he does not see the use.[36]

This soldierly blindness involves an agnostic's abdication before a
Final Judgment – the "supposed final valuation" which "we may
leave to the unknown."[37] In the actual practice of war it involves an
abdication before the judgment on the battlefield: might makes right.
But as a model of human judgment in more everyday civil cases, it
puts a whole new meaning into our commonplaces about "blind
justice." For this blind faith would not caution the human judge to be
impartial; rather it simply teaches him that he must accept and act
upon his own inevitable ideological blindnesses.

THE SENSE OF AN ENDING

Perhaps a close look at the movement of one paragraph – the third
one from Holmes Junior's "Natural Law" – can best illustrate how
the model of war intervenes in his thought to cut off any potential
openings into conversational form or any recognition of uncertainty.
From the first sentence, a typically alliterative and cryptic aphorism,
we see that a legal definition of objective "certainty" – as opposed to
purely subjective belief – will be the goal:

Certitude is not the test of certainty. We have been cock-sure of many things that were not so. If I may quote myself again, property, friendship, and truth have a common root in time. One can not be wrenched from the rocky crevices into which one has grown for many years without feeling that one is attacked in one's life. What we most love and revere generally is determined by early associations. I love granite rocks and barberry bushes, no doubt because with them were my earliest joys that reach back through the past eternity of my life. But while one's experience thus makes certain preferences dogmatic for oneself, recognition of how they came to be so leaves one able to see that others, poor souls, may be equally dogmatic about something else.

Thus far this could be a speech at the Autocrat's table. For Holmes Senior too loved to stress the power of childhood associations – his too specifically tied to New England granite and berries. And the extension of the "root" metaphor – one's being rooted and then uprooted like the bushes – adds power and vigor to the opinion by making new the organic images beneath its surface: again very typical of the Doctor. Even the Autocratic self-citation (another enactment of this speaker's topic: the way that our "conceit" makes it hard for us to leave our own experience) seems familiar, as does the self-mocking humor of the last sentences, which seem to recognize the exaggerations in "one's own" provincialism with jokes about "the past eternity of my life" and the grudging notice of those other "poor souls" who just cannot seem to see through our eyes.

But in Holmes Senior's works we would expect a sudden interruption at just this point. Another voice would butt in to play upon that "natural" root imagery, to respond to that self-quoted opinion, and to launch into a harangue – equally "dogmatic," as predicted – on other themes central to the Doctor's thought: the need to break out of a single voice and out of the familial birthplace; the importance of periodic uprooting and transplanting. These are not simply themes of Holmes Senior's talk; they are, as we have seen, movements inherent in his model of the conversational process. After bringing us to this juncture, though, Holmes Junior characteristically digs in his heels. He finds that he cannot change his mind, he cannot give up the floor to another voice. Speaking during one war (in 1918), he is clearly thinking of his own Civil War days: from the beginning his imagery has been calling up the irreconcilable differences between America's North and South. Able to envision no "conversation of a culture" between such incommensurable "certitudes," he turns to the solution of force, in sentences that themselves have a new urgent force. And here again war emerges as a model defining a form of skepticism (a recognition of one's inborn blindnesses) that does not preclude active judgment. The paragraph continues,

And this again means skepticism. Not that one's belief or love does not remain. Not that we would not fight and die for it if important – we all, whether we know it or not, are fighting to make the kind of world that we should like – but that we have learned to recognize that others will fight and die to make a different world, with equal sincerity or belief. Deep-seated preferences cannot be argued about – you cannot argue a man into liking a glass of beer – and therefore, when differences are sufficiently far reaching, we try to kill the other man rather than let him have his way. But this is perfectly consistent with admitting that, so far as appears, his grounds are just as good as ours.[38]

A small voice might raise a large question here: even if we grant that war must replace conversation for questions of "far-reaching. . . differences" – first principles – couldn't we still talk about that glass of beer? Of course, the Justice often likes to shock us by combining neat, rational references to logic and "perfect" consistency with sudden, searing tonal shifts: all at once we find we are killing the other man or fighting for a bone. But it is astonishing how often the "greater" model of martial law is invoked by Holmes Junior even for "lesser" questions about civil law or about what he mockingly calls "municipal regulations," in fact even for the most minor questions of taste (that beer again) or intellectual specialization. When Harold Laski asked Holmes' opinion of Jane Austen (obviously too small, too talky, too much of the drawing room for the old warrior), the Justice refused even to answer his questioner and instead could only repeat once again his dictum that "in cases of differences between ourselves and another there is nothing to do except in unimportant matters to think ill of him and in important ones to kill him."[39]

Here we have lost any sense of a middle ground, of the possibility of a heterogenous community built around compromise or conversation. The only test of the "Truth" of a position, the Justice always says, is one's willingness to die for it: the "soldier's faith," which allows one "to be ready to give one's life" even in time of peace. If Austen lovers would organize and sacrifice their lives for their cause, that is the only way they could change Holmes' opinion. The only way to resolve a conflict is to fight it out the way the North and South did – with the party that wins then imposing its will on the losers. "It seems clear to me," writes Holmes in another well-known motto, "that the *ultima ratio*, not only *regum*, but of private persons, is force."[40] A mark of the Justice's deep craving for certainty is his repetition of these same extreme opinions again and again, from decade to decade, often in exactly the same words. Removed from debate or conversational interaction, his single-voiced sentences become well-chiseled formulae, his ideas become simplified, solid counters. The following passage from a letter, for example, begins with a weak attempt to incorporate the interlocutors of a dialogue form, but soon dismisses all outside voices, turning to the more characteristic Holmesian style, a series of abrupt declarative assertions.

I loathe war – which I described when at home with a wound in our Civil War as an organized bore – to the scandal of the young women of the day who thought that Captain Holmes was wanting in patriotism. But I do think that man at present is a predatory animal. I think that the sacredness of human life is a purely municipal ideal of no validity outside the jurisdiction. I believe that force, mitigated so far as may be by good manners, is the *ultima ratio*, and between two groups that want to make inconsistent kinds of world I see no remedy except force. I may add that every society rests on the death of men.[41]

This might be the voice of Holmes Senior's Autocrat – but with little irony and no interruption. Since the verbs in these sentences are abstract rather than active, the main charge here comes from the shock of the ideas themselves. But if they seem to cry out for some interruptive response, we sense that these are not the epigrams of a drawing-room voice playing to its audience in a social setting; this is a mind that has abolished almost all social and personal relations to concentrate on specialized thought, working in isolation on the problem at hand, making remarkably few gestures even to the addressee of the letter. Everything begins with "I think" and "I believe" – foregrounding the extreme self-consciousness of this subjectivity. This author is his own best authority; he is constantly citing himself, relying upon the rigid propositions that he has been able to forge out of a surrounding chaos – and the only text he glosses is that of his personal experience during the Civil War.

When Holmes Junior's transformation as a soldier led Motley to imagine what might become of the nation "when a whole community transforms itself into an army," he could hardly have known how prophetic a vision this would be.[42] For, as Justice, Holmes does in fact tend to define the community on the model of an army. What he often refers to as a separate realm – the jurisdiction of the "purely municipal ideals" noted above – seems actually to be based upon and invaded by the operations of an all-surrounding world of brute military force. Government is defined on the pattern of the Lincoln administration, which, at the peak of war crisis, had to use extra-ordinary means to assure its continued control. When Holmes writes that "Truth [is] the majority vote of that nation that could lick all others," he implies that the majority rules at home in just the same way that the dominant national power rules abroad.[43] Even the home country's civil law is based, then, on the seemingly extralegal. Rogat worries that Holmes' vision often seems to involve simply "a crude system of social control, resting on naked power." Certainly the Justice suggests a reduction of law to brute physical force in several letters to Laski: "The only limit that I can see to the power of the law-maker is the limit of power as a question of fact"; "All law means I will kill you if necessary to make you conform to my requirements." Faced with questions about the proper role of lawful government, he could only repeat, "What proximate test of excel-lence can be found except . . . conformity to the wishes of the dominant power."[44]

Some theorists and judges might want to try to distinguish brute social power from legal process and to see the maintenance of a distinction between civil and martial law to be the prime goal of a constitutional system.[45] But even in peacetime Holmes often justifies strong governmental measures by analogy to the greater powers of the state during war. Making his harsh judgment promoting eugenics and state-ordered programs of sterilization in *Buck v. Bell*, for example, he writes,

We have seen more than once that the public welfare may call upon the best citizens for their lives. It would be strange if it could not call upon those who already sap the strength of the state for these lesser sacrifices . . . in order to prevent our being swamped with incompetence . . . Society can prevent those who are manifestly unfit from continuing their kind . . . Three generations of imbeciles are enough.[46]

The "society" that speaks here is founded on the sacred violence of human "sacrifice." And this sovereign power leaves little room for consideration of even some very basic "rights": "The most funda-mental of the supposed pre-existing rights – the right to life – is sacrificed without scruple not only in war, but whenever the interest of society, that is, of the predominant power in the community, is thought to demand it."[47] Contrasted with the bleak clarity of this battlefield vision, advocacy of various humanitarian rights always seemed to Holmes Junior to be "drool," the sort of "squashy sentimentalism" that he said made him "puke."[48] Talk of John Dewey, for example, brings out the formulaic retort: "He talks of the exploitation of man by man – which always rather gets my hair up . . . All society rests on the death of men. If you don't kill 'em one way you kill 'em another – or prevent their being born."[49]

When Holmes does come around to defending some rights, war is still the model for justification. Admitting that "All my life I have sneered at the natural rights of man . . . the bills of rights in Constitutions," he finally is able to recognize some basis for these ideas when reminded that "they embody principles that men have died for."[50] What subtends any "legal rights," he notes elsewhere, "is the fighting will of the subject to maintain them."[51] And again: "I understand by human rights what a given crowd will fight for (successfully)."[52]

Another letter to Laski explaining his *Abrams* decision puts the Justice's position on freedom of speech in these same terms – it is a fighting faith that helps him to overcome skeptical doubts: "Little as I believe in it as a theory, I hope I would die for it." What makes Holmes so tentative here is both his skepticism about *a priori* absolutes and the brooding omnipresence of that strong military vision which takes over the letter after even this minor assertion – so that a law defending the "right" to speech of diverse voices comes to seem a puny, pale-faced, indoor ideal, something like the give-and-take of a drawing-room chat in comparison to the violent struggle of a Civil War battle:

> . . . on their premises it seems logical to me in the Catholic Church to kill heretics and [for] the Puritans to whip Quakers – and I see nothing more wrong in it from our ultimate standards than I do in killing Germans when we are at war. When you are thoroughly convinced that you are right – wholeheartedly desire an end – and have no doubt of your power to accomplish it – I see nothing but municipal regulations to interfere with your using your power to accomplish it.[53]

But what leads Holmes to fight against total war and for "municipal regulations" in this instance is that he can see free speech as itself a fighting faith – based on a verbal model of battle. The *Abrams* dissent defines "free trade in ideas" as the "best test of truth" because it too involves conflict based on power: "the power of the thought to get itself accepted in the competition of the market." And the related dissent in *Vegelahn v. Guntner* links a defense of labor's right to threaten harm against an employer to an overriding defense of the violent competition of this unregulated marketplace: any union or company must have the right to try to kill off a weaker antagonist, the right to struggle toward "victory in the battle of trade." The point is in fact the same as in Holmes' advocacy of railroad merger in the *Northern Securities* case: he simply does not want to penalize the strong for their strength or to take away from them what is for him the most basic right – the right to fight "the battle of life."[54]

But it would be unfair to leave Holmes Junior without a final recognition that the strength and certainty of these achieved opinions represent hard-fought and momentary victories forged out of the rather violent struggle of an uncertain and ongoing inner debate. Reviewing the Holmes–Pollock correspondence, Daniel Boorstin catches very aptly the background sense of the Justice's mind that emerges between the lines of the abrupt assertions of the letters: "More and more it appears that Mr. Justice Holmes's belief in conflict and in free competition among ideas was connected somehow with the conflicts in his own life and with his difficulty in deciding what he really believed . . . The uncertainty, the doubt, and the enquiry continued for the whole of the fifty-eight years of the correspondence."[55]

Perhaps a look at one last snippet from this correspondence can serve as a reminder of this background quality to Holmes' thought – and then as a final example of his characteristic writerly response to this predicament. Reacting to Louis Brandeis' suggestion that he bone up on some facts and statistics about the real life of textile workers, the Justice finds himself once again turning in circles of paralyzing indecision – even as he tries to articulate the most basic principles of his legal philosophy. Here his thoughts break out for a moment into a form of inner dialogue that recalls the talk at his father's breakfast-table: "I hate facts. I always say the chief end of man is to form general propositions – adding that no general proposition is worth a damn. Of course a general proposition is simply a string of facts and I have little doubt that it would be good for my immortal soul to plunge into them."[56] We could begin to read this in a caricatural boardinghouse voice, until the gruff soldierly phrase "worth a damn" forces us into a sudden change of tone, and a sudden retroactive recognition that the phrase "I hate facts" is not joking or ironic but heartfelt. While Doctor Holmes would whimsically attack "facts" because they tend, like "general propositions," to "stop all debate," his son wants to uphold these "general propositions" as opposed to "facts" – again citing himself in an effort to make this abstract, oft-repeated proposition about propositions the "end of man" and the end of this inner conversation.

In the second of Doctor Holmes' breakfast-table works, the Professor tries on page one to start a discussion of "the great end of being," but he is interrupted before he can even finish his first sentence. And we have seen that the Master promises throughout the third table-talk work to finish his sentence, "The chief end of man is . . . ," but even his last-chapter attempt at summation is cut short by other voices always working against conversational closure:

"The one central fact in the Order of Things which solves all questions is –"
At this moment we were interrupted by a knock at the Master's door. (*CW,* III, 339)

Holmes Junior's "propositions" are chiefly intended as a defense against just this sort of irresolution, but his own inner dialogue on "the end of man" continues in this letter to Pollock when the distinction between "facts" and generalizations dissolves. The Justice must then lift himself out of the conflict entirely by shifting to another distinction: that between present, plebeian "facts" and immortal, gentlemanly literature. Facts might be good for his "immortal soul," but, he continues, "I hate to give up the chance to read this and that, that a gentleman should have read before he dies. I don't remember that I ever read Machiavelli's *Prince* – and I think of the Day of Judgement."[57] Having failed to assert his own judgment of the ends of man, Holmes Junior turns by reflex to the remedial vision of a greater end: the Last Judgment. Recurring often throughout his letters, these jokes about the need to finish reading Dante, Machiavelli, Thucydides, and so on, before the great Final Examination above, have a serious side to them: thought of books, of reading and of writing, always implies for Holmes Junior a strong "sense of an ending." While the Doctor made a point of reading for his own delight, skipping around in books, always avoiding the duty of reading from beginning to end as part of his rejection of the work ethic and of Calvinist theology, his son developed a religion of books that made it a rigid duty to get to the end of any work he started to read. Like Dante and Machiavelli, he was governed by an analogy between the order of the book and the order of sacred history. As a reader, then, he would reject his father's prodigal digressiveness to accept the role of a pilgrim moving toward the conversion of an unknown, unknowable allegorical end. This is why the thought of the end of a book so often conjures for the Justice a vision of the end of the world – along with some secularized Calvinist suggestions that, before this end, good hard cramming for the Final Exam might improve one's chances for "election." A reader-pilgrim cannot know the meaning of a narrative until he arrives at its conclusion, a soldier cannot know the plan of a military campaign until it is over (when, in retrospect, it will appear that the "message was divine"), and speakers in dialogue cannot come to any decision until the verbal conflict is resolved. In the same spirit, Justice Holmes as writer will always appeal out of the labyrinth of conversational doubt and irresolution with a special sense of the urgent need for some end.

We have in the literary stances of Holmes Senior and Holmes Junior a neat comparison: one raises the problems of conversation and the other raises the problems of its resolution. But how do we balance the unresolved debate in this case? Certainly we can understand the urgency and admire the courage of Holmes Junior's attempt to answer the deep questions left to him by his antebellum fathers. But we must admit that there is also an important honesty and humanity in the attempt to comprehend a tension of opposing voices – the "conversation of a culture" – rather than too suddenly to put on one's military mustache and march blindly into judgment.

Notes

I THE CONVERSATION OF A CULTURE:
STRANGE POWERS OF SPEECH

1 Emerson, "Domestic Life," *Society and Solitude*, in *The Complete Works of Ralph Waldo Emerson*, ed. Edward Waldo Emerson (Boston: Houghton Mifflin, 1904) VII: 107–09. Underlining the focus on talk here, the earlier journal entry containing these same phrases locates the "true character" of the age not in the "dwelling-house" but in "the conversation of a true philosopher": see *The Journals and Miscellaneous Notebooks of Ralph Waldo Emerson*, ed. A. W. Plumstead, Harrison Hayford (Cambridge: Harvard University Press, 1969) VII: 277.

2 The phrase "interior oratory" is cited from Bloom, "Mr. America," *New York Review of Books*, 22 November 1984: 21. Emerson describes Webster-inspired "moments of Eloquence" in a letter to Carlyle of 8 August, 1839: see Joseph Slater, ed., *The Correspondence of Emerson and Carlyle* (New York: Columbia University Press, 1964) 246. Emerson's well-known description of the "Lecture room as the true church" is from his *Journals* of 1839: *Journals and Miscellaneous Notebooks* VII: 277.

3 The culture's sense of itself as a "Golden Age" of eloquence is clear in the title of one of the leading contemporary studies of mid-century eloquence: Edward G. Parker, *The Golden Age of American Oratory* (Boston: Whittmore, Niles, and Hall, 1854).

4 For general treatments of some of the speech areas surveyed here, see Barnet Baskerville, *The People's Voice: The Orator in American Society* (Lexington: University Press of Kentucky, 1979); Daniel J. Boorstin, "American Ways of Talking," in *The Americans: The National Experience* (New York: Random House, 1965) 275–324; Russel Blaine Nye, "Poetry and the Public Arts," in *Society and Culture in America, 1830–1860* (New York: Harper and Row, 1974) 115–57; Constance Mayfield Rourke, *Trumpets of Jubilee* (New York: Harcourt, Brace, 1927); David S. Reynolds, "American Performances: Theater, Oratory, Music," in *Walt Whitman's America* (New York: Knopf, 1995) 154–93.

5 Contemporary responses to Choate cited in Nye, "Poetry," 144. See also Robert A. Ferguson, *Law and Letters in American Culture* (Cambridge: Harvard University Press, 1984) 78–79, 82–84.

6 Boorstin, "American Ways," 310–11.

7 On the era's tendency to recreate or to try to "impersonate" oratory from the Revolutionary past, in what Daniel Boorstin has termed "posthumous ghost-writing," we might note here that the most famous Revolutionary speech, Patrick Henry's "Call to Arms" – "Give me liberty, or give me death" – had to be created or reconstructed nearly half a century after the event by his biographer William Wirt; that James Otis' well-known speech on the Writs of Assistance – "Taxation without representation is tyranny" – was forged from scant notes by William Tudor; and that Daniel Webster's 1826 tribute to the eloquence of Adams invented the "classic" speech it then re-enacts. See Boorstin, "American Ways," 308–10; Baskerville, *The People's Voice*, 8, 22–27.

8 The phrase "spoken into existence" is from an oft-cited 1842 review discussed in Christopher Looby, *Voicing America: Language, Literary Form, and the Origins of the United States* (Chicago: University of Chicago Press, 1996) 18. Looby's book examines, primarily through eighteenth-century examples, some implications of this tendency to take "vocal utterance . . . as a privileged figure for the making of the United States."

9 Tanner, *Scenes of Nature, Signs of Men* (New York: Cambridge University Press, 1987) 173; Adams cited in Lewis P. Simpson, ed., *The Federalist Literary Mind* (Baton Rouge, LA: Louisiana State University Press, 1962) 171; Ferguson, *Law and Letters*, 83.

10 Matthiessen, *American Renaissance* (New York: Oxford University Press, 1941) 18.

11 Tuckerman, *North American Review* 75 (October 1852): 338; first anthologist of American oratory is cited in Baskerville, *The People's Voice*, 3; second editor is Samuel Knapp, cited in Boorstin, "American Ways," 312. Mid-century publishers produced numerous anthologies defining an American oratorical tradition and celebrating the era's triumphs of eloquence, including: James Spear Loring, *The Hundred Boston Orators*, 2nd edn. (Boston: Jewett, 1853) and Parker, *The Golden Age of American Oratory*.

12 Alcott's description of "the American invention" comes in an 1856 journal entry, cited in Matthiessen, *American Renaissance*, 23; Emerson, "Eloquence," *Letters and Social Aims*, in *Complete Works* VIII: 132; the other Emerson lecture/essay titled "Eloquence" appears in *Society and Solitude*, in *Complete Works* VII: 59–100.

13 The apt word "yellocution" is coined by Huck Finn in chapter 31 of Twain's *Adventures of Huckleberry Finn*: Guy Cardwell, ed., *Mississippi Writings* (New York: Library of America, 1982) 830. The Wendell Phillips anecdote is cited in Baskerville, *The People's Voice*, 2.

14 Alexis de Tocqueville, *Democracy in America*, ed. Richard D. Heffner (New York: New American Library, 1956) 109. (I have altered some phrasings in an effort to bring the translation closer to the French original.)

Such obnoxious interlocutors seemed to meet Tocqueville every-where he turned; the same story of failed conversation recurs again and again throughout his study, testifying to his own fear of contact with everyday Americans as well as to the American tendency to pontificate: "Nothing is more embarrassing, in the ordinary inter-course of life, than this irritable patriotism of the Americans . . ."; or later, "I have often remarked, in the United States, that it is not easy to make a man understand that his presence may be dispensed with; . . . I contradict an American at every word he says, to show him that his conversation bores me; he instantly labors with fresh pertinacity to convince me: I preserve a dogged silence, and he thinks I am meditating deeply on the truths which he is uttering." Tocqueville, *Democracy in America*, 105, 224.

For Dickens' more graphic descriptions of similar encounters, based upon his experiences during an 1842 American tour, see *The Life and Adventures of Martin Chuzzlewit* (London: Macmillan, 1910). "Everything is lectured upon, from the destinies of humanity down to the proper method of making a pumpkin-pie," observed another exasperated Englishman, Edward Hingston, the biographer of Artemus Ward, evoking the scenes which inspired Dickens' most wicked parodies. Hingston cited in Neil Harris, *Humbug: The Art of P. T. Barnum* (Boston: Little, Brown, 1973) 74.

15 Rourke, *Trumpets of Jubilee*, vii, 175; see also Rourke, *American Humor* (New York: Harcourt, 1931); Wilbur Joseph Cash, *The Mind of the South* (New York: Knopf, 1941) 51; Ann Douglas, *The Feminization of American Culture* (New York: Knopf, 1977) 341.

16 Alcott cited in Lawrence Buell, *Literary Transcendentalism: Style and Vision in the American Renaissance* (Ithaca: Cornell University Press, 1973) 77.

17 Alcott "Diary for 1838," cited in Buell, *Literary Transcendentalism*, 81; *Tablets* (Boston: Roberts, 1868) 76.

18 Emerson, "Domestic Life," *Complete Works* VII: 107–09.

19 Emerson journal entry cited in Louis Biancolli, ed., *The Book of Great Conversations* (New York: Simon and Schuster, 1948) ix.

20 Emerson, "Circles," *Complete Works* II: 311.

21 Emerson, 1848 journal entry, in *The Journals and Miscellaneous Notebooks of Ralph Waldo Emerson* IX: 28–29.

22 Emerson, "Circles," *Complete Works* II: 310–11.

23 Conversation is a necessary complement to oratory as society is a necessary complement to solitude, according to Emerson's basic vision of Polarity, or Alternation – a vision of the life process which is itself fundamentally dialogical: "Solitude is naught & society is naught. Alternate them & the good of each is seen . . . Undulation, Alternation, is the condition of progress, of life" (*Journals* VII: 14).

24 Buell, *Literary Transcendentalism*, 79, 92; Wade, *Margaret Fuller: Whetstone of Genius* (New York: Viking, 1940) 78. For a general treatment of the Transcendentalist's interest in conversation, see Buell, "From Conversation to Essay," in *Literary Transcendentalism*, 77–101.

25 On parlor life in Victorian America, see Katherine C. Grier, *Culture and Comfort: People, Parlors, and Upholstery 1850–1930* (Rochester: Strong Museum, 1988); Thomas J. Schlereth, *Victorian America: Transformations in Everyday Life, 1876–1915* (New York: HarperCollins, 1991) 118–21; Richard Ohmann, *Selling Culture: Magazines, Markets, and Class at the Turn of the Century* (New York: Verso, 1996) 140–54. The phrase "parlor culture" is used by Ohmann, *Selling Culture*, 154 and also by Schlereth, *Victorian America*, 118. For a ground-breaking study of "salon culture" in British America (and its relation to a lively network of "private society" talk groups such as coffeehouses, tea-tables, and clubs), see David S. Shields, *Civil Tongues and Polite Letters in British America* (Chapel Hill: University of North Carolina Press, 1997).

26 The phrase "parlor people" is used in Grier, *Culture and Comfort*, 19.

27 For the phrase "a world full of parlors" and a survey of "public parlors" in mid-century hotels, steamboats, and trains, see Grier, *Culture and Comfort*, 53.

28 For a useful study of mid-century pride in the republican institution of the American Plan developed in American Hotels, see Boorstin, "Palaces of the Public," in *The Americans: The National Experience*, 144–47.

29 Blumin, *The Emergence of the Middle Class: Social Experience in the American City, 1760–1900* (Cambridge: Cambridge University Press, 1989) 192.

30 This overview of relations between nineteenth- and eighteenth-century venues for American conversation is indebted to David Shields' important study of the foundational role played by various "discursive institutions" and arenas for polite conversation in the colonies. On the later proliferation of a nexus of "competing counterpublics" that forces a revision of Habermas' model of a "single, comprehensive public sphere," see Nancy Fraser, "Rethinking the Public Sphere: A Contribution to the Critique of Actually Existing Democracy," in Craig Calhoun, ed., *Habermas and the Public Sphere* (Cambridge, MA: MIT Press, 1992) 115–17, 124.

31 On the Saturday Club, see Edward Waldo Emerson, *The Early Years of the Saturday Club, 1855–1870* (Boston: Houghton Mifflin, 1918). On the mid-century popularity of the conversation club, see Buell, *Literary Transcendentalism*, 79. For extended descriptions of aristocratic and literary salons in New England and New York, see Rourke, *Trumpets of Jubilee*, 126, 285–91, 308–10. On the conversation sessions which were the Transcendentalists' first organized activity, see Joel Myerson, "A History of the Transcendental Club," *Critical Essays on American Transcendentalism*, ed. Philip F. Gura, Joel Myerson (Boston: G. K. Hall, 1982) 596–608. For detailed descriptions of New York talk groups like the Knickerbocker Circle and the Bohemian Circle at Pfaff's, see: Perry Miller, *The Raven and the Whale: The War of Words and Wits in the Era of Poe and Melville* (New York: Harcourt, Brace, 1956) 11–33; Gay Wilson Allen,

The Solitary Singer: A Critical Biography of Walt Whitman (New York: New York University Press, 1967) 228–31, 269–70.

32 On fancy parlors in some mid-century Firemen's Halls, see Grier, *Culture and Comfort*, 51–53; on Whitman's interest in the noisy scene at Firemen's Halls, see Allen, *The Solitary Singer*, 206.

33 On the emergence of the saloon as a new social institution in the 1870s, see Roy Rosenzweig, *Eight Hours for What We Will* (New York: Cambridge University Press, 1983) 35–64, 240–49. On the saloon as a form of "private club" offering a "rough masculine conviviality," see Blumin, *The Emergence of the Middle Class*, 217–18.

34 On the rapid growth of women's associations during the nineteenth century, see Karen J. Blair, *The History of American Women's Voluntary Organizations, 1810–1960: A Guide to Sources* (Boston: G. K. Hall, 1989); also Shields, *Civil Tongues and Polite Letters*, 326.

35 On the cultural work of colonial women's tea societies, see Shields, *Civil Tongues and Polite Letters*, 99–140.

36 On the diverse ways in which nineteenth-century American women of various classes and ethnicities developed their own discursive "publics," see Mary P. Ryan, *Women in Public: Between Banners and Ballots, 1825–1880* (Baltimore: Johns Hopkins University Press, 1990). On associations of elite bourgeois women as a "counter civil society," see Fraser, "Rethinking the Public Sphere," 115.

37 Karen J. Blair, *The Clubwoman as Feminist: True Womanhood Redefined, 1868–1914* (New York: Holmes and Meier, 1980).

38 For published accounts of the conversations in Alcott's school, see Alcott, *Conversations with Children on the Gospels*, 2 vols. (Boston: Munroe, 1836–37) and Elizabeth Palmer Peabody, *Record of a School* (1836; New York: Arno, 1969). On Alcott and Fuller as "professional conversationalists," see Buell, *Literary Transcendentalism*, 82. For details about Alcott's "parlour teaching" and "ministry of talk," see Frederick C. Dahlstrand, *Amos Bronson Alcott* (Rutherford, NJ: Fairleigh Dickinson University Press, 1982) 156–57, 215–19, 224–25, 250–53, 300–13.

39 On the conversational form of the discussion sections stressed as the basis of new methods for teaching reading and speaking, see Gladys L. Borchers and Lillian R. Wagner, "Speech Education in Nineteenth-Century Schools," in Karl R. Wallace, *History of Speech Education in America* (New York: Appleton–Century–Crofts, 1954) 277–300.

40 On mid-century groups that made reading a social activity, see Shields, *Civil Tongues and Polite Letters*, 323 and Mary Kelley, *Private Woman, Public Stage: Literary Domesticity in Nineteenth-Century America* (New York: Oxford University Press, 1984).

41 Ann Douglas criticizes mid-century clergymen for their accommodation to what she sees as the "feminized," narcissistic, commercial culture embodied in salon talk forms; see, for example, Douglas, *The Feminization of American Culture*, 42–44, 190–94. Henry Ware, Jr., on the ideal of

"Christian conversation," is cited in Douglas, *The Feminization of American Culture*, 192.

42 See Shields, *Civil Tongues and Polite Letters*, 320–21. With Griswold's *The Republican Court* (New York: Appleton, 1855), other books commenting on salon culture through the example of Martha Washington's levee included E[lizabeth] F. Ellet, *The Court Circles of the Republic* (Hartford: Hartford Publishing Co., 1869) and Anne Hollingsworth Wharton, *Salons Colonial and Republican* (Philadelphia: 1900) and *Martha Washington* (New York, Scribner's, 1897).

43 Fuller's translation of Eckermann's *Conversations with Goethe* (Boston: Hilliard, Gray, 1839); *The Table-Talk of Martin Luther*, trans. and ed. William Hazlitt (London, 1846; rpt. London: Bell, 1902). On the American reception of works of printed table-talk, see Buell, *Literary Transcendentalism*, 79. Emerson's remarks on Luther and conversation appear in his "Clubs," *Complete Works* VII: 236, where the general point about the era's valuation of table-talk is made very clearly: "Jesus spent his life discoursing with humble people . . . Luther spent his life so; and it is not his theologic works . . . but his Table-Talk, which is still read by men. Dr. Johnson was a man of no profound mind . . . yet his conversation as reported by Boswell has a lasting charm . . . One of the best records of the great German master who towered over all his contemporaries in the first thirty years of this century, is his conversations as recorded by Eckermann; and the Table-Talk of Coleridge is one of the best remains of his genius" (236–37).

44 William Mills Todd III, "A Russian Ideology," *Stanford Literary Review*, 1 (Spring 1984): 86, 104, 91. See also Todd, *Fiction and Society in the Age of Pushkin: Ideology, Institutions, and Narrative* (Cambridge: Harvard University Press, 1986).

45 Daniel J. Boorstin, *The Image: A Guide to Pseudo-Events in America* (New York: Harper and Row, 1964) 15.

46 Fern, *Ruth Hall and Other Writings*, ed. Joyce W. Warren (New Brunswick: Rutgers University Press, 1988) 207.

47 On the popularity of written forms of "imaginary dialogue," see Buell, *Literary Transcendentalism*, 93.

48 Porter, "Social Discourse and Nonfictional Prose," in Emory Elliott, ed. *The Columbia Literary History of the United States* (New York: Columbia University Press, 1985) 349.

49 On the relations between some antebellum social reform movements and the "spontaneity" associated with talk, see Lewis Perry, " 'We Have Had Conversation in the World': The Abolitionists and Spontaneity," *Canadian Review of American Studies* 6 (Spring 1975): 3–26.

50 Hawthorne, "Rappacini's Daughter," *Nathaniel Hawthorne: Selected Tales and Sketches* (New York: Holt, Rinehart, Winston, 1964) 278.

51 See Francis Hodge, *Yankee Theater: The Image of America on the Stage, 1825–1850* (Austin: University of Texas Press, 1964) 61–71, 153–211.

52 Elizabeth Johns, *American Genre Painting: The Politics of Everyday Life* (New Haven: Yale University Press, 1991).

53 Habermas, *The Structural Transformation of the Public Sphere*, trans. Thomas Burger (Great Britain: Polity, 1989).

54 Aaron Fogel, *Coercion to Speak: Conrad's Poetics of Dialogue* (Cambridge: Harvard University Press, 1985) 17, 261.

55 On the republican critique of clubs, see Shields, *Civil Tongues and Polite Letters*, 325.

56 Buell, *Literary Transcendentalism*, 85.

57 This "Boswell" motto appeared before each serial installment of the *Autocrat* papers in the *Atlantic*, and on the title page as subtitle of the book versions of that work: Holmes, *The Autocrat of the Breakfast-Table* in *The Writings of Oliver Wendell Holmes*, 13 vols. (Boston: Houghton Mifflin, 1892), 1: t.p. Hereafter cited in the text as *CW*.

58 Van Wyck Brooks, "Dr. Holmes's Boston," *Harper's* (July 1940): 142. James, Sr., cited in Brooks, *The Flowering of New England* (1936; New York: Dutton, 1952) 368.

59 Annie Fields, *Authors and Friends* (Boston, 1896; rpt. New York: AMS Press, 1969) 110; Barrett Wendell writes that, "Early in life [Holmes] acquired the reputation of being the best talker ever heard in Boston; and this he maintained unbroken to the very end . . . In his later life his conversation and his wit alike, always spontaneous and often of a quality which would have been excellent anywhere, are said sometimes to have been overwhelming." (*A Literary History of America* [New York: Scribner's, 1900] 410); Edwin P. Hoyt, *The Improper Bostonian: Dr. Oliver Wendell Holmes* (New York: Morrow, 1979) 13; Brooks, *The Flowering of New England*, 368. Recent studies can only catalogue the many superlative judgments rendered previously. Barry Menikoff writes: "The most brilliant conversationalist of a not undistinguished circle, for a quarter of a century he dominated New England letters." (*Fifteen American Authors Before 1900: Bibliographic Essays on Research and Criticism*, eds. Robert A. Rees and Earl N. Harbert [Madison: University of Wisconsin Press, 1971] 212.) And the *Oxford Companion to American Literature* observes, "As a witty, urbane conversationalist, he reigned supreme in Boston society and club life and became the unofficial poet laureate of all important gatherings in the intellectual 'hub of the Universe.'": ed. James D. Hart (New York: Oxford University Press, 1983) 339.

60 Wendell, *A Literary History of America*, 409; *The Nation*, 11 Oct. 1894, cited in Rees and Harbert, *Fifteen American Authors*, 216; Vernon Parrington, *Main Currents in American Thought: The Romantic Revolution in America, 1800–1860*, 3 vols. (New York: Harcourt, Brace, 1927) ii: 451–52; Mark DeWolfe Howe, *Justice Oliver Wendell Holmes: The Shaping Years, 1841–1870*, 2 vols. (Cambridge: Harvard University Press, 1957) i: 13; Van Wyck Brooks, "Dr. Holmes's Boston," 141–42.

The frequent reappearance of this phrase, "Dr. Holmes' Boston," testifies to what was once a strong identification of Holmes and his city; at least one collection of the Doctor's writings about Boston uses this phrase as its title: Caroline Ticknor, ed., *Doctor Holmes's Boston* (Boston: Houghton Mifflin, 1915). Hereafter cited in the text as *DHB*.

61 Henry James, "Mr. and Mrs. James T. Fields," *Atlantic* 116 (July 1915): 25–27. In his history of the *Atlantic Monthly*, M. A. DeWolfe Howe also notes that Holmes was "the one indispensable contributor" to the new journal; see *The Atlantic Monthly and its Makers* (Boston: Atlantic Monthly Press, 1919) 18.

62 Schlegels' *Athenaeum* fragment 116, in *Friedrich Schlegel's Lucinde and the Fragments*, trans. Peter Firchow (Minneapolis: University of Minnesota Press, 1971) 175.

63 "The Autocrat Gives a Breakfast to the Public," *Atlantic*, December 1858, reprinted in *The Autocrat's Miscellanies*, ed. Albert Mordell (New York: Twayne, 1959) 30–31.

64 "I am large, I contain multitudes" is Whitman's boast near the end of his "Song of Myself," in *Leaves of Grass*, eds. Sculley Bradley and Harold Blodgett (New York: W. W. Norton, 1973) 88.

   Holmes and Whitman put their own stamps on the stereotypes of the age; of course in the mid-century "Yankee theater" their highly theatrical, exaggerated personae would have been arch-antagonists. But the inclusiveness of Holmes' talk form nonetheless allows him to open a place even to unlettered "Walt." Remembering that Holmes himself had hailed Emerson's Phi Beta Kappa Oration as "our Declaration of Literary Independence," a host speaker in *Over the Teacups* finally has to admit that Whitman has only taken that independence and that democratic spirit to its limit, and he finds room for him too in the talk at the breakfast-table: "But there is room for everybody and everything in our huge hemisphere. Young America is like a three-year-old colt with his saddle and bridle just taken off. The first thing he wants to do is *roll*. He is a droll object, sprawling in the grass with his four hoofs in the air; but he likes it, and it won't harm us. So let him roll, – let him roll!" (*CW*, IV, 233, 237–38)

65 Wilde has his character Ernest ask naively of his interlocutor, "But do you seriously propose that every man should become his own Boswell? What would become of our industrious compilers of Lives and Recollections in that case?" ("The Critic as Artist," in *Intentions*, 16th edn. [London, 1891; London: Methuen, 1947] 98.)

   Another famous remark, used by Wilde and often attributed to him as a defining statement of aestheticism – "Give us the luxuries of life, and we will dispense with its necessaries" – also had its source in Holmes' *Autocrat*, in a passage where the Autocrat is actually citing an aphorism by Motley (*CW*, I, 125). Wilde's sense of his strong connection to Holmes was also evident when, preparing for his 1882 trip to America, he urged

Lowell to provide him with a letter of introduction to the Doctor, and then dined with Holmes, who also took him to the Saturday Club. Later that year, the two met again, reportedly engaging in an extended battle of witty repartee before the "amazed" guests at a large party given by Julia Ward Howe in Newport (Richard Ellmann, *Oscar Wilde* [London: Hamish Hamilton, 1987] 192–93).

Though Holmes was an avid reader of Boswell on Johnson, he may have been inspired to use of the "Boswell" motto by a passage in Emerson's "The Method of Nature," which the Doctor cites in his biography of the poet: "Why then goest thou as some Boswell or literary worshipper to this saint or that?" (*Ralph Waldo Emerson* [Boston: Houghton Mifflin, 1885] 138.) But Holmes like Wilde is less interested in the democratic self-assertion or narcissistic self-worship implied by the idea of serving as a Boswell to oneself than in the way that a Boswell-like self-interrogation can open into new aspects of self-criticism, self-division, self-consciousness.

2 "TO CHANGE THE ORDER OF CONVERSATION":
INTERRUPTION AND VOCAL DIVERSITY
IN HOLMES' AMERICAN TALK

1 Holmes explains this reference to a prior interruption in remarks prefatory to the *Autocrat* papers. He had begun a trial run for the *Autocrat* in the 1830s:
"The interruption referred to in the first sentence of the first of these papers was just a quarter of a century in duration.
"Two articles entitled 'The Autocrat of the Breakfast Table' will be found in the 'New England Magazine,' . . . The date of the first of these articles is November, 1831, and that of the second, February, 1832."
2 Tannen, "Who's Interrupting: Issues of Dominance and Control," *You Just Don't Understand: Women and Men in Conversation* (New York: Morrow, 1990) 188–215. See also Tannen, *Conversational Style: Analyzing Talk Among Friends* (Norwood, NJ: Ablex, 1984).
3 For a much more detailed study of this debate, including extended analyses of the positions of Alcott, Hazlitt, Emerson, and Fuller, see Peter Gibian, *The Golden Age of American Conversation: Literary Writing in a Talk-Based Culture* (New York: Oxford University Press, forthcoming 2002).
4 For broad, basic characterizations of earlier English conversational ideals, see: Habermas, *The Structural Transformation of the Public Sphere*, trans. Thomas Burger (Great Britain: Polity, 1989); Herbert Davis, "The Conversation of the Augustans," in *The Seventeenth Century: Studies in the History of English Thought and Literature from Bacon to Pope*, ed. Richard Foster Jones (Stanford: Stanford University Press, 1951) 181–97; Peter Gay, "The Spectator as Actor: Addison in Perspective," *Encounter* 29

(1967): 27–32; William Matthews, "Polite Speech in the Eighteenth Century," *English* 1 (1937): 493–511.

5 For parallel speculation on the contrasts between English and American talk forms, see Tocqueville, *Democracy in America*, ed. Richard D. Heffner (New York: New American Library, 1956) 221–24, 234.

6 Habermas traces a parallel development along these lines in France, Germany, and England, and we might add that Enlightenment progressives in Spain also defined their ideals by reference to new "institutions" of conversation (such as the Society of Friends of the Nation) dedicated to the promotion of free intellectual exchange. For a detailed study of parallel developments in eighteenth-century America, see Shields, *Civil Tongues and Polite Letters in British America* (Chapel Hill: University of North Carolina Press, 1997).

7 For the London reviews of Holmes as the "American Sterne," see Eleanor M. Tilton, *Amiable Autocrat*, 259. Holmes hoped to place himself in the line of what he saw as a Sterne tradition in America. His notes to the first *Autocrat* paper, for instance, show him to be less interested in the Revolutionary ancestors remembered in Copley portraits than in an underground family succession of wits, humorists, and story-tellers whom he would like to commemorate as American "Yoricks." Part Three of this study looks more closely at intellectual affinities between Holmes and Sterne, focussing on the interactions between levity and gravity in their mode of philosophic comedy.

8 To promote conversation has always been to promote association – and "association" was certainly a key word with special meanings in mid-century America. American readers who responded so overwhelmingly to Holmes' table-talks must have felt that they could find there something that was lacking in their lives – rushing to join this fictional "club" for the same reasons Tocqueville found them joining all sorts of political and cultural associations in the period. The Doctor introduced his talk form with an extended defense of clubs, and in conjunction with a new journal, which was founded out of the same hopes that Tocqueville had expressed for newspapers in American life. For the Frenchman had noted, just as Holmes would, that a newspaper readership could bring the widespread and diverse citizens of a democracy together in a new version of the club form:

> Wandering minds, which had long sought each other in darkness, at length meet and unite . . . Means must then be found to converse every day without seeing each other . . . A newspaper, therefore, always represents an association which is composed of its habitual readers . . . The fact that the newspaper keeps alive is proof that at least the germ of an association exists in the minds of its readers. (Tocqueville, *Democracy in America*, 202–09)

Of course Holmes' club of readers too can only keep alive a germ of this hope: many contemporary Americans were bemoaning the dominant centrifugal and atomistic tendencies of their age. Was America becoming a nation of wordless Bartlebys? For those interested in promoting "association," though, conversation could seem to offer the ground for a last defense of common-sense benevolence and sympathy against the Lockean contract built upon self-interest, and for the cohesive forces of Whig Sentiment against the anti-institutional and anti-Union tendencies of Jacksonian individualism. Was America losing the old sense of republican fraternity and the public life? At least Boston still retained the older ideal of sociability, and Holmes in his table-talk works offered to share it – or an image of it – with the larger country.

9 "The Autocrat Gives a Breakfast to the Public," *Atlantic*, December 1858, reprinted in *The Autocrat's Miscellanies*, ed. Albert Mordell (New York: Twayne, 1959) 30–31.

10 Hazlitt's important role in transforming the conversation tradition, at a crucial juncture in the early nineteenth century, with his new definitions of a "conversational style" in writing, is discussed later in this chapter. For more recent work in this line, see Richard Bridgman, *The Colloquial Style in America* (New York: Oxford, 1966); Eugene Hnatko, "Sterne's Conversational Style," *The Winged Skull*, eds. A. H. Cash and J. M. Stedmond (London: Methuen, 1971) 229–36; Louis T. Milic, "Observations on Conversational Style," *English Writers of the Eighteenth Century*, ed. John H. Middendorf (New York: Oxford University Press, 1971) 273–87.

11 Ian Watt, "Introduction," in Sterne, *The Life and Opinions of Tristram Shandy, Gentleman* ed. Ian Watt (Boston: Houghton Mifflin, 1965) xviii.

12 On the "war of the dictionaries" and nineteenth-century debates about language see Kenneth Cmiel, *Democratic Eloquence: The Fight over Popular Speech in Nineteenth-Century America* (Berkeley: University of California Press, 1990), and Thomas Gustafson, *Representative Words: Politics, Literature, and the American Language, 1776–1865* (New York: Cambridge University Press, 1992).

13 See especially *The Dialogic Imagination*, ed. Michael Holquist, trans. Caryl Emerson and Michael Holquist (Austin: University of Texas Press, 1981); *Problems of Dostoevsky's Poetics*, trans. R.W. Rotsel (New York: Ardis, 1973). Chapter Three explores the relationships between Holmes' table-talk works and Bakhtin's model of carnivalesque dialogue in more detail.

14 Pratt, "Arts of the Contact Zone," *Profession 91*, ed. Phyllis Franklin (New York: Modern Language Association of America, 1991) 33–40.

15 Willis cited in Boorstin, "Palaces of the Public," in *The Americans: The National Experience* (New York: Random House, 1965) 147.

16 Boorstin "Palaces of the Public," 143, 136.

17 Boorstin, "Palaces of the Public," 134, 144–46.

18 Statistics and contemporary terminology on boardinghouse life here cited in John Modell and Tamara K. Hareven, "Urbanization and the Malleable Household: An Examination of Boarding and Lodging in American Families," in *The American Family in Social-Historical Perspective*, ed. Michael Gordon, 2nd edition (1973; rpt. New York: St. Martin's,

1978) 51–68. See also Schlereth, *Victorian America: Transformations in Everyday Life*, 1876–1915 (New York: Harper Collins, 1991) 103–06.

19 Northall cited in Neil Harris, *Humbug: The Art of P. T. Barnum* (Boston: Little, Brown, 1973) 37–38.

20 Boorstin, "Palaces of the Public," 144.

21 Thomas De Quincey, "Conversation," in David Masson, ed., *The Collected Writings of Thomas De Quincey*, 14 vols. (Edinburgh: A. and C. Black, 1889–90) x: 281–82.

22 On the shift in talk goals from coffeehouse or café to club, see Richard Sennett, *The Fall of Public Man* (New York: Knopf, 1977) 81–84.

23 See Hazlitt, "On the Conversation of Authors," "On the Differences Between Writing and Speaking," "On Familiar Style," and "Conversations of James Northcote, Esq.," in *The Collected Works of William Hazlitt*, eds. A. R. Waller and Arnold Glover (London: J. M. Dent, 1903).

24 Emerson, "Circles," *The Complete Works of Ralph Waldo Emerson*, ed. E. W. Emerson (Boston: Houghton Mifflin, 1904) II: 310.

25 De Quincey's essay on "Conversation" first appeared in *Tait's Magazine* (October, 1847) but was expanded in 1860; *Collected Writings* x: 264, 268–69, 281–82, 286.

For many contemporary descriptions of Coleridge as "the most impressive talker of his age," see: Richard W. Armour and Raymond F. Howes, eds., *Coleridge the Talker* (Ithaca: Cornell University Press, 1940). Several British periodicals of the 1830s, like *Fraser's Magazine*, introduced a form of "Round Table" imaginary dialogue which clearly developed as a parody of Coleridge's talk: though Coleridge was their patron saint, their humorous monological dialogues were intended to prick the bubble of idolatry which surrounded him. The English stage caricaturist Charles Mathews also toured with a very popular impersonation of Coleridge as a loquacious "humor." Holmes may well have been inspired by such works of English humor when he wrote his first, trial "Autocrat Papers" in 1831.

In *The Poet*, Holmes is very explicit about situating the Autocrat's relative the Master in the imperial line of "three famous talkers of Great Britain": "Samuel the First, Samuel the Second, and Thomas, last of the Dynasty." The long discussion of this "talking dynasty" (of Johnson, Coleridge, and Caryle) which follows makes clear Holmes' recognition that the conversational autocrat is, like Roger de Coverley, an obsolete relic of an age which has passed (*CW*, III, 262–63).

In the American past, when eighteenth-century newspapers adopted the persona of a conversation club, they also often singled out one character as superintendent of the talk. In Franklin's *New-England Courant* he was Janus – "a Doctor in the chair," or a "perpetual Dictator" – another forerunner of Holmes' Autocrat. Shields, *Civil Tongues and Polite Letters in British America* (Chapel Hill: University of North Carolina Press, 1997) 267.

26 "History knows no monologist like Napoleon," writes the editor of selections from the Emperor's conversations: Louis Biancolli, ed., *The Book of Great Conversations* (New York: Doubleday, 1948) 197–98.

27 Holmes cited in: *Addresses at the Inauguration of Cornelius Felton as President of Harvard College, July 19, 1860* (Cambridge: Sever and Francis, 1860) 121–22.

28 In the parodic minutes of a Parisian "Société Polyphysiophilosophique" contributed to the *Autocrat* by "Benjamin Franklin," the "membre à questions" is clearly much to be preferred to the Webster-like "membre à 'Bylaws'," who uses his religion of the Constitution to quash any warm expression from the others: "C'est un empereur manqué, – un tyran . . . Il n'y a qu'un mot pour ce membre audessus de "Bylaws." Ce mot est pour lui ce que l'Om est aux Hindous. C'est sa religion; il n'y a rien audelà. Ce mot là c'est la CONSTITUTION!"

Holmes' added notes to the first number of the Autocrat also celebrate the fact that the Saturday Club was a talk group without "Constitution or bylaws" (*CW*, 1, 136–37).

29 On the development in Boston circles of these "Christian conversations," described in relation to the Unitarian Henry Ware, Jr., and the sentimental novelist Susan Warner, see: Douglas, *The Feminization of American Culture* (New York: Knopf, 1977) 43, 190–95.

3 "COLLISIONS OF DISCOURSE" 1: THE ELECTRODYNAMICS OF
   CONVERSATION – A CARNIVAL OF VERBAL FIREWORKS

1 James Russell Lowell, "Elsie Venner," *The Round Table* (Boston: Gorham, 1913) 68; Annie Fields, *Authors and Friends*, 146; Parrington, *Main Currents in American Thought: The Romantic Revolution in America, 1800 1860*, 3 vols. (New York: Harcourt, Brace, 1927) 459; Tilton, *Amiable Autocrat: A Biography of Dr. Oliver Wendell Holmes* (New York: Henry Schuman, 1947) 210; S. I. Hayakawa and Howard Mumford Jones, eds., *Oliver Wendell Holmes: Representative Selections* (New York: American Book Company, 1939) ciii.

2 Holmes, "The Autobiographical Notes," in John T. Morse, Jr., *Life and Letters of Oliver Wendell Holmes* (Boston: Houghton Mifflin, 1897) 1, 50–51. Hereafter cited in the text as *AN*. See also Tilton, *Amiable Autocrat*, 52–54.

3 Bakhtin, *Problems of Dostoevsky's Poetics* trans. R. W. Rotsel (New York: Ardis, 1973) 101. On the theory of carnival, see pp. 88, 100–06 in this book, and Bakhtin, *Rabelais and his World* trans. Hélène Iswolsky (Cambridge: M.I.T. Press, 1968) 4–14.

4 Bakhtin, "From the Prehistory of Novelistic Discourse," in Michael Holquist, ed., *The Dialogic Imagination* trans. Caryl Emerson and Michael Holquist (Austin: University of Texas Press, 1981) 50, 80.

5 Bakhtin, *Problems of Dostoevsky's Poetics*, 102–03.

6 Bakhtin, "From the Prehistory of Novelistic Discourse," 52–53, 72–73, 80–82. See also his *Problems of Dostoevsky's Poetics*, 98–99, 131.

7 Bakhtin, *Rabelais*, 355, 360–61; see also *Problems of Dostoevsky's Poetics*, 93. On Holmes' book collection, see Tilton, *Amiable Autocrat*, 374, 385. On Holmes and the *Hippocratic Novel*, see Tilton, *Amiable Autocrat*, 134.

8 Bakhtin, *Problems of Dostoevsky's Poetics*, 107, 110, 101; *Rabelais*, 34–37.

9 Emerson, *Journals* VII: 61; "Society and Solitude," in *Complete Works* VII: 14.

10 For the citation from Thomas Appleton, see Leslie Stephen, "Oliver Wendell Holmes," *Studies of a Biographer*, 4 vols. (New York: Putnam's, 1907) II: 171; James Russell Lowell, *The Complete Writings of James Russell Lowell*, 16 vols. (Boston: Houghton Mifflin, 1904) XII: 78.

11 Bakhtin, *The Dialogic Imagination*, 66, 80, 431.

12 Tilton, *Amiable Autocrat*, 277.

13 For descriptions of these meetings by Motley and Lowell, see Hoyt, *The Improper Bostonian: Dr. Oliver Wendell Holmes* (New York: Morrow, 1979) 109–10, 168, 204–06; Tilton, *Amiable Autocrat*, 179, 218, 237, 277.

14 Donald E. Pease observes that the decade of the 1850s was "a time when Americans found their personal conversations filled with dissension and opposition." *Visionary Compacts: American Renaissance Writings in Cultural Context* (Madison: University of Wisconsin Press, 1987) 157.

15 Bakhtin, *Problems of Dostoevsky's Poetics*, 98.

16 For Holmes' whispering in school, see Tilton, *Amiable Autocrat*, 18, 23. For Mitchell's troubles while exiting, see Anna R. Burr, *Weir Mitchell: His Life and Letters* (New York: Duffield, 1929) 146.

17 Fuller, cited in James Freeman Clarke, Ralph Waldo Emerson, and William H. Channing, eds., *Memoirs of Margaret Fuller Ossoli*, 2 vols. (Boston: Phillips, Sampson, 1852) I: 296.

Fuller is here articulating a core element of Romantic language theory, which she had probably absorbed from extensive readings in the German and English Romantics so congenial to many Americans in the mid-century. Friedrich Schlegel, for example, presents a classic statement of this conception common to many early nineteenth-century Romantic thinkers: "So profound . . . is this intrinsic dualism and duplicity . . . rooted in our consciousness, that even when we are alone we still think as two, . . . This colloquy with self, or generally, this internal dialogue, is . . . the natural form of human thinking" (*The Philosophy of Life, and Philosophy of Language*, ed. J. B. Robertson, trans. A. J. Morrison (London, 1847; rpt. New York: AMS Press, 1973) 380.

18 Bakhtin, *Problems of Dostoevsky's Poetics*, 98.

19 Holmes' uses of the terms "unconscious," "sub-conscious," and "underground workshop of the mind," from "Mechanism in Thought and Morals" (*CW*, VIII), are discussed in detail in Chapter Seven of this study.

20 The phrase "oceans of similitudes" is from the *Autocrat* (*CW*, I, 84).

21 This Enlightenment movement is very typical of Holmes: the most characteristic example is his anti-clerical mock-parable of turning-over-the-stone, in the *Autocrat*, where again the dark of unscrutinized belief is brought out to the light of day (*CW*, I, 111–13).

22 Holmes' phrase "the committee of the self" is from his "Mechanism in Thought and Morals" (*CW*, VIII, 289).

23 This conversation between the Member and the Master opens Chapter one of *The Poet at the Breakfast-Table* (*CW*, III, 1–5).

4 "COLLISIONS OF DISCOURSE" II: ELECTRIC AND OCEANIC "CURRENTS" IN CONVERSATION – THE CULTURAL WORK OF HOLMESIAN TALK

1 Parrington, *Main Currents in American Thought: The Romantic Revolution in America, 1800–1860*, 3 vols. (New York: Harcourt, Brace, 1927) II: 456–57.

2 This becomes only too schematically clear through the rest of the *Poet*, for the explosive potential that the Master is introducing here is later personified by That Boy, who emerges as one of the heroes of the book as he frequently uses his Pop-Gun as a "boricide" to interrupt any overly prolix speakers at the table. When the conservative Member of the Haouse yells "Order! Order!" after one of the boy's fireworks intrusions, we are told that the Master looked "half approvingly" at the rude Boy; another time, when That Boy shoots his gun just as the Member is bragging about how he "hit his constitooents in their most vital . . ." we sense that, though the youth's act may mirror that of anarchist assassins in the culture at large, Holmes here identifies with that response in conversation. The Boy's "squibs and crackers" may have touched off a powder keg – the Member picks him up, shakes him, and breaks his toy gun – but the real, dangerous violence is clearly latent in the stance of the reactionary politician (*CW*, III, 237, 72, 236).

3 Parrington, *Main Currents*, 456–57.

4 Oliver Wendell Holmes, letter of 29 Nov. 1846, reprinted in Morse, *Life and Letters of Oliver Wendell Holmes* (Boston: Houghton Mifflin, 1897) I: 298.

5 Lowell, *The Round Table* (Boston: Gorham, 1913) 68; Richard Rorty, *Philosophy and the Mirror of Nature* (Princeton: Princeton University Press, 1979). Rorty cites, as one of his sources for the phrase "the conversation of a culture," Michael Oakeshott, "The Voice of Poetry in the Conversation of Mankind," in his *Rationalism and Politics, and Other Essays* (New York: Basic Books, 1962).

6 Van Wyck Brooks, "Dr. Holmes: Forerunner of the Moderns," *The Saturday Review of Literature* (27 June 1936): 1–12. Material from this article later reappeared in slightly different form in Brooks' *The Flowering of New England* (1936; New York: Dutton, 1952) 501, 504.

7 All citations from the essay "Clubs," *The Complete Works of Ralph Waldo*

Emerson VII: 224, 225, 234, 227–28, 250, 419–20n, 421n (my italics), 232–33, 422n.

8 This anecdote about the dinner with the Stowes is widely repeated. An early, first-hand description can be found in Thomas Wentworth Higginson, *Cheerful Yesterdays* (Boston: Houghton Mifflin, 1898) 179–80. For other similar renderings, see Tilton, *Amiable Autocrat: A Biography of Dr. Oliver Wendell Holmes* (New York: Henry Schuman, 1947) 250–51; M. A. DeWolfe Howe, *The Atlantic Monthly and Its Makers* (Boston: Atlantic Monthly Press, 1919) 24; Larzer Ziff, *Literary Democracy* (New York: Viking, 1981) 59. For the story of that last alumni dinner, see Tilton, *Amiable Autocrat*, 382.

9 Reports on "the most famous picnic in American literary history" diverge widely; my version is an attempted merging of various accounts. Several of the participants at this picnic wrote memoirs of it. These are excerpted in detail in: Tilton, *Amiable Autocrat*, 220–24; Hoyt, *The Improper Bostonian*, 136–42; Miller, *The Raven and the Whale: The War of Words and Wits in the Era of Poe and Melville* (New York: Harcourt, Brace, 1956) 280–91. Because Holmes could often speak on both sides of an issue, and because it was often hard to tell if he was joking or serious, participants have left contradictory notes on his conversation – at this event as at many others. But certainly the general tone of the talk at this Berkshire picnic is clear.

10 It should be noted that this idea of British superiority was not at all the Doctor's single, final, or "true" view on the subject. Indeed, he reviewed this "hot" topic often – from a variety of positions in the debate. He seems to have his Berkshire argument with Melville in mind when, in the *Autocrat*, after raising the possibility of comparing human physiognomies and elm trees in England and America in order to study differences in the "creative force" on both sides of the Atlantic, he admits that he actually favored his interlocutor's position: "It may turn out the other way [that Anglo-Saxons don't die out when transplanted here], as I have heard one of our literary celebrities argue, – and though I took the other side, I liked his best, – that the American is the Englishman reinforced" (*CW*, I, 236–38).

11 E. P. Whipple cited in Edward Waldo Emerson, *The Early Years of the Saturday Club: 1855–1870* (Boston: Houghton Mifflin, 1918) 91–92, 121–22.

12 Walt Whitman, "Song of Myself," *Leaves of Grass*, eds. Sculley Bradley and Harold Blodgett (New York: W. W. Norton, 1973) 88 ; Ralph Waldo Emerson, "Self-Reliance," *Complete Works* II: 57.

13 Friedrich Schlegel, *Athenaeum Fragments*, no. 220. Like the scientist–writer Holmes, Schlegel defines *Witz* as a mode of science that extends a spirit of sociability into everything it touches: "Wit is absolute social feeling . . ." and "Wit is logical sociability" (*Lyceum Fragments*, nos. 9, 54). And the perpetual divisive or combinative activity in wit's social-scientific

laboratory is then always seen in terms of electrical explosiveness: "Wit is an explosion of the confined [compound] spirit" (*Lyceum*, no. 90); and again, "A witty idea is a disintegration of spiritual substances which, before being suddenly separated, must have been thoroughly mixed. The imagination must first be satiated with all sorts of life before one can electrify it with the friction of free social intercourse so that the slightest friendly or hostile touch can elicit brilliant sparks and lustrous rays – or smashing thunderbolts" (*Lyceum*, no. 34). *Friedrich Schlegel's Lucinde and the Fragments*, trans. Peter Firchow (Minneapolis: University of Minnesota Press, 1971) 191, 144, 149, 153, 146.

14 Bakhtin, *Problems of Dostoevsky's Poetics*, trans R. W. Rotsel (New York: Ardis, 1973) 103–4.

15 For the cited phrases "Nihilist incendiary" and "a sort of reincarnation of Voltaire," see: M. A. DeWolfe Howe, *The Atlantic Monthly and its Makers*, 29, 31. Holmes' dialogue with the mid-century medical establishment is the subject of Chapter Six.

5 A CONVERSATIONAL APPROACH TO TRUTH: THE DOCTOR IN DIALOGUE WITH CONTEMPORARY TRUTH-SAYERS

1 Bakhtin, *Problems of Dostoevsky's Poetics*, trans. R. W. Rotsel (New York: Ardis, 1973) 90, 103.

2 Habermas, *The Structural Transformation of the Public Sphere*, trans. T. Burger (Great Britain: Polity, 1989) xi–xii, 36–37.

3 Rorty, *Philosophy and the Mirror of Nature* (Princeton: Princeton University Press, 1979) 317, 386.

4 Rorty, *Philosophy and the Mirror of Nature*, 373, 11–12, 317–18, 390.

5 The Professor reacted strongly to some especially violent attacks along these lines with strident definitions of his "democratic" reasons for attacking specialization, and ringing defenses of the freedom of skeptical and progressive "talk": "Religion and government seem to me the two subjects which of all others should belong to the common talk of people who enjoy the blessings of freedom . . . Every now and then some members [of the graver profession] seem to lose common sense and common humanity. The laymen have to keep setting the divines right constantly . . . Every generation dissolves something new and precipitates something once held in solution from that great storehouse of temporary and permanent truths . . . You may observe this: that the conversation of intelligent men of the stricter sects is strangely in advance of the formulae that belong to their organizations" (*CW*, II, 107, 113, 122–23). On Holmes' debate with the theologians, see M. A. DeWolfe Howe, *The Atlantic Monthly and Its Makers* (Boston: Atlantic Monthly Press, 1919) 29–31; Tilton *Amiable Autocrat: A Biography of Dr. Oliver Wendell Holmes* (New York: Henry Schuman, 1947) 250. On the related cultural debate between the new conversational style (of minis-

ters and laymen) and the older theological style, see Douglas, *The Feminization of American Culture* (New York: Knopf, 1977) 279–80. Douglas joins the orthodox clergymen in lamenting the loss of their specialized journals and treatises, and the weakening of their language.

6 All Rorty citations on the "hardness" of facts here are from "Criticism Without Theory: MLA Version," manuscript of a talk given at Stanford University, February 1983, 3–5. For a later version of this argument, see Rorty, "Texts and Lumps," *New Literary History* 17.1 (Autumn 1985): 1–16.

7 On Holmes' collection of books of learned, scientific para-doxa such as Renaissance anthologies of table-talk *facetiae*, seventeenth-century collections of paradoxical scientific aphorisms (dialogues between several unpopular or unusual views intended to help readers to stretch their mental muscles), and Rabelais' *Hippocratic Novel*, see Tilton, *Amiable Autocrat*, 374, 385. On the function of these early paradox dialogues, "encyclopedias of the light and grave in science," see R. L. Colie, "Some Paradoxes in the Language of Things," *Reason and the Imagination: Studies in the History of Ideas, 1600–1800*, ed. J. A. Mazzeo (New York: Columbia University Press, 1962) 93–128.

8 Holmes, *Ralph Waldo Emerson* (Boston: Houghton, Mifflin, 1885) 51. Hereafter cited parenthetically in the text as *RWE*.

9 Van Wyck Brooks, "Dr. Holmes' Boston," *Harper's* (July 1940): 142.

10 Among the critics who have noted that Holmes' descriptions of Brahminism or aristocracy were intended in some ways as provocative critiques of those elites which might draw out a shocked response from them are: Van Wyck Brooks, "Dr. Holmes: Forerunner of the Moderns," 13–15; and Larzer Ziff, *Literary Democracy* (New York: Viking, 1981) 59. In an interview outlining his ambitious project for a study of "America's aristocrats," Arthur R. Gold observes that Doctor Holmes is "a key source . . . the best place to start," since he gave us the term "Brahmin" along with "a rather mischievous definition of the 'aristocracy'." But then Gold, though he notes Holmes' stress on the primary role of inherited money in defining the American intellectual "aristocracy," describes one aspect of Holmes' vision as a "kind of racism," thus ignoring the ways in which the Doctor's "mischievous" stress on the economic basis of this "caste" system undermines any sense of its basis in blood or race. See William E. Cain, "Studying America's Aristocrats: An Interview with Arthur R. Gold," *American Literary History* 2:2 (Summer 1990): 360–62.

11 This and other relevant Jacksonian literature is cited in Richard Hofstadter, *Anti-intellectualism in American Life* (New York: Knopf, 1963) 159. Hofstadter defines the issues in the election of 1828 very starkly: "The last President to stand in the old line of government by gentlemen, Adams became the symbol of the old order and the chief victim of the reaction against the learned man" (ibid., 157). Tilton's biography

presents revealing information about Holmes' reactions to this 1828 election in the chapter on his Harvard years; see Tilton, *Amiable Autocrat*, 34–49. Catherine Drinker Bowen vividly recreates the atmosphere of these Harvard years in *Yankee from Olympus: Justice Holmes and his Family* (Boston: Little, Brown, 1945) 51–55.

12 Shields, *Civil Tongues and Polite Letters in British America* (Chapel Hill: University of North Carolina Press, 1997) 175, 180. For more detailed analysis of club life in British America, see ibid., 175–208.

13 Whipple's descriptions of the Saturday Club's organization cited in Edward W. Emerson, *The Early Years of the Satuday Club, 1855–1870* (Boston: Houghton Mifflin, 1918) 121.

14 On the role of an earlier "secular priesthood" in New England, see George M. Fredrickson, *The Inner Civil War: Northern Intellectuals and the Crisis of the Union* (New York: Harper and Row, 1965) 29. Chapter 12 surveys the ways in which Oliver Wendell Holmes, Jr. would turn against and transform his father's Brahmin ideal while defining another crucial shift in the role of the intellectual in American life at the end of the nineteenth century.

15 Ralph L. Rusk, ed., *The Letters of Ralph Waldo Emerson* (New York: Columbia University Press, 1939) v: 17.

16 In "Bread and the Newspaper," Holmes complains that a critic has labeled his "Brahmins" a "bloated aristocracy," and stresses again that on the contrary "they are very commonly pallid, undervitalized, shy, sensitive creatures, whose only birthright is an aptitude for learning" (*CW*, VIII, 9). Van Wyck Brooks, "Dr. Holmes: Forerunner of the Moderns," 13.

17 Hofstadter, *Anti-intellectualism in American Life*, 29–33.

18 Parrington, *Main Currents in American Thought: The Romantic Revolution in America, 1800–1860*, 3 vols. (New York: Harcourt, Brace, 1927) II: 455.

19 Habermas, *The Structural Transformation of the Public Sphere*, trans. Thomas Burger (Great Britain: Polity, 1989) 9.

20 Rorty, *Philosophy and the Mirror of Nature*, 317, 12.

   We will see in Chapter Twelve, when a distinction between Holmes Senior and Holmes Junior involves a distinction between a "free play of ideas" and a "free trade in ideas," that the Doctor's works can serve as nice test cases pointing up some of the problems and limits of Rorty's model.

   Many critics have raised difficult questions about the political implications of what Rorty calls "conversation" – questions also very relevant to the vision of Doctor Holmes: in a real world of political, economic, and social power, who determines the subject and form of the dialogue, who gets to take an active part, and do all voices have an equal sway? For an incisive analysis along these lines, see Jo Burrows, "Conversational Politics: Rorty's Pragmatist Apology for Liberalism," *Reading Rorty*, ed. Alan Malachowski (Oxford: Basil Blackwell, 1990). Frank

Lentricchia finds that, while they may have possessed critical power in the mid-nineteenth century, "Rorty's values of ungrounded cultural conversation have been decisively co-opted by late capitalist economy": "Rorty's Cultural Conversation," *Raritan*, 3 (Summer 1983): 139. And William E. Connolly too locates the danger here in Rorty's tendency (shared with Holmes) to isolate the "realm of the intellectual" from political or social lives: "Mirror of America," *Raritan*, 3 (Summer 1983): 124–35. See also: David L. Roochnik, "The Impossibility of Philosophical Dialogue," *Philosophy and Rhetoric*, 19.3 (1986); Robert Hollinger, ed., *Hermeneutics and Praxis* (Notre Dame: University of Notre Dame Press, 1985).

6 CONVERSATION AND "THERAPEUTIC NIHILISM": THE DOCTOR IN DIALOGUE WITH CONTEMPORARY MEDICINE

1 Tocqueville, *Democracy in America*, ed. R. D. Heffner (New York: New American Library, 1956) 117. Henry James made an observation parallel to Tocqueville's about the differences between conversation in mid-century New England and in Paris, which might help us to appreciate the Doctor's role as a sort of "foreign agitator" within his Boston circles. For whether he was born with it, or whether he developed it during his lively student years in Paris, Holmes' antithetical spirit in talk always tended to counteract bland agreement, working to draw out disagreements and differences often left unexpressed by his timid countrymen:

There were opinions in Woolett, but only three or four. The differences were there to match; if they were doubtless deep, though few, they were quiet – they were, as might be said, almost as shy as if people had been ashamed of them. People showed little diffidence about such things, on the other hand, in the Boulevard Malesherbes, and were so far from being ashamed of them – or indeed of anything else – that they often seemed to have invented them to avert those agreements that destroy the taste of talk.

Henry James, *The Ambassadors* (Boston: Houghton Mifflin, 1960) 113.
2 For a classic description of Victorian culture as a culture of coherences, see W. L. Burn, *The Age of Equipoise: A Study of the Mid-Victorian Generation* (New York: W. W. Norton, 1964).
3 Although he was one of the leading cultural spokesmen in mid-century America, Holmes' ironic table-talk writings in fact worked to develop strong challenges to many fundamental "Victorian" values. If, as historian Daniel Walker Howe observes, "Victorian ideals . . . taught people to work hard, to postpone gratification, to repress themselves sexually, to 'improve' themselves, to be sober, conscientious, even compulsive," the Doctors' humorous conversations and poems tend to portray such ideals as dangerously constrictive – in fact medically unhealthy – and to undermine them at every opportunity. The tendencies of this unsettling and disorderly conversational form also

certainly pose severe challenges to what Howe describes as "the Victorians' high valuation of order"; we will see that Holmes' speakers specifically attack the ordering impulses behind the asylum and the penitentiary, mock attempts to prohibit alcohol, and in general ridicule promoters of prudish self-denial or self-control. And his breakfast-table will then later prove to be open to free discussion even of the most shattering vision of disorder in the century: Darwin's theory of evolution. If at times the Autocrat can wax emotional about protecting the Victorian home as the shrine of moral values and personal identity, more often (as we will see) the "house-breaking" movements of his talk form finally work to explode out of any static, insulated domesticity. If an occasional country-bred breakfast-table voice may speak for a conservative, sentimentalist desire to return to the traditional culture epitomized in an "Old Oaken Bucket" or a "Village Blacksmith," the more dominant voice at this table is clearly that of urban cosmopolitan innovation. In general, then, the multivoiced, ironic structure and playful atmosphere of Holmes' table-talk simply does not allow much place for the tones of moral seriousness, self-righteousness, or earnestness traditionally associated with Victorianism or with the Victorian Sage. See Howe, "American Victorianism as a Culture," *American Quarterly* 27: 5 (December 1975): 521–25.

4 William R. Hutchison, "Cultural Strain and Protestant Liberalism," *American Historical Review* 76 (April 1971): 386–411; Howe, "American Victorianism," 525; David Grimsted, ed., "Introduction," *Notions of the Americans, 1820–1860* (New York: Braziller, 1970) 16–17. T. J. Jackson Lears, *No Place of Grace: Antimodernism and the Transformation of American Culture, 1880–1920* (New York: Pantheon, 1981) also studies a number of later nineteenth-century movements as anti-modernist reactions revealing the widespread anxieties aroused by many aspects of contemporary "progress."

5 William Ellery Channing is cited in Bowen, *Yankee from Olympus: Justice Holmes and his Family* (Boston: Little, Brown, 1945) 51.

6 Providing a useful contrast to Holmes' late nineteenth-century view of the telegraph and telephone, Thoreau delivers one of the great anti-conversation aphorisms of the mid-century when remarking on the advent of the telegraph, in *Walden* – "We are in great haste to construct a magnetic telegraph from Maine to Texas; but Maine and Texas, it may be, have nothing important to communicate." Thoreau, *Walden and Other Writings*, ed. William Howarth (New York: Modern Library, 1981) 47.

7 Holmes' letter with him "cross as a wild-cat" is cited in Tilton's good discussion of this traumatic period, *Amiable Autocrat: A Biography of Dr. Oliver Wendell Holmes* (New York: Henry Schuman, 1947) 48–49. We will return for further analysis of Holmes' turn away from his father's Calvinism in Chapter Nine.

8 *The Early Years of the Saturday Club, 1855–1870* (Boston: Houghton Mifflin, 1918) 144.

9 For descriptions of Holmes' Paris days, and citations from his revealing letters home, see Tilton, *Amiable Autocrat,* 87–97.

10 On the Parisian "clinical method" see: Erwin H. Ackerknecht, *Medicine at the Paris Hospital, 1794–1848* (Baltimore: Johns Hopkins University Press, 1967); Richard H. Shryock, "Medicine and Public Health," *The Nineteenth-Century World: Readings from the History of Mankind,* eds. Guy Métraux and François Crouzet (New York: New American Library, 1963) 193–253; Richard Shryock, *Medicine and Society in America: 1660–1860* (New York: New York University Press, 1960) 124–32; Michel Foucault, *The Birth of the Clinic: An Archaeology of Medical Perception,* trans. A. M. Sheridan Smith (New York: Pantheon, 1973). On the influence of the skepticism of the Paris school on American medical theory and practice, and on later debates between clinicians and bacteriologists, see John Harley Warner, *The Therapeutic Perspective: Medical Practice, Knowledge, and Identity in America, 1820–1885* (Cambridge: Harvard University Press, 1986). For Holmes' relations with the Paris clinicians, see Tilton, *Amiable Autocrat,* 101–05.

11 Holmes' most extended discussion of Rush comes in "Currents and Counter-Currents in Medical Science" (*CW,* ix). Though Holmes' attacks were well known and strongly phrased, criticisms of Rush were widespread in the nineteenth century, as a new generation of doctors sought to define their own position (and as Boston physicians sought to undercut Philadelphia's earlier medical preeminence). As early as 1800, William Cobbett could report in a study of the effectiveness of Rush's treatments in a yellow fever epidemic that Rush's system is "one of the great discoveries . . . which have contributed to the depopulation of the earth." And at least two pamphlets in the next decades had suggested that this First Doctor's harsh treatments had been responsible for the death of our First President, Washington. See: Shryock, *Medicine and Society in America,* 118–23; R[ichard] H. S[hryock], "Benjamin Rush," *The Dictionary of American Biography,* ed. Dumas Malone, 20 vols. (New York: Scribner's, 1935) 227–31.

12 Holmes' whole point as a medical historian here is to undermine our common-sense notions of medical science as objective and neutral, going "its own straightforward inductive path" without regard to the fluctuations of other historically-based events. He reminds us that,

> The truth is, that medicine, professedly founded on observation, is as sensitive to outside influences, political, religious, philosophical, imaginative, as is the barometer to the changes of atmospheric density . . . Look for a moment while I clash a few facts together, and see if some sparks do not reveal by their light a closer relation between the Medical Sciences and the Conditions of Society and the general thought of the time, than would at first be suspected. (*CW,* ix, 177)

Commenting on Holmes' analysis of the "Bowie-knife" spirit behind "heroic" practice, historian John Haller notes that, "European observers like Tocqueville and James Bryce no doubt would have commended Holmes for his perceptive view of heroic therapeutics." John A. Haller, Jr., *American Medicine in Transition: 1840–1910* (Urbana: University of Illinois Press, 1981) 99.

The Doctor must have been aware, though, that his thinking placed him in some ways far ahead of actual practice in his day. For even his 1861 remark, in "Border Lines of Knowledge in Some Provinces of Medical Science," that venesection had become obsolete in England and America, could only have been wishful thinking: many not at the cutting edge of medical theory continued to use extreme surgery and bloodletting well into the 1870s. Historian David Cowen comments that Holmes' remark was "figuratively too sanguine and literally not sanguine enough." See John H. Warner, "'The Nature-Trusting Heresy': American Physicians and the Concept of the Healing Power of Nature in the 1850s and 1860s," *Perspectives in American History* 2 (1977–78): 32. And Warner notes elsewhere that while, by the 1860s, the earlier monistic *explanations* for heroic practice had tended to dissolve in the face of clinical attacks, in fact many physicians remained strongly attached to the *principle* of heroic therapies. Such doctors, finding therapeutic nihilism simply impossible, would often attempt to use the new science to develop new rationales for continuing use of older cures such as mercury treatments or blood letting. See Warner, *The Therapeutic Perspective*.

13 It should probably be mentioned here that Holmes always had a secondary reason for taking up the cases of naturopathic cures, infinitesimal doses, Perkins' Metallic Tractors, and the "King's touch": these cases allowed him to play with intriguing imagery and to get off some good lines. Of Berkeley's peculiar passion, for example, he observes: "[Berkeley] was an illustrious man, but he held two very odd opinions: that tar water was everything, and that the material universe was nothing" ("Homeopathy and its Kindred Delusions," *CW*, IX, 15).

14 Again, as in the case of Rush, Holmes' specific targets here are "heroic" Philadelphia doctors: Profs. Hugh Hodge and Charles Meigs, leaders in the field of Female Diseases, who brought out a series of books and pamphlets countering Holmes (e.g., Hodge, *On the Non-Contagiousness of Puerperal Fever*, 1852). For them, the heterogenic contagion theory arose out of the "jejeune dreaming of sophomore writers," and they sought to "exalt the value and dignity of our profession" by once again blaming the victim: childbed fever was "conceived" autogenically by and within the pregant women that it attacked – probably another "disease of the womb," another sign of womens' congenital infirmity and of their need for the strong intervention of male professionals. John A. Haller, Jr., *American Medicine in Transition 1840–1910*, 164; Barbara Ehrenreich and

Deidre English, *Complaints and Disorders: The Sexual Politics of Sickness* (Old Westbury: Feminist Press, 1973) 11–40. On the cruelty of some "heroic" surgical practices in gynecology and obstetrics which could arise out of the views of Holmes' Philadelphia antagonists, see: G. J. Barker-Benfield, "The Spermatic Economy: A Nineteenth-Century View of Sexuality," *The American Family in Social-Historical Perspective* ed. David Gordon (New York: St. Martin's, 1973) 336–72. In later years, some right-wing applications of contagion theory would also be attacked from the reformist left by "environmentalist" progressives whose campaigns to improve living conditions in urban slums were deflated by doctors suggesting that all that was needed to help the poor was a program of vaccinations.

Though standard, the phrase "one of the most important documents . . ." used here is cited from a long discussion of the "Contagion" essay in: Richard W. Wertz and Dorothy C. Wertz, *Lying-In: A History of Childbirth in America* (New York: Free Press, 1977) 121.

15 This typical characterization of the "philosophy" of the speech is from Edward O. Otis, cited in Rees and Harbert, *Fifteen American Authors Before 1900: Bibliographic Essays on Research and Criticism* (Madison: University of Wisconsin Press, 1971) 227. For the Medical Society reaction, see Warner, *The Therapeutic Perspective*, 291–324.

16 Thomas, *The Youngest Science: Notes of a Medicine-Watcher* (New York: Viking, 1983) 85. Thomas is a New England doctor-writer very much in the Holmes tradition, and his meditations on these particular issues develop along the lines set out in the mid-nineteenth century by Doctor Holmes and his Harvard teachers.

17 Charles Rosenberg, "The Therapeutic Revolution: Medicine, Meaning and Social Change in Nineteenth-Century America," in *The Therapeutic Revolution: Essays in the Social History of American Medicine*, eds. Morris Vogel and Charles Rosenberg (Philadelphia: University of Pennsylvania Press, 1979) 20.

18 Holmes' humbling strictures on the limits of medical intervention have, of course, become standard fare in most introductory classes at English-speaking medical schools – though since the 1950s modern medicine has developed some positive arts for life-saving intervention. For Holmes' position as spokesman for "therapeutic nihilism" or for the "Nature-Trusting Heresy," and for the above-cited responses to his position, see: Warner, " 'The Nature-Trusting Heresy' "; and Shryock, *Medicine and Society in America*, 131. On the more general consequences of such a stance of "spectatorship" as it was developed as an approach to all of life in the generation of Henry James, Henry Adams, and Oliver Wendell Holmes, Junior, see: Yosal Rogat, "The Judge as Spectator," *The University of Chicago Law Review* 31 (Winter 1964): 213–56.

19 Charles E. Rosenberg, *The Cholera Years: The United States in 1832, 1849, and 1866*, (Chicago: University of Chicago Press, 1962) 67, 152, 154–55.

20 Bick, "A Note on the Medical Works of Oliver Wendell Holmes," *Annals of Medical History* 4 (1932): 487–508.

21 See Holmes, "The Stereoscope and the Stereograph," *Atlantic* 3: 20 (June 1859): 738–48. On Holmes and the implications of stereoscopy, see Jonathan Crary, *Techniques of the Observer: On Vision and Modernity in the Nineteenth Century* (Cambridge, MA: MIT Press, 1990) 125. Holmes' fascination with the new technologies of vision is also evident in his speculative writings on the philosophical implications of photography: see "Sun-Painting and Sun-Sculpture; With a Stereoscopic Trip across the Atlantic," *Atlantic* 8: 45 (July 1861): 14–28; "Doings of the Sunbeam," *Atlantic* 12: 69 (July 1863): 9–12.

22 Rosenberg, *The Cholera Years*, 76–81, 143, 164; Erwin H. Ackerknecht, "Anti-contagionism between 1821 and 1867," *Bulletin of the History of Medicine* 22 (1948): 562–93. If some contagionists later applied germ theory as part of a right-wing, anti-environmentalist agenda denying the need for public health reforms, this does not seem to have been the direction of Holmes' thinking.

23 Tilton, *Amiable Autocrat*, 187; Shryock, *Medicine and Society in America*, 133. See also Martin S. Pernick, *A Calculus of Suffering: Pain, Professionalism, and Anesthesia in Nineteenth-Century America* (New York: Columbia University Press, 1985).

24 The phrase about "taking away the old . . ." is from Shryock, *Medicine and Society in America*, 124–25.

25 Philip Cash, "Pride, Prejudice, and Politics," in Werner Sollors, ed. *Blacks at Harvard* (New York: New York University Press, 1993) 22.

26 Tilton, *Amiable Autocrat*, 192. For documentary material on the Harriot K. Hunt episode, see Gerda Lerner, ed., *The Female Experience: An American Documentary* (Indianapolis: Bobbs-Merrill, 1977) 397–400.

27 Ullman, *Martin R. Delany: The Beginnings of Black Nationalism* (Boston: Beacon Press, 1971) 118.

28 For further details on these attempts to admit black medical students at Harvard, see Cash, "Pride, Prejudice, and Politics," 22–31 and Ullman, *Martin R. Delany*, 113–21. One can only hope that the ugly lines in the letter Holmes was directed to send to the Colonization Society – informing them that "this experiment" had satisfied the faculty that "the intermixing of the white and black races in their lecture rooms, is distasteful to a large portion of the class and injurious to the interests of the school" – were dictated to him by the governing body and not reflections of his own position, since they go so strongly against the grain of his more characteristic personal vision favoring "intermixing": Holmes letter cited in Cash, "Pride, Prejudice, and Politics," 29. Some incomplete accounts of this episode at Harvard make it sound as though it was Holmes who opposed the female and black students, without noting that Holmes was the key supporter of these moves, in fact standing alone in support of Hunt and apparently taking the bold initial

step of admitting Delany on his own. After Delany (a strong personality who stated directly that he planned to practice not in Liberia but in America) had been rejected because of his race at several medical schools (Jefferson, the University of Pennsylvania, Geneva, Albany, and Berkshire), Holmes met him in his office and admitted him to Harvard the same day: Cash, "Pride, Prejudice, and Politics," 24–26.

29 Michel Foucault, *The Birth of the Clinic*; Michel Foucault, *Madness and Civilization: A History of Insanity in the Age of Reason*, trans. Richard Howard (New York: Random House, 1965).

Lewis Thomas, in *The Youngest Science*, seems to be one of the few medical commentators to have noticed, as part of his criticism of today's increasingly sanitized, technologized, and thus dehumanized medical practice, that at its origins, when it involved a diagnostic rather than a therapeutic approach, the clinical method could actually foster the sort of close doctor–patient conversation so sorely lacking in current practice: "in former times doctors talked extensively and comfortingly to patients because, beyond the diagnosis, there was little that they had to offer." Of course Thomas is harking back to a golden-age spirit which would have been far from dominant even in "former times"; this vision of medicine as a care-and-comfort operation and a largely verbal interchange was probably mainly a New England tradition – a tradition epitomized and promoted by Dr. Holmes. Seeking to revive that tradition, Thomas holds up as a model for today's doctors – just as Holmes had done for the newly "professionalized" physicians of his day – the central importance of the bedside care provided by the neglected nursing profession.

30 This passage is from a Holmes letter of 8 May 1862 to Silas Weir Mitchell, reprinted in: Anna R. Burr, *Weir Mitchell: His Life and Letters* (New York: Duffield, 1929) 82–83. The imagery of that phallic snake, here probably a boa constrictor, recurs frequently in Holmes' letters to Mitchell, since they shared a fascination with snakes, especially rattlers. (Mitchell began his career with lab work on snake venom, which Holmes read with interest because of his literary use of rattlesnake imagery in *Elsie Venner*.) But here, as elsewhere, the Doctor seems to be developing this shared image as a vain warning to the young disciple about the dangers inherent in the scientific stance.

This passage is now occasionally cited by historians as a contemporary recognition of the masculine and aggressive elements latent in nineteenth-century experimental science. Some feminist scholars, though, in their desire to find enemies in the past, have seemed to misread Holmes' characteristically ironic position in this passage. Ehrenreich and English, for example, introduce the citation as a direct statement of belief: "Holmes Sr., a regular doctor and early champion of scientific medicine, described his attitude toward scientific investigation in the language of undisguised sexual sadism." But they then end their quote unscrupulously just before the hyphen, thus deleting the Doctor's disavowal of such a stance. The rest of their book, however, provides ample testimony that Holmes was not so univocally "regular": many of their main critiques of the male-dominated profession are amplified by forceful citations from other writings of the Doctor. Barbara Ehrenreich and Deidre English, *For Her Own Good: 150 Years of Experts' Advice to Women* (New York: Anchor, 1979) 76.

Other critics, by contrast, take this sort of passage in Holmes as evidence that he was too "feminized," too trapped on the women's side of the separate sexual spheres, to be a man, to be able to assert without guilt his own active "phallicism, professionalism." See Gail Thain Parker, "Sex, Sentiment, and Oliver Wendell Holmes," *Women's Studies* 1: 1 (1972): 57.

31 Foucault, *The Birth of the Clinic*, xviii.

32 William M. Johnston, *The Austrian Mind: An Intellectual and Social History, 1848–1983* (Berkeley: University of California Press, 1972) 228.

33 Foucault, *The Birth of the Clinic*, xviii, xi ; Shryock, *Medicine and Society in America* 124, 159.

34 Dr. Jackson is cited in Tilton, *Amiable Autocrat*, 78; Bowen, *Yankee from Olympus*, 190. For Holmes' attendance upon Louis, see Tilton, *Amiable Autocrat*, 99–100.

35 Even after Pasteur's germ theory had given firm support to the Doctor's speculations about "contagion," Holmes retained a characteristic skepticism about these findings. Though he is relieved that "the little army of microbes was marched up to support my position," his metaphoric language here suggests that we must recognize that this "proof" too may soon be succeeded by other theories which will make this one seem but a quaint story. In his view, the history of science is a battle between successive stories rather than a cumulative progress of ever more adequate truths.

Thomas W. Higginson observed that, though the Doctor introduced the microscope in his medical classes, he himself used the tool in the manner of those microscopists who are "the poets of science." The Doctor's anatomy lectures at Harvard were most noted for his very unscientific flights of metaphor – mixing detailed observation with highly imaginative visual imagery. His associate, Professor Dwight, remarked that, "None but Holmes could have compared the microscopical coiled tube of a sweat-gland to a fairy's intestine." One student at these highly popular courses wrote that, "Every muscle, bone, or organ suggests some witty story": the fimbriated end of the Fallopian tube was like the fringe of a poor woman's shawl; the mesentery, like old-fashioned shirt ruffles; and so on. Mocking overtechnical jargon, using rhyme and ribaldry as mnemonic devices, Holmes here was most centrally engaged in a playful challenge to the truth-claims of the foundational language prescribed by Royal Society science or by clinical medicine.

Holmes' letter on the "little army of microbes" cited in Hayakawa and Jones, *Oliver Wendell Holmes: Representative Selections* (New York: American Book Company, 1939) xxxiii; Higginson, *Old Cambridge* (New York: Macmillan, 1900) 94; Tilton, *Amiable Autocrat*, 195–96.

36 Norman Cousins, *Anatomy of an Illness as Perceived by the Patient: Reflections on Healing and Regeneration* (New York: Norton, 1979) 26.

7 THE SELF IN CONVERSATION: THE DOCTOR IN DIALOGUE WITH CONTEMPORARY PSYCHOLOGY

1 The description of this as the "first great psychiatric revolution" is from Andrew Scull, ed., *Madhouses, Mad-doctors, and Madmen: The Social History of Psychiatry in the Victorian Era* (Philadelphia: University of Pennsylvania Press, 1981) 1; the phrases "age of the asylum" and "cult of asylum" are from David J. Rothman, *The Discovery of the Asylum: Social Order and Disorder in the New Republic* (Boston: Little Brown, 1971) xiii, 130. See also Shryock, *Medicine and Society in America: 1660–1860* (New York: New York University Press, 1960) 129–30.

2 For a full treatment of the lifelong dialogue between Holmes Senior and Holmes Junior on these issues, see Chapter Twelve.

3 [Holmes], "A Visit to the Asylum for Aged and Decayed Punsters," *Atlantic* (January 1861): 113–17. No author's name is listed as byline for this piece, but it is attributed to Holmes for many reasons: it refers to Holmes' beloved Hasty Pudding Club at Harvard and recalls his pun-filled participation in that club's burlesque mock trials; it seems to repeat material from one of his earlier burlesque Lyceum lectures; its concluding joke – "a capital pun-is-meant" – is included in notes in the Holmes collection at the Houghton Library; it shares references to the dictionary wars with the *Autocrat*, and also parallels the famously pun-loving Doctor's well-known set-piece on "the pun question" in the *Autocrat* – which takes us through similar mock trials and carnivalizations of judgment: *CW*, I, 11–14.

4 Tocqueville and Wayland are cited in Rothman, *The Discovery of the Asylum*, 89, 96. On the centrality of architecture as the tool of these new treatments, see: Rothman, *The Discovery of the Asylum*, 83–92; Nancy J. Tomes, "A Generous Confidence: Thomas Story Kirkbride's Philosophy of Asylum Construction and Management," in Scull, *Madhouses, Mad-doctors, and Madmen*, 121–43. The Leuret anecdote appears in Michel Foucault, *Mental Illness and Psychology*, trans. Alan Sheridan (New York: Harper and Row, 1976) 72.

5 For the 1869 dating of the birth of this branch of medicine, see Eliot Hearst, *The First Century of Experimental Psychology* (New York: Wiley, 1979). The two professors of "mental science" to become new associates of Holmes at Harvard were John E. Tyler (1871) and James Jackson Putnam (1873–75); see Tilton, *Amiable Autocrat: A Biography of Dr. Oliver*

Wendell Holmes (New York: Henry Schuman, 1947) 303. On the influence of the Civil War in the birth of neuro-psychiatry, see: William Malamud, "The History of Psychiatric Therapies," and Albert Deutsch, "Military Psychiatry: The Civil War, 1861–1865," in *One Hundred Years of American Psychiatry* (New York: Columbia University Press, 1944) 291, 367–84, 390–96. On Broca and localization, see Nathan Hale, Jr., *Freud and the Americans: The Beginnings of Psychoanalysis in the United States, 1876–1917* (New York: Oxford University Press, 1971) 49–51. Holmes' "Mechanism in Thought and Morals" appears in *CW*, VIII.

6 In his study of Holmes' "medicated" or psychiatric novels, the psycho-analyst Clarence P. Oberndorf notes that many of the Doctor's insights into the motives and forces in our mental life could only have emerged out of his close, "firsthand observations" of the verbal texture of patient histories, and so reflect the "hours spent in intimate talks with patients, comparable to psychoanalytic sessions." See *The Psychiatric Novels of Oliver Wendell Holmes* (New York: Columbia University Press, 1943) 55.

7 In the *Autocrat*, for example, Holmes' speakers often examine the mean-ings of slips of the tongue in their own social talk, and anticipate the serious themes of the *Mechanism* study through speculation on examples of a repetition compulsion in their own conversation – suggesting that the brain is a "Babbage's calculating machine" with its "ruts and grooves" governed by an "express train of associations" – or on the sense of repetition in *déjà vu*, showing that an automatic "mathematical rule" may govern the "regular cycles" of thought as well as of the body. Even the tendency to use adjectives in triads prompts a hypothesis about the dominance of "the automatic and instinctive principles in body, mind, and morals" over the more limited "self-determining" move-ments of consciousness. *CW*, I, 7–8, 65–66, 73, 85.

8 The Holmes Papers at Harvard's Houghton Library contain a notebook with what seems to be a sketch of the Doctor's autobiography; near the opening of the section on his youth (1809–15), Holmes feels it important to include another aphorism about the basic physiological dualism in the human constitution: "Each of us in two halves: the liver (right) side and the spleen (left) side."

9 Several critics have remarked, in very general terms, that Holmes' unscientific, exploratory writings often seem to anticipate the advanced work of later theorists. Van Wyck Brooks writes that in *Elsie Venner* and in his table-talk Doctor Holmes "played into the hands of Dr. Freud": see, "Dr. Holmes: Forerunner of the Moderns," *The Saturday Review of Literature* (27 June 1936): 16. Edmund Wilson, in a series of letters on Holmes, gives the Doctor's "medicated novels" an important role in the birth of the psychological novel as a genre, and H. Bruce Franklin notes that Holmes' "brilliant psychiatric theories" were first tested not in scientific papers but in these "science fiction" novels as well as in the *Mechanism* speech: *Future Perfect: American Science Fiction of the Nineteenth*

Century (New York: Oxford University Press, 1966) 218. Clarence Oberndorf, finding that "in certain essentials Holmes' theory and philosophy of approach to psychological problems is prophetic of psychoanalysis and anticipated Freud's formulations and the psycho-analytic psychiatry which grew out of it," explains that the many specific parallels he finds between the insights of Freud and Holmes probably arose out of Holmes' daily experience of social conversation and of medical "talking exams": *The Psychiatric Novels of Oliver Wendell Holmes.* Similarly, Karl P. Wentersdorf, in "The Underground Workshop of O. W. Holmes," *American Literature* 35 (March 1963): 11, judges that the Doctor's new conceptions arose out of the fertilizing interconnections between his roles as writer and as scientist: "Holmes seems to have been the first to combine the sensitivity and insight of a literary artist with the specialized knowledge and probing curiosity of a scientist whose theories foreshadowed important later developments in the field of psychology." M. E. Grenander, "Doctors and Humanists: Transactional Analysis and Two Views of Man," *Journal of American Culture* 3 (Fall 1980): 475, also concludes that the Doctor's literary reflections, especially in the "three Johns" passage, looked forward to later ideas of transactional analysis: "More than a century ago Oliver Wendell Holmes voiced an idea that recurs today. His approach was direct, his language simple and witty. But the concept he proposed was solidly constructed. It was later elaborated by Harry Stack Sullivan. Drs. Berne and Harris were touted as leaders in the field, pioneers of a new outlook. When their theories are stripped of their mechanical metaphors, however, they are seen to be the latest restatement of the simple words of a clear-sighted humanist who lived many years before them."

10 The idea of staging such an interdisciplinary conversation still intrigues many psychologists. Morton F. Reiser, for example, opens his *Mind, Brain, Body: Toward a Convergence of Psychoanalysis and Neurobiology* (New York: Basic Books, 1985) by stating "a challenge" very similar to Holmes': "Do psychoanalysis and neurobiology . . . have anything to say to each other?"

But a partisan reviewer finds even after Reiser's study that the answer to his question is simply: "Very little." The enterprise remains crucial, but in some ways, as these two specialized fields have advanced, we have lost ground in the effort to open up a conversation between them. See: B. A. Farrell, "Snails on the Couch," *New York Review of Books* (18 July 1985): 36.

11 Hale gives the "crisis" these exact dates in his *Freud and the Americans: The Beginnings of Psychoanalysis in the United States.* Richard Shryock puts this revolt more vaguely at the "turn of the century" in his "Medicine and Public Health," in *The Nineteenth-Century World: Readings from the History of Mankind,* eds. Guy Métraux and François Crouzet (New York: New American Library, 1963). See also Ernest R. Hilgard, *Psychology in*

America: A Historical Survey (San Diego: Harcourt, Brace, Jovanovich, 1987). On early conceptions of the "unconscious" which come out of this crisis of the somatic model, see: Henri F. Ellenberger, *The Discovery of the Unconscious: The History and Evolution of Dynamic Psychiatry* (New York: Basic Books, 1970).

12 Certainly, in preparing his *Mechanism* lecture, Holmes would have been very aware of the tradition of Harvard Phi Beta Kappa speeches that preceeded his. His effort to define at least some possibilities of freedom for mental movement within the new mechanistic vision may indeed owe some debt to Edward Everett's 1824 oration on the role of the American intellectual in the formation of a national culture freed from that of England and, more centrally, to Emerson's 1837 celebration of the liberating power of "The American Scholar" (a speech which Doctor Holmes heard from his seat on the stage behind Emerson, and later praised as "our intellectual Declaration of Independence"). But Holmes' version of the Phi Beta Kappa report on the state of the American mind also speaks for the much more constricted vision of post-bellum America – a vision which leaves very little room for expansion or free play of the intellect or spirit.

13 Hale, *Freud and the Americans*, 121–22, 117.

14 The Holmes Papers in Harvard's Houghton Library include a series of letters from Mitchell (inquiring about statistics on the "white race," on tendencies to "degeneracy" in American women [and the avoidance of such degeneration in the line of New England aristocratic "signers,"] and so on); an 1859 letter is signed "very greatly your debtor."

15 For a large selection of Mitchell's correspondence with Holmes, see: Burr, *Weir Mitchell: His Life and Letters* (New York: Duffield, 1929). For comment on Mitchell's career as a writer, and on his sense of discipleship to Holmes, see: Joseph Lovering, *Silas Weir Mitchell* (New York: Twayne, 1971). For Hale's comments on the "important . . . psychological elements" implied by Mitchell's mentalist therapeutics, see: *Freud and the Americans*, 60. The cited passage from *Dr. North and His Friends* (New York: The Century Co., 1903) is on page 294.

16 Prince cited and discussed in Hale, *Freud and the Americans*, 53, 67, 87, 89, 91, 120, 126–29.

17 On James' sense of the relations between the "social Self" and other "constituents of the Self," see "The Consciousness of Self," *The Principles of Psychology* vol. 1 (Cambridge: Harvard University Press, 1981) 280–83.

18 Gay Wilson Allen, *William James* (Minneapolis: University of Minnesota Press, 1970); Hale, *Freud and the Americans*, 90, 110, 114, 127; Tilton, *Amiable Autocrat*, 377.

19 James cited and analyzed in Hale, *Freud and the Americans*, 128.

20 Holmes' Notebook for *The Poet* cited in Tilton, *Amiable Autocrat*, 313. The letter to Mitchell is in Morse, *Life and Letters of Oliver Wendell Holmes* (Boston: Houghton Mifflin, 1897) II, 15.

21 Brooks, "Dr. Holmes: Forerunner of the Moderns," 11–12.
22 James, *The Varieties of Religious Experience* (New York: Longmans, Green and Co., 1902) 234–35.
23 Rieff, *Freud: The Mind of the Moralist* (Chicago: University of Chicago Press, 1979).

8 THE BIPOLAR DYNAMICS OF HOLMES' HOUSEHOLD
DIALOGUES: LEVITY AND GRAVITY

1 P. L. Travers, *Mary Poppins* (New York: Harcourt, Brace, 1934) 29–48.
2 Lowell, *The Round Table* (Boston: Gorham, 1913) 68–69, 73–76.
3 Joel Dana Black, "The Second Fall: The Laws of Digression and Gravitation in Romantic Narrative and Their Impact on Contemporary Encyclopaedic Literature," Dissertation Stanford University, 1979.
4 Black, "The Second Fall," 223, 275–76.
5 Jonathan Edwards, "Sinners in the Hands of an Angry God," *Jonathan Edwards: Basic Writings*, ed. Ola E. Winslow (New York: New American Library, 1966) 157.
6 Sigurd Burckhardt, "*Tristram Shandy*'s Law of Gravity," *ELH* 28 (1961): 70–71.
7 Schlegel, fragment 108, *Lucinde and the Fragments*, trans. P. Firchow (Minneapolis: University of Minnesota Press, 1971) 236.
8 Review of Holmes as "American Sterne" cited in Tilton, *Amiable Autocrat: A Biography of Dr. Oliver Wendell Holmes* (New York: Henry Schuman, 1947) 259.
9 Fliegelman, *Prodigals and Pilgrims: The American Revolution against Patriarchal Authority, 1750–1800* (Cambridge: Cambridge University Press, 1982) 39, 62.
10 Lowell, *The Round Table*, 73–74.
11 *Quarterly Review*, Jan. 1895, cited in Rees and Harbert, *Fifteen American Authors Before 1900: Bibliographic Essays on Research and Criticism* (Madison: University of Wisconsin Press, 1971) 215.
12 *Christian Examiner* comments about Holmes' "levity" cited in Franklin T. Baker, ed., "Introduction," *The Autocrat of the Breakfast-Table* (New York: Macmillan, 1928) ix.
13 The description of the Shandy family life as one of "diametrically opposed temperaments, perpetual misunderstandings, and mutual devotion" is given by Ian Watt, ed., "Introduction," *The Life and Opinions of Tristram Shandy, Gentleman*, ed. Ian Watt (Boston: Houghton Mifflin, 1965) xxii.
14 Whitman's poem was first published, in an early version, in the Christmas edition (24 December 1859) of the New York *Saturday Press*.
15 Holmes, *Ralph Waldo Emerson* (Boston: Houghton Mifflin, 1885) 82–83.
  The Doctor's revisionist reading of Emerson in this biography describes the bard's mental life as a rich interaction between eighteenth-

century wit and nineteenth-century enthusiasm, and applauds Emerson for his successful internal balancing of the twin urges of gravity and levity – a success characteristically seen by Holmes in playful, boyish images of an airy flight that maintains firm contact with the ground: Emerson, he writes, "never let go of his balloon."

16 On Clemen's early uses and readings of *The Autocrat*, see: Justin Kaplan, *Mr. Clemens and Mark Twain* (New York: Simon and Schuster, 1966) 80, 92–93, 325. On Twain's "comic dialectic," see Cox, *Mark Twain: The Fate of Humor* (Princeton: Princeton University Press, 1966) 205.

17 Twain, *Selected Shorter Writings of Mark Twain*, ed. Walter Blair (Boston: Houghton Mifflin, 1962) 13–18, 135–50. For more detailed readings of the Twain works, see Peter Gibian, "Levity and Gravity in Twain: The Bipolar Dynamics of the Early Tales," *Studies in American Humor* ser. 3: 1 (1994): 80–94.

18 The phrase "Newton of the Mind" is used by Peter Gay to describe a major impulse in psychological thought during the Enlightenment. Gay, *The Enlightenment: The Science of Freedom*, vol. II (New York: Knopf, 1969) 174–86.

19 Indeed Holmes does notice this electrodynamic effect often – it is a whim that seems to preoccupy him both as a scientist and as a conversational writer. As we noted earlier, his *Mechanism* essay uses an almost exact repetition of the Autocrat's church scene to describe the dialogic relations between layers of mental currents – between the continuous involuntary murmurings of the autonomic system and the more conscious "talking thought" which it "influences"; "The automatic flow of thought is often singularly favored by the fact of listening to a weak, continuous discourse, with just enough ideas in it to keep the mind busy on something else. The *induced current* of thought is often rapid and brilliant in the inverse ratio of the force of the inducing current" (*CW*, VIII, 292).

20 Holmes' portrait of himself as a hyperactive little bird seems particularly apt. A similar picture recurs frequently in descriptions of Holmes given by familiar readers or by his conversational partners. Emerson describes the Doctor as a bee or a hummingbird in his highly metaphorical conversation, buzzing quickly from rhetorical flower to flower (Emerson, "Clubs," *Complete Works*, 422). Franklin Baker cites a Holmes acquaintance who remembers this physically tiny (about 5'2" or 5'3" tall) doctor-dilettante as "a hummingbird sipping the one honeyed drop from every flower" (Baker, ed. *The Autocrat*, xi). Virginia Woolf quotes another friend's picture of a "small, compact, little man . . . buzzing about like a bee, or fluttering like a hummingbird, exceedingly difficult to catch" ("Oliver Wendell Holmes," *Collected Essays*, vol. IV [London: Hogarth, 1967) 46]. And Tilton offers the capsule vision of a flighty butterfly who seems always to "hover" around the era's dogmas but never to "alight" (Tilton, *Amiable Autocrat*, 207).

21 The lesson is the same in the many Holmes defenses of the "levity" of digression: we might recall here once again his poem "The Crooked Footpath," in which the "truant child" whose prodigal self-culture digresses from "school and church" and the paternal home in a "devious" trail of "aimless, wayward curves" finally finds that,

> Through all the wanderings of the path,
> We still can see our Father's door! (*CW,* ii, 102–03)

9 HOLMES' HOUSE DIVIDED: HOUSE-KEEPING AND HOUSE-BREAKING

1 Of course, Douglas typically condemns all of these men who move away from religious orthodoxy into writing as feminized, impotent idlers, frail boys who hide under their mothers' skirts, perpetual children who evade masculine responsibility: Douglas, *The Feminization of American Culture* (New York: Knopf, 1977) 284–89, 466–68.

2 Tilton's medical analogy here actually inverts the normal process of inoculation. See Tilton, *Amiable Autocrat: A Biography of Dr. Oliver Wendell Holmes* (New York: Henry Schuman, 1947) 27.

3 Tilton, *Amiable Autocrat*, 44–45.

4 Tilton, *Amiable Autocrat*, 4.

5 On Isaac Watts, see Fliegelman, *Prodigals and Pilgrims: The American Revolution against Patriarchal Authority, 1750–1800* (Cambridge: Cambridge University Press, 1982) 19–21, 170–71.

6 Bowen, *Yankee from Olympus: Justice Holmes and his Family* (Boston: Little, Brown, 1945) 38–39.

7 Bowen, *Yankee from Olympus*, 4, 39.

8 For these descriptions of the Wendell heritage, see: Hoyt, *The Improper Bostonian: Dr. Oliver Wendell Holmes* (New York: Morrow, 1979) 25.

9 Bowen, *Yankee from Olympus*, 32, 40, 60, 65, 70.

10 Tilton, *Amiable Autocrat*, 80.

11 The Doctor's friend Leslie Stephen mentions this "smallest fevers" joke to show again how Holmes' verbal levity tended to undercut the gravity associated with his profession: "he had not the excessive gravity we desire in doctors." *Studies of a Biographer*, vol. ii (New York: Putnam's, 1907) 170. And Lowell also remembers the general bafflement at the light tone of this Doctor: in medicine, Holmes "suffered by giving evidence of too much wit." Lowell, *The Round Table* (Boston: Gorham, 1913) 73–75.

12 On Holmes' contemporary reputation as the "Laughing Doctor," see: Oberndorf, *The Psychiatric Novels of Oliver Wendell Holmes* (New York: Columbia University Press, 1943) 1. For this orthodox outrage at his "levity of tone," see: Baker, *The Autocrat of the Breakfast-Table* (New York: Macmillan, 1928) ix.

13 Laurence Sterne, *The Life and Opinions of Tristram Shandy, Gentleman*, ed.

James A. Work (Indianapolis: Bobbs-Merrill, 1940) 26. Hereafter cited in the text as *TS*.

14 Holmes letter cited in Tilton, *Amiable Autocrat*, 6, with further information in a note on 389.
15 Tilton, *Amiable Autocrat*, 10.
16 Yvor Winters, *Maule's Curse: Seven Studies in the History of American Obscurantism* (Norfolk: New Directions, 1938) 38.
17 In Chapter Twelve we will see that such a Calvinist approach, making it seem a central duty to read *through* the great works from beginning to end, became an obsession for Oliver Wendell Holmes, Jr. – one of the many telling divergences between this father and son.
18 Harold Bloom, *The Anxiety of Influence: A Theory of Poetry* (New York: Oxford, 1973).
19 For the description of this "aristocratic reader," see Barthes, *The Pleasure of the Text*, trans. Richard Miller (New York: Hill and Wang, 1975) 13. For more extended analysis of the effects of "writerly reading," as described here, see Barthes, *S/Z*, trans. Richard Miller (New York: Hill and Wang, 1974) 16, 11. Of course this need not be seen solely as a modern discovery: Emerson in "The American Scholar" is happy to observe that "There is then creative reading as well as creative writing" (*Complete Works*, I, 93).
20 Barthes, *S/Z* 13, 15.
21 For some of the ideas about "carnivalization" alluded to here, see: Bakhtin, *Problems of Dostoevsky's Poetics*, trans. R. W. Rotsel (New York: Ardis, 1973) 105–06.
22 Tilton, *Amiable Autocrat*, 249.
23 Gregory Bateson, *Steps to an Ecology of Mind* (New York: Ballantine, 1972).
24 Edwards, "Sinner in the Hands of an Angry God," *Basic Writings*, ed. O. E. Winslow (New York: New American Library, 1966) 157.
25 *Hegel: Texts and Commentary*, trans. Walter Kaufmann (Garden City: Doubleday, 1966) 20.
26 Bachelard, *La formation de l'esprit scientifique: contribution à une psychanalyse de la connaissance objective* (Paris: J. Vrin, 1960).
27 Emerson, "Circles," *Complete Works*, II, 304–05.
28 Emerson, "Nature," *Complete Works*, I, 76.
29 Emerson, "Circles," *Complete Works*, II, 318.
30 Tilton, *Amiable Autocrat*, 304.
31 Beecher, *A Treatise on Domestic Economy* (New York: Harper, 1849).
32 Heman Humphrey, "Family Government and National Government," *Antebellum American Culture: An Interpretive Anthology*, ed. David Brion Davis (Lexington: Heath, 1979) 9–13.
33 Emerson, "Intellect," *Complete Works*, II, 330.
34 Gaston Bachelard, *The Poetics of Space*, trans. Maria Jolas (New York: Orion, 1964) 112–17.

10 "CUTTING OFF THE COMMUNICATION": FIXATIONS AND
FALLS FOR THE WALLED-IN SELF — HOLMES IN DIALOGUE WITH
STERNE, DICKENS, AND MELVILLE

1 Much of the most relevant data for the now-common identification of
   Holmes and Mr. Scribe is provided in the letters and journals collected
   by Jay Leyda, filling in the background for dates surrounding Melville's
   illness. Holmes treated Melville in June 1855 and the Melville story
   appeared in *Putnam's Monthly*, March 1856.
       For further background on the story, see: Jay Leyda, *The Melville Log: A
   Documentary Life of Herman Melville, 1819–1891*, 2 vols. (New York:
   Harcourt, 1951) II: 502–04; Merton M. Sealts, Jr., "Herman Melville's 'I
   and My Chimney,'" *American Literature* 13 (May 1941): 142–54; Sealts,
   "Melville's Chimney, Reexamined," in *Themes and Directions in American
   Literature*, ed. Ray B. Browne and Donald Pizer (Lafayette: Purdue
   University Studies, 1969) 80–102; Leon Howard, *Herman Melville: A
   Biography* (Berkeley: University of California Press, 1951) 223–25. For a
   full bibliography on autobiographical readings of this story, see: Allan
   Moore Emery, "The Political Significance of Melville's Chimney," *New
   England Quarterly* (June 1982): 201–28.
2 Herman Melville, *Selected Tales and Poems*, ed. Richard Chase (New York:
   Holt, 1950) 164, 189, 173. Hereafter cited in text as *HM*.
3 Burckhardt, "*Tristram Shandy*'s Law of Gravity," *ELH* 28 (1961): 77, 82.
4 Burckhardt, "*Tristram Shandy*'s Law of Gravity," 72.
5 Burckhardt, "*Tristram Shandy*'s Law of Gravity," 72.
6 Burckhardt, "*Tristram Shandy*'s Law of Gravity," 75, 88.
7 Charles Dickens, *Great Expectations*, ed. Angus Calder (Hammondsworth:
   Penguin, 1965) 229.

11 BREAKING THE HOUSE OF ROMANCE: HOLMES IN DIALOGUE
WITH HAWTHORNE

1 Emerson and Melville cited in Richard H. Brodhead, *The School of
   Hawthorne* (New York: Oxford University Press, 1986) 45–46.
2 Fields, *Authors and Friends* (Boston, 1896; rpt. New York: AMS Press,
   1969) 131.
3 Holmes seems to be playing out this dialogue with Hawthorne about the
   temptation of Catholicism when, in the context of the Hawthorne-
   inspired novel *Elsie Venner*, he presents an extended, intimate "talking
   exam" between a medical counselor, Doctor Kittredge, and a Unitarian
   minister who, weakened by extended illnesses, reveals that he has long
   been struggling with a deep attraction to the Old Church (*CW*, V,
   401–11).
4 Stoehr, *Hawthorne's Mad Scientists* (Hamden, Conn.: Archon, 1978)
   103–34.

5 The phrase "disenchantment of the world," from a study by Keith Thomas, is cited in this medical context in: Paul Starr, *The Social Transformation of American Medicine* (New York: Basic, 1982) 35.

6 For the "dungeon" image, see Hawthorne's letter to Longfellow of 4 June 1837: *The Letters, 1813–1843*, in Thomas Woodson, L. Neal Smith, and Norman Holmes Pearson, eds., *Works of Nathaniel Hawthorne* 23 vols. (Columbus: Ohio State University Press, 1984) xv: 251; on opening an "intercourse with the world," see Hawthorne, "Preface to the 1851 Edition of *Twice-told Tales*," *Nathaniel Hawthorne's Tales*, ed. James McIntosh (New York: Norton, 1987) 290–91.

7 Hawthorne, "The Custom-House," *The Scarlet Letter*, eds. Sculley Bradley, Richmond C. Beatty, and E. Hudson Long (New York: Norton, 1961) 13. Hereafter cited parenthetically within the text.

8 Hawthorne, *The House of Seven Gables*, ed. Hyatt H. Waggoner (Boston: Houghton Mifflin, 1964) 224–25. Hereafter cited parenthetically within the text.

9 "Hawthorne," *Atlantic*, 5 (May 1860) 614–22. Hereafter cited parenthetically within the text.

10 Stoehr, *Hawthorne's Mad Scientists*, 124–25.

11 It is interesting to note that Alcott, another loquacious conversationalist, pictured Hawthorne in very similar terms as a coy figure locked in isolation by a maidenly reserve: Hawthorne was "the most diffident of men," Alcott told audiences at his talk sessions, "As coy as a maiden, he could only be won by some cunning artifice, his reserve was so habitual, his isolation so entire, the solitude so vast": Alcott cited in Dahlstrand, *Amos Bronson Alcott* (Rutherford, NJ: Fairleigh Dickinson University Press, 1982) 313.

12 Stoehr, *Hawthorne's Mad Scientists*, 124.

13 Stoehr, *Hawthorne's Mad Scientists*, 124.

12 CONCLUSIONS: HOLMES SENIOR IN DIALOGUE
WITH HOLMES JUNIOR

1 Holmes, Jr., "The Soldier's Faith," in Max Lerner, ed., *The Mind and Faith of Justice Holmes: His Speeches, Essays, Letters, and Judicial Opinions* (Boston, 1943) 24.

2 Descriptions of the talk around the Holmes family dinner-table are given in several of Holmes Junior's letters, noted by the Justice's biographer Howe. Howe also cites the recollection of Holmes Senior's grandson, Edward J. Holmes, about the quality of the talk always heard on every visit to the home of the Doctor and the future Justice: it was, he writes, "the most brilliant conversation that I have ever heard or ever expect to hear, with absolutely fair give and take and only one criterion, the skill in presentation of an argument. Father admired son and son admired father . . ."; Howe, *Justice Oliver Wendell Holmes: The Shaping*

Years, 1841–1870, 2 vols. (Cambridge: Harvard University Press, 1957) 1: 19. The anecdote about the marmalade prize for the best table-talk appears in Bowen, *Yankee from Olympus: Justice Holmes and his Family* (Boston: Little, Brown, 1945) 110.

3 See, for example, Edward J. Bander, ed., *Justice Holmes Ex Cathedra* (Charlottesville: Michie, 1966).

4 Bowen takes this heroic appellation (apparently suggested to her by an Elizabeth S. Sergeant essay) as the title for her biography of the Justice. But many of Holmes' contemporaries also commented on his godlike, Olympian stature. Edmund Wilson notes that Holmes Junior had truly become, by the 1920s, a "sage . . . a god of the national pantheon"; Wilson, *Patriotic Gore: Studies in the Literature of the American Civil War* (New York: Oxford University Press, 1962) 779. G. Edward White makes a similar observation about a later period: "The years from 1932 to 1940 witnessed the apotheosis of Holmes"; White, "The Rise and Fall of Justice Holmes," *The University of Chicago Law Review* 39 (1971): 51, 62. According to Saul Touster, Holmes' often-noted "Olympian aloofness" and "the mythos his *person* seemed to create" had their origins in his experiences during the Civil War; Touster, "In Search of Holmes from Within," *Vanderbilt Law Review* 18 (1965): 470–71.

While the Autocrat had to serve as his own Boswell, the Yankee Justice soon found himself surrounded by foster-son law clerks and admiring younger judges who indeed enshrined his every "opinion" – whether issued from the bench, in a letter, or during table-talk – as that of consecrated authority, to be passed down as part of the American legal tradition.

5 T. J. Jackson Lears, *No Place of Grace: Antimodernism and the Transformation of American Culture, 1880–1920* (New York: Pantheon, 1981) 47.

6 See "Mechanism in Thought and Morals" (*CW*, VIII), and also the "Three Johns" passage in *The Autocrat* (*CW*, 1, 53–54).

7 One well-known Holmes set piece, for example, involves a failed tribunal on the "pun question." In this tour de force of ironic wordplay, the Autocrat puts on the mask of gravity, pretending to want to banish all puns as enemies of the conversational community. But, of course, punning is one of Holmes' specialities, and this long polemic develops as an extraordinary tissue built almost entirely out of puns – so that the condemnation of subversive wordplay also operates as a celebration of it. Finally, the matter is brought to trial – but the puns still won't stop. For the presiding judge at this saturnalia is the jokester Joe Miller, author of the classic "Jest-Book"; because he is more interested in the "jests" than in the "just," his punning verdict – "Jest so" – only further confuses justice and "jestice." Amidst great confusion the offending pun is "ordered burned by the sheriff," but an anonymous boarder gets in the last word, mumbling something about the "Macaulay-flowers of literature" even after the Autocrat feels he has closed the case; *The Autocrat* (*CW*, 1, 11–13).

The carnival spirit of these recurring mock-trial scenes – carnivaliza-tions of all judgment, but especially of legal judgment – seems to have developed during Holmes Senior's college years at Harvard. He spent much time enjoying what he experienced as the "festive indulgences and gay license" of the "revelries" among other "young bacchanalians" at Harvard student clubs. Often the random repartee of the Hasty Pudding Club would be organized into mock trials, and Holmes' ready wit apparently gave him a central role speaking on both sides of many of these carnival cases – his pun-filled, ambiguous defenses of free love and prosecutions of opera dancers were most noted. Perhaps the session that reveals most clearly the general attitude toward authority among this generation of students was an all-college debate in 1828 on the question: Can one President govern the entire United States? Holmes was a prominent voice in this discussion – though he apparently did not care which side he argued on – and in the end the noes had it: these young Harvard students, engaged in an ongoing series of undecidable, multi-voiced debates, would finally find that the nation was too big and too diverse to be ruled by or united under one figure. See *AN* 50–51; Tilton, *Amiable Autocrat*, 52–54; Bowen, *Yankee from Olympus*, 52.

8 The relevant essays of this series are: "Mechanism in Thought and Morals" (*CW*, VIII, 260–314), "Crime and Automatism" (*CW*, VIII, 322–60), and "Jonathan Edwards" (*CW*, VIII, 361–401).

9 For an opposed view, see Arnold L. Goldsmith, "Oliver Wendell Holmes, Father and Son," *Journal of Criminal Law, Criminology, and Police Science* 48, 4 (Nov.–Dec. 1957): 394–98.

10 Holmes, "The Autocrat Gives a Breakfast to the Public," in Mordell, ed. *The Autocrat's Miscellanies* (New York: Twayne, 1959) 30–31.

11 See Yosal Rogat, "Mr. Justice Holmes: A Dissenting Opinion," *Stanford Law Review* 15 (1963): 3, 254.

12 Motley letter of 31 Aug. 1862, quoted in George M. Fredrickson, *The Inner Civil War: Northern Intellectuals and the Crisis of Union* (New York: Harper, 1965) 175–76.

13 Fredrickson, *The Inner Civil War*, 172, 209.

14 Hofstadter, *Anti-Intellectualism in American Life* (New York: Knopf, 1963) 30.

15 Holmes to Charles Evans Hughes, quoted in Merlo J. Pusey, *Charles Evans Hughes*, 2 vols. (New York, 1951) 1: 287.

16 Wilson, *Patriotic Gore*, 650.

17 The Holmes motto about this verbal "instinct for the jugular" was actually adopted from Rufus Choate. It is discussed in Wilson, *Patriotic Gore*, 760.

18 Holmes, Jr., "Natural Law," in *Collected Legal Papers* (New York: Harcourt Brace, 1920) 310, 314–15.

19 Holmes to Felix Frankfurter, 26 June 1928, quoted in G. Edward White, *The American Judicial Tradition* (New York, 1976) 156; Wilson, *Patriotic Gore*, 781.

20 Asked why he often wrote standing up, Holmes replied, "If I sit down, I write a long opinion and don't come to the point as quickly as I could"; Harry C. Shriver, ed., *What Gusto: Stories and Anecdotes about Justice Oliver Wendell Holmes* (Potomac, Md.: 1970) 10. Holmes citations from: "The Soldier's Faith," in *The Mind and Faith of Justice Holmes*, 19; Holmes to Pollock, 1 Feb. 1920, in Mark deWolfe Howe, ed., *The Holmes–Pollock Letters: The Correspondence of Mr. Justice Holmes and Sir Frederick Pollock, 1874–1932*, 2 vols. (Cambridge: Harvard University Press, 1941, 1946) ii: 36; Holmes, "Natural Law," 310; Holmes, *Abrams* v. U.S., in *Mind and Faith*, 312; Holmes, Jr., *The Common Law*, ed. Mark deWolfe Howe (Cambridge: Harvard University Press, 1963) 1.

21 This motto about the writing of "small diamonds" or "jewels five words long" is cited in Yosal Rogat, "The Judge as Spectator," *University of Chicago Law Review* 31 (1964): 253.

22 The phrase "sense of an ending" is from Frank Kermode, *The Sense of an Ending: Studies in the Theory of Fiction* (New York: Oxford University Press, 1967). For Rogat's estimate of the relative brevity of Holmes' opinions, see his "Mr. Justice Holmes," 9.

23 Rorty, *Philosophy and the Mirror of Nature* (Princeton: Princeton University Press, 1979) 317–18.

24 This introduction to Holmes' first essay, "Books," published in *The Harvard Magazine* for December 1858 (the peak period for Holmes Senior's breakfast-table papers) is cited in Howe, *Justice Holmes: The Shaping Years*, 43–44.

25 Holmes, Jr., "Answer to Resolutions of the Bar (1897)," in Lerner, ed., *Mind and Faith of Justice Holmes*, 39. The Justice's preoccupation with the model of war, in this example and many others, is discussed in Daniel Boorstin, "The Elusiveness of Mr. Justice Holmes," *New England Quarterly* 14 (September 1941): 481–83.

26 Lerner, ed., *Mind and Faith of Justice Holmes*, 312, 390.

27 Holmes, Jr., "Natural Law," in *Collected Legal Papers*, 314.

28 Rogat, "Mr. Justice Holmes," 293, 6; Rogat, "The Judge as Spectator," 251.

29 Biddle quoted in G. Edward White, "The Rise and Fall of Justice Holmes," 68.

30 Wilson, *Patriotic Gore*, 668.

31 Holmes, "The Soldier's Faith," in Lerner, ed., *Mind and Faith of Justice Holmes*, 24, 21, 23.

32 Holmes, "The Soldier's Faith," 23.

33 Mark deWolfe Howe, ed., *Touched With Fire: Civil War Letters and Diary of Oliver Wendell Holmes, Jr.* (Cambridge: Harvard University Press, 1947) 142.

34 The refrain in the Doctor's class-day poem for 1851 is "The Boys of '29"; in 1854, it is "The man would be a boy again"; in 1856, "While we've youth in our hearts we can never grow old!"; and even in 1866 the

song can conclude that "His Honor, His Worship, are boys like the rest." Just before the Civil War, Holmes' class-song observes: "We're twenty to-night!/We've a trick, we young fellows, you may have been told,/Of talking (in public) as if we were old:/That boy we call 'Doctor,' and this we call 'Judge' " – though the piece ends with the question: "Shall we ever be men?" Holmes, *Songs and Poems of the Class of 1829* (Boston: Prentiss and Deland, 1868).

35 George B. Forgie, *Patricide in the House Divided: A Psychological Interpretation of Lincoln and His Age* (New York: Norton, 1979) 11.

36 Holmes, Jr., "The Path of the Law," in *Collected Legal Papers*, 187–88; Holmes, Jr., "The Soldier's Faith," in Lerner, ed., *Mind and Faith of Justice Holmes*, 21, 20.

37 Holmes, Jr., "Natural Law," in *Collected Legal Papers*, 316. This 1918 essay ends with a return to the Civil War language of "The Soldier's Faith": even if, writes Holmes, we are "private soldiers [who] have not been told the plan of campaign, or even that there is one . . . we still shall fight"; 315–16. And the same model recurs in a letter to Pollock, 18 June 1925, clearly defining the Justice's basic position of agnosticism before the workings of a God again characteristically pictured as a great General: "I think the proper attitude is that we know nothing of cosmic values and bow our heads – seeing reason enough for doing all we can and not demanding the plan of campaign of the General – or even asking whether there is any general or any plan"; Howe, ed., *Holmes–Pollock Letters* II: 163.

38 Holmes, "Natural Law," in *Collected Legal Papers*, 311–12.

39 Holmes to Laski, 5 Aug. 1926, in Mark deWolfe Howe, ed., *The Holmes–Laski Letters: The Correspondence of Mr. Justice Holmes and Harold J. Laski, 1916–1935*, 2 vols. (Cambridge: Harvard University Press, 1953) II: 862–63.

40 Holmes, Jr., *The Common Law*, 38.

41 Holmes to Pollock, 1 Feb. 1920, in Howe, ed., *Holmes–Pollock Letters* II: 36.

42 Motley quoted in Fredrickson, *The Inner Civil War*, 175–76.

43 Holmes, "Natural Law," 310.

44 Rogat, "The Judge as Spectator," 225; Howe, ed., *Holmes–Laski Letters*, I: 115 (3 Dec. 1917), I: 16 (7 Sept. 1916); Holmes, Jr., "Montesquieu," in *Collected Legal Papers*, 258.

45 Rogat makes this point very strongly; see Rogat, "Mr. Justice Holmes." My sense of Holmes Junior's legal thought is greatly indebted to this article and to Rogat's other important essay on the Justice, "The Judge as Spectator."

46 Lerner, ed., *Mind and Faith of Justice Holmes*, 358.

47 Holmes, Jr., "Natural Law," in *Collected Legal Papers*, 314.

48 Holmes quoted in White, "The Rise and Fall of Justice Holmes," 58.

49 Holmes to Laski, 14 June 1922, in Howe, ed., *Holmes–Laski Letters* I: 431.

50 Holmes to Laski, 15 Sept. 1916, in Howe, ed., *Holmes–Laski Letters* I: 21.

51 Holmes, Jr., "Natural Law," in *Collected Legal Papers*, 313.
52 Holmes to Laski, 3 Dec. 1917, in Howe, ed., *Holmes–Laski Letters* I: 115. This axiom is repeated in a 23 July 1925, letter to Laski; I: 762.
53 Holmes to Laski, 26 Oct. 1919, in Howe, ed., *Holmes–Laski Letters* I: 217.
54 Lerner, ed., *Mind and Faith of Justice Holmes*, 312, 114.
55 Boorstin, "The Elusiveness of Mr. Justice Holmes," 484, 486.
56 Holmes to Pollock, 26 May 1919, in Howe, ed., *Holmes–Pollock Letters* II: 13.
57 Holmes to Pollock, 26 May 1919, in Howe, ed., *Holmes–Pollock Letters* II: 14.

Index